THE STATE OF PRESCHOOL

Table of Contents

VISIT OUR WEBSITE FOR ACCESS TO ALL DATA WWW.NIEER.ORG

Executive Summary

At a time when quality preschool education is widely recognized as an engine of success for our nation's children, the disparity in availability of that engine within and among the states is startling. A difference of a few miles can make the difference between being guaranteed access to high-quality preschool and having no access at all. And, where state-funded programs exist, preschool spending per child in one state can be nearly 10 times as high as in another. Across our nation, high-quality and readily available state-funded preschool programs are the exception rather than the rule. If quality prekindergarten education is "the little engine that could," that engine too often lacks fuel, suffers from substandard design, and, in many places, has no track on which to run.

In developing *The State of Preschool: 2004 State Preschool Yearbook*—our second annual report on state prekindergarten—NIEER found that the number of children attending state-funded preschool programs rose from 693,000 in school year 2001–2002 to 738,000 in 2002–2003. Although this finding is heartening, state-funded preschool programs only reached about 10 percent of the nation's 3- and 4-year-olds. Couple that with the fact that 10 states account for three-quarters of all the children served, and it becomes painfully obvious that some states are much worse than others when it comes to offering preschool education. The state preschool picture across the United States is one of haves and have-nots, with notable regional differences as shown in Figure 1 below. Access to a good education depends on where a child lives and the income of the family. Parents looking for a state where state-funded preschool is universally available will find only two states from which to choose.

Though total enrollment in state-funded programs rose, spending per preschool student fell as funding failed to keep pace with enrollment, particularly in states with budget shortfalls that opted to cut funding to preschool programs. The instability of funding is particularly disturbing—and unwise, given that few other state expenditures are so important to our children's future or return so much on the state's investment. There would be public outcry were such cuts levied on kindergarten or first grade. The education of younger children is no less deserving of protection from the vicissitudes of year-to-year swings in the economy.

Despite the instability of funding, some states did make gains. For example, New Jersey, North Carolina, and Louisiana increased funding substantially. In terms of access, Louisiana, Kansas, and North Carolina made noteworthy gains.

FIGURE 1: ACCESS FOR 4-YEAR-OLDS AND STATE SPENDING PER CHILD ENROLLED BY REGION

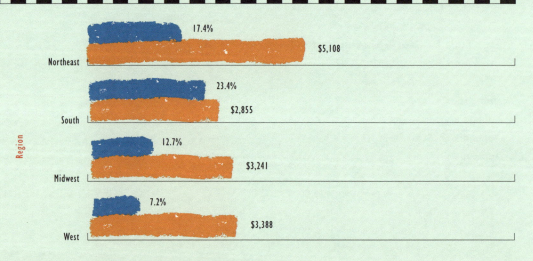

4

States With No Program

Alaska	New Hampshire
Florida	North Dakota
Idaho	Rhode Island
Indiana	South Dakota
Mississippi	Utah
Montana	Wyoming

Major findings from our study can be grouped into three main categories as follows:

Access

- In 2002–2003, 38 states funded one or more state prekindergarten initiatives, serving a total of nearly 740,000 children (about 45,000 more than the previous year). Access was uneven across states, with 10 states accounting for over three-quarters of enrollment.

- State prekindergarten initiatives served more than six times as many 4-year-olds as 3-year-olds in 2002–2003. Twenty states enrolled at least 10 percent of their 4-year-olds in state preschool programs, but only 3 states served at least 10 percent of their 3-year-olds.

- Georgia and Oklahoma continued to be the only states that made prekindergarten universally available to children. Across the United States, only one out of 10 children ages 3 and 4 were participating in state preschool programs, as most states targeted programs to serve economically or otherwise disadvantaged children.

- Twelve states (see box above) do not have a state-funded prekindergarten program.

Quality

- States need to initiate or improve policies that establish stronger quality standards. Only one state, Arkansas, met all 10 of NIEER's quality benchmarks, whereas 20 state initiatives met five or fewer benchmarks.

- State policies regarding quality standards were inconsistent. For example, one state may emphasize comprehensive services and another, teacher qualifications.

- Only 13 state prekindergarten initiatives required teachers to have both a bachelor's degree and specialized training in early childhood education. In addition, only 13 programs required teachers to be paid on a public school salary scale, even though adequate compensation is necessary for attracting and retaining the most qualified and effective teachers.

Resources

- State funding for prekindergarten initiatives totaled $2.54 billion in 2002–2003. Over three-fifths of this funding was from five states—California, Georgia, New Jersey, New York, and Texas. Inadequate funding severely limited access and quality in most states.

- State spending per child enrolled in state-funded preschool ranged from less than $1,000 in Maryland to more than $8,700 in New Jersey. State spending per child averaged about $3,500—less than half the total funding provided per child in federal Head Start or public K–12 education.

- Between 2001–2002 and 2002–2003, total state spending (adjusted for inflation) rose by $90 million, or 4 percent. However, state funding *per child* enrolled decreased by $90, and 21 states decreased total spending.

Conclusions and Recommendations

Vast disparities exist in quality, access, and resources across the states. Some states, such as Arkansas, Illinois, New Jersey, and Oklahoma, have moved far beyond others in at least one of these areas. In contrast, a "dirty dozen" states fail to provide any state program at all. Children in highly rural western states have particularly poor access to preschool education because of a lack of state support. The need for preschool education does not cease when family incomes exceed the income thresholds for targeted state (and federal) programs. Children in these families constitute a large underserved population and deserve access to high-quality preschool programs. There is good reason to believe that our nation would benefit from making such programs more widely available.

Because, after parents, the primary responsibility for education rests with the states, it is the states that should develop policies that seek to address this large need. The costs of these policies are modest relative to overall state budgets. If states were to increase access so that 80 percent of all 4-year-olds were served in state-funded programs (including preschool special education) or Head Start for at least a half day, the full cost would be an additional $15 billion. If states simply paid for the same share of preschool education that they do for K–12, the cost would be only $8.75 billion above current annual spending. This is just a bit more than one penny per dollar of current state spending.

The following policy recommendations are offered as a means of promoting equal access to high-quality education for the nation's 4-year-olds:

- All states should increase funding to improve access and quality. If states included prekindergarten in their public K–12 funding formulas, every state in the nation could provide a good education for 80 percent of its 4-year-olds with a national investment of less than $9 billion in state funds.

- States must improve their standards for prekindergarten education if programs are to produce the large gains in learning and development that the nation seeks. Teachers are required to have a BA and specialized training in preschool education in only 13 state preschool initiatives, whereas all public K–12 teachers must hold 4-year degrees and be state licensed or certified by the end of the 2005–2006 school year. States should apply high standards to all programs, so that no child can slip through the cracks.

- State-funded preschool has vast potential to contribute to economic growth and prosperity. States should make adequate funding for these programs a priority so that prekindergarten initiatives are less reliant on local support. When funding depends on local investment, services for the most disadvantaged children are often the most compromised.

- The federal government should increase support specifically for prekindergarten programs by offering to match state government spending that is accompanied by high standards. Such financial incentives could promote integration of various federal and state programs. Currently, federal programs that support the education of young children are inadequately funded to serve all targeted children.

- States need to create better data systems that provide the critical information policymakers need to make informed decisions about expanding and improving preschool. Most states cannot report unduplicated enrollment counts across early childhood education programs, nor can they track funding across multiple sources. Such shortcomings in information gathering do not exist for children in grades K–12. The federal government should support states in creating or improving data systems for prekindergarten programs.

- Effective change requires careful planning. Improvements in access and quality will most likely have their desired effects if sufficient time, funding, facilities, and personnel are provided to meet changing needs.

This report may be viewed in its entirety on the NIEER website at www.nieer.org.

TABLE 1: STATE RANKINGS AND QUALITY CHECKLIST SUMS

State	Access for 4-Year-Olds Rank	Access for 3-Year-Olds Rank	Resources Rank	Quality Standards Checklist Sum (Maximum of 10)
Alabama	35	none served	14	8
Alaska	no program	no program	no program	no program
Arizona	29	none served	28	4
Arkansas	26	12	21	10
California	21	13	17	4
Colorado	15	18	25	4
Connecticut	18	9	4	4
Delaware	22	none served	5	7
Florida	no program	no program	no program	no program
Georgia	2	none served	12	6
Hawaii	25	none served	15	5
Idaho	no program	no program	no program	no program
Illinois	10	5	23	9
Indiana	no program	no program	no program	no program
Iowa	30	20	22	5
Kansas	14	none served	34	4
Kentucky	7	3	27	7
Louisiana	12	none served	10	7.5
Maine	16	none served	32	3
Maryland	8	14	37	8
Massachusetts	17	2	9	6
Michigan	13	none served	19	5
Minnesota	36	19	2	8
Mississippi	no program	no program	no program	no program
Missouri	31	11	30	4
Montana	no program	no program	no program	no program
Nebraska	33	17	31	6
Nevada	38	24	13	4
New Hampshire	no program	no program	no program	no program
New Jersey	11	1	1	8.3
New Mexico	34	23	33	4
New York	5	25	16	5.6
North Carolina	28	none served	6	9
North Dakota	no program	no program	no program	no program
Ohio	20	7	8	6.5
Oklahoma	1	none served	29	8
Oregon	27	10	3	6
Pennsylvania	37	none served	not available	2
Rhode Island	no program	no program	no program	no program
South Carolina	4	15	35	8
South Dakota	no program	no program	no program	no program
Tennessee	32	21	7	8
Texas	3	8	26	3
Utah	no program	no program	no program	no program
Vermont	19	6	36	6
Virginia	24	none served	20	5
Washington	23	16	11	6
West Virginia	6	4	18	5
Wisconsin	9	22	24	3.3
Wyoming	no program	no program	no program	no program

TABLE 2: CHANGES IN ENROLLMENT AND FUNDING FOR STATE PRESCHOOL PROGRAMS FROM 2001–2002 TO 2002–2003

STATE	CHANGE IN ENROLLMENT FOR 4-YEAR-OLDS		CHANGE IN ENROLLMENT FOR 3-YEAR-OLDS		CHANGE IN TOTAL STATE SPENDING		CHANGE IN STATE SPENDING PER CHILD ENROLLED	
	number enrolled	percent of state population	number enrolled	percent of state population	inflation-adjusted dollars	percent	inflation-adjusted dollars	percent
Alabama	504	0.90%	0	none served	$1,724,030	60.3%	-$146	-3.9%
Alaska	0	no program	0	no program	$0	0.0%	$0	0.0%
Arizona	-185	-0.53%	0	none served	-$106,617	-1.1%	$80	3.4%
Arkansas	14	0.07%	-94	-0.24%	$2,632,689	39.8%	$908	43.4%
California	-1,476	0.17%	-272	0.01%	$2,484,514	1.0%	$142	4.5%
Colorado	139	-0.17%	176	0.22%	$3,503,160	12.6%	$99	3.6%
Connecticut	392	0.96%	25	0.06%	-$5,599,846	-13.6%	-$1,323	-19.1%
Delaware	0	0.53%	0	none served	$44,154	1.0%	$53	1.0%
Florida	0	no program	0	no program	$0	0.0%	$0	0.0%
Georgia	2,287	0.86%	0	none served	$8,009,640	3.3%	-$12	-0.3%
Hawaii	-315	-1.51%	0	none served	-$689,341	-17.5%	$325	10.3%
Idaho	0	no program	0	no program	$0	0.0%	$0	0.0%
Illinois	3,366	2.88%	-382	-0.08%	-$6,432,584	-3.8%	-$285	-8.9%
Indiana	0	no program	0	no program	$0	0.0%	$0	0.0%
Iowa	89	0.46%	-33	-0.03%	-$985,432	-12.5%	-$467	-13.8%
Kansas	3,203	8.86%	0	none served	$4,713,723	101.6%	-$359	-17.3%
Kentucky	858	3.83%	1,343	3.18%	-$826,040	-1.7%	-$377	-13.2%
Louisiana	5,449	9.07%	0	none served	$18,769,208	58.5%	-$346	-8.1%
Maine	0	1.14%	0	none served	$432,240	19.1%	$300	19.1%
Maryland	0	0.84%	0	0.02%	-$593,285	-3.0%	-$29	-3.0%
Massachusetts	-1,405	-1.08%	-1,405	-1.22%	-$26,169,120	-26.3%	-$871	-17.5%
Michigan	-765	0.11%	0	none served	-$2,463,380	-2.8%	$3	0.1%
Minnesota	74	0.19%	47	0.10%	-$1,320,950	-7.0%	-$544	-7.5%
Mississippi	0	no program	0	no program	$0	0.0%	$0	0.0%
Missouri	-512	-0.55%	-832	-1.10%	-$4,717,012	-30.5%	-$283	-11.4%
Montana	0	no program	0	no program	$0	0.0%	$0	0.0%
Nebraska	227	1.04%	217	0.94%	$759,960	56.7%	-$883	-31.6%
Nevada	171	0.47%	107	0.31%	$1,686,409	128.4%	$645	21.2%
New Hampshire	0	no program	0	no program	$0	0.0%	$0	0.0%
New Jersey	3,486	3.70%	3,526	3.33%	$109,695,251	40.3%	$1,320	17.8%
New Mexico	-842	-3.10%	-308	-1.21%	-$111,240	-6.9%	$959	119.1%
New York	7,723	5.19%	-4,405	-1.74%	-$15,633,880	-6.0%	-$386	-10.3%
North Carolina	5,031	4.46%	0	none served	$23,517,523	351.0%	-$584	-10.8%
North Dakota	0	no program	0	no program	$0	0.0%	$0	0.0%
Ohio	442	0.60%	-498	-0.27%	-$15,724,876	-12.9%	-$656	-12.7%
Oklahoma	2,181	3.79%	0	none served	$1,675,204	2.6%	-$135	-5.4%
Oregon	51	0.09%	251	0.55%	-$2,350,080	-8.3%	-$1,168	-15.2%
Pennsylvania	59	0.15%	0	none served	not available	not available	not available	not available
Rhode Island	0	no program	0	no program	$0	0.0%	$0	0.0%
South Carolina	674	2.90%	605	1.21%	-$1,786,020	-7.3%	-$216	-14.2%
South Dakota	0	no program	0	no program	$0	0.0%	$0	0.0%
Tennessee	642	0.89%	-42	-0.07%	-$462,000	-3.0%	-$1,162	-20.3%
Texas	15,491	3.79%	-6,079	-2.04%	-$2,560,688	-0.6%	-$207	-7.0%
Utah	0	no program	0	no program	$0	0.0%	$0	0.0%
Vermont	24	1.18%	87	1.72%	-$93,719	-6.6%	-$224	-15.8%
Virginia	8	-0.01%	0	none served	-$1,160,938	-6.0%	-$202	-6.1%
Washington	238	0.30%	69	0.09%	$881,975	3.4%	-$41	-1.0%
West Virginia	749	4.69%	125	0.79%	$3,031,424	13.4%	$20	0.6%
Wisconsin	3,326	5.65%	-18	-0.01%	-$1,037,690	-2.0%	-$745	-20.5%
Wyoming	0	no program	0	no program	$0	0.0%	$0	0.0%
50 States	**51,398**	**1.7%**	**-7,790**	**-0.2%**	**$92,736,368**	**3.8%**	**-$90**	**-2.5%**

The State of Preschool

The *2004 State Preschool Yearbook* is the second in this annual NIEER series evaluating state-funded preschool programs. It describes state-funded prekindergarten in the 2002–2003 school year. Last year's *State Preschool Yearbook* focused on programs for the 2001–2002 school year and established a baseline against which we may now measure progress. Tracking these trends is essential, since the role states play in preschool education will increasingly affect how successfully America's next generation will compete in the knowledge economy.[1]

As this year's report demonstrates, the states vary greatly in how they pick up where federal and private programs leave off. There is a wide gap between states like Oklahoma and Georgia, which make programs available for all 4-year-olds, and states like Indiana, South Dakota, and Utah, which provide no state programs.[2] In the middle are states like Colorado, Iowa, and Washington with programs developed for at-risk and economically disadvantaged populations.[3]

The *State Preschool Yearbooks* have been developed by NIEER to serve as a resource for everyone from policymakers to advocates to researchers. Because state and local governments bear great responsibility for education in the United States, evaluating the approaches taken by, and progress of, the states is essential. From the start, NIEER's *Yearbook* initiative has contributed to a robust dialogue about prekindergarten and the growing role of states in program development. We believe that this dialogue enables policymakers to make more informed decisions about state-funded preschool.

The *Yearbook* data were collected from an intensive survey of the states. Information is presented regarding three key characteristics of prekindergarten programs: access, quality standards, and resources.

- *Access:* Access remains far from universal across the country. It varies not only between states, but also within them. The ability to attend preschool depends greatly on family income and where families live. We use enrollment of children at the ages of 3 and 4 to measure the extent to which states offer opportunities for preschool participation.

- *Quality Standards:* The quality of preschool education determines its educational value. Yet, many preschool programs in the United States are poor or mediocre. High state standards are essential for ensuring that preschool programs provide quality education. The *Yearbook* compares state quality standards against a research-based checklist of benchmarks.

- *Resources:* Resources, as measured by state expenditures for preschool, indicate each state's commitment to expanding access and ensuring educational adequacy. State spending per child in a prekindergarten program is a key determinant of program quality and a measure of state support for access to a good preschool education.

This *Yearbook* is organized into three major sections. The first section provides background information on preschool education in the United States, a description of our data collection and analytical methods, a national summary of our findings, and national policy recommendations. The second section presents detailed reports identifying each state's policies with respect to preschool access, quality standards, and resources. In addition to basic program descriptions, these state profiles describe unique features of a state's program and recent changes that can be expected to alter the future *Yearbook* statistics on a program. Unlike last year's *Yearbook*, the states without state-funded programs also have their own profile pages. The last section contains the appendices, including tables that report the complete survey data obtained from every state, as well as Head Start and child care data.

PRESCHOOL IN THE UNITED STATES: AN OVERVIEW

Preschool participation in the United States has with rare exception moved steadily upward throughout the last four decades, as shown in Figure 2. In 1965, about 5 percent of 3-year-olds and 17 percent of 4-year-olds attended some form of preschool. By 2002, about 40 percent of 3-year-olds and 66 percent of 4-year-olds attended preschool.[4] Much of the growth in preschool education has occurred beyond the purview of state-provided public education. In sharp contrast to elementary school and even kindergarten, early childhood education remains primarily outside the public schools. Prekindergarten education takes place in private programs, federal Head Start, and public schools.

While availability has grown, access to affordable, high-quality preschool education is highly unequal across the country. Despite the best efforts of an array of federal and state programs targeting the disadvantaged, less than half of children in poverty attend preschool at ages 3 and 4.[5] Prekindergarten is also less available to a potentially larger group of families whose incomes hover just above the eligibility requirements for targeted programs but who cannot afford private preschool. These families with modest incomes find it difficult to afford a good private preschool, and many of their children miss out on this opportunity.[6]

FIGURE 2: KINDERGARTEN AND PRESCHOOL PARTICIPATION BY AGE 1965–2001

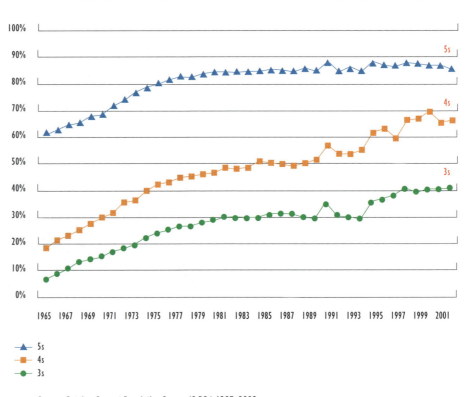

Source: October Current Population Survey (C.P.S.) 1965–2002.
Note: Some children enter Kindergarten at age 6 and are not included here.

In labor force
Not in the labor force

Source: Current Population Survey (C.P.S.) 1967–2002
Data for the following years have been interpolated: 1977–1981, 1983, 1984 and 1986.

What Drives Preschool Participation

Contrary to the oft-held view that working mothers—and a concomitant need for child care—drive the demand for preschool, research demonstrates that the prevailing motivator for increased preschool attendance is parents' desire to better educate their children.[7] As shown in Figure 3, the rate of participation in preschool by children of mothers not in the labor force, while somewhat lower than the rate for children of employed mothers, has grown at virtually the same rate since the late 1960s. Although child care demand plays some role in increased preschool participation, it appears to be of decidedly secondary importance.

FIGURE 4: PRESCHOOL PARTICIPATION BY FAMILY INCOME 2001

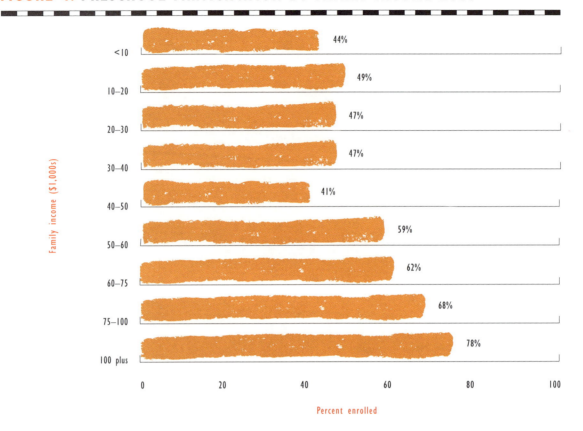

Despite a variety of government programs, family income remains a prime determinant of preschool participation. Because of state prekindergarten and Head Start, rates of preschool participation vary relatively little over the bottom end of the income scale, as shown in Figure 4.[8] However, there is a significant dip at the $40,000 to $50,000 income level. Preschool education opportunities appear to be least available to children in families with moderate incomes. Participation rises with income thereafter, but most Americans have less access to preschool than the wealthiest.

Mothers' education is also highly predictive of preschool participation. Among 4-year-olds whose mothers have a 4-year college degree, 76 percent attend preschool. Sixty-five percent of 4-year-olds whose mothers graduated from high school attend preschool and 49 percent of those whose mothers dropped out of high school attend preschool. Thus, despite the public programs we have today, the less education a child's parents have (and thus the more the child might gain from preschool attendance), the less likely it is that a child will attend prekindergarten.

Private Preschool Programs

Preschool education has expanded in both the private and public sectors, although at different rates. In 1990, private programs served 64 percent of the children attending preschool programs. During the 1990s, public programs grew more rapidly and by 1995 only 52 percent of the children attending preschool were in private programs. Private programs maintained a small edge in total preschool enrollment thereafter.[9] Private preschool programs are operated by for-profit organizations, independent nonprofit organizations, or religious organizations. They operate under a wide variety of names including nursery school, preschool, day care, and child care, and most are part-day programs. Regulation is primarily by state child care agencies, but varies by state and within states by auspice. Some states exempt religious or private school programs from child care licensing standards. Like their regulation and funding, the educational quality of private programs is highly variable and tends to be lower on average than for public programs.[10]

Head Start

Since the program was launched in 1965, federal Head Start has provided many low-income families with free education for their young children and comprehensive services. From 1975 to 1990, the program grew slowly. In 1975, Head Start enrolled 5 percent of the nation's 3- and 4-year-olds. By 1990 enrollment had risen to 7 percent. Head Start grew faster in the 1990s, and in the year 2000 served 11 percent of all 3- and 4-year-olds. During the 2003 fiscal year, Head Start reported funding more than 900,000 children, nearly 800,000 of whom were ages 3 and 4.[11] Despite this growth, Head Start does not reach all of the eligible preschoolers. Furthermore, Head Start's program standards fall short of what is required to ensure that programs are highly effective. Head Start teacher qualifications and compensation are of particular concern. Only recently has Congress required that half of Head Start teachers have even a 2-year college degree. Head Start teachers still earn about half the average public school teacher's salary. Without fully qualified teachers (those with BA degrees and specialization in early childhood education) who are adequately paid, Head Start will not be nearly as effective as it could be.[12]

State Prekindergarten Programs

With notable exceptions, the states have been slow to recognize the revolution in preschool education and to address a new reality with policies that provide equal access to effective programs. Most states with preschool programs followed the federal government's lead and targeted children with the greatest needs. Typically, states support two types of preschool programs—one providing preschool special education for children with disabilities and the other providing preschool education to children in low-income families or children otherwise identified as being at high risk for school failure. States began to create entitlements to a free education for 3- to 5-year-old children with disabilities in the 1970s. Illinois, Michigan and Wisconsin were the first states to do so in 1973–1974.[13] Federal legislation passed in 1986 provided federal funds as incentives for all states to provide a free appropriate education to young children with disabilities by 1991–1992. The law was highly effective: the 24 states already providing such services were joined by 25 more in 1991–1992, and the one remaining state mandated services in 1992–1993. Enrollment rose steadily over the years and by 2002 reached 382,290 in the 50 states (387,293 in states, U.S. territories and military bases), or 5 percent of all 3- and 4-year-olds. Most were served in public schools, but some were served in Head Start or private programs.

Movement Toward Preschool for All

Growth accelerated in preschool programs for at-risk children through the 1990s. Following a logical progression, some states began to expand eligibility from at-risk groups to all children. Georgia created the first statewide universal prekindergarten (UPK) program in 1995. Oklahoma, New York, and West Virginia followed suit, though New York has not fully funded its program and West Virginia plans for a phase-in by 2012. In 2002, Florida voters approved a constitutional amendment entitling all 4-year-olds to a free, high-quality prekindergarten education by 2005. That date looms large in the wake of Florida's failed attempt at universal prekindergarten legislation in the first half of 2004. Also active is Massachusetts, which made its first move toward universal preschool in 2004 by passing legislation to create the Office of Early Education and Care charged with developing a state-funded preschool program for all children.

During the 2002–2003 program year, as during the 2001–2002 program year, states were using a wide variety of models to provide prekindergarten services to 3- and 4-year-olds. This *Yearbook* compares the different models in use, highlights the strengths and weaknesses of those models, and identifies the opportunities and challenges that lie ahead for state prekindergarten initiatives.

Prekindergarten Data Systems

The data in this report do not provide the complete picture of all publicly funded early childhood programs. Although detailed data about state prekindergarten, Head Start, and preschool special education programs are included, there are many additional types of resources that states use in support of early childhood education. The *Yearbook* provides limited details about these other resources because most states do not have adequate data systems to track this information.

Louisiana is an example of a state that gathers more complete data about a range of programs serving 4-year-olds, by local parish and statewide. The state also compares the number of children served by state, federal, and local programs to the estimated number of at-risk children.

Despite this promising effort, most other states lack data systems that allow children and funds to be tracked across programs.

1   Shonkoff, J.P., & Phillips, D.A. (Eds.) (2000). *From neurons to neighborhoods: The science of early childhood development.* Washington, DC: National Academy Press. Bowman, B., Donovan, M., & Burns, S. (Eds.) (2001). *Eager to learn: Educating our preschoolers.* Washington, DC: National Academy Press.

2   Barnett, W.S., Robin, K., Hustedt, J., & Schulman, K. (2003). *The state of preschool: 2003 state preschool yearbook.* New Brunswick, NJ: National Institute for Early Education Research, Rutgers University.

3   Barnett et al. (2003).

4   Barnett, W.S., & Yarosz, D.J. (2004). Who goes to preschool and why does it matter? *Preschool Policy Matters, 8.* New Brunswick, NJ: National Institute for Early Education Research, Rutgers University.

5   Barnett, W.S., Brown, K., & Shore, R. (2004). The universal vs. targeted debate: Should the United States have preschool for all? *Preschool Policy Matters, 6.* New Brunswick, NJ: National Institute for Early Education Research, Rutgers University.

6   Barnett & Yarosz (2004).

7   Barnett & Yarosz (2004).

8   Barnett & Yarosz (2004).

9   U.S. Statistical Abstract and Current Population Survey, October 2001. The CPS tracks "nursery school" enrollment. Comparison with data from the National Household Education Survey conducted by the National Center for Education Statistics for all center-based programs suggests that perhaps 10 percent of child care center enrollment is not reported as nursery school. It seems reasonable that the CPS numbers may slightly underestimate the percentage of private programs as a result.

10 Barnett, W.S., Tarr, J., Lamy, C., & Frede, E. (2001). *Fragile lives, shattered dreams: A report on implementation of preschool education in New Jersey's Abbott districts.* New Brunswick, NJ: National Institute for Early Education Research, Rutgers University. Cost, Quality and Outcomes Study Team. (1995). *Cost, quality, and outcomes in child care centers: Public report.* Denver: University of Colorado at Denver, Economics Department. Zill, N., Resnick, G., Kim, K., McKey, R., Clark, C., Pai-Samant, S., Connell, D., Vaden-Kiernan, M., O'Brien, R., & D'Elio, M. (2001). *Head Start FACES: Longitudinal findings on program performance. Third progress report.* Washington, DC: Administration on Children, Youth and Families, U.S. Department of Health and Human Services.

11 U.S. Department of Health and Human Services, Administration for Children and Families, Head Start Bureau. (2004). *Head Start program fact sheet fiscal year 2003.* Retrieved September 19, 2004, from http://www.acf.hhs.gov/programs/hsb/research/2004.htm.

12 Barnett, W.S. (2003). Better teachers, better preschools: Student achievement linked to teacher qualifications. *Preschool Policy Matters, 2.* New Brunswick, NJ: National Institute for Early Education Research, Rutgers University. National Institute for Early Education Research (2003). Investing in Head Start teachers. *Preschool Policy Matters, 4.* New Brunswick, NJ: National Institute for Early Education Research, Rutgers University.

13 Trohanis, P. (2002). Progress in providing services to young children with special needs and their families. *NECTAC Notes, 12,* 1–18. Chapel Hill, NC: National Early Childhood Technical Assistance Center.

HIGH-QUALITY PRESCHOOL PROGRAMS: WHAT'S IN IT FOR THE STATES?

In a world shaped by global competition, preschool programs play an increasingly vital role in the education of our children—and, ultimately, the competitiveness of our states and nation. More parents and policy-makers recognize the potential for educating children during the period of rapid growth and development that occurs before age 5. It is then that children can improve the foundational capabilities in ways that can dramatically change their lives for the better.

Numerous studies demonstrate that high-quality preschool programs produce large gains in school readiness for economically disadvantaged children. That translates to improved achievement and behavior in school. Long-term follow-up studies show that children from disadvantaged families who attend high-quality pre-school programs acquire more education, earn more money, and become more responsible citizens than children from similar families who do not attend high-quality preschool.[1]

A growing body of evidence shows that preschool education has similar benefits for children who are not poor, though those benefits may not be as pronounced.[2] Not to be underestimated are societal gains that go beyond those realized by children in their individual lives. Such gains accrue to society in the form of a better-educated, more productive workforce, enhancing the ability of states and communities to sustain economic growth and compete with the world's best. Other benefits include stronger families and communities.

The educational problems addressed by high-quality preschool programs are experienced by many children who are not economically disadvantaged. In Maryland, for example, only 52 percent of all children entering kindergarten in 2002 were deemed "fully ready."[3] In 2003, 37 percent of our nation's fourth graders scored below "basic" on the reading portion of the National Assessment of Educational Progress. The problems of grade repetition and high school dropout are remarkably high even in middle-income families. The expansion of prekindergarten to serve children who are less disadvantaged may still produce savings at the state level, as costs associated with additional educational services are reduced.

As the case for state investment in quality prekindergarten programs grows more compelling, the fact remains that few programs exist of the quality necessary to bring about the potential benefits. Public financial support has been limited. Budget constraints led some states to decrease their financial commitments to quality prekindergarten between 2001–2002 and 2002–2003. This comes at a time when parents feel squeezed by the high costs of quality programs.

> "We can, and should, be creating a preschool system that would be good enough for everyone. Public preschools should be built the same way we constructed our highway system: the same road available to all Americans, rich and poor."
>
> John Merrow, editorial in *USA Today*

Too many children in the United States lack access to any preschool program at all and too many others do not have access to a high-quality educational program. Most existing public programs are targeted in an attempt to reach the most disadvantaged children. While those programs have shown positive results among populations served, there is an even larger population of under-served children from families who are either missed by targeted programs or whose family income is just above eligibility requirements. Neither targeted programs nor most public school systems serve this segment of the population when it comes to preschool education.[4]

Parents must deal with the reality that high-quality preschool education is expensive. Americans pay a higher percentage of costs for preschool programs than for higher education.[5] In fact, parents in the United States bear more of the cost in comparison to their counterparts in other developed countries.[6]

A national poll of 3,230 voters conducted for NIEER in 2001 revealed strong public sentiment for increased state responsibility for high-quality preschool programs. Nearly 90 percent of respondents supported the view that states should provide funding for preschool programs so all parents could afford to enroll their children in high-quality programs. In addition, 85 percent agreed that states should ensure the quality of preschool programs by setting high standards for learning and teacher qualifications.

Investing in Pre-K: An Economic Development Strategy

States searching for economic development strategies should first look to high-quality preschool, which can provide higher educational returns to the students, greater financial returns to our communities and families, and a more productive workforce to help shoulder future financial responsibilities. Cost-benefit analyses have found that preschool programs for disadvantaged children can be sound public investments with real, inflation-adjusted public returns as high as 12 percent, and combined public and private returns of 16 percent. Researchers at the Federal Reserve Bank of Minneapolis urge states to invest in early education programs as an economic development strategy based on the exceptionally high payoff. In this economic research, the Federal Reserve researchers found that early childhood investments make more sense than spending on venture capital funds, subsidizing new industries such as biotechnology, building new stadiums or providing tax incentives for businesses.

1 Barnett, W. S. (1998). Long-term effects on cognitive development and school success. In W. S. Barnett & S. S. Boocock (Eds.), *Early care and education for children in poverty: Promises, programs, and long-term results* (pp. 11–44). Albany, NY: SUNY Press. Bowman, B. T., Donovan, M. S., & Burns, M.S. (Eds.). (2001). *Eager to learn: Educating our preschoolers*. Washington, DC: National Academy Press.
2 Innes, F., Denton, K., & West, J. (2001, April). *Child care factors and kindergarten outcomes: Findings from a national study of children*. Paper presented at the Annual Meeting of the Society for Research in Child Development, Minneapolis, MN. Peisner-Feinberg, E., Burchinal, M.R., Clifford, R.M., Culkin, M.L., Howes, C., Kagan, S.L., Yazejian, N., Byler, P., Rustici, J., & Zelazo, J. (1999). *The children of the Cost, Quality, and Outcomes Study go to school*. Chapel Hill: University of North Carolina at Chapel Hill, Frank Porter Graham Child Development Center. Sammons, P., Sylva, K., Melhuish, E., Siraj-Blatchford, I., Taggart, B., & Elliot, K. (2002). *Measuring the impact of preschool on children's cognitive progress over the pre-school period*. (Technical paper 8a). London: Institute of Education, University of London. Sammons, P., Sylva, K., Melhuish, E., Siraj-Blatchford, I., Taggart, B., & Elliot, K. (2003). *Measuring the impact of preschool on children's social/behavioral development over the pre-school period*. (Technical report 8b). London: Institute of Education, University of London.
3 Bowler, M. (2003). Fifty-two percent of kindergartners in Maryland judged "fully ready." *Baltimore Sun*.
4 Barnett, W.S., & Yarosz, D.J. (2004). Who goes to preschool and why does it matter? *Preschool Policy Matters, 8*. New Brunswick, NJ: National Institute for Early Education Research, Rutgers University.
5 Cooper, S., & Dukakis, K. (2004). *Kids can't wait to learn: Achieving voluntary preschool for all in California* (Preschool California). Retrieved September, 2004, from http://www.preschoolcalifornia.org/pg51.cfm.
6 Kagan, S., & Neuman, M. (2003). Integrating early care and education. *Educational Leadership, 60* (7), 58–63.

METHODOLOGY

The data in this report were collected primarily through surveys of state prekindergarten administrators and focus on the 2002–2003 program year. During the spring of 2004, surveys were sent to administrators of the state-funded preschool initiatives covered in NIEER's previous *State Preschool Yearbook*. We also checked with other sources to determine whether any new initiatives had been started since the 2001–2002 program year or whether we had omitted any initiatives in that report. All initiatives included in the current report meet the criteria outlined in the survey, which define state prekindergarten initiatives as initiatives that are funded and directed by the state to support group learning experiences for preschool-age children, usually ages 3 and 4. For more information about these criteria, please see "What Qualifies As A State Preschool Program" on page 23.

This report covers most of the same initiatives as last year, with a few exceptions. Three initiatives in Louisiana (LA4, Starting Points, and the Nonpublic Schools Early Childhood Development Program) that were covered with only brief descriptions last year are given full data pages for 2002–2003. Minnesota's School Readiness Program, which was included last year, is not included this year. After a closer look at that program, we determined it did not meet our definition of a state prekindergarten initiative because it supported a range of services rather than primarily prekindergarten classes and because the state did not collect sufficient data to determine how much funding was used for prekindergarten classes.

Our survey included yes/no questions, questions that asked state administrators to select which of several choices best described their program, and open-ended questions. Where data were already available from the previous *State Preschool Yearbook* or from other sources, we filled in the responses for the states and simply asked them to verify that the information remained valid during the 2002–2003 program year.

The survey included questions on the topics of access, eligibility requirements, access for children with special needs, program standards, personnel, resources, monitoring and evaluation, state-level scholarships for teachers, state-level staffing, and important changes to the program since the previous survey. Most of the questions addressed the same issues as last year's survey. However, the wording of many questions—such as those on eligibility criteria, operating schedules, and comprehensive services—was revised to make them clearer and gather more precise data. Several new questions were added as well, requesting information on the use of other funding sources to serve children in the state-financed prekindergarten program, wrap-around care, monitoring and evaluation, and recent changes. Due to alterations in the survey, the data gathered this year are not completely comparable to data in last year's report, although largely similar information was collected in both years.

After completed surveys were returned, we followed up with state administrators to clarify any questions about their responses. Later, we contacted them again to provide an opportunity to verify the data we had gathered. At that time, we asked them to review tables containing all of the data for their program, as well as a written description of their program. We also requested data on funding and enrollment for 2003–2004 if available. Administrators' survey responses, including answers for items not covered in the state profiles, are shown in Appendix A.

Although most of the data in this report were collected through the survey, there are a few exceptions. For the data on curriculum standards, we referred to a 2003 analysis conducted for NIEER by Mid-continent Research for Education and Learning (McREL). McREL reviewed state documents to assess prekindergarten standards in each state. The analysis examined only standards focused on prekindergarten. If state prekindergarten standards were incorporated into a broader age range (such as prekindergarten through third grade), such standards were considered to be too general to guide instruction and were therefore excluded from the McREL analysis.

The Head Start Bureau in the U.S. Department of Health and Human Services was the source of data on federal Head Start spending and enrollment for 2002–2003 as well as enrollment data used to calculate spending per 3- and 4-year-old in states that fund Head Start programs profiled in this report. Additional Head Start data are provided in Appendix B.

The U.S. Office of Special Education Programs was the source of data on special education enrollment in the Individuals with Disabilities Education Act Preschool Grants program (IDEA Section 619 of Part B) in 2002–2003. These data are presented in Appendix C.

Photo: RC Peters

Total federal, state, and local expenditures on K–12 education in 2002–2003 were calculated by NIEER based on data from the National Education Association's "Rankings and Estimates: Rankings of the States 2003 and Estimates of School Statistics 2004." Total K–12 spending for each state includes current operating expenditures as well as annual capital outlays and interest on school debt. This provides a more complete picture of the full cost of K–12 than including only current operating expenditures, which underestimate the full cost. Our estimate of K–12 expenditures is also more comparable to total prekindergarten spending per child because this funding generally must cover all costs, including facilities. Total spending per child in K–12 was calculated for each state by dividing expenditures by fall 2002 enrollment. We estimated the breakdown of total spending by source, using percentages of revenue receipts from federal, state and local sources in each state.

Populations of 3- and 4-year-olds in each state were obtained from the Census Bureau's Population Estimates Data Sets. Estimates of populations at each single year of age as of July 2002 were used to calculate the percentages of 3- and 4-year-olds enrolled in state preschool, federal Head Start, and special education. The Census Bureau data were also used to calculate spending per 3- and 4-year-old in each state. These figures were calculated using enrollment data broken down by age. When a state did not report separate enrollment numbers for 3-year-olds and 4-year-olds, the age breakdown was estimated using the proportion of children at each age in states that served both 3- and 4-year-olds and did provide data by age. For estimating separate funding amounts for 3-year-olds and for 4-year-olds, it was assumed that spending was proportional to enrollment—so that, for example, if 50 percent of children enrolled were age 3, 50 percent of spending was assumed to be directed to children age 3.

States are given rankings in three areas: the percentage of 4-year-olds enrolled in state prekindergarten initiatives (Access Ranking—4s), the percentage of 3-year-olds enrolled (Access Ranking—3s), and state spending per child enrolled (Resources Ranking). The measures of access for 3- and 4-year-olds were calculated, as described above, using state data on enrollment in the prekindergarten initiatives and Census population data. The measure of resources was calculated by dividing state prekindergarten funding (including TANF funding directed toward the state preschool initiative) by enrollment. All states that provided data are ranked, starting with "1" for the state with the greatest percentage of its children enrolled in the state prekindergarten program or the most spent per participant. States that did not serve children at age 3 receive notations of "none served" on the ranking of access for 3-year-olds. The 12 states that do not fund a preschool initiative are omitted from all rankings, and instead receive notations of "no program" on their state profile pages. Finally, Pennsylvania is omitted from the ranking on spending per child, as the state was unable to provide a funding amount specific to prekindergarten.

District of Columbia

This report also includes data on the District of Columbia's prekindergarten initiative. In a number of ways, the District of Columbia's prekindergarten efforts are more comparable to those of other cities—many of which also have their own extensive prekindergarten programs that are locally initiated, funded, and controlled—than to prekindergarten efforts in the 50 states. Although other local prekindergarten programs are not addressed in this report, the District's program is covered, since the District has a unique status as a city without a state. Yet the District's program is not ranked with the states on access or resources, and the program is only covered in the profile pages; no data for the program are included in Appendix A.

WHAT QUALIFIES AS A STATE PRESCHOOL PROGRAM?

Our *Yearbook* focuses on state-funded preschool initiatives as defined by the following criteria:

- The initiative is funded, controlled, and directed by the state.

- The initiative serves children of prekindergarten age, usually 3 and/or 4. Although initiatives in some states serve broader age ranges, programs that serve infants and toddlers only (such as Early Head Start) are excluded.

- Early childhood education is the primary focus of the initiative. This does not exclude programs that offer parent education, but does exclude programs in which the main focus is parent education.

- The initiative offers a group learning experience to children at least two days per week.

- State-funded preschool education initiatives must be distinct from the state's system for subsidized child care. However, preschool initiatives may be <u>coordinated</u> with the subsidy system for child care.

- The initiative is <u>not</u> primarily designed to serve children with disabilities.

- State supplements to the federal Head Start program are considered to constitute *de facto* state preschool programs if they substantially expand the number of children served. State supplements to fund quality improvements, extended days, or other program enhancements and that expand enrollment minimally are not considered equivalent to a state preschool program.

While ideally this report would identify all prekindergarten funding streams at the state, local, and federal levels, there are a number of limitations on the data that make this extremely difficult to do. For example, prekindergarten is only one of several types of educational programs toward which local districts can target their Title I funds. Many states do not track how Title I funds are used at the local level and the extent to which they are spent on prekindergarten. Another challenge involves tracking total state spending for child care, using a variety of available sources, such as CCDF dollars, TANF funds, and any state funding above and beyond the required matches for federal funds. Also, although some of these child care funds may be used for high-quality, educational, center-based programs for 3- and 4-year-olds that closely resemble programs supported by state prekindergarten initiatives, it is nearly impossible to determine what proportion of the funds are spent this way.

Age Groupings Used in this Report

Children considered to be *3 years old* during the 2002–2003 school year are those who were eligible to enter kindergarten two years later, during the 2004–2005 school year. Children considered to be *4 years old* during the 2002–2003 school year were eligible to enter kindergarten one year later, during the 2003–2004 school year. Children considered to be *5 years old* during the 2002–2003 school year were already eligible for kindergarten at the beginning of the 2002–2003 program year.

Viewing the access, quality standards and resources findings of this *Yearbook* from a national perspective provides an overall summary of the status of state prekindergarten initiatives during the 2002–2003 program year. At the same time, it paints a picture of vastly different programs across the states, with varying levels of access, quality and funding provided for the nation's children.

Access to state prekindergarten was measured by the percentages of 3- and 4-year-olds enrolled in state programs. The total number of 3- and 4-year-old children served by 44 state prekindergarten programs in 2002–2003 rose to 711,000, up from the 667,000 children served in the previous year. Like the previous year, the children served were predominately 4-year-olds, with 616,618 or 16.1 percent of the nation's 4s enrolled (Figure 5). There was tremendous variation in the enrollment figures of the individual states. Again in 2002–2003, two states, Georgia and Oklahoma, enrolled more than half their 4-year-olds (Figure 9, p. 29). In 2002–2003, 10 additional states enrolled more than 20 percent of their 4s, eight states enrolled 10–20 percent; and 18 states enrolled less than 10 percent. Twelve states funded no state prekindergarten program at all. Although most state prekindergarten programs primarily serve 4-year-olds, some states are moving toward providing prekindergarten for 3-year-olds as well. In 2002–2003, Massachusetts, New Jersey and Kentucky enrolled more than 10 percent of their 3s.

Louisiana experienced the largest increase in the percentage of 4-year-olds enrolled, with an additional 9 percent of its 4-year-olds enrolled in state preschool. Texas, New Jersey, Louisiana and North Carolina all increased enrollment by more than 5,000 children compared to the previous year. The number of children served by the prekindergarten programs in both Kansas and North Carolina more than doubled. However, large decreases in access occurred in some states. For example, enrollment declined by more than 10 percent in both Massachusetts and Missouri, resulting in a combined 3,500 fewer children served in those states.

FIGURE 5: STATE PRE-K, HEAD START, AND SPECIAL EDUCATION ENROLLMENT AS A PERCENTAGE OF TOTAL U.S. POPULATION

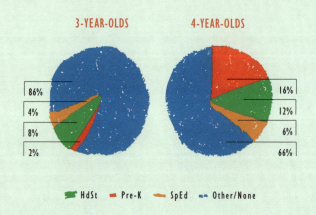

3-YEAR-OLDS   4-YEAR-OLDS

86%   4%   8%   2%

16%   12%   6%   66%

HdSt   Pre-K   SpEd   Other/None

FIGURE 6: TEACHER TRAINING REQUIREMENTS*

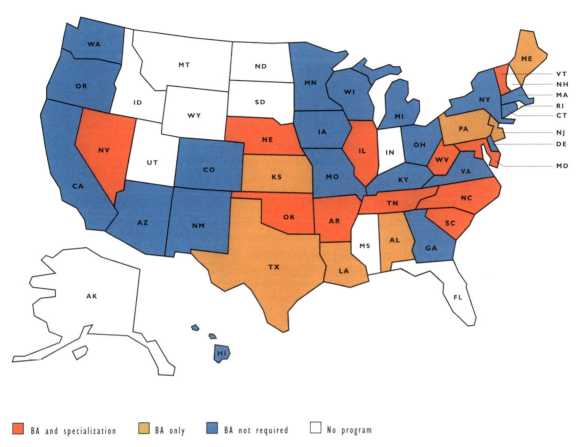

■ BA and specialization ■ BA only ■ BA not required □ No program

* In states with multiple prekindergarten initiatives, the lowest permissable training requirement is shown.

The quality of state preschool programs depends on the standards required by each state. In this report, 10 benchmarks—based on scientific evidence—are compared to quality standards set by policy in each state. Table 4 on page 44 lists the benchmarks for quality met by each state. Only Arkansas met all 10 benchmarks. Three state programs met 9 out of 10 benchmarks: Illinois, New Jersey's Abbott program, and North Carolina. Twelve out of 44 programs met less than half of the benchmarks. Many states fell short on teacher qualifications (Figure 6). For example, only 23 of the 44 programs required their preschool teachers to have 4-year college degrees, just as they do for kindergarten teachers. Furthermore, only 13 programs required a teacher with a bachelor's degree and specialized training in early childhood education. The total number of state programs that meet each benchmark, as charted in Figure 7 (p. 27), demonstrates that most states lack adequate quality standards for their children.

States spent $2.54 billion in 2002–2003, slightly more than the $2.37 billion spent in the prior year. Again, dramatic variations can be seen in resources made available by states—with five states accounting for more than 60 percent of total state spending. State spending per child was calculated by dividing total state spending by the number of children enrolled in the state preschool initiative. When state spending per child is taken into account (Table 5, p. 51), it is clear that the levels of resources made available by most states are not sufficient to provide a high-quality program. Nationally speaking, the amount spent per child enrolled in state-funded preschool averaged $3,451—well short of the national average of $9,173 spent per child for K–12 education (Figure 8). Out of 38 states, only one spent at least as much per child as the federal Head Start program. Sometimes the funding stream for state-supported preschools is supplemented by local funding. However, if preschool programs were funded in the same way that states fund K–12 education, local funding would reliably supplement state funding for preschool. The hodgepodge of funding mechanisms currently in use causes doubts about states' support for quality programs and equitable access to the high-quality programs that do exist.

The biggest increases in expenditures were in New Jersey, North Carolina and Louisiana. New Jersey increased spending by more than $100 million between 2001–2002 and 2002–2003, accounting for the majority of the nominal dollar difference in national spending on preschool. The biggest declines in total state funding were in Massachusetts, New York and Ohio, each of which reduced spending for state preschool by more than $15 million during 2002–2003, compared to adjusted spending for 2001–2002.

The access, quality standards and resources sections that follow discuss these issues in much greater detail.

Photo: RC Peters

FIGURE 7: NUMBER OF STATE PRE-K INITIATIVES MEETING BENCHMARKS

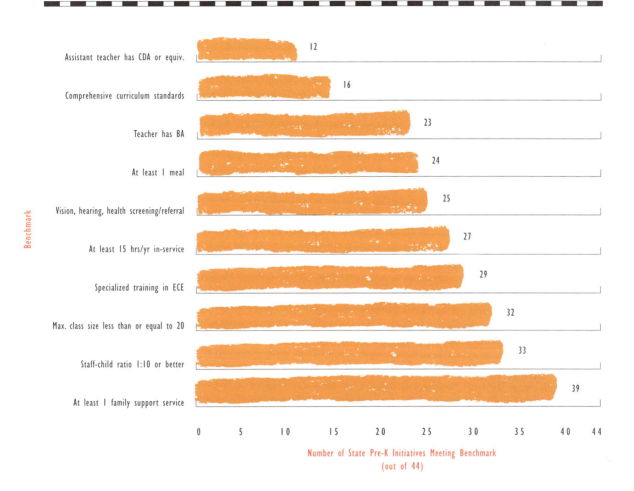

Benchmark	Number of State Pre-K Initiatives Meeting Benchmark (out of 44)
Assistant teacher has CDA or equiv.	12
Comprehensive curriculum standards	16
Teacher has BA	23
At least 1 meal	24
Vision, hearing, health screening/referral	25
At least 15 hrs/yr in-service	27
Specialized training in ECE	29
Max. class size less than or equal to 20	32
Staff-child ratio 1:10 or better	33
At least 1 family support service	39

Number of State Pre-K Initiatives Meeting Benchmark
(out of 44)

FIGURE 8: NATIONAL SPENDING PER CHILD ENROLLED

	$ thousands
Pre-K*	$3,451
HdSt	$7,089
K–12**	$9,173

State Contribution   Local Contribution   Federal Contribution

* Pre-K programs may receive additional funds from federal or local sources that are not included in this figure.

** K–12 expenditures include capital spending as well as current operating expenditures.

ACCESS

Approximately 740,000 children were enrolled in state prekindergarten initiatives in 2002–2003. The number of children served ranged widely, with Delaware, Hawaii, Nevada, and New Mexico each serving fewer than 1,000 children, while Texas served more than 150,000 children. Ten states accounted for more than three-quarters of the children participating in state prekindergarten programs, and even these states served only a fraction of their preschool-age populations. Overall, state prekindergarten initiatives reached about 10 percent of the nation's population of 3- and 4-year-olds. Most of those participants were 4 years old, representing 16 percent of 4-year-olds in the United States. A mere 2 percent of 3-year-olds were served in state prekindergarten initiatives.

Eligibility Criteria

Most states targeted their programs to low-income children and children with other background factors that place them at risk for starting school behind their peers. However, there were nine states that did not set eligibility criteria for at least one of their state prekindergarten initiatives. Having no eligibility criteria does not mean all children are actually able to participate—Georgia and Oklahoma are the only two states that made prekindergarten universally available to 4-year-olds. In the other states, access was still limited by the availability of state funds to support prekindergarten and districts' willingness to offer it. Some states, such as Nevada, New York (for its Universal Prekindergarten Program), and West Virginia, which technically allowed all children to be eligible, in fact often gave priority to low-income and at-risk children—although New York and West Virginia plan to make prekindergarten universally available eventually.

Whereas many states used family income as one of the factors (or the only factor) in determining eligibility, they did not all use the same income cutoff. Commonly used income eligibility criteria were the cutoff for free lunch (130 percent of the federal poverty level), which was used in three states (Iowa, Kansas, and Kentucky), or the cutoff for reduced-price lunch (185 percent of poverty), which was used by 11 state initiatives. Eleven other state initiatives used alternative income criteria, with the cutoff set at levels ranging from 100 percent of poverty for the Head Start models in Delaware, Minnesota, Oregon, and Wisconsin, to 125 percent of state median income in Massachusetts. Both of New Jersey's state prekindergarten initiatives used free or reduced-price lunch eligibility to determine which districts qualified for programs, although all children in qualifying districts were allowed to participate.

Most of the states that set income eligibility criteria required only a certain proportion of participating children to meet these criteria or allowed at least some children to qualify based on other factors. For example, only half of the children enrolled in Vermont's prekindergarten initiative were required to meet the income eligibility criteria; the remainder qualified for the program based on other risk factors such as exposure to violence or substance abuse, low parental education levels, limited English proficiency, or developmental delay.

The eight remaining state initiatives did not set income eligibility criteria and instead took into account a range of risk factors. In several of these states, the risk factors used and the relative weight given to these factors were determined at the local level. Factors frequently taken into account included disability or developmental delay, limited English proficiency, low parental education levels, low birth weight, and experience of abuse or neglect. Some states, such as Louisiana (for its 8(g) program) and Illinois, used developmental screenings to determine whether children had risk factors that qualified them to participate.

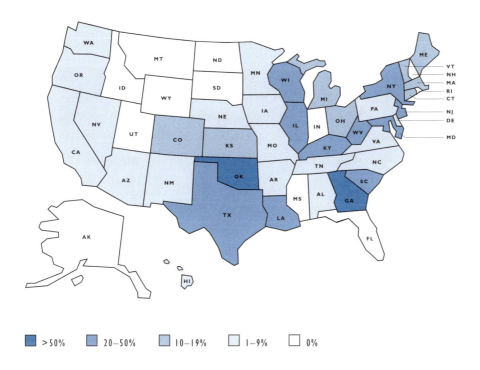

■ >50%   ■ 20–50%   ■ 10–19%   □ 1–9%   □ 0%

Age Requirements

Although all state prekindergarten initiatives served 4-year-olds, in 2002–2003 there were 27 programs that offered services to children in other age groups as well. Twenty-two of these initiatives served only children at ages 3 and 4. Five additional states served even younger children. Arkansas, Minnesota, Nevada, and New Mexico served children from birth to age 5, while Nebraska served children from 6 weeks of age.

Some states that allowed 3-year-olds to participate limited their access. For example, Hawaii and Kentucky served 3-year-olds only if they had special needs, and West Virginia had plans to adopt a similar approach as of July 2004. Colorado required 4-year-olds to have only one risk factor to qualify for the program, but 3-year-olds were required to have three risk factors to participate. Washington allowed 3-year-olds to enroll only after all 4-year-olds whose families wanted them to participate had been served. Arizona allowed children younger than 4 to be served, but in practice generally served only 4-year-olds in its state program.

Among the 20 state initiatives that served children younger than 4 years old and reported enrollment data by age for 2002–2003, 3-year-olds accounted for 40 percent or more of total enrollment for only three state initiatives—programs in Massachusetts and Vermont, as well as New Jersey's Abbott program. In most states reporting data, 3-year-olds made up less than one-third of the enrollment. Seventeen state initiatives restricted access exclusively to 4-year-olds.

EVALUATING PRESCHOOL POLICY: WHY TARGETING INEVITABLY FALLS SHORT

For four decades, publicly funded preschool initiatives have primarily operated on the targeted program model. This is not without reason, as the premise of targeting is a worthy one. In concept, it focuses limited resources to deliver preschool programs only to children most in need—whether they are disadvantaged by economics, disability, or other circumstances.

At both state and federal levels, policymakers have been attracted to targeted programs because they "look good on paper" since the total commitment of public funds is less than if such programs were provided for all children. Conventional wisdom has held that targeting is more likely to gain political support than preschool programs for all.

However, this policy model has met with mixed success when put into practice. After decades of operation, many targeted programs have not been able to identify and serve the majority of children who qualify for them. So mobile are today's families, both geographically and economically, that targeting a high percentage of those who qualify has proven to be an almost insurmountable task.

A prime example is the federal Head Start program. Forty years after its inception—and 10 years after Congress authorized full funding—there are not enough slots to serve all eligible children. Enrollment remains at less than 60 percent of the number of preschool-age children in poverty. The actual number of children in poverty served by Head Start at any given time may in fact drop below 50 percent. This is because families with children move in and out of poverty and not all Head Start children (particularly those with disabilities) must come from low-income families. Such realities on the ground sorely test the operating model of targeted preschool programs.

The model used by child care programs to determine eligibility also poses problems. When this type of model is used, shifting family circumstances including mothers' employment status confound the process of determining eligibility. Changes in mothers' employment status may lead children to cycle in and out of programs, though their need for a good education does not change.

There is also mounting evidence of unmet demand for (and unequal access to) quality preschool among families whose incomes are somewhat above the qualification levels for targeted programs. Recent evidence suggests this group may represent a larger population of children than those who qualify for targeted programs.[1] Children from these families often lack access to the patchwork of programs that represents preschool in America. On one hand, they do not qualify for targeted programs; on the other, their parents cannot afford to pay for high-quality preschool programs even if they exist in their neighborhoods.

EVALUATING PRESCHOOL POLICY: WHY TARGETING INEVITABLY FALLS SHORT

Recent research demonstrates that the need for quality preschool programs does not dramatically diminish once families exceed the income eligibility requirements for targeted programs. Rather, the school readiness gap (see figure 10) is surprisingly persistent and drops only gradually for all children except those with family incomes in the top 20 percent of all Americans.[2]

This inefficiency in providing access to quality early education—and the growing awareness among business and policy leaders of preschool's importance to future productivity—has spurred a reexamination of targeting. Of course, "one size fits all" will never be good prekindergarten policy; some children require broader and more intensive services than others. Still, more states should follow the lead of Oklahoma and Georgia to expand access for all children and at the same time ensure that children with the greatest needs are included in prekindergarten and receive the services necessary to fully support their learning and development.

1 Barnett, W.S., & Yarosz, D.J. (2004) Who goes to preschool and why does it matter? *Preschool Policy Matters, 8.* New Brunswick, NJ: National Institute for Early Education Research, Rutgers University.
2 Barnett, W.S., Brown, K., & Shore, R. (2004) The universal vs. targeted debate: Should the United States have preschool for all? *Preschool Policy Matters, 6.* New Brunswick, NJ: National Institute for Early Education Research, Rutgers University.

FIGURE 10: ACADEMIC ABILITIES OF ENTERING KINDERGARTENERS BY FAMILY INCOME

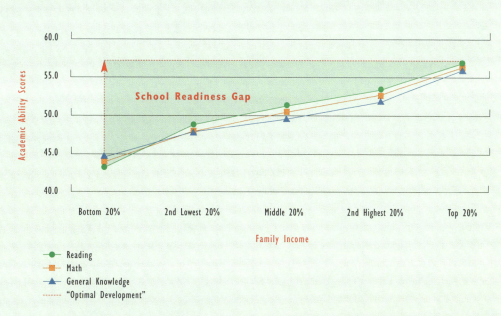

Source: U.S. Department of Education, National Center for Education Statistics, Early Childhood Longitudinal Study, Kindergarten Class of 1998–99, Fall 1998.

Serving Children with Special Needs

Most states served children with special needs in state prekindergarten classrooms through a combination of state prekindergarten funding along with other local, state, and/or federal sources such as IDEA funding. However, several states—Arizona, Colorado, Connecticut, Georgia, Iowa, Kansas, Nebraska, New Jersey (for its Abbott program), Oregon, Pennsylvania, and Virginia—reported that children with special needs may be served in state prekindergarten classrooms but only using funding other than state prekindergarten dollars.

Many states were not able to provide data on the percentage of children enrolled in state prekindergarten initiatives who had Individualized Education Plans (IEPs) for meeting their special needs. Of the 26 state initiatives for which there were data, the percentage of children with IEPs ranged from 3 percent in California and South Carolina to 63 percent in Kentucky. The median for the states reporting data was 10 percent.

Enrollment Supported with Other Sources

Many of the children enrolled in state prekindergarten programs were partially supported with other funding sources, such as federal IDEA, Head Start, or TANF funds, or local sources. For example, Iowa reported that of the 2,355 children served, 286 were supported with local sources and 379 with IDEA funding.

Most states reported using some other funding sources to help support services for participating children, but they were often unable to provide complete, specific data on the number of children benefiting from each of these sources. A few states also indicated that some children beyond those counted in the state prekindergarten enrollment totals were being served in the same classrooms as state prekindergarten children, but using other sources of funding. Once again, these states were generally not able to provide specific data on the number of children served or amount of funding from these other sources.

Availability of Programs Across Communities

Children's ability to participate in prekindergarten depends on availability of programs in their communities. Only three states required prekindergarten to be offered in all of their school districts (Kentucky, Maryland, and South Carolina). Another four states offered prekindergarten in all of their counties, and five states offered prekindergarten in at least 90 percent of their towns, counties, or school districts.

In contrast, 14 states had state prekindergarten programs available in fewer than half of their districts or communities. Nebraska's prekindergarten program was offered in just 5 percent of school districts and Pennsylvania's program was available in only 6 percent of districts.

A few states, including Connecticut, New Jersey, and Texas, did not require prekindergarten to be offered in all districts, but did require it in certain districts. For example, schools in Texas were required to offer prekindergarten if there were at least 15 eligible 4-year-olds (children who qualified for free or reduced-price lunch, were unable to speak and understand English, or were homeless) in the district.

Parent Fees

Most state prekindergarten initiatives served children free of charge to families. However, nine state initiatives had (or allowed districts the option of having) sliding fee scales, which charge parents fees based on income. Connecticut charged fees to all families, but most other states charged fees only to certain families or under certain circumstances. For example, Hawaii and Ohio charged fees only to families whose incomes were above 100 percent of the federal poverty level, and Iowa, Kentucky, and Louisiana's LA4 program collected fees only from families who did not meet income eligibility criteria.

Hours of Operation

State prekindergarten programs most commonly operated on a half-day basis, 5 days per week during the school year. However, a number of state initiatives operated on a different schedule, offering longer hours or fewer days per week. In addition, many states coordinated with other programs and resources to provide full-day, full-year services to meet the needs of families with working parents.

Only 10 state initiatives operated on a full school-day schedule or for longer hours. Twelve state initiatives operated on a part-day schedule, and Delaware's programs operated between 4 and 6 hours per day. In Connecticut, at least 60 percent of slots in each community were required to be full-day slots. For the remaining 20 state initiatives, daily operating hours were locally determined. However, many of these state initiatives required programs to operate for a minimum number of hours per day or per week—usually about 2.5 or 3.5 hours per day—and one state initiative required a minimum number of hours of operation per year.

Several states that offered both full-day and half-day options varied the amount of funding provided to programs based on hours of operation. For example, Connecticut paid $7,000 per child for full-day programs and $4,500 per child for half-day programs. New York's Experimental Prekindergarten Program provided 45 percent more for full-day classes than for half-day classes. In Oklahoma, full-day programs received nearly twice as much funding per child as half-day programs.

More than half (23) of the state initiatives operated 5 days per week. Colorado and Michigan's programs operated fewer than 5 days per week. The rest of the state initiatives (19) had locally determined weekly schedules. However, some of these initiatives required programs to operate for at least 4 days per week.

Most states' prekindergarten programs operated for the academic year. While a number of states allowed the specific schedule to be determined locally, programs in these states still typically operated for the academic year. A few states had a significant number of programs operating on a full-year schedule. These include Hawaii, Connecticut (which required at least 60 percent of slots to be full-year), Massachusetts (where about 60 percent of programs operated for the calendar year), New Mexico, and Vermont (where prekindergarten programs offered in child care centers generally operated year-round).

While state prekindergarten initiatives were typically funded to operate on a part-day, part-year schedule, in 34 state initiatives children were able to receive wrap-around services. These wrap-around services were usually provided in coordination with other resources and programs, and were not funded by the state prekindergarten initiative itself. The most commonly cited sources of funding for wrap-around care were federal Child Care and Development Funds and tuition charged to parents. Most states were not able to provide data on how many of the children enrolled in their prekindergarten programs were receiving wrap-around services. Among those states that did provide data, the percentage of enrolled children in wrap-around care ranged from 5 percent in California and Maryland to an estimated 90 percent in Hawaii.

Program Settings

Although the large majority of children enrolled in state prekindergarten programs are served in public school settings, many children are also being served in other locations, such as child care centers and Head Start programs. Each type of setting has certain advantages. For example, public schools can allow programs to take advantage of existing resources, such as experienced staff, buildings, and playgrounds. Child care centers may be better able to provide full-day services for children with working parents. Head Start programs can offer prekindergarten programs access to their comprehensive services and other resources. As shown in Figure 11, of the states that were able to report data, 71 percent of children were served in public schools, 18 percent in private child care centers, 7 percent in Head Start programs, less than 1 percent in faith-based programs, less than 1 percent in family child care, and 3 percent in other settings.

Out of the 39 state initiatives for which data were reported, 25 served half or more of their children in public school settings. These state initiatives include 11 in which all, or virtually all, children were served in public school settings.

Still, in some state prekindergarten initiatives, a large percentage of children were served in private child care settings. More than 40 percent of children participating in initiatives in Connecticut, Georgia, Massachusetts, New Jersey (for its Abbott program), and North Carolina were served in private child care.

FIGURE 11: PERCENTAGE OF STATE PRESCHOOL ENROLLEES BY TYPE OF PROGRAM SETTING

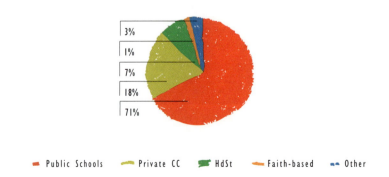

3%
1%
7%
18%
71%

■ Public Schools ━ Private CC ▧ HdSt ━ Faith-based ▪▪ Other

Photo: RC Peters

Some states served many of their children in Head Start programs. In addition to the state Head Start models in Delaware, Ohio, Oregon, and Wisconsin, 11 state initiatives each had 10 percent or more of enrolled children receiving state prekindergarten services in Head Start settings.

Only four states reported using family child care to deliver state prekindergarten services. Even in states that did, only a small percentage of children were served in this type of setting—7 percent in Massachusetts, and 2 percent or less for New York's Universal Prekindergarten Program, Ohio's Head Start program, and Washington's Early Childhood Education and Assistance Program.

Most states were not able to provide data on the proportion of children enrolled in faith-based settings. Among those that did provide data, only Louisiana's Nonpublic Schools Early Childhood Development Program, which had nearly all children enrolled in such settings, had a large proportion of children served in this type of program. Connecticut had 14 percent of its children in faith-based settings, and the other six states reporting data for this category had 5 percent or less of their children in faith-based programs.

Twelve state initiatives had a home-based option during the 2002–2003 program year. The number of children enrolled in this type of component ranged from 20 children in Washington to 4,719 in Arkansas.

Changes in Access from 2001–2002 to 2002–2003

The number of children enrolled in state prekindergarten programs grew from approximately 693,000 in 2001–2002 to more than 738,000 in 2002–2003, an increase of 45,000 children, or 6.5 percent. Twenty-six states showed increases in enrollment. In about half of these states, the increase was less than 10 percent, but several states reported increases of 50 percent or more. However, enrollment decreased in nine states. Although many of these states saw only a small drop in the number of children served, decreases in other states were relatively large. For example, New Mexico's enrollment dropped more than 50 percent, from 2,000 to 850, and Massachusetts reduced its enrollment by 10 percent, or more than 2,000 children. Enrollment in three states was unchanged (Delaware, Maine, and Maryland).

Despite the overall growth in enrollment, the number of 3-year-olds participating in state prekindergarten programs actually declined. Although the proportion of 4-year-olds in the U.S. enrolled in state prekindergarten programs increased from 14.4 percent in 2001–2002 to 16.1 percent in 2002–2003, the proportion of 3-year-olds dropped slightly from 2.7 percent to 2.5 percent. Many of the programs that expanded most rapidly served only 4-year-olds, and some of the programs that served both 3-year-olds and 4-year-olds placed more emphasis on serving 4-year-olds. For example, the number of 4-year-olds in Texas' prekindergarten program increased by more than 15,000, but the number of 3-year-olds decreased by 6,000. New York's EPK program served 3,400 more 4-year-olds but 4,400 fewer 3-year-olds. Arkansas, Iowa, and Tennessee also each had small decreases in the number of 3-year-olds served whereas enrollment of 4-year-olds in their programs rose.

Due to some differences in the way information was collected in 2001–2002 and 2002–2003, data related to other aspects of access to prekindergarten are not completely comparable between the two time periods. However, based on the information available, there do not appear to have been major shifts in state policies and practices for prekindergarten access. States maintained generally the same approaches on issues such as which districts or communities offered prekindergarten, eligibility criteria, operating schedules, use of sliding fee scales, and settings in which programs operate.

Although state policies and practices involving access to prekindergarten have been largely stable, a few states have begun to make changes in certain areas. For example, Maryland revised its eligibility criteria so that, as of 2003–2004, local districts are required to provide prekindergarten to all 4-year-olds who qualify for free or reduced-price lunch or who are homeless. In North Carolina, individual programs currently determine eligibility criteria, but by 2004–2005, at least 80 percent of participants must be from families at or below 75 percent of state median income.

A few states have started to implement changes to other aspects of their programs. For instance, Illinois, Maryland, West Virginia, and Wisconsin have indicated that they plan to start making greater use of settings outside the public schools in providing prekindergarten.

TABLE 3: STATE RANKINGS BY PRE-K ACCESS FOR 4-YEAR-OLDS

Access for 4-Year-Olds Rank	State	Percent Enrolled in State Prekindergarten (2002–2003)			Percent Enrolled in State Prekindergarten, Head Start, or IDEA Preschool Grants Programs (2002–2003)		
		4-year-olds	3-year-olds	Total (3s and 4s)	4-year-olds	3-year-olds	Total (3s and 4s)
1	Oklahoma	59.4%	0.0%	29.7%	82.4%	16.4%	49.5%
2	Georgia	54.3%	0.0%	27.0%	68.1%	11.6%	39.7%
3	Texas	43.0%	4.1%	23.5%	57.6%	14.7%	36.1%
4	South Carolina	32.3%	1.9%	17.1%	51.1%	16.4%	33.7%
5	New York	29.7%	0.6%	15.2%	56.2%	14.1%	35.2%
6	West Virginia	28.9%	9.5%	19.2%	57.9%	27.4%	42.7%
7	Kentucky	27.7%	10.5%	19.1%	60.8%	29.5%	45.1%
8	Maryland	26.3%	2.0%	14.2%	39.9%	11.5%	25.7%
9	Wisconsin	24.8%	1.0%	12.9%	43.0%	14.8%	28.9%
10	Illinois	24.4%	8.0%	16.2%	41.5%	19.9%	30.7%
11	New Jersey	24.1%	14.6%	19.4%	35.4%	23.2%	29.3%
12	Louisiana	20.9%	0.0%	10.5%	43.2%	17.1%	30.1%
13	Michigan	19.2%	0.0%	9.7%	39.2%	13.6%	26.5%
14	Kansas	14.7%	0.0%	7.3%	32.6%	13.1%	22.8%
15	Colorado	13.8%	1.5%	7.6%	28.7%	10.3%	19.4%
16	Maine	10.8%	0.0%	5.5%	39.4%	17.6%	28.6%
17	Massachusetts	10.5%	10.6%	10.5%	25.5%	20.9%	23.2%
18	Connecticut	10.4%	3.4%	6.9%	24.2%	12.7%	18.5%
19	Vermont	9.8%	7.0%	8.4%	26.6%	19.9%	23.3%
20	Ohio	9.5%	6.2%	7.9%	26.6%	19.1%	22.8%
21	California	8.7%	2.2%	5.5%	25.0%	11.2%	18.2%
22	Delaware	8.5%	0.0%	4.2%	24.6%	10.1%	17.3%
23	Washington	6.9%	1.8%	4.4%	21.8%	10.0%	15.9%
24	Virginia	6.3%	0.0%	3.1%	20.1%	8.0%	14.0%
25	Hawaii	6.2%	0.0%	3.1%	21.1%	10.8%	15.9%
26	Arkansas	6.1%	2.4%	4.3%	35.3%	19.9%	27.7%
27	Oregon	5.8%	3.0%	4.4%	22.7%	13.4%	18.1%
28	North Carolina	5.6%	0.0%	2.8%	21.9%	8.9%	15.3%
29	Arizona	5.1%	0.0%	2.5%	23.7%	9.9%	16.8%
30	Iowa	4.5%	1.3%	2.9%	20.5%	12.1%	16.3%
31	Missouri	4.3%	2.4%	3.4%	22.2%	16.1%	19.2%
32	Tennessee	3.2%	1.1%	2.1%	22.0%	10.1%	16.0%
33	Nebraska	2.5%	1.5%	2.0%	20.2%	14.2%	17.2%
34	New Mexico	2.5%	0.8%	1.6%	28.3%	14.3%	21.2%
35	Alabama	2.2%	0.0%	1.1%	23.8%	11.9%	17.9%
36	Minnesota	2.1%	1.3%	1.7%	18.0%	12.1%	15.1%
37	Pennsylvania	1.8%	0.0%	0.9%	18.9%	11.7%	15.3%
38	Nevada	1.5%	0.7%	1.1%	11.1%	6.3%	8.7%
No Program	Alaska	0.0%	0.0%	0.0%	22.3%	16.9%	19.6%
No Program	Florida	0.0%	0.0%	0.0%	16.2%	9.3%	12.8%
No Program	Idaho	0.0%	0.0%	0.0%	19.4%	8.1%	13.7%
No Program	Indiana	0.0%	0.0%	0.0%	15.3%	9.6%	12.5%
No Program	Mississippi	0.0%	0.0%	0.0%	43.2%	28.7%	35.9%
No Program	Montana	0.0%	0.0%	0.0%	27.1%	17.0%	22.1%
No Program	New Hampshire	0.0%	0.0%	0.0%	10.9%	7.7%	9.3%
No Program	North Dakota	0.0%	0.0%	0.0%	31.0%	17.8%	24.5%
No Program	Rhode Island	0.0%	0.0%	0.0%	23.3%	11.6%	17.5%
No Program	South Dakota	0.0%	0.0%	0.0%	26.9%	19.9%	23.3%
No Program	Utah	0.0%	0.0%	0.0%	14.9%	7.2%	11.0%
No Program	Wyoming	0.0%	0.0%	0.0%	30.5%	19.8%	25.1%
	50 State Population	16.1%	2.5%	9.3%	34.0%	13.8%	23.9%

37

For details about how these figures were calculated, see the Methodology section and Roadmap to State Profile Pages.

QUALITY STANDARDS

Research shows that children who have previously attended high-quality preschool education programs are more successful in kindergarten. Quality in a prekindergarten program depends on several factors including curriculum standards, personnel requirements, program structure, and the availability of family support services. For example, high levels of teacher education are associated with more positive outcomes for preschool students. Quality standards for state-funded preschool initiatives are typically specified in state-level policies that identify the minimum requirements. Findings from our survey show that policies relating to quality standards vary considerably from state to state—and sometimes within a state, in states with multiple prekindergarten initiatives.

Quality Standards Checklist

We used a 10-item Quality Standards Checklist to compare standards of quality across different state prekindergarten initiatives. Previous research has shown that the components of this checklist contribute to the quality of prekindergarten programs, and research findings were used in developing benchmarks for each item. The benchmarks do not represent high standards of excellence or an exhaustive list of quality elements. Rather, they indicate important minimum standards for educationally effective programs, particularly those serving disadvantaged children.

State prekindergarten programs received a summary score indicating the number of items for which state policies met or exceeded the relevant benchmarks. Possible quality summary scores range from a minimum of zero to a maximum of 10. This scoring system is simply a count of quality components—it does not imply that each item is of equal value or is interchangeable. We strongly recommend that state policies be evaluated based on standards for each component of the checklist rather than solely on the basis of summary scores. Our Quality Standards Checklist is composed of the following benchmarks:

- *Curriculum standards*—the state must have comprehensive curriculum standards that are specific to prekindergarten and cover the domains of language/literacy, mathematics, science, social/emotional skills, cognitive development, health and physical development, and social studies.[1]
- *Teacher degree requirement*—lead teachers in both public and private settings must be required to hold at least a BA.[2]
- *Teacher specialized training requirement*—preservice requirements for lead teachers should include specialized training in prekindergarten. Such training might involve licensure/endorsement in the prekindergarten area or a degree or credential in early childhood, such as a CDA. Kindergarten endorsements and elementary teaching certificates did not qualify as specialized training in a pre-school area.[2]
- *Assistant teacher degree requirement*—assistant teachers are required to hold at least a CDA or equivalent training, in both public and private settings.[3]
- *Teacher in-service requirement*—teachers must be required to attend an average of at least 15 clock hours of professional development per year. In-service training received in fulfillment of state recertification requirements was counted toward a program's teacher in-service requirement.[4]

- *Maximum class size*—class sizes must be limited to no more than 20 children, for both 3- and 4-year-olds.[5]
- *Staff–child ratio*—at least one staff member must be present per 10 children in a classroom, for both 3- and 4-year-olds.[6]
- *Screening/referral requirements*—programs are required to provide both screening and referral services covering at least vision, hearing, and health.[7]
- *Required support services*—programs must offer (either directly or through active referral) at least one type of additional support service for families of participants or the participants themselves. Types of services may include parent conferences or home visits, parenting support or training, referral to social services, and information relating to nutrition.[8]
- *Meal requirements*—all participants must be offered at least one meal per day, including any meals offered due to requirements not specifically set by the preschool program. Snacks were not counted as meals.[9]

This year's Quality Standards Checklist is adapted from the checklist used in NIEER's *2003 State Preschool Yearbook* and is largely unchanged in its emphasis. The item labeled "Required Support Services" replaces the item labeled "Family Support Service Requirements" in the 2003 *Yearbook*, reflecting a broader emphasis on the types of support services offered to participants and their families.[10]

Details about how programs fared on each of the component benchmarks are discussed below and reported in Table 4 (p. 44) for each of the 44 state-funded initiatives. State-financed prekindergarten initiatives varied considerably in meeting the benchmarks and received a wide range of scores on the Quality Standards Checklist. Summary scores were as high as 10 in Arkansas, and as low as 2 in Pennsylvania.

Curriculum Standards

States identify and prioritize specific content areas for educational programs through the adoption of curriculum standards. Since curriculum standards are set at the state level, all prekindergarten programs funded by any given state must follow a common set of curriculum standards. This is true even in states that fund more than one preschool initiative. Curriculum standards were found to be comprehensive in 12 of the 38 states that funded prekindergarten initiatives.

Personnel Requirements

Educational requirements for prekindergarten teachers are important indicators of a state's commitment to supporting quality early education services. Research shows that teachers and staff members with higher levels of education provide higher quality learning environments in their preschool classrooms. However, personnel requirements vary considerably from state to state, and many state policies do not meet the minimum benchmarks.

In 23 of the 44 state-financed preschool initiatives profiled in this report, all lead teachers were required to hold a bachelor's degree. In eight more state preschool initiatives—those in Iowa, Massachusetts, Michigan, Missouri, Oregon, Virginia, and Washington, as well as New York's Universal Prekindergarten program—lead teachers were required to hold a bachelor's degree only when teaching in public school settings. Each of these additional programs had a two-tier system in which teacher degree requirements were more stringent for teachers in public school settings than they were for teachers in nonpublic settings.

Overall, more than two-thirds of the state preschool initiatives required teachers working in public school settings to have at least a BA. New York's initiatives had the most stringent requirements for prekindergarten teachers in public schools. Teachers trained after 1978 were required to have master's degrees. New Mexico was the only state that did not require a degree or credential of preschool teachers in public schools—all other states required at least an associate's degree, a CDA, or equivalent training.

Bachelor's degrees were required of teachers in fewer than half of the state initiatives allowing children to be served in prekindergarten programs operating in private school settings. Among the 21 state initiatives not requiring a BA, only three required an AA for all teachers in nonpublic settings. The CDA (or equivalent training) was the most common requirement among programs not requiring a BA. In five state initiatives, there was no specific degree or credential requirement that applied to all teachers in nonpublic settings, although four of these programs either set requirements for teachers in certain types of nonpublic settings (e.g., Head Start) or required teachers to complete a minimal amount of coursework.

In 29 of the 44 state-financed preschool initiatives, teachers were required to receive specialized training in prekindergarten. Requirements for specialized training were closely tied to teacher degree requirements. In programs that required teachers to hold a bachelor's degree, specialized training typically took the form of licensure, certification, or an endorsement in early childhood or a closely related area. In programs that did not require a BA, specialized training usually involved earning a CDA.

Degree requirements for assistant teachers were minimal, and were less stringent than those for lead teachers in all states except New Mexico. New Mexico did not set a minimum educational requirement for lead or assistant teachers. Only 12 of the 44 state prekindergarten initiatives required assistant teachers to have at least a CDA or equivalent training. In some states, the educational requirements for assistant teachers differed in public and private settings. Although requirements in public schools were generally more rigorous, the differences in requirements were relatively minor. For example, assistant teachers in Missouri's state prekindergarten initiative were required to have a high school diploma plus vocational certification in early childhood education when working in public schools, but were required to have only a high school diploma when working in nonpublic settings. Vermont set the most rigorous educational requirements in public schools, as assistant teachers in such settings were required to have a BA. Across the states, the most common educational requirement for assistant teachers was a high school diploma or its equivalent. In eight state prekindergarten initiatives there were no minimum educational requirements that applied to assistant teachers in all program settings, and in three additional programs the requirements were determined locally in at least some circumstances. Pennsylvania's program did not require assistant teachers to be present in the classroom.

Although requirements for teacher in-service training varied considerably from one state prekindergarten initiative to the next, 27 of the 44 initiatives required teachers to participate in an average of at least 15 hours of in-service training per year. In some cases, the reported in-service requirements were determined by state regulations for recertification. Alabama set the highest annual in-service requirement—40 clock hours per year. Six state initiatives had no annual requirement for teacher in-service training.

Class Size and Staff–Child Ratio

Small class sizes are associated with more effective programs. The benchmark of capping class sizes at no more than 20 students was met by 32 of 44 state preschool initiatives. When programs served both 3- and 4-year-olds, they typically followed the same requirements for maximum class sizes for children in both age groups. Of the programs that did not, most followed Head Start's requirements for a maximum class size of 17 for 3-year-olds and a maximum class size of 20 for 4-year-olds. Regardless, when maximum class sizes differed by the age of child, requirements always specified a smaller group size for 3-year-olds than for 4-year-olds.

The state preschool programs that required the smallest group size were Colorado's program and New Jersey's Abbott program. Each of these initiatives required that group sizes be no larger than 15 children for both 3- and 4-year-olds. In nine state prekindergarten programs, there was no statewide requirement regarding maximum class size, in which cases requirements may be determined at the local level. However, some of these state initiatives offered specific guidance—for example, encouraging programs to follow recommendations of the National Association for the Education of Young Children.

Low staff–child ratios are also associated with effective early childhood education programs. Staff–child ratio requirements were closely related to the class size requirements followed by state prekindergarten initiatives. Three-quarters (33 of 44) of the state preschool initiatives had requirements in place that set a 1:10 staff–child ratio or better. When programs served both 3- and 4-year-olds, they typically followed the same staff–child ratio requirements for children in both age groups. However, when this was not the case, requirements always specified a lower staff–child ratio for 3-year-olds than for 4-year-olds.

The lowest overall staff–child ratio requirement was the 2:15 requirement set by New Jersey's Abbott program. In a few states, even lower ratios were required for classes with larger group sizes. For example, New York's Universal Prekindergarten and Experimental Prekindergarten programs required staff–child ratios of either 1:9 or 3:20. In seven of the initiatives covered by this report, there was no minimum state requirement for staff–child ratios (in which cases requirements may be determined at the local level). With one exception, the initiatives without state-specified staff–child ratio requirements also did not set maximum requirements for class size.

Comprehensive Services

The remaining components of our Quality Standards Checklist focused on the types of comprehensive services provided by state preschool initiatives. The additional support services offered to preschoolers and their families can help promote learning and child development. As with state policies regarding curriculum standards, personnel requirements, and program structure, there was a good deal of variability in the types of comprehensive services offered across different state programs.

Twenty-five of the 44 state preschool initiatives required programs to provide all enrolled children with both screening and referral services covering vision, hearing, and general physical health. A number of initiatives went beyond this benchmark by offering additional types of services, including dental and developmental screening and referral. Among the state preschool programs not meeting our benchmark of screening and referral for vision, hearing, and health, six offered at least one type of screening and referral service. Five more programs allowed screening and referral services to be determined at the local level, and the remaining eight did not mandate screening and referral services for vision, hearing, or health.

Support services for families were offered through 39 of the 44 state prekindergarten programs. The only state programs that did not require at least one type of support service were those in Arizona, Maine, Missouri, Pennsylvania, and West Virginia. The majority of state policies mandate multiple types of family support services. Some of the most frequently required support services were parent involvement activities, parenting support or training, parent conferences/home visits, referral to social services, health services for children, and transition to kindergarten activities.

Finally, in 24 of the 44 state preschool initiatives, all children were offered at least one meal per day. While not requiring meals for all participants, an additional 13 programs offered meals under certain circumstances, particularly when children attended programs that offered longer class days or were operating during mealtimes. In the remaining state preschool programs, there were no meal requirements or only snacks were offered.

Photo: RC Peters

Quality Standards Overview and Changes from 2001–2002 to 2002–2003

Overall, program standards for quality varied widely from initiative to initiative. Of 44 state-financed prekindergarten initiatives across the U.S., the Arkansas Better Chance program was the only initiative to meet all 10 of our benchmarks for quality. Initiatives in Illinois and North Carolina, as well as the New Jersey Abbott program, met 9 of 10 benchmarks. Pennsylvania's program received the lowest quality score, meeting only 2 of the 10 benchmarks. Taking all state-funded prekindergarten initiatives into account, the median Quality Standards Checklist summary score was 6 of 10, indicating that there is marked room for improvement in quality standards of many state prekindergarten programs.

In terms of individual elements of the Quality Standards Checklist, the benchmark for required family support services was met by the most (39 of 44) state preschool initiatives, while the benchmark for assistant teacher degree requirements was met by the fewest (12 of 44). Only 12 states—representing 16 prekindergarten initiatives—had promulgated comprehensive preschool curriculum standards. Each of the other benchmarks was met by between one-half and three-quarters of the state preschool initiatives.

It is important to note that the Quality Standards Checklist is a measure of state *policy*, and does not necessarily represent actual practices in prekindergarten programs. In some cases, program quality may widely exceed the standards set at the state level, and in other cases many providers may fail to comply with state requirements. Nevertheless, our data on state policies clearly indicate a need for improvement. Such policies are the means by which states establish acceptable levels of quality to which every child served is entitled. Inadequate standards mean that fewer children will receive an effective preschool education.

When comparing the policies of state prekindergarten initiatives that were followed in 2001–2002 with those followed in 2002–2003, it is apparent that policies change very slowly. State preschool standards are essentially unchanged from the previous year, despite the inadequacies of most of them. Only one state initiative specifically reported a policy change for the 2002–2003 program year that resulted in its meeting an additional benchmark on the Quality Standards Checklist. A number of other states received higher scores on the Quality Standards Checklist in 2002–2003, and two states received lower scores, due to improvements in NIEER's survey questions or the information provided by states. The single policy change reported in response to NIEER's survey was made by Louisiana's 8(g) Student Enhancement Block Grant Program, which changed its staff–child ratio requirement from 1:15 to 1:10.

1   Current practice too frequently underestimates children's capabilities to learn during the preschool years. Clear and appropriate expectations for learning and development across all domains are essential to an educationally effective preschool program. Bowman, B. T., Donovan, M. S., & Burns, M. S. (Eds.). (2001). *Eager to learn: Educating our preschoolers.* Washington, DC: National Academy Press. Frede, E. C. (1998). Preschool program quality in programs for children in poverty. In W. S. Barnett & S. S. Boocock (Eds.), *Early care and education for children in poverty: Promises, programs, and long-term results* (pp. 77–98). Albany, NY: SUNY Press. Kendall, J. S. (2003). Setting standards in early childhood education. *Educational Leadership 60*(7), 64–68.

2   Based on a review of the evidence, a committee of the National Research Council recommended that preschool teachers have a BA with specialization in early childhood education (Bowman et al., 2001). Burchinal, M. R., Cryer, D., Clifford, R. M., & Howes, C. (2002). Caregiver training and classroom quality in child care centers. *Applied Developmental Science, 6*, 2–11. Barnett, W. S. (2003). Better teachers, better preschools: Student achievement linked to teacher qualifications. *Preschool Policy Matters, 2.* New Brunswick, NJ: National Institute for Early Education Research, Rutgers University. Whitebook, M., Howes, C., & Phillips, D. (1989). *Who cares? Child care teachers and the quality of care in America* (Final report of the National Child Care Staffing Study). Oakland, CA: Child Care Employee Project.

3   Preschool classrooms typically are taught by teams of a teacher and an assistant. Research focusing specifically on the qualifications of assistant teachers is rare, but the available evidence points to a relationship between assistant teacher qualifications and teaching quality. There is much evidence on the educational importance of the qualifications of teaching staff generally. Bowman et al. (2001). Burchinal et al. (2002). Barnett (2003). Whitebook et al. (1989). The CDA has been recommended to prepare assistant teachers who are beginning a career path to become teachers rather than permanent assistants. Kagan, S. L., & Cohen, N. E. (1997). *Not by chance: Creating an early care and education system for America's children* [Abridged report]. New Haven, CT: Bush Center in Child Development and Social Policy, Yale University.

4   Good teachers are actively engaged in their continuing professional development. Bowman et al. (2001). Frede (1998). Whitebook et al. (1989) found that teachers receiving more than 15 hours of training were more appropriate, positive, and engaged with children in their teaching practices.

5   The importance of class size has been demonstrated for both preschool and kindergarten. A class size of 20 is larger than the class size shown in many programs to produce large gains for disadvantaged children. Barnett, W. S. (1998). Long-term effects on cognitive development and school success. In W. S. Barnett & S. S. Boocock (Eds.), *Early care and education for children in poverty: Promises, programs, and long-term results* (pp. 11–44). Albany, NY: SUNY Press. Bowman et al. (2001). Finn, J. D. (2002). Class-size reduction in grades K–3. In A. Molnar (Ed.), *School reform proposals: The research evidence* (pp. 27–48). Greenwich, CT: Information Age Publishing. Frede (1998). NICHD Early Child Care Research Network. (1999). Child outcomes when child care center classes meet recommended standards for quality. *American Journal of Public Health, 89*, 1072–1077. National Association for the Education of Young Children. (1998). *Accreditation criteria and procedures of the National Association for the Education of Young Children.* Washington, DC: Author.

6   A large literature establishes linkages between staff–child ratio, program quality, and child outcomes. A ratio of 1:10 is larger than in programs that have demonstrated large gains for disadvantaged children and is the largest generally accepted by professional opinion. Barnett (1998). Bowman et al. (2001). Frede (1998). NICHD Early Child Care Research Network (1999). National Association for the Education of Young Children (1998).

7   For some children, preschool provides the first opportunity to detect vision, hearing, and health problems that may impair a child's learning and development. This opportunity should not be missed. Meisels, S. J., & Atkins-Burnett, S. (2000). The elements of early childhood assessment. In J. P. Shonkoff & S. J. Meisels (Eds.), *Handbook of early childhood intervention* (pp. 231–257). New York: Cambridge University Press.

8   Families are the primary source of support for child development and the most effective programs have partnered with parents. Bowman et al. (2001). Frede (1998).

9   Good nutrition is essential for healthy brain development and for children's learning. Shonkoff, J. P., & Phillips, D. A. (Eds.). (2000). *From neurons to neighborhoods: The science of early childhood development.* Washington, DC: National Academy Press.

10 In the 2003 *Yearbook*, state preschool initiatives were considered to offer family support services if they required parent conferences or provided any support services to enrolled families. In the current report, our definition of support services was slightly broadened. Programs received credit for requiring additional support services if they offered any of the following: parent conferences, home visits, education services or job training for parents, parenting support or training, parent involvement activities, health services for parents or children, information about nutrition, referral to social services, transportation, transition to kindergarten activities, other specified support services, or if additional services were required by the state but specified only at the local level.

TABLE 4: 2002–2003 STATE PRE-K QUALITY STANDARDS

State	Comprehensive curriculum standards	Teacher has BA	Specialized training in Pre-K	Assistant teacher has CDA or equiv.	At least 15 hrs/yr in-service	Maximum class size ≤ 20	Staff-child ratio 1:10 or better	Vision, hearing, health scr./ref.	At least 1 support service	At least 1 meal	Quality Standards Checklist Sum 2002–2003
Alabama		✓		✓	✓	✓	✓	✓	✓	✓	8
Arizona	✓		✓			✓	✓				4
Arkansas	✓	✓	✓	✓	✓	✓	✓	✓	✓	✓	10
California			✓		✓		✓		✓		4
Colorado			✓			✓	✓		✓		4
Connecticut			✓			✓	✓		✓		4
Delaware			✓		✓	✓	✓	✓	✓	✓	7
Georgia			✓			✓	✓	✓	✓	✓	6
Hawaii	✓		✓	✓					✓	✓	5
Illinois	✓	✓	✓	✓	✓	✓	✓	✓	✓		9
Iowa						✓	✓	✓	✓	✓	5
Kansas		✓		✓				✓	✓		4
Kentucky			✓		✓	✓	✓	✓	✓	✓	7
Louisiana (8g)	✓	✓			✓	✓	✓		✓	✓	7
Louisiana (LA4/SP)	✓	✓			✓	✓	✓	✓	✓	✓	8
Louisiana (NSECD)	✓	✓				✓	✓		✓	✓	6
Maine		✓		✓	✓						3
Maryland	✓	✓	✓		✓	✓	✓	✓	✓		8
Massachusetts	✓				✓	✓	✓	✓	✓		6
Michigan			✓	✓		✓	✓		✓		5
Minnesota	✓		✓	✓		✓	✓	✓	✓	✓	8
Missouri			✓		✓	✓	✓				4
Nebraska		✓	✓	✓		✓	✓		✓		6
Nevada		✓	✓		✓				✓		4
New Jersey (Abbott)	✓	✓	✓		✓	✓	✓	✓	✓	✓	9
New Jersey (ECPA)	✓	✓			✓			✓	✓		5
New Mexico					✓			✓	✓	✓	4
New York (EPK)	✓	✓	✓		✓	✓	✓		✓	✓	8
New York (UPK)	✓				✓	✓	✓		✓		5
North Carolina		✓	✓	✓	✓	✓	✓	✓	✓	✓	9
Ohio (HdSt)			✓		✓	✓	✓	✓	✓	✓	7
Ohio (Public School)			✓		✓			✓	✓	✓	5
Oklahoma	✓	✓	✓		✓	✓	✓		✓		8
Oregon			✓			✓	✓	✓	✓	✓	6
Pennsylvania		✓			✓						2
South Carolina		✓	✓		✓	✓	✓	✓	✓	✓	8
Tennessee		✓	✓	✓	✓	✓	✓		✓	✓	8
Texas	✓	✓							✓		3
Vermont		✓	✓			✓	✓	✓	✓		6
Virginia						✓	✓	✓	✓	✓	5
Washington			✓	✓			✓	✓	✓	✓	6
West Virginia		✓	✓		✓	✓			✓		5
Wisconsin (4K)		✓			✓				✓		3
Wisconsin (HdSt)			✓			✓	✓	✓	✓	✓	6
Totals	16	23	29	12	27	32	33	25	39	24	

Note: Alaska, Florida, Idaho, Indiana, Mississippi, Montana, New Hampshire, North Dakota, Rhode Island, South Dakota, Utah, and Wyoming are not included in this table because they do not fund state prekindergarten initiatives. For more details about quality standards and benchmarks, see Roadmap to State Profile Pages.

RESOURCES

The preschool programs shown by research to produce large gains in learning and development that the nation seeks, particularly for its most disadvantaged students, were well funded. To be equally effective, state-funded preschool programs must have sufficient funding to: hire and retain good teachers and assistant teachers, keep class size reasonable, provide strong educational leadership and supervision, and put the other elements of a quality education in place. Obviously, money alone does not guarantee educational excellence, but without enough money educational excellence is not possible on a large scale. The amount of funding is a key indicator of state commitment to high-quality preschool education for 3- and 4-year-olds.

Total state spending is an important determinant of both access and quality, and states may make tradeoffs between the two. Total state spending on preschool has increased considerably over the past decade. This has enabled states to greatly increase the number of children served in preschool programs. Funding per child enrolled is the critical indicator for quality. Despite overall increases in state spending, the amount spent per child has stayed low relative to per-child spending for the model programs they seek to emulate, such as the federal Head Start program and public K–12 education.

One of the limitations of the existing data on preschool funding is the lack of information about federal and local funds going into state-funded preschool programs. This year's survey added questions in an effort to identify spending amounts from specific federal, state, and local funding streams. We found that, although federal and local funds are widely used to support preschool in most states that fund programs, the amount of money received from these sources is generally not tracked. As a result, most states cannot provide reliable estimates of total funding. We also added questions this year about mechanisms used by states to distribute funds to eligible agencies. As in our previous *Yearbook*, we collected data on local match requirements.

State preschool programs require resources beyond those that go directly into classrooms and local agencies. Standards must be developed and set at the state level. Data systems must be developed and operated for educational and financial accountability. And, when building programs, it is vital to provide adequate resources for the development of a high-quality teacher force, as many preschool teachers have far less education than is typical in K–12 education. Thus, one additional funding category for which we collected information is scholarships for preschool educators.

State Spending

For this year's report, total state spending figures include all funds reported from state sources as well as Temporary Assistance for Needy Families (TANF) funds directed to preschool at states' discretion. Data on state preschool spending do not include money received from federal sources such as the Child Care and Development Fund (CCDF) and the Individuals with Disabilities Education Act (IDEA), or local sources such as district funds and parent fees. Preschool spending figures presented on the state profile pages are not estimates of total spending, but reflect each state's level of financial commitment to preschool. The resources ranking is based on state spending per child enrolled, calculated by dividing total state funding by total enrollment. Spending per child in states with multiple programs was calculated by dividing the sum of state spending by the sum of enrollment across all programs profiled. As an indication of per-capita spending on preschool education, we report state spending per 3-year-old, and state spending per 4-year-old, derived by multiplying state funding by the percent of enrollees in each age category, then dividing that product by total state population at the corresponding single year of age.

States contributed a total of about $2.54 billion to their preschool programs during 2002–2003, exclusive of preschool special education funding. Individual state spending varied considerably, from about $1.5 million in New Mexico and Vermont to more than $400 million in Texas. Among the 37 states that reported funding for preschool, average total state spending was just under $70 million. More than 60 percent of national spending on preschool came from five states: New Jersey, Texas, Georgia, California, and New York. Spending in Texas and New Jersey was more than 50 percent greater than that of any other state. Although the most populous states generally provided the largest state contributions to preschool, there were some exceptions. For example, Oklahoma ranked tenth in total state spending although 26 states have larger populations of 3- and 4-year-olds.

As shown in Table 5 (p. 51), state spending per child enrolled in preschool ranged from less than $1,000 in Maryland to more than $8,700 in New Jersey. Average state spending per child across the 37 states for which data were available was $3,451. Twelve of the 13 states not included in this calculation do not fund preschool. Data were unavailable for Pennsylvania. Only nine states provided more than $4,000 per child. Four of these offer state Head Start programs (Delaware, Minnesota, Ohio, and Oregon), which provide comprehensive and family support services that raise the cost of supporting each child enrolled. Whereas New Jersey served more than 20 percent of its 4-year-olds, each of the five other leading states in this category served less than 10 percent of its population.

During 2002–2003, funding per child for both public K–12 education and federal Head Start far exceeded state spending on preschool in most states. The average state share to support a child in K–12 was $3,935, and total K–12 spending, which includes federal and local money as well as capital spending, was $9,173. Only Connecticut, Nevada, New Jersey, Ohio, Oregon, and Tennessee funded each child in state preschool at a level that matched or surpassed the state share for a child in K–12, and total funding per child in K–12 exceeded state preschool spending in every state. Per child spending on preschool was at least $3,500 less than total K–12 spending in all but 5 states.

Federal Head Start also received considerably more money per child than state preschool programs. State funding for a child in preschool was lower than federal funding for Head Start in 36 of 37 states for which these data were available. Nationally, federal Head Start programs received more than double the support per child in comparison to state preschool programs. Although Head Start served fewer 3- and 4-year-olds than state preschool during 2002–2003, federal Head Start grantees received more than $6 billion to provide services to participants, 87 percent of whom were 3 or 4 years old.

The size of the 3- and 4-year-old population differs dramatically by state. Thus, we compared funding across states by calculating per-capita spending for each year of age separately. Although no state currently funds preschool programs for all 3- and 4-year-olds, this method of calculation provides a useful indicator of state financial commitment relative to the entire preschool population. Per-capita spending figures are presented in Table 5. Twenty-five states offered some preschool services for 3-year-olds, but only six provided more than $200 of support per 3-year-old in the state. New Jersey made more than three times the per capita investment of any other state for 3-year-olds. The majority of state funds for preschool were directed to services for 4-year-olds, and all states with a program served children in this age group. Spending per 4-year-old was greater than $500 in 12 states, and exceeded $1,000 in four—Georgia, New Jersey, Oklahoma, and Texas. Georgia and New Jersey spent considerably more than other states, supporting preschool with an average of more than $2,000 for each 4-year-old resident.

Funds from Federal or Local Sources

Most states reported that some federal or local funds had been used to supplement state support for preschool during 2002–2003. Generally, states were not able to specify how much money was spent on preschool from these sources, and, therefore, they could not accurately report total spending on state Pre–K from all sources. In some cases, state administrators did not know whether specific federal or local sources were being used to support preschool. At least seven states directed TANF funds to preschool, supporting nine different preschool initiatives. Of all federal and local sources, states were most often able to specify funding amounts for TANF. Three programs, two in Louisiana and one in Ohio, were entirely or almost entirely supported with TANF dollars. Additionally, more than half of state preschool funds in Tennessee came from TANF, and these funds constituted about 30 percent of total preschool spending in Massachusetts.

The federal funding stream most frequently used to support state preschool was IDEA. Out of 44 programs profiled in this report, 24 used IDEA money to fund services for some participants. IDEA funds were generally used to supplement or replace state funds for children who required special services. Many programs (18) also were reported to use Title I funds. Unfortunately, state preschool administrators were rarely able to estimate how much funding was received from either Title I or IDEA. West Virginia used more than $8 million from Title I to fund preschool, which was one-third as large a contribution as state funding. Finally, child care (CCDF) funds supported preschool in at least seven states, with a specific amount reported for three of those states. Washington directed more than $5 million in CCDF money to support its state preschool initiative, representing an almost 20 percent increase over state funds alone.

At least 80 percent of programs used local money to help pay for preschool. As was the case with federal funds, few states were able to quantify support received from local sources. More than two-thirds of programs received in-kind contributions from localities, which may include services such as transportation, provision of meals, or maintenance of facilities. About one-third of programs were partially supported by parent fees, usually collected on a sliding scale based on family income. Connecticut and Massachusetts each reported using more than $10 million in parent fees to help fund their programs.

Although 35 programs were reported to receive some support from local funds, only eight required a local match. Percentages of funding required from local sources ranged from 11 percent for New York's EPK program to 40 percent of total funding in Arkansas. Alabama required that localities match half of the amount granted by the state. Some states allowed local matches to be either in cash or in-kind. In Wisconsin's 4K program, the local share of general school revenue was reported as a local match for preschool. Local funds are likely to be required in any state that funds a preschool initiative through the regular public school funding formula. The local match requirement in Virginia depended on a composite index of local ability to pay, so that wealthier localities generally have to pay for a higher percentage of overall program cost. In Kentucky, nearly $20 million in local funds were used to fund preschool, though no match was required.

Types of Agencies Eligible to Receive Funding

The manner in which states distribute resources to preschool programs may affect both the accessibility and quality of services. In most cases, the state distributes funds directly to operating agencies, which may or may not be allowed to subcontract with other providers. During 2002–2003, preschool initiatives in Kansas, Louisiana 8(g), Maine, New York (EPK), and Pennsylvania were operated exclusively through public schools. In these programs, only public schools were eligible to receive state funds and no subcontracting was permitted. In 36 of the 44 state initiatives, services were offered through a combination of public and private providers. Private agencies received funds directly from the state in 20 programs. Head Start, private or family child care, and faith-based centers were each eligible to receive funds directly in more than one-third of state programs. In 16 other initiatives, the state gave funds only to public schools, but schools subcontracted with private providers. Public schools were not involved with the provision of services in Hawaii's Preschool Open Doors Project, which distributes subsidies directly to parents, or in Louisiana's Nonpublic Schools Early Childhood Development Program, which operates out of nonpublic facilities.

Subcontracting with multiple types of agencies was allowed in about three-quarters of the programs profiled. Head Start centers and private child care were the providers most frequently used for subcontracting. More than half of all programs permitted subcontracting with faith-based centers, although some states did not allow services offered by these providers to include religious content. Programs that allow subcontracting in policy may in practice distribute different proportions of funds to eligible agencies. For example, more than half of all funds for New York's UPK program were distributed to subcontractors, whereas in South Carolina and Illinois a very small percentage of funds was directed to outside providers.

Other Types of Support for Preschool

No commitment a state can make to early childhood education is more important than recruiting and retaining highly qualified preschool teachers. To demonstrate such commitment, resources must be allocated to provide competitive salary and benefit packages for preschool teachers. Thirteen programs required all teachers to be paid on the public school district salary scale, including eight of the 12 programs that met at least eight benchmarks on NIEER's Quality Checklist. Approximately one-third of state prekindergarten initiatives applied the public salary scale only to preschool teachers employed by a public school system or those who taught in a public school. Teachers employed by agencies such as Head Start or other private agencies were generally not required to be paid public school teacher salaries. In 14 programs, the public school salary scale did not apply to preschool teachers regardless of program setting, and Pennsylvania allowed districts to decide this issue locally.

Scholarship or loan forgiveness programs were available to some preschool teachers in 23 states. These programs encourage professional development and reflect a financial commitment to promote high-quality preschool. Of 11 states that were able to provide specific data, only Arkansas, Colorado, and Massachusetts awarded more than 200 scholarships. In some states, such as Iowa and West Virginia, scholarships were only available to teachers in nonpublic settings who had not yet attained a BA. Assistant teachers in Nebraska and Wisconsin's 4K program were eligible for T.E.A.C.H. scholarships, but lead teachers in these two programs could not receive such support.

States were asked to report the number of full-time professional staff members employed at the state level who administered early childhood education programs. Resources devoted to administrative staff can contribute to program quality by funding teacher support and supervision as well as program monitoring and evaluation efforts. Of the 34 states for which data were available, 18 employed fewer than five full-time staff members to administer early childhood programs. In most states, administrative staff worked within a single agency or entity, such as the Department of Education, even when overseeing multiple programs. Approximately 300 administrators were employed nationally, each responsible on average for 2,500 preschoolers. In Texas, a single individual administered a program that served nearly 150,000 children. Such initiatives clearly depend on local public school administration to support the preschool program.

Monitoring and Evaluation

Preschool programs can be held accountable for compliance with quality standards through systems of monitoring and evaluation. During 2002–2003, states monitored their programs using a variety of approaches, including site visits, financial audits, and desktop reviews of other program records. About one-third of the state initiatives required site visits by state monitors at least once per year, including eight state initiatives that required two or three site visits per year. New Jersey's Abbott program, which required the most frequent site visits (one per week), uses "mentor" teachers who act as coaches for less experienced staff. Thirteen states did not require any site visits.

The vast majority of states reviewed financial or other program records (or both) at least once per year, including some states that reviewed records quarterly or monthly. Several states, including Arizona, Hawaii, Maine, Missouri, Texas, and West Virginia, did not require record reviews.

For most state initiatives, the monitoring requirements were the same regardless of the type of program providing services. However, there were some exceptions. For example, programs in nonpublic school settings in Illinois received additional visits from state monitors. For New York's UPK program, the state monitored programs provided by school districts directly, but districts were responsible for monitoring any agencies with which they subcontracted to provide services.

Along with monitoring, states also ensure accountability for their preschool programs through evaluations. Of 28 state initiatives that had completed evaluations, most assessed both child progress and program quality. The majority of state preschool evaluations that were completed by 2002–2003 were required and funded by the state, but most were conducted by an independent organization such as a university or private research firm. Other initiatives were evaluated either by the state or jointly by the state and an independent organization.

Summary

During 2002–2003, state preschool programs continued to experience inadequate funding, especially when compared to other types of educational initiatives for children, such as federal Head Start or public K–12 schools. Lack of resources affects programs directly by limiting access and quality. Staffing and budget constraints at the administrative level restrict monitoring and evaluation efforts and severely limit available data on state preschool programs. State preschool initiatives are part of broader systems of early education that usually involve several programs and funding streams, and multiple levels of government. Few states have data systems that provide unduplicated enrollment counts across programs or specific funding information across sources. Given these challenges, it is difficult to estimate the total amount of resources directed to each program, or to evaluate the efficiency with which these resources are being used.

Changes from 2001–2002

Differences in state funding for preschool from fiscal year 2002 to fiscal year 2003 can be examined in terms of nominal (unadjusted) dollars, or with spending figures for 2002 adjusted for inflation. In unadjusted figures, states spent about $165 million more on preschool during fiscal year 2003, and spending per child rose by about $15. However, when 2002 dollars are adjusted, the increase in total spending is reduced to approximately $90 million or 4 percent, and funding per child *decreases* by $90 for 2003. A similar pattern of change occurred for federal Head Start, although both total funding and spending per child decreased slightly in 2003 when comparing adjusted dollars. Of course, changes in funding are related to enrollment, and federal Head Start saw a small drop in funded enrollment during 2003, whereas participation in state preschool programs increased by about 7 percent.

Using 2002 adjusted figures, North Carolina, Nevada, and Kansas more than doubled total spending on preschool for 2003. In North Carolina, funding for the *More at Four* program increased by 350 percent, but state support for the Smart Start initiative has been significantly reduced. The largest spending increase occurred in New Jersey, where funding for preschool was nearly $110 million greater during 2003. The second largest increase was $24 million in North Carolina. Nationally, 16 states increased preschool spending for 2003 while funding decreased in 21 states. In six states—Missouri, Massachusetts, Hawaii, Connecticut, Ohio, and Iowa—spending on preschool dropped more than 10 percent between 2002 and 2003. In unadjusted dollars, 14 states decreased funding for preschool. Pennsylvania was not able to provide data for these analyses.

Only 12 states showed increases in spending per child enrolled in state preschool initiatives during the 2002–2003 program year. Spending increased by more than 10 percent in six states, including New Jersey— despite its having led the nation in spending per child during 2002. Among states that spent more per child during 2003, the percentage of change was greatest in New Mexico and Arkansas. Fifteen states lowered spending per child by at least 10 percent for the 2003 fiscal year. In Nebraska, Wisconsin, and Tennessee, the decline in state spending per child exceeded 20 percent.

The proportion of preschool funds directed to services for 4-year-olds as compared to 3-year-olds was relatively constant from 2002 to 2003. The vast majority of resources was spent in service of 4-year-olds, as would be expected given that nearly seven 4-year-olds were served in state preschool initiatives for every one 3-year-old enrolled. Spending per capita for 4-year-olds increased by more than 50 percent in North Carolina, Kansas, Nevada, and Louisiana, while the largest decreases were seen in Massachusetts and Missouri. The few states that contributed significantly to preschool for 3-year-olds during 2002, such as New Jersey, Massachusetts, and West Virginia, continued to do so during 2003.

TABLE 5: RANKINGS OF STATE PRE-K RESOURCES PER CHILD ENROLLED

Resources Rank	State	$ per child enrolled in state Pre-K	$ per 3-year-old in the state	$ per 4-year-old in the state
1	New Jersey	$8,739	$1,373	$2,009
	FEDERAL HEAD START	$7,089	FEDERAL HEAD START	
2	Minnesota	$6,672	$96	$149
3	Oregon	$6,525	$197	$379
4	Connecticut	$5,601	$191	$584
5	Delaware	$5,287	$0	$449
6	North Carolina	$4,819	$0	$271
7	Tennessee	$4,573	$49	$147
8	Ohio	$4,514	$292	$416
9	Massachusetts	$4,104	$436	$430
10	Louisiana	$3,922	$0	$820
11	Washington	$3,897	$69	$270
12	Georgia	$3,824	$0	$2,075
13	Nevada	$3,686	$25	$57
14	Alabama	$3,638	$0	$79
15	Hawaii	$3,478	$0	$215
16	New York	$3,347	$20	$996
17	California	$3,317	$72	$288
18	West Virginia	$3,309	$313	$957
19	Michigan	$3,306	$0	$636
20	Virginia	$3,090	$0	$195
21	Arkansas	$2,998	$70	$184
22	Iowa	$2,925	$39	$133
23	Illinois	$2,905	$231	$708
24	Wisconsin	$2,881	$44	$700
25	Colorado	$2,864	$42	$395
26	Texas	$2,746	$112	$1,192
27	Kentucky	$2,484	$261	$688
28	Arizona	$2,432	$0	$123
29	Oklahoma	$2,368	$0	$1,406
30	Missouri	$2,198	$52	$95
31	Nebraska	$1,909	$28	$49
32	Maine	$1,875	$0	$203
33	New Mexico	$1,765	$14	$44
34	Kansas	$1,721	$0	$253
35	South Carolina	$1,303	$25	$421
36	Vermont	$1,197	$84	$117
37	Maryland	$936	$19	$246
NA	Pennsylvania	NA	NA	NA
No program	Alaska	$0	$0	$0
No program	Florida	$0	$0	$0
No program	Idaho	$0	$0	$0
No program	Indiana	$0	$0	$0
No program	Mississippi	$0	$0	$0
No program	Montana	$0	$0	$0
No program	New Hampshire	$0	$0	$0
No program	North Dakota	$0	$0	$0
No program	Rhode Island	$0	$0	$0
No program	South Dakota	$0	$0	$0
No program	Utah	$0	$0	$0
No program	Wyoming	$0	$0	$0

NA=Not available (State did not provide data.)

For details about how these figures were calculated, see the Methodology section and Roadmap to State Profile Pages.

Policy Recommendations

Throughout America, children share a common need for a good early childhood education, and their families face common challenges in obtaining this education for them. Education for 4-year-olds can no longer be thought of as a luxury in any state, nor should it be viewed as a service that can only benefit poor children. Using a variety of models, a number of states have made progress on key aspects of state prekindergarten programs. However, much remains to be done. We offer specific recommendations for state and federal government policy to promote the effective education of young children.

1. States should increase funding for prekindergarten programs to improve access to a quality education. The 12 states without prekindergarten programs should each start one, and states that already have programs should increase their efforts. Oklahoma (which ranks 42nd in per-capita income) has demonstrated that even states with modest resources can make a good education available to all 4-year-olds. The Oklahoma prekindergarten program, together with Head Start and preschool special education, serves 82 percent of the state's 4-year-olds. All of the children enrolled in Oklahoma's state program are provided with fully qualified early childhood teachers. Georgia is not far behind in providing access. If every state followed Oklahoma by including prekindergarten in its state K–12 funding formula, 80 percent of all 4-year-olds in the United States could be served with an increase of only $9 billion in state funds.

2. High standards are necessary for educational excellence. States must improve their standards for prekindergarten education. Again, some states have demonstrated that this is possible. For example, Arkansas met all 10 of our benchmarks for state policy regarding quality. As the most important benchmarks relate to teacher quality, it is noteworthy that only 13 programs require all teachers to have a BA and specialized training in preschool education. All states should adopt this standard. Many states require this standard for some programs or have a high percentage of fully qualified teachers. Unfortunately, when this is not required, the most disadvantaged children are most likely to end up with poorly qualified teachers. Other elements of quality are also important and are detailed in our description of the Quality Standards Checklist.

3. Funding for state prekindergarten programs is too often a low priority. No other state-funded programs have greater potential to contribute to economic growth and prosperity. Yet, states spend more than $1 trillion each year on other priorities. States could adequately fund prekindergarten programs for all 4-year-olds by reallocating only about one percent of their total spending. Without sufficient resources, programs are forced to limit the number of children they serve and to skimp on quality. Inadequate state funding can also lead to heavy reliance on local funding to finance programs. Given the vast differences in local financial capacity, this has the potential to produce serious gaps and inequities in access to effective preschool education.

4. The federal government's role in prekindergarten education must continue to evolve and improve. Important federal supports for the education of young children include Head Start, child care funding through several programs, preschool special education funds, and Title I. However, despite the proliferation of overlapping federal programs, they do not provide enough funding to adequately serve all targeted children. As with most state prekindergarten programs, Head Start standards for teachers fall short, and programs struggle to pay salaries sufficient to attract and keep highly qualified teachers. Child care programs barely address the issues of educational quality at all. Although it is important to plan for the integration of education and child care, this poses difficulties. A large portion of child care funds are used to serve older children or children whose parents work outside normal school hours. Therefore, most child care funds are not available to fund preschool education. The federal government could increase support specifically for prekindergarten programs by offering to match state government spending that is accompanied by high standards. Rather than seeking to force integration of various federal and state programs, the federal government could experiment with financial incentives for program integration.

5. States need better data on prekindergarten enrollment. Most states cannot accurately identify how many 3- and 4-year-olds receive how much education and from which programs. Although it is highly desirable that the existing programs be braided together to give young children good education and care, the result is that an unduplicated count of the number of children served is not available in many states. Financial information is no easier to come by. For children in grades K–12, it is possible to identify the state, local, and federal share of expenditures for a year of education. Most states cannot provide this information for their state prekindergarten initiatives. More detailed data are critical for policymakers to make fully informed decisions about how to expand and improve prekindergarten and how to coordinate resources so that they are used in the most efficient way possible. As many of the difficulties arise from lack of coordination among multiple federal programs, the federal government should support states in creating better data systems.

6. Advance planning is essential to effecting change in prekindergarten programs. States should look ahead to determine what improvements are needed and how to implement changes so that they bring about the desired effects. For example, if a state expands funding to serve more children, planning is essential to ensure that local districts and communities are able to inform families and enroll children, and to ensure that new teachers and facilities are available. If teacher qualification standards are raised, states may need to provide financial support, time, and training to enable teachers to meet the new regulations, as well as increased compensation to attract and retain teachers with higher credentials.

Photo: RC Peters

Leading States for Prekindergarten

Several states stand out as leaders in providing prekindergarten. Each of these states is noteworthy for making prekindergarten widely accessible, setting high quality standards, providing the resources to implement high standards, or investing substantial new funding in its initiatives in recent years. These states' prekindergarten initiatives have some shortcomings, and there is room for improvement as they work toward opening up high-quality prekindergarten programs to more children. Still, the states are taking some promising steps forward and offer models for others to follow.

Arkansas

In 2002–2003, the Arkansas Better Chance (ABC) program was the only initiative that met all 10 of NIEER's quality benchmarks. Although enrollment decreased slightly between 2001–2002 and 2002–2003, total spending rose by 40 percent and spending per child enrolled rose by 43 percent. Total funding dropped by a small amount in 2003–2004, but the state will greatly expand its prekindergarten investment in 2004–2005 as part of a broader education reform measure. State spending will increase from about $9 million in 2003–2004 to about $50 million in 2004–2005. Funds will be targeted to schools where students are not performing well on statewide exams.

Arkansas helps ensure high-quality prekindergarten not only by setting strong standards but through other steps as well. The state annually monitors and evaluates all center-based programs using the Early Childhood Environment Rating Scale (ECERS), and programs must score an overall average of 5.5 out of 7. The state also requires preschool teachers to be paid on the public school salary scale and provides scholarships to nearly 600 prekindergarten teachers, about one-quarter of whom are ABC staff working toward their CDA credentials.

Illinois

Although funding for the state's Prekindergarten Program for At-Risk Children decreased between 2001–2002 and 2002–2003, Illinois appropriated about $27.5 million in additional funding for the initiative for 2003–2004. With this new money, the state was able to enroll about 8,000 more children in the prekindergarten program. Illinois' program is also notable for its commitment to quality, meeting 9 of NIEER's 10 quality benchmarks. In the one area it falls short—meal requirements—programs are required to provide snacks and, while it is not mandated, most full-day programs also provide lunch.

In addition, the state is now encouraging agencies outside the public schools to provide prekindergarten by allowing them to compete directly for funding, rather than permitting them to receive funding only through subcontracts with the schools. These agencies will still have to comply with all the same quality standards that apply to public schools, including having teachers certified in early childhood education who are paid according to the public school salary scale.

New Jersey

As a result of a court ruling in a school finance equity case, New Jersey is making high-quality prekindergarten available to all 3- and 4-year-olds in the 30 lowest-income districts in the state (referred to as the Abbott districts, and expanded to include one additional district in 2004). The Abbott prekindergarten program's quality standards, which must follow standards laid out by the state Supreme Court, meet all but one of NIEER's quality benchmarks. Abbott programs employ certified teachers who are paid salaries equivalent to other public school teachers. Enrolled children receive comprehensive services and attend 6 hours per day, with wrap-around services available using funds from the Department of Human Services. State spending per pupil is more than $8,700, which is higher than the amount provided by any other state initiative.

Although the state has been successful in addressing prekindergarten needs in its lowest-income areas, it is still lagging behind in covering other districts. The state has a secondary prekindergarten program for 102 districts other than the Abbott districts, but this program enrolls only about one-fifth as many children as the Abbott prekindergarten program. In addition, the quality standards do not match up with those for the Abbott districts, although the state is working to align the two sets of standards.

New Jersey is seeking to expand prekindergarten to additional non-Abbott districts through its new Early Launch to Learning Initiative (ELLI). The state has set aside $15 million that could be used to serve 4,000 low-income preschoolers throughout the state in fiscal year 2005. The long-term goal is to make prekindergarten available to all 4-year-olds in New Jersey by 2010.

Oklahoma

In Oklahoma, all 4-year-olds are eligible to participate in prekindergarten if their district offers it. Districts that choose to provide prekindergarten receive funding from the state for each 4-year-old served, just as they would for any K–12 student. The state prekindergarten initiative has expanded rapidly since 1998 when it was opened up to all 4-year-olds. In 2002–2003, the program was available in more than 90 percent of school districts. These districts served 28,000 children, or 59 percent of all 4-year-olds in the state—a higher percentage served than by any other state. Oklahoma's program has continued to expand, enrolling more than 30,000 children in 2003–2004. The initiative is limited to 4-year-olds and does not serve 3-year-olds.

The state has taken some important steps to ensure the quality of its programs, including requiring all teachers to have bachelor's degrees with certification in early childhood education and paying them salaries equivalent to those of other public school teachers. However, the program lacks statewide requirements for health screenings and referrals. The state continues to work on strengthening other aspects of this initiative, for example by increasing collaboration with Head Start and child care programs to offer services.

States to Watch

A number of states are worth watching to see if they follow through with current plans for strengthening and expanding prekindergarten. Although there are initial signs of progress in these states, there is also reason for caution. In some cases, these states have yet to commit resources to increasing access to prekindergarten or to lay out specific plans to achieve their goals.

Developments in *Florida* deserve particular attention. In 2002, voters approved a ballot measure requiring prekindergarten to be made universally available for all 4-year-olds by 2005. Although this was a landmark measure, the state has yet to adopt an implementation plan or identify a funding source even as the deadline fast approaches. A proposal passed by the Legislature in the 2004 session failed to set adequate quality standards and was ultimately vetoed. Fulfilling the voter mandate will require the state to serve an estimated 90,000 additional 4-year-olds not served by other publicly funded programs. Florida lacks a state prekindergarten initiative to build upon because it eliminated its separate prekindergarten initiative and the associated quality standards in 2001.

Several other states have taken promising steps forward, although these are often only first steps:

Maryland plans to increase access to prekindergarten over the next several years, with the goal of making it available to all eligible 4-year-olds by 2007–2008. The state emphasizes coordination of its various prekindergarten funding streams.

Policy changes are planned for *New York's* Universal Prekindergarten program (UPK) that would raise standards to fulfill at least two of NIEER's quality benchmarks that the program did not meet in the year covered by this report. Legislation drafted in 1997 required all UPK teachers to be certified in early childhood education by 2002. The state has made progress toward achieving this goal, with an estimated 80 percent of UPK teachers certified during 2002–2003, but implementation of the requirement has been postponed until September 2005. In addition, assistant teachers in UPK programs located in public schools will be required to complete 18 credit hours toward an AA or BA within 4 years of their hiring date. The change in assistant teacher requirements went into effect in February 2004. Other states, such as Kentucky and West Virginia, plan to make policy changes in the next few years that would improve their prekindergarten quality standards. In some cases, the vast majority of providers already meet the higher standards, so the new requirements may not be particularly expensive or problematic to fulfill.

In *North Carolina*, funding and enrollment for the *More at Four* program—which meets 9 out of 10 quality benchmarks on NIEER's checklist—have grown steadily. The program, which served 1,240 children in 2001–2002, is expected to serve 12,000 children in 2004–2005. Meanwhile, funding has increased from $6.5 million for 2001–2002 to approximately $50 million for 2004–2005. Yet, some of this expansion of *More at Four* has come at the expense of the state's comprehensive early childhood program, Smart Start, which has experienced a decrease in funding from $231 million in 2000–2001 to $191 million in 2003–2004.

Photo: RC Peters

Pennsylvania established a new Education Accountability Block Grant in 2004 that school districts can use to support prekindergarten. The block grant provides a total of $200 million, two-thirds of which will be targeted toward early childhood, with individual school districts determining exactly how their funds will be spent. More than $9 million of the block grant funds will be used to provide prekindergarten to about 3,400 children in 40 school districts.

In 2004, **Virginia** significantly increased the amount of funding available to districts for prekindergarten. The goal is to make prekindergarten available to more at-risk 4-year-olds through either Head Start or the state program. While the state previously provided funds to serve 60 percent of at-risk 4-year-olds not enrolled in federal programs such as Head Start or Title I, state funding will now allow districts to serve 90 percent of at-risk 4-year-olds not served by Head Start. However, it is up to districts whether they access the funds and offer prekindergarten programs.

West Virginia intends to make prekindergarten universally available for all 4-year-olds by 2012–2013. Enrollment in the state's prekindergarten program has already increased somewhat over the past few years, from 6,853 children in 2001–2002 to 7,924 children in 2003–2004. The program currently serves only about one-third of the state's 4-year-olds.

Wisconsin has been promoting its Four-Year-Old Kindergarten (4K) program, which is open to all 4-year-olds if schools choose to offer it. The number of children enrolled in 4K has grown from about 12,700 children in 2001–2002 to more than 16,000 in 2002–2003 to nearly 17,000 children in 2003–2004. However, the increase in enrollment has not been accompanied by a similar increase in funding. State funds for 4K remained relatively flat from 2001–2002 to 2002–2003, leading to a 20 percent decline in spending per child. Although most children are served within the public schools, the state is working to encourage collaboration with community-based settings such as child care and Head Start centers to meet the increased demand.

Enrollment in each of several additional states, including **Alabama**, **Kansas**, **Louisiana**, **Nebraska**, and **Nevada**, grew by more than 50 percent between 2001–2002 and 2002–2003. However, there is still much more room for further expansion of these state prekindergarten initiatives. Louisiana's four prekindergarten initiatives reached more than 20 percent of the state's 4-year-olds in 2002–2003, and Kansas' initiative served 15 percent of its 4-year-olds, but neither of these states' programs serves 3-year-olds. Alabama, Nebraska, and Nevada each served 2.5 percent or less of their 4-year-olds in 2002–2003.

Roadmap to State Profile Pages

For each state that has a prekindergarten initiative, we present one page with a description of the state's program followed by a page with data on the program's key features.

On the top of the first page for each state are five bar graphs:
- The first bar shows the percentage of the state's 4-year-olds enrolled in the state program in 2002–2003.
- The second bar shows the percentage of the state's 4-year-olds enrolled in 2003–2004, when data were available.
- The third bar shows how many of the 10 benchmarks in the Quality Standards Checklist were met by the state's prekindergarten policies as of 2002–2003.
- The fourth bar shows the state's spending per child enrolled in the state prekindergarten initiative in 2002–2003.
- Finally, the fifth bar shows the state's spending per child enrolled in 2003–2004, if data were available.

Next to the bar graphs representing the 2002–2003 enrollment and spending data are arrows pointing up or down or an equal sign. These symbols indicate whether there has been an increase, decrease, or no change in the percentage of 4-year-olds enrolled in the state's prekindergarten program or in state spending per participant compared to 2001–2002. Most of the 2001–2002 data used for comparison purposes come from NIEER's *2003 State Preschool Yearbook*; however, spending figures from our earlier report were adjusted for inflation. There are also some exceptions in cases where states revised data or reported data differently. In such cases we adjusted the data to ensure comparability across program years.

The bar graphs are followed by a narrative describing the main features of the state's initiative, including its origins, the types of settings in which prekindergarten can be offered, and the eligibility criteria for children. The narrative also notes unique or particularly interesting aspects of the state initiative that may not be highlighted elsewhere in the report. Where information is available, new developments in funding and enrollment are also discussed, including specific data for 2003–2004. Some of the descriptive information in the paragraphs was originally included in *Seeds of Success* from the Children's Defense Fund and the *Quality Counts 2002* issue of *Education Week*.

At the bottom of the first page of each state profile are three numbers showing how the state ranks against other states on the following measures:

- The percentage of the state's 4-year-old population enrolled in the state's prekindergarten program (Access Ranking—4s)
- The percentage of the state's 3-year-old population enrolled in the state's prekindergarten program (Access Ranking—3s)
- State expenditures per child enrolled in the program (Resources Ranking)

Information for states that have more than one prekindergarten initiative is presented slightly differently and is explained on the individual state pages. Louisiana, New Jersey, New York, Ohio, and Wisconsin have more than one initiative reported here.

States that do not fund state prekindergarten initiatives have been given their own state profile pages for the first time in this year's report. For most of these states, the space usually filled by a description of a state's initiative is left blank, and the table on quality standards is left blank. However, these profiles do provide information on special education enrollment, federally funded Head Start enrollment, and state-funded Head Start enrollment. Information on K–12 spending and federal Head Start spending is also provided. Where applicable, state Head Start spending is reported.

The sections below provide an introduction to information contained in data tables on the state profile pages and explain why these elements are important when discussing prekindergarten initiatives.

Access

The first item in the Access data table is total state program enrollment. This is the number of children enrolled on a given day. Following that is the percentage of school districts (or in some cases, counties or communities) that offer state prekindergarten programs. This information indicates the extent of the initiative's geographic coverage. Next, the table shows what, if any, income requirement is used in determining eligibility for the program.

Data on the hours of operation (hours per day and days per week) and operating schedule (academic year or full year) are shown as another measure of access. Parents working full time may find it difficult to get their children to and from a program that operates only a few hours per day. The number of hours children participate in preschool also matters for other reasons—for example, it can influence how much impact a program has on children's development and learning.

The Access data table also shows enrollment of 3- and 4-year-old children in two federally funded programs outside the state prekindergarten initiative. These are preschool special education and Head Start. The final item in the table reports how many children are in Head Start slots funded by the state.

Two pie charts in the Access section illustrate the percentages of 3-year-olds and 4-year-olds in the state enrolled in the state prekindergarten initiative, special education, or Head Start. The remaining children are categorized as enrolled in "Other/None." These children may be enrolled in another type of private or publicly funded program (e.g., state-subsidized child care) or may not be attending a center-based program at all. For the purposes of these charts, it was assumed that there was no overlap across the three types of programs. In fact, children may be enrolled in more than one program. However, there is no way to determine the extent to which this occurs. Therefore, the proportion of children enrolled in one of these three major programs may be overestimated.

Quality Standards Checklist

States' policies in 10 critical areas related to quality are shown. For each area, states receive a checkmark when their policy meets or exceeds the related benchmark standard. On the right-hand side of the page, a road sign displays the total number of benchmarks met by the state. A separate section of this report explains why these 10 areas of quality were chosen for assessing state policies and how the benchmarks were set. Two caveats are important to note. First, these data reflect policy, not practice. A state with good policies may have some programs that fail to comply with these policies, whereas, conversely, a state with weak policies may have many programs that exceed state standards. Evaluating implementation of standards is outside the scope of this report. Second, this is not an exhaustive list of all the important elements of a good prekindergarten program, so meeting all 10 standards is not necessarily sufficient for ensuring a high-quality program. However, each of these standards is essential, and no state's prekindergarten policies should be considered fully satisfactory unless every one of the 10 benchmarks is met.

Resources

A table in the Resources section shows total state spending for the prekindergarten initiative, whether a local match is required, state spending per child participating in the program, amount of state Head Start funding, and state spending per 3-year-old and per 4-year-old. These measures offer different views of a state's resources for prekindergarten that together provide a more complete picture. For example, total spending by a small state may appear relatively low, but may prove to be fairly high relative to its population. A state with a high total funding level for its prekindergarten initiative may have a low per-pupil spending level if it enrolls a large number of children. As a result, children may not be receiving the extent or intensity of services they need for the prekindergarten program to have a substantial impact. Inadequate funding per student may also require local communities to cover the funding shortfall in order to ensure a good preschool program. This can create problems when low-income communities lack resources—often the very same communities whose children most need the extra boost provided by high-quality prekindergarten.

A bar chart in the resources section compares prekindergarten funding to federal Head Start funding and K–12 funding. Different colors indicate different sources of funding—state, local, and federal. A separate color is used to indicate any TANF funds that a state directs toward its prekindergarten initiative. While TANF funds are federal dollars, it is the state that decides whether to devote these funds to prekindergarten as opposed to other purposes. Although many states use other local and federal sources to support state prekindergarten, data on the amounts of these other funds used are only occasionally available. When states were able to provide such information, it is included in the bar charts as well.

ACCESS

Total state program enrollment - Number of children in state program
School districts that offer state program - - - - - - - - - - - - - - - - - Percentage of school districts in state where program is offered
(may include programs not provided by district itself)
Income requirement - Maximum family income for participants
Hours of operation - Hours per day and days per week programs operate
Operating schedule - Annual schedule of operation (academic year or entire calendar year)
Special education enrollment - - - - - - - - - - - - - - - - - Number of 3- and 4-year-olds served by the Preschool Grants Program of the
Individuals with Disabilities Education Act
Federally funded Head Start enrollment - - - - - - - - - Number of slots for 3- and 4-year-olds in Head Start funded with federal money
State-funded Head Start enrollment - - - - - - - - - - - - - Number of slots for 3- and 4-year-olds in Head Start funded with state money

QUALITY STANDARDS CHECKLIST

POLICY   STATE PRE-K REQUIREMENT

Curriculum standards - - - - - Type of preschool-specific curriculum standards adopted by state (comprehensive, not comprehensive, or none)
Teacher degree requirement - Minimum teacher educational level
Teacher specialized training requirement - - - - - - - - - - - - - - - - - Area of specialization for degree or credential required of teacher
Assistant teacher degree requirement - Minimum assistant teacher educational level
Teacher in-service requirement - - - - - - - - - - - - - Annual requirement for ongoing in-service professional development and training
Maximum class size - Maximum number of children per classroom
 3-year-olds
 4-year-olds
Staff-child ratio - Minimum ratio of staff to children in classroom
 3-year-olds
 4-year-olds
Screening/referral requirements - - - - - - - - - - - - - Areas in which screenings or referrals are required (vision, hearing, health, etc.)
Required support services - - - - Additional support services required to be provided to families of enrollees, including parent conferences
Meal requirements - Specific meals required daily

RESOURCES

Total state Pre-K spending - Total state funds spent on state Pre-K program
Local match required? - - - - - - - - - - - - - - Whether state requires local providers to match state monetary contribution to program
and amount of any match required
State spending per child enrolled - - - - - - - - - - - - - - - - - - Amount of state funds spent per child participating in Pre-K program
State Head Start spending (when applicable) - - - - - - - - - - - - - Total state funds spent to supplement federal Head Start program
State spending per 3-year-old - - - - - - - - - - - - - - - - - - Amount of state funds spent on Pre-K program per 3-year-old in state
State spending per 4-year-old - - - - - - - - - - - - - - - - - - Amount of state funds spent on Pre-K program per 4-year-old in state

GLOSSARY OF ABBREVIATIONS

AA	Associate of Arts
BA	Bachelor of Arts
BS	Bachelor of Science
CC	Child Care
CCDBG	Child Care and Development Block Grant
CCDF	Child Care and Development Fund
CD	Child Development
CDA	Child Development Associate
DHHS	Department of Health and Human Services
DK	Don't Know (denotes that respondent was not able to provide information requested in a survey question)
DOE	Department of Education
DPI	Department of Public Instruction
DSS	Department of Social Services
EC	Early Childhood
ECE	Early Childhood Education
ECERS(-R)	Early Childhood Environment Rating Scale (-Revised)
ECSE	Early Childhood Special Education
EE	Elementary Education
ELL	English Language Learner
ESL	English as a Second Language
Exp.	Experience
FPL	Federal Poverty Level
FTE	Full-time Equivalent
FY	Fiscal Year
GED	General Equivalency Diploma
HdSt	Head Start
HSD	High School Diploma
IDEA	Individuals with Disabilities Education Act
IEP	Individualized Education Plan
IFSP	Individualized Family Service Plan
K	Kindergarten
LEA	Local Education Agency
LEP	Limited English Proficiency
MA	Master of Arts
MOE	Maintenance of Effort
Mos.	Months
N–	Denotes that the age range covered by a teaching license begins at nursery (e.g., N–4 = nursery–grade 4)
NA	Not Applicable
NAEYC	National Association for the Education of Young Children
NCLB	No Child Left Behind
P–	Denotes that the age range covered by a teaching license begins at preschool (e.g., P–4 = preschool–grade 4)
Pre-K	Prekindergarten
RFP	Request for Proposal
SDE	State Department of Education
SES	Socio-economic Status
SMI	State Median Income
SpEd	Special Education
TANF	Temporary Assistance to Needy Families
USDA	United States Department of Agriculture

State Profiles

- Enrollment
- Quality
- Access
- Standards
- Resources

Alabama

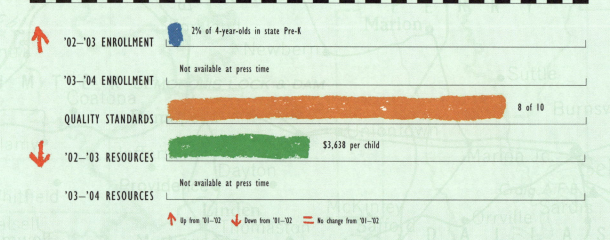

↑	'02–'03 ENROLLMENT	2% of 4-year-olds in state Pre-K
	'03–'04 ENROLLMENT	Not available at press time
	QUALITY STANDARDS	8 of 10
↓	'02–'03 RESOURCES	$3,638 per child
	'03–'04 RESOURCES	Not available at press time

↑ Up from '01–'02   ↓ Down from '01–'02   ＝ No change from '01–'02

In 2000, the Alabama Pre-Kindergarten Pilot Program began serving 4-year-olds using a mixture of state, federal, and local funding sources. The local contribution for these programs is particularly notable, as localities are required to provide matching funds totaling at least 50 percent of the state funding amount for each program. Programs are operated by schools, private child care centers, child care management agencies, Head Start providers, universities, and housing authorities. There are no set eligibility criteria, and in 2002–2003, programs were offered in 63 out of the state's 67 counties. All 4-year-olds who live in these counties are eligible to participate.

Administrators of the Alabama Pre-Kindergarten Pilot Program are particularly proud of the program's efforts to raise awareness of the need for—and quality of—prekindergarten programs across the state.

ACCESS RANKING—4s	ACCESS RANKING—3s	RESOURCES RANKING
35	None Served	14

ACCESS

Total state program enrollment - - - - - - - - - - - - - - 1,260
School districts that offer state program - - - - - 94% (counties)
Income requirement - - - - - - - - - - - - - - - - - - - None
Hours of operation - - - - - - - - - - - - - Full-day, full-week
Operating schedule - - - - - - - - - - - - - - - Academic year
Special education enrollment - - - - - - - - - - - - - - 3,763
Federally funded Head Start enrollment - - - - - - - - 15,742
State-funded Head Start enrollment - - - - - - - - - - - - - 0

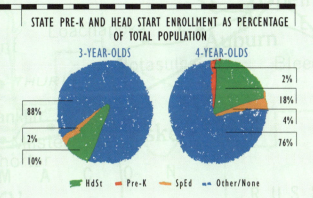

STATE PRE-K AND HEAD START ENROLLMENT AS PERCENTAGE
OF TOTAL POPULATION

3-YEAR-OLDS
88%
2%
10%

4-YEAR-OLDS
2%
18%
4%
76%

■ HdSt   ■ Pre-K   ■ SpEd   ■ Other/None

QUALITY STANDARDS CHECKLIST

POLICY	STATE PRE-K REQUIREMENT	BENCHMARK	DOES REQUIREMENT MEET BENCHMARK?
Curriculum standards - - - - - - - - - - - - - - - - - - - None		Comprehensive	☐
Teacher degree requirement - - - - - - - - - - - - - - - BA		BA	☑
Teacher specialized training req. - Degree in ECE, ECSE, EE, or CD		Specializing in Pre-K	☐
Assistant teacher degree requirement - - - - - - - - - - CDA		CDA or equivalent	☑
Teacher in-service requirement - - - - - - - - - 40 clock hours		At least 15 hours/year	☑
Maximum class size		20 or lower	☑
3-year-olds - NA			
4-year-olds - 18			
Staff-child ratio		1:10 or better	☑
3-year-olds - NA			
4-year-olds - 1:9			
Screening/referral requirements - Vision, hearing, general health, and dental		Vision, hearing, and health	☑
Required support services - - - - - - 2 parent conferences and support services [1]		At least 1 service	☑
Meal requirement - - - - - - - - - - - - - - Lunch and snack		At least 1/day	☑

TOTAL:

8

of 10

RESOURCES

Total state Pre-K spending - - - - - - - - - - - - - $4,584,500 [2]
Local match required? - - - - - - - - Yes; 50% of granted amount
State spending per child enrolled - - - - - - - - - - - $3,638 [3]
State spending per 3-year-old - - - - - - - - - - - - - - - - $0
State spending per 4-year-old - - - - - - - - - - - - - - - $79 [3]

* Pre-K programs may receive additional funds from federal or local sources that are not included in this figure.
** K–12 expenditures include capital spending as well as current operating expenditures.

Data are for the '02–'03 school year, unless otherwise noted.

SPENDING PER CHILD ENROLLED

PRE-K* $6,465
HDST $6,275
K–12** $6,810

0   2   4   6   8   10   12   14
$ thousands

■ State Contribution   ■ Local Contribution   ■ Federal Contribution   ■ TANF Spending

1 Support services include parenting support or training, parent involvement activities, health services for children, and transition to kindergarten activities.
2 This figure includes $1 million in TANF funds.
3 These estimates include both state and TANF funds.

Alaska

NO PROGRAM

ACCESS RANKING—4s	ACCESS RANKING—3s	RESOURCES RANKING
	No Program	

ACCESS

Total state program enrollment - - - - - - - - - - - - - - - 0

School districts that offer state program - - - - - - - - - - NA

Income requirement - NA

Hours of operation - NA

Operating schedule - NA

Special education enrollment - - - - - - - - - - - - - 1,015

Federally funded Head Start enrollment - - - - - - - - 2,323

State-funded Head Start enrollment - - - - - - - - - - - 403 I

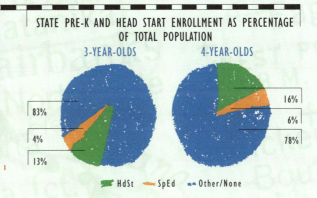

STATE PRE-K AND HEAD START ENROLLMENT AS PERCENTAGE OF TOTAL POPULATION

3-YEAR-OLDS: 83%, 4%, 13%

4-YEAR-OLDS: 16%, 6%, 78%

HdSt   SpEd   Other/None

QUALITY STANDARDS CHECKLIST

No Program

RESOURCES

Total state Pre-K spending - - - - - - - - - - - - - - - - $0

Local match required? - - - - - - - - - - - - - - - - - - - NA

State spending per child enrolled - - - - - - - - - - - - - $0

State Head Start spending - - - - - - - - - - - - $6,276,000

State spending per 3-year-old - - - - - - - - - - - - - - - $0

State spending per 4-year-old - - - - - - - - - - - - - - - $0

* Pre-K programs may receive additional funds from federal or local sources that are not included in this figure.
** K–12 expenditures include capital spending as well as current operating expenditures.
Data are for the '02–'03 school year, unless otherwise noted.

I Alaska did not track the number of children served through its Head Start supplement. As a result, this figure is an estimate based on the number of non-federally funded children in Alaska reported in Head Start's 2002–2003 Program Information Report, and proportions of Alaska's Head Start enrollees who were 3 or 4 years old.

SPENDING PER CHILD ENROLLED

PRE-K* $0

HDST $6,674

K–12** $10,338

0   2   4   6   8   10   12   14

$ thousands

State Contribution   Local Contribution   Federal Contribution

Arizona

'02–'03 ENROLLMENT — 5% of 4-year-olds in state Pre-K

'03–'04 ENROLLMENT — 5% of 4-year-olds in state Pre-K

QUALITY STANDARDS — 4 of 10

'02–'03 RESOURCES — $2,432 per child

'03–'04 RESOURCES — $2,434 per child

↑ Up from '01–'02   ↓ Down from '01–'02   ▬ No change from '01–'02

Arizona has provided funding for prekindergarten since 1991. Since 1996, prekindergarten funds have been one component of the Early Childhood Block Grant (ECBG), which also finances full-day kindergarten and provides supplements for grades K to 3. Only public schools may receive direct funding from the state, although preschool programs may be operated in Head Start and private child care centers through subcontracts with public schools. Some school districts choose to supplement state funds with local funding sources, including district general funds. All providers must be accredited by a state-approved accrediting organization, such as the National Association for the Education of Young Children. Children are eligible for the ECBG preschool program if they come from low-income backgrounds (with family incomes below 185 percent of the federal poverty level) and are not yet eligible for kindergarten. Nearly all participants are 4 years old.

Early learning standards have been a recent focus of the program, with the publication of the Arizona Early Childhood Education Standards. These new early learning standards cover six areas: social/emotional, physical, language and literacy, math, science, and arts. While not required, the early learning standards are promoted by the Arizona Department of Education, which collects information about how programs use the standards to implement curriculum and inform instruction.

In the 2003–2004 school year, $10,542,475 in ECBG funding was used to provide prekindergarten services to 4,332 children.

ACCESS RANKING—4s	ACCESS RANKING—3s	RESOURCES RANKING
29	None Served	28

ACCESS

Total state program enrollment - - - - - - - - - - - - - - - 4,092

School districts that offer state program - - - - - - - - - - - 8%

(school districts and charter schools) [1]

Income requirement - - - - - - - - - - - - - - - - - - - 185% FPL

Hours of operation - - - - - - - - - - - Determined locally [2]

Operating schedule - - - - - - - - - - - Determined locally [2]

Special education enrollment - - - - - - - - - - - - - - - 6,289

Federally funded Head Start enrollment - - - - - - - - - 16,895

State-funded Head Start enrollment - - - - - - - - - - - - - - 0

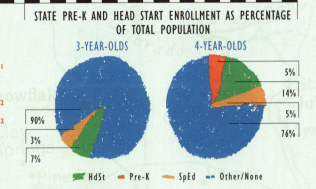

STATE PRE-K AND HEAD START ENROLLMENT AS PERCENTAGE OF TOTAL POPULATION

3-YEAR-OLDS

90%
3%
7%

4-YEAR-OLDS

5%
14%
5%
76%

■ HdSt ■ Pre-K ■ SpEd ■ Other/None

QUALITY STANDARDS CHECKLIST

POLICY	STATE PRE-K REQUIREMENT	BENCHMARK	DOES REQUIREMENT MEET BENCHMARK?
Curriculum standards - - - - - - - - - - -	Comprehensive	Comprehensive	✓
Teacher degree requirement - - - - - - - - - - - - - - -	CDA [3]	BA	☐
Teacher specialized training requirement - Meets CDA requirements [3]		Specializing in Pre-K	✓
Assistant teacher degree requirement - - - - - - - - - -	None	CDA or equivalent	☐
Teacher in-service requirement - - - - - - - -	12 clock hours	At least 15 hours/year	☐
Maximum class size		20 or lower	✓
3-year-olds - - - - - - - - - - - - - - - - - - -	20 [3]		
4-year-olds - - - - - - - - - - - - - - - - - - -	20 [3]		
Staff-child ratio		1:10 or better	✓
3-year-olds - - - - - - - - - - - - - - - - - - -	1:10 [3]		
4-year-olds - - - - - - - - - - - - - - - - - - -	1:10 [3]		
Screening/referral requirements - - - - - - - - - - - -	None	Vision, hearing, and health	☐
Required support services - - - - - - - - - - - - - -	None	At least 1 service	☐
Meal requirement - - - - - - - - - - - - - - - - -	Varies [4]	At least 1/day	☐

TOTAL:

4

of 10

RESOURCES

Total state Pre-K spending - - - - - - - - - - - - - - $9,953,752

Local match required? - No

State spending per child enrolled - - - - - - - - - - - $2,432

State spending per 3-year-old - - - - - - - - - - - - - - NA [5]

State spending per 4-year-old - - - - - - - - - - - - - - $123 [5]

SPENDING PER CHILD ENROLLED

PRE-K* ▬ $2,432

HDST ▬ $7,580

K–12** ▬ $6,424

0 2 4 6 8 10 12 14

$ thousands

▬ State Contribution ▬ Local Contribution ▬ Federal Contribution

* Pre-K programs may receive additional funds from federal or local sources that are not included in this figure.
** K–12 expenditures include capital spending as well as current operating expenditures.

Data are for the '02–'03 school year, unless otherwise noted.

1 This figure is calculated based on the total number of school districts and charter schools in Arizona. However, only 329 districts and charter schools participate in the Early Childhood Block Grant Program, as most charter schools do not receive ECBG funding. A subset of the schools funded by the ECBG offer the prekindergarten program.

2 The vast majority of programs operate 5 days per week for the academic year.

3 This requirement represents NAEYC standards. All programs must be accredited.

4 The state licensing agency requires licensed programs, including all ECBG Pre-K programs, to provide breakfast, lunch and snacks depending upon the length of time and the time of day that a child attends a program.

5 For the purpose of these calculations, all spending was considered to be directed toward 4-year-olds, because nearly all enrollees are age 4.

Arkansas

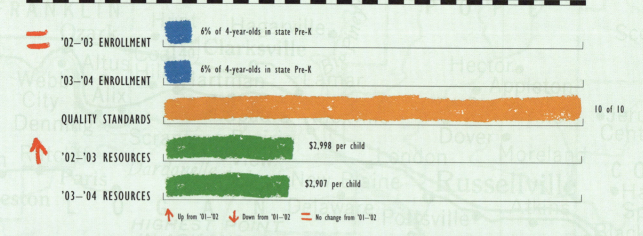

'02–'03 ENROLLMENT		6% of 4-year-olds in state Pre-K
'03–'04 ENROLLMENT		6% of 4-year-olds in state Pre-K
QUALITY STANDARDS		10 of 10
'02–'03 RESOURCES		$2,998 per child
'03–'04 RESOURCES		$2,907 per child

↑ Up from '01–'02   ↓ Down from '01–'02   = No change from '01–'02

The Arkansas Better Chance (ABC) program started in 1991 as part of a state initiative supported by a dedicated sales tax for the Educational Excellence Trust Fund. Since 2001, the program has been funded in part by 80 percent of the monies received through an excise tax on package beer. In addition, localities are required to provide matching funds equal to 40 percent of total funding. While the majority of programs operate in public schools, the state also provides direct funding to Head Start agencies, private child care centers, universities, education cooperatives, community mental health centers, and developmental disability centers. Children from birth to age 5 are eligible to participate if they are from low-income families or at risk due to abuse or neglect, low birth weight, limited English proficiency, or other circumstances.

A recent ABC task force recommendation identified core quality components, established a clear unit rate per child, and specified that children in center-based programs should receive at least 7.5 hours of services per day. The model also brought teacher and aide salaries in line with compensation for these positions in public schools.

With $8,972,517 in state funds for center-based ABC programs, 862 3-year-olds and 2,224 4-year-olds were enrolled during the 2003–2004 school year. As part of a broader education reform measure that was adopted in response to a school finance equity ruling, Arkansas recently passed legislation that will greatly expand the availability of prekindergarten. Starting in 2004–2005, the state will provide $40 million in new funds. Districts that have at least 75 percent of their children scoring below proficient levels in literacy and math on the State Benchmark exams and children in schools that have been designated as being in school improvement status will receive priority for funding.

ACCESS RANKING—4s	ACCESS RANKING—3s	RESOURCES RANKING
26	12	21

ACCESS

Total state program enrollment - - - - - - - - - - - - - 3,086 [1]

School districts that offer state program - - - - - - - - 63% [2]

Income requirement - - - - - - - - - - - - - - - - 156% FPL [3]

Hours of operation - - - - - - - - - - - - - - Full-day, full-week

Operating schedule - - - - - - - - - - - - - - - Academic year

Special education enrollment - - - - - - - - - - - - - 6,694

Federally funded Head Start enrollment - - - - - - - - 10,283

State-funded Head Start enrollment - - - - - - - - - - - - 0

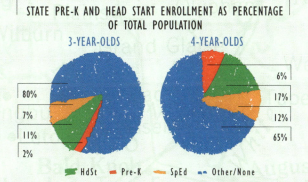

STATE PRE-K AND HEAD START ENROLLMENT AS PERCENTAGE OF TOTAL POPULATION

3-YEAR-OLDS
- 80%
- 7%
- 11%
- 2%

4-YEAR-OLDS
- 6%
- 17%
- 12%
- 65%

■ HdSt　■ Pre-K　■ SpEd　■■ Other/None

QUALITY STANDARDS CHECKLIST

POLICY	STATE PRE-K REQUIREMENT	BENCHMARK	DOES REQUIREMENT MEET BENCHMARK?
Curriculum standards	Comprehensive	Comprehensive	✓
Teacher degree requirement	BA	BA	✓
Teacher specialized training requirement	P–4 teacher license [4]	Specializing in Pre-K	✓
Assistant teacher degree requirement	CDA	CDA or equivalent	✓
Teacher in-service requirement	30 clock hours	At least 15 hours/year	✓
Maximum class size		20 or lower	✓
3-year-olds	20		
4-year-olds	20		
Staff-child ratio		1:10 or better	✓
3-year-olds	1:10		
4-year-olds	1:10		
Screening/referral requirements	Vision, hearing, and health	Vision, hearing, and health	✓
Required support services	1 parent conference and support services [5]	At least 1 service	✓
Meal requirement	Lunch and snack	At least 1/day	✓

TOTAL:
10
of 10

RESOURCES

Total state Pre-K spending - - - - - - - - - - - $9,250,285 [6]

Local match required? - - - - - - - - - Yes—40% of total funding

State spending per child enrolled - - - - - - - - - - - $2,998

State spending per 3-year-old - - - - - - - - - - - - - - $70

State spending per 4-year-old - - - - - - - - - - - - - $184

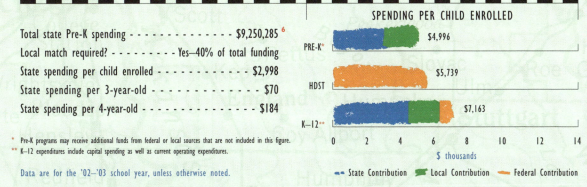

SPENDING PER CHILD ENROLLED

- PRE-K* : $4,996
- HDST : $5,739
- K–12** : $7,163

0　2　4　6　8　10　12　14
$ thousands

■■ State Contribution　■ Local Contribution　■ Federal Contribution

* Pre-K programs may receive additional funds from federal or local sources that are not included in this figure.

** K–12 expenditures include capital spending as well as current operating expenditures.

Data are for the '02–'03 school year, unless otherwise noted.

1　This enrollment figure only includes children in the center-based component of the program. ABC also has a home-based component, but the enrollment for this component is not included here.

2　Programs are offered in 68 out of 75 (91%) counties.

3　This is equivalent to an income of $23,523 for a family of three.

4　The P–4 teacher license covers birth to fourth grade.

5　Support services include education services or job training for parents, parenting support or training, parent involvement activities, health services for children, information about nutrition, referral to social services, and transition to kindergarten activities. Funding specific to parent engagement is included in the Core Quality Component model for ABC programs. Home visits, however, are not required.

6　This figure represents spending on the center-based component of the ABC program.

California

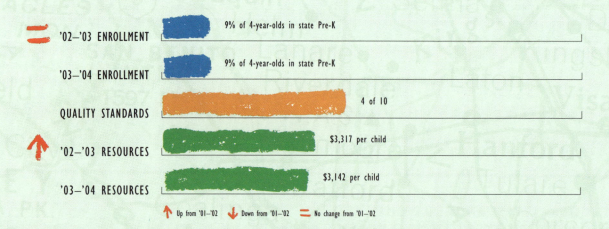

'02–'03 ENROLLMENT		9% of 4-year-olds in state Pre-K
'03–'04 ENROLLMENT		9% of 4-year-olds in state Pre-K
QUALITY STANDARDS		4 of 10
'02–'03 RESOURCES		$3,317 per child
'03–'04 RESOURCES		$3,142 per child

↑ Up from '01–'02   ↓ Down from '01–'02   ═ No change from '01–'02

Established in 1965, the California State Preschool Program provides child care and development programs for the state's 3- to 5-year-old children from low-income families. Programs are funded through a competitive grant process and administered by school districts, Head Start agencies, and private child care providers. Children are eligible to participate if their family's income falls below 230 percent of the federal poverty level. Children who are receiving protective services, who have been abused, neglected, or exploited, or who are at risk for abuse or neglect are also eligible to participate, regardless of income, and are given top priority.

California administrators view the State Preschool Program as one of several state early childhood programs designed to meet the varied needs of children and families and that together comprise a broader child development system. Although the State Preschool Program primarily supports part-day services, coordination with federally and state-funded child care assistance programs provides funds to help parents working full time cover the costs of extended hours of care. In addition, the state provided $247,196,000 to support 30,370 full-time slots for 3- and 4-year-olds in General Child Care programs, bringing total state funding for prekindergarten and child care to $496,718,000 in 2002–2003. General Child Care programs have the same curriculum standards and program requirements as the State Preschool Program, but are targeted to working parents who need full-day care for their children.

The components of high-quality programming are laid out for child development programs in the Prekindergarten Learning and Development Guidelines, which were published in 2000. Programs are required to record children's development using the Desired Results system, and then use the findings to plan the curriculum and developmentally appropriate activities.

The State Preschool Program was provided with $303.8 million in state funds to support a total of 96,685 slots during the 2003–2004 school year. However, because some contractors lacked staff or facilities to fill all of their slots, approximately 75,000 children were enrolled and not all of the funds were spent on preschool.

An additional early childhood initiative was approved in 1998 through the California Children and Families Act. Also known as First 5, this initiative established a dedicated tobacco tax to fund programs promoting early childhood development, from prenatal care to age 5. First 5 funds are allocated by county commissions and may be used for services including early care and education, parent education, family support, or child health needs. California also reserved $200 million over four years for a School Readiness Initiative.

ACCESS RANKING—4s	ACCESS RANKING—3s	RESOURCES RANKING
21	13	17

ACCESS

Total state program enrollment - - - - - - - - - - - - - 75,231 [1]

School districts that offer state program - - - - - 95% (counties) [2]

Income requirement - - - - - - - - - - - - - - - - - - 230% FPL [3]

Hours of operation - - - - - - - - - - - - - Determined locally [4]

Operating schedule - - - - - - - - - - - - - - - Academic year [5]

Special education enrollment - - - - - - - - - - - - - 34,701

Federally funded Head Start enrollment - - - - - - - - 90,496

State-funded Head Start enrollment - - - - - - - - - - - - - 0

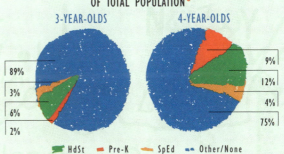

STATE PRE-K AND HEAD START ENROLLMENT AS PERCENTAGE OF TOTAL POPULATION [6]

3-YEAR-OLDS

89%
3%
6%
2%

4-YEAR-OLDS

9%
12%
4%
75%

▇ HdSt   ▇ Pre-K   ▇ SpEd   ⊶ Other/None

QUALITY STANDARDS CHECKLIST

POLICY	STATE PRE-K REQUIREMENT	BENCHMARK	DOES REQUIREMENT MEET BENCHMARK?
Curriculum standards	Not comprehensive	Comprehensive	☐
Teacher degree requirement	CDA [7]	BA	☐
Teacher specialized training requirement	Meets CDA requirements [7]	Specializing in Pre-K	☑
Assistant teacher degree requirement	CD Asst. Tchr. Permit [8]	CDA or equivalent	☐
Teacher in-service requirement	105 clock hours/5 years	At least 15 hours/year	☑
Maximum class size		20 or lower	☐
3-year-olds	No limit [9]		
4-year-olds	No limit [9]		
Staff-child ratio		1:10 or better	☑
3-year-olds	1:8		
4-year-olds	1:8		
Screening/referral requirements	None [10]	Vision, hearing, and health	☐
Required support services	2 parent conferences and support services [11]	At least 1 service	☑
Meal requirement	Varies [12]	At least 1/day	☐

TOTAL:

4

of 10

RESOURCES

Total state Pre-K spending - - - - - - - - - - - - - $249,522,000 [1]

Local match required? - - - - - - - - - - - - - - - - - - - No

State spending per child enrolled - - - - - - - - - - - $3,317 [13]

State spending per 3-year-old - - - - - - - - - - - - - - $72 [13]

State spending per 4-year-old - - - - - - - - - - - - - $288 [13]

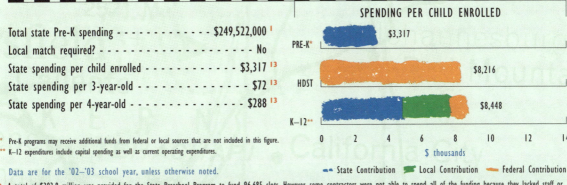

SPENDING PER CHILD ENROLLED

PRE-K* — $3,317

HDST — $8,216

K–12** — $8,448

$ thousands

⊶ State Contribution   ▇ Local Contribution   ▇ Federal Contribution

* Pre-K programs may receive additional funds from federal or local sources that are not included in this figure.

** K–12 expenditures include capital spending as well as current operating expenditures.

Data are for the '02–'03 school year, unless otherwise noted.

1   A total of $303.8 million was provided for the State Preschool Program to fund 96,685 slots. However, some contractors were not able to spend all of the funding because they lacked staff or facilities, because working families opted for full-day instead of part-day programs, or due to other reasons. These figures reflect unallocated and under-earned contracts.
2   There are a total of 476 contracts or agencies providing State Preschool services. The program is offered in 320 out of 1,165 (27%) Local Education Agencies, which include school districts, county offices of education, and community colleges.
3   The income cutoff applies to all children except those who receive protective services, who are identified as abused, neglected, exploited, or who are at risk for abuse or neglect.
4   Programs are required to operate a minimum of 3 hours per day, 5 days per week.
5   Children must be served for at least 175 days per year (equivalent to a school year), but an agency is permitted to operate for up to 250 days per year.
6   Percentages of children in Pre-K reflect only those served in state preschool, and do not include 30,370 slots in General Child Care programs. An estimated 3.4% of 3-year-olds and 13.6% of 4-year-olds were enrolled in either state Pre-K or General Child Care during 2002–2003.
7   The Associate Teacher Permit requires 12 credits in ECE or child development and 50 days of work experience in an instructional capacity. A CDA credential issued in California may be substituted for this requirement. The Associate level teacher may function as the lead teacher in a classroom and the permit may be renewed one time for a 5-year period. The full Child Development Teacher Permit requires a minimum of 40 semester units of education of which a minimum of 24 units must be in ECE or child development. A CDA credential may be used as 9 semester units toward the required 24.
8   The Child Development Assistant Teacher Permit requires 6 credits in early childhood education or child development.
9   Class size is not statutorily controlled, but is typically limited to 24 in order to meet the staff-child ratio requirement of 1:8.
10 A physical exam is required for program entry. Health and social services referral and follow-up to meet family needs are required.
11 Support services include parenting support or training, parent involvement activities, health services for children, referral to social services, and transition to kindergarten activities.
12 Each contractor must provide meals and/or snacks that meet nutritional requirements specified by the federal Child and Adult Care Food Program or the National School Lunch Program. Most programs offer a meal, and virtually all programs provide a snack.
13 These figures reflect state spending for preschool programs only. During 2002–2003, state spending across both Pre-K and General Child Care programs was $4,704 per child enrolled, $168 per 3-year-old and $692 per 4-year-old.

Colorado

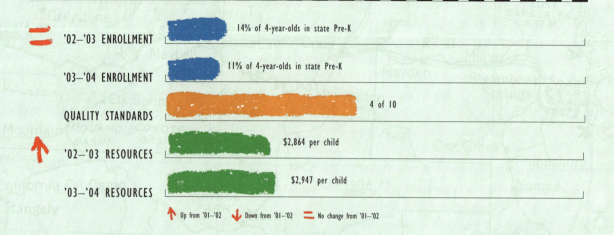

'02–'03 ENROLLMENT	14% of 4-year-olds in state Pre-K
'03–'04 ENROLLMENT	11% of 4-year-olds in state Pre-K
QUALITY STANDARDS	4 of 10
'02–'03 RESOURCES	$2,864 per child
'03–'04 RESOURCES	$2,947 per child

↑ Up from '01–'02   ↓ Down from '01–'02   = No change from '01–'02

I n an effort to reduce the dropout rate in the state, the Colorado Preschool Program (CPP) began in 1988. While some CPP funds are used to provide full-day kindergarten in certain districts (serving 1,494 children in 2002–2003), funding is used primarily to provide at-risk children with a half-day, comprehensive prekindergarten program. Additional funding sources, such as federal Head Start funds, may be combined with state CPP funds to extend the length of the program day or to provide extra services to children. Among the risk factors used to determine eligibility are homelessness, drug or alcohol abuse by a family member, low parental education, and eligibility for free or reduced-cost lunch. Four-year-olds must have at least one risk factor to be eligible, while 3-year-olds must have at least three risk factors to qualify. Only public schools may receive funding directly from the state. Local school districts may subcontract with Head Start and community-based child care providers to provide CPP classes.

The 2003 legislative session resulted in a 2,000-slot reduction in the number of children served in the Colorado Preschool Program. A total of 936 3-year-olds and 7,047 4-year-olds were served by CPP, using $26,589,159 in state funds during the 2003–2004 school year.

A consortium of statewide organizations has been formed to create the framework for a cohesive, effective early childhood system in Colorado. This Early Childhood State Systems Team includes representatives from the Colorado Department of Education, the Colorado Department of Human Services, the Colorado Department of Public Health and Environment, Educare, and a number of other organizations. Activities of the consortium include work on a public engagement campaign and a plan for measuring outcomes and quality within the early childhood system.

ACCESS RANKING—4s	ACCESS RANKING—3s	RESOURCES RANKING
15	18	25

ACCESS

Total state program enrollment - - - - - - - - - - - - - - - 10,923 [1]

School districts that offer state program - - - - - - - - - - 87%

Income requirement - None

Hours of operation - - - - - - - - - Half-day, less than 5 days/week [2]

Operating schedule - - - - - - - - - - - - - - - - Academic year

Special education enrollment - - - - - - - - - - - - - - - 5,507

Federally funded Head Start enrollment - - - - - - - - - 9,133

State-funded Head Start enrollment - - - - - - - - - - - - - 0

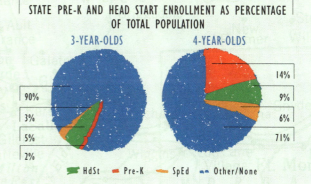

STATE PRE-K AND HEAD START ENROLLMENT AS PERCENTAGE OF TOTAL POPULATION

3-YEAR-OLDS: 90%, 3%, 5%, 2%

4-YEAR-OLDS: 14%, 9%, 6%, 71%

■ HdSt ■ Pre-K ■ SpEd ■ Other/None

QUALITY STANDARDS CHECKLIST

POLICY	STATE PRE-K REQUIREMENT	BENCHMARK	DOES REQUIREMENT MEET BENCHMARK?
Curriculum standards	Not comprehensive	Comprehensive	☐
Teacher degree requirement	CDA [3]	BA	☐
Teacher specialized training requirement	Meets CDA requirements	Specializing in Pre-K	☑
Assistant teacher degree requirement	None	CDA or equivalent	☐
Teacher in-service requirement	10 clock hours	At least 15 hours/year	☐
Maximum class size		20 or lower	☑
3-year-olds	15		
4-year-olds	15		
Staff-child ratio		1:10 or better	☑
3-year-olds	1:8		
4-year-olds	1:8		
Screening/referral requirements	Health only; vision and hearing determined locally	Vision, hearing, and health	☐
Required support services	1 parent conference and support services [4]	At least 1 service	☑
Meal requirement	Varies [5]	At least 1/day	☐

TOTAL: 4 of 10

RESOURCES

Total state Pre-K spending - - - - - - - - - - - - - $31,287,685 [6]

Local match required? - - - - - - - - - - - - - - - - - - - No

State spending per child enrolled - - - - - - - - - - - $2,864 [7]

State spending per 3-year-old - - - - - - - - - - - - - - $42

State spending per 4-year-old - - - - - - - - - - - - - - $395

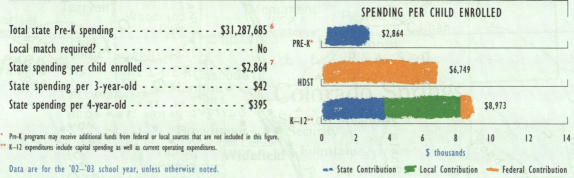

SPENDING PER CHILD ENROLLED

PRE-K* : $2,864

HDST : $6,749

K-12** : $8,973

$ thousands

■– State Contribution   ■ Local Contribution   ■– Federal Contribution

* Pre-K programs may receive additional funds from federal or local sources that are not included in this figure.

** K–12 expenditures include capital spending as well as current operating expenditures.

Data are for the '02–'03 school year, unless otherwise noted.

1 This figure includes 1,494 5-year-olds served in full-day kindergarten programs.

2 Most programs operate 4 days per week with the fifth day funded to provide home visits, teacher planning time, or staff training. Full-day programs have difficulty allocating time for home visits.

3 In the event that a teacher with a CDA is not available, an AA in early childhood education or child development becomes the minimum requirement.

4 Support services include parenting support or training, parent involvement activities, health services for parents and children, information about nutrition, referral to social services, and transition to kindergarten activities.

5 Meals and nutritious snacks must be served at suitable intervals. Children who are in the program for more than 4 hours per day or during evenings must be offered a meal that meets at least one-third of the child's daily nutritional needs.

6 CPP is funded by the School Finance Act. Funding for school districts is provided first by local sources, including revenues, property taxes and specific ownership taxes. State monies are then used to fund any shortfall. The state share is about 61% of total program funding.

7 This amount is an average that is reflective of school finance money only. In FY 2002–2003, funding levels for CPP ranged from $2,587 to $6,000 per child, depending on the funding level for the school district.

Connecticut

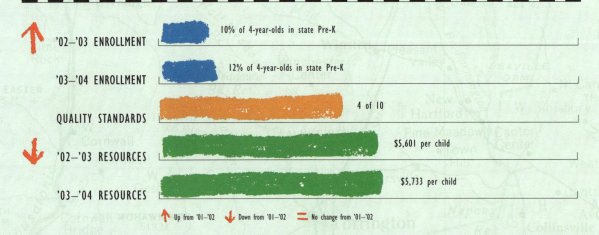

'02–'03 ENROLLMENT — 10% of 4-year-olds in state Pre-K

'03–'04 ENROLLMENT — 12% of 4-year-olds in state Pre-K

QUALITY STANDARDS — 4 of 10

'02–'03 RESOURCES — $5,601 per child

'03–'04 RESOURCES — $5,733 per child

↑ Up from '01–'02   ↓ Down from '01–'02   ▬ No change from '01–'02

Connecticut has provided funds for School Readiness programs since 1997 to increase access to high-quality preschool programs. Three- and 4-year-olds are eligible to participate. At least 60 percent of children served in each community must have family incomes at or below 75 percent of the state median income. Families participating in the program are charged fees on a sliding scale basis. Communities are allowed to exempt families in part-day programs from paying fees, and the state has issued guidelines on other types of exemptions.

The state allocates funds to priority school districts and awards competitive grants to schools considered to have severe needs. The mayor or superintendent designates a fiscal agent to receive the funds and local School Readiness Councils provide guidance on how to distribute the funds to individual programs. Programs may be offered in public schools, child care centers, and Head Start centers that are accredited or have state approval. At least 60 percent of slots must be full-day, full-year slots.

Professional development opportunities for staff, as well as other efforts, have contributed to the establishment and implementation of preschool standards. A recent focus has been to link these standards with the Preschool Assessment Framework.

In 2003–2004, School Readiness programs received approximately $37,576,500 from the state to fund 6,554 slots for 3- and 4-year-olds.

Connecticut also supplemented Head Start funds in 2003–2004 with $4.5 million in state general funds. While most of these funds were used to enhance services to existing classrooms, they also supported an estimated 332 additional Head Start slots for 3- and 4-year-olds.

ACCESS RANKING—4s	ACCESS RANKING—3s	RESOURCES RANKING
18	9	4

ACCESS

Total state program enrollment - - - - - - - - - - - - - - 6,369

School districts that offer state program - - - 26% (communities)

Income requirement - 60% of students must be at or below 75% SMI

Hours of operation - - - - - - - - - - - Determined by type of slot [1]

Operating schedule - - - - - - - - - Determined by type of slot [1]

Special education enrollment - - - - - - - - - - - - - - 4,812

Federally funded Head Start enrollment - - - - - - - - - 5,505

State-funded Head Start enrollment - - - - - - - - - - - 332 [2]

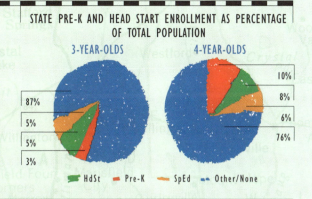

STATE PRE-K AND HEAD START ENROLLMENT AS PERCENTAGE OF TOTAL POPULATION

3-YEAR-OLDS: 87%, 5%, 5%, 3%

4-YEAR-OLDS: 10%, 8%, 6%, 76%

■ HdSt ■ Pre-K ■ SpEd ■ Other/None

QUALITY STANDARDS CHECKLIST

POLICY	STATE PRE-K REQUIREMENT	BENCHMARK	DOES REQUIREMENT MEET BENCHMARK?
Curriculum standards	Not comprehensive	Comprehensive	☐
Teacher degree requirement	BA or CDA (public), CDA (nonpublic) [3]	BA	☐
Teacher specialized training requirement	[see footnotes] [3]	Specializing in Pre-K	☑
Assistant teacher degree requirement	None [4]	CDA or equivalent	☐
Teacher in-service requirement	75 CEUs/5 years (public), 1% of hours worked (nonpublic) [5]	At least 15 hours/year	☐
Maximum class size		20 or lower	☑
3-year-olds	20		
4-year-olds	20		
Staff-child ratio		1:10 or better	☑
3-year-olds	1:10		
4-year-olds	1:10		
Screening/referral requirements	Health [6]	Vision, hearing, and health	☐
Required support services	2 parent conferences and support services [7]	At least 1 service	☑
Meal requirement	Varies [8]	At least 1/day	☐

TOTAL:

4

of 10

RESOURCES

Total state Pre-K spending - - - - - - - - - - - - - $35,674,423

Local match required? - - - - - - - - - - - - - - - - - - - No

State spending per child enrolled - - - - - - - - - - - - $5,601

State Head Start spending - - - - - - - - - - - - - - $4,500,000

State spending per 3-year-old - - - - - - - - - - - - - $191 [9]

State spending per 4-year-old - - - - - - - - - - - - - $584 [9]

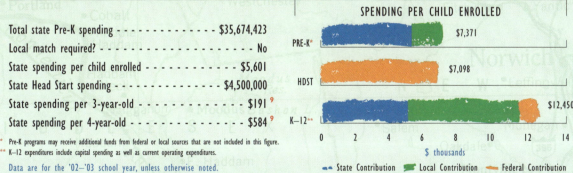

SPENDING PER CHILD ENROLLED

PRE-K*: $7,371

HDST: $7,098

K–12**: $12,450

$ thousands

■- - State Contribution   ■ Local Contribution   ■ Federal Contribution

* Pre-K programs may receive additional funds from federal or local sources that are not included in this figure.

** K–12 expenditures include capital spending as well as current operating expenditures.

Data are for the '02–'03 school year, unless otherwise noted.

1. Each community chooses its own specific combination of slots. Types of slots include full-day, full-year (10 hours per day, 50 weeks per year), part-day, part-year (2.5 hours per day, 180 days per year), and extended-day (extends the hours, days, and weeks of a non-School Readiness program to meet full-day requirements). At least 60% of slots in each community must be full-day, full-year. All programs operate 5 days per week, and about 75% of programs are full-day.
2. This figure represents an estimate based on the number of state-funded slots in Head Start reported by the state, and proportions of Connecticut's federal Head Start enrollees who were 3 or 4 years old.
3. Programs operating in public schools are required to have a certified teacher present for at least 2.5 hours per day. Three types of certification are accepted: Elementary with a Pre-K endorsement, Nursery–K, or Special Education with an endorsement in Pre-K–12. For the remainder of the day, the teacher present must have a CDA plus 9 credits in early childhood.
4. Assistant teachers must meet teacher requirements if they act in the capacity of lead teacher for part of the day, which they generally do in full-day programs.
5. School Readiness program requirements also mandate that teachers take two courses or workshops in ECE and receive training on an annual basis in serving children with disabilities. In addition, they must present documentation that they have attended at least one workshop on emerging pre-literacy skills and one on diversity.
6. All children in the School Readiness program must have an annual well-child check up that conforms to EPSDT standards. Some communities provide vision, hearing, and dental check-ups.
7. Support services include educational services or job training for parents, parenting support or training, relevant parent workshops, health services for children, information about nutrition, referral to social services, and transition to kindergarten activities. In addition, all programs must have written collaborative agreements with community agencies to serve families' needs.
8. Programs are required to serve one snack to children who attend less than 5 hours per day, and one snack plus one meal to children in class for 5 to 8 hours per day. Children on the premises more than 8 hours per day require one snack and two meals or two snacks and one meal. Either the program or the parent can provide food for all meals.
9. Connecticut did not break its total enrollment figure into specific numbers of 3- or 4-year-olds. As a result, these calculations are estimates, based on proportions of enrollees who were ages 3 and 4 in states that served 3-year-olds and provided age breakdowns for 2002–2003.

Delaware

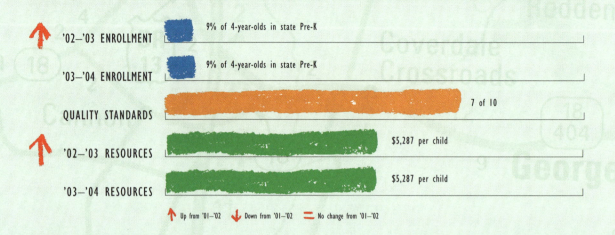

↑ '02–'03 ENROLLMENT	9% of 4-year-olds in state Pre-K
'03–'04 ENROLLMENT	9% of 4-year-olds in state Pre-K
QUALITY STANDARDS	7 of 10
↑ '02–'03 RESOURCES	$5,287 per child
'03–'04 RESOURCES	$5,287 per child

↑ Up from '01–'02   ↓ Down from '01–'02   = No change from '01–'02

In 1994, the Early Childhood Assistance Program (ECAP) was established to increase the number of Head Start-eligible 4-year-olds who have access to comprehensive early childhood services prior to kindergarten. Head Start programs, public schools, nonprofit agencies, private child care centers, and community colleges receive ECAP funds from the state. ECAP offers the same services as the federal Head Start program, follows the same performance standards, and uses similar eligibility criteria. As in Head Start, at least 90 percent of the children enrolled must come from families below the federal poverty line. Ten percent of the slots may be filled by children who are from families above the federal poverty line and exhibit other risk factors including, but not limited to, an identified disability.

The state Department of Education has developed and published the Delaware Early Learning Foundations, a curriculum framework for instructional planning in preschool. This framework was adopted in August 2003, and is mandatory for state-funded educational programs. The Delaware Early Learning Foundations framework is aligned with K–12 standards and performance indicators.

With $4,456,700 in state funding, ECAP served 843 4-year-olds in 2003–2004.

ACCESS RANKING–4s	ACCESS RANKING–3s	RESOURCES RANKING
22	None Served	5

ACCESS

Total state program enrollment - - - - - - - - - - - - - 843

School districts that offer state program - - - - 100% (counties) [1]

Income requirement - - 90% of children must be below 100% FPL

Hours of operation - - - - - - - - - - - - - - Half-day, full-week

Operating schedule - - - - - - - - - - - - - - - - Academic year

Special education enrollment - - - - - - - - - - - - - - 1,065

Federally funded Head Start enrollment - - - - - - - - 1,541

State-funded Head Start enrollment - - - - - - - - - - - 843 [2]

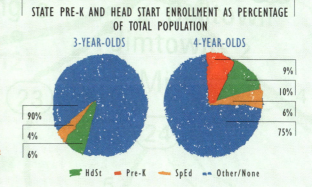

STATE PRE-K AND HEAD START ENROLLMENT AS PERCENTAGE OF TOTAL POPULATION

3-YEAR-OLDS 4-YEAR-OLDS

90%
4%
6%

9%
10%
6%
75%

■ HdSt   ■ Pre-K   ■ SpEd   ■ Other/None

QUALITY STANDARDS CHECKLIST

POLICY	STATE PRE-K REQUIREMENT	BENCHMARK	DOES REQUIREMENT MEET BENCHMARK?
Curriculum standards	None	Comprehensive	☐
Teacher degree requirement	CDA	BA	☐
Teacher specialized training requirement	Meets CDA requirements	Specializing in Pre-K	☑
Assistant teacher degree requirement	HSD	CDA or equivalent	☐
Teacher in-service requirement	15 clock hours [3]	At least 15 hours/year	☑
Maximum class size		20 or lower	☑
3-year-olds	NA		
4-year-olds	20		
Staff-child ratio		1:10 or better	☑
3-year-olds	NA		
4-year-olds	1:10		
Screening/referral requirements	Hearing, vision, general health, developmental, and behavioral	Vision, hearing, and health	☑
Required support services	4 parent conferences and support services [4]	At least 1 service	☑
Meal requirement	Breakfast and lunch	At least 1/day	☑

TOTAL:
7
of 10

RESOURCES

Total state Pre-K spending - - - - - - - - - - - - $4,456,700

Local match required? - - - - - - - - - - - - - - - - - - - No

State spending per child enrolled - - - - - - - - - - $5,287

State Head Start spending - - - - - - - - - - - - $4,456,700 [5]

State spending per 3-year-old - - - - - - - - - - - - - - - $0

State spending per 4-year-old - - - - - - - - - - - - - - $449

SPENDING PER CHILD ENROLLED

PRE-K* $5,287

HDST $5,663

K–12** $11,650

0   2   4   6   8   10   12   14
$ thousands

■- State Contribution   ■ Local Contribution   — Federal Contribution

* Pre-K programs may receive additional funds from federal or local sources that are not included in this figure.

** K–12 expenditures include capital spending as well as current operating expenditures.

Data are for the '02–'03 school year, unless otherwise noted.

1 While the program is not targeted to particular school districts, communities, or towns, it is available in each of Delaware's three counties. In 2002–2003, at least two programs were available in each county.

2 This number represents ECAP enrollment. All state-funded Head Start enrollment is through ECAP.

3 This represents the requirement to meet state child care licensing standards. There is no specific ECAP requirement.

4 Support services include parenting support or training, parent involvement activities, health services for children, information about nutrition, referral to social services, transition to kindergarten activities, and medical and dental services.

5 ECAP is a state-funded Head Start model. All state Pre-K spending is therefore directed toward Head Start programs.

Florida

NO PROGRAM

Although Florida had a state prekindergarten initiative for more than 20 years, it does not currently have a state-funded program that fits the definition used in this report. In 1978, Florida launched its first state prekindergarten initiative with the creation of the State Migrant Prekindergarten Program, which supplemented federal Title I funds. The state expanded its support for prekindergarten in 1987 by establishing the Prekindergarten Early Intervention Program to serve low-income 3- and 4-year-olds. As of October 2000, these two programs were serving more than 20,000 children. In 2001, the programs were incorporated into the School Readiness Program, a broader early childhood initiative begun in 1999.

The School Readiness Program distributes federal and state resources to local councils, which are then responsible for determining how funds will be used to support and coordinate services for young children in their communities. Participating providers are no longer mandated to follow the specific quality standards that were required under the former prekindergarten programs, although they must follow applicable licensing standards.

Total funding for the School Readiness Program was about $700 million for fiscal year 2003–2004. Most of these funds were derived from federal and state TANF and CCDF contributions, although state general revenue funds accounted for $170.9 million of the total amount. The state does not collect data on the number of children receiving each particular type of service funded by the School Readiness Program.

A voter mandate requires Florida to make prekindergarten available to all 4-year-olds by 2005. However, the legislature and the governor have not yet settled on a plan for implementing universal prekindergarten.

ACCESS RANKING—4s	ACCESS RANKING—3s	RESOURCES RANKING
No Program		

ACCESS

Total state program enrollment - - - - - - - - - - - - - - - - 0
School districts that offer state program - - - - - - - - - - NA
Income requirement - NA
Hours of operation - NA
Operating schedule - NA
Special education enrollment - - - - - - - - - - - - - - 18,320
Federally funded Head Start enrollment - - - - - - - - - 32,957
State-funded Head Start enrollment - - - - - - - - - - - - - 0

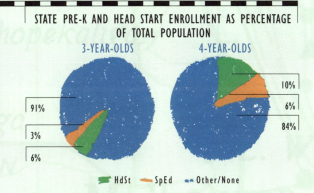

STATE PRE-K AND HEAD START ENROLLMENT AS PERCENTAGE OF TOTAL POPULATION

3-YEAR-OLDS
91%
3%
6%

4-YEAR-OLDS
10%
6%
84%

HdSt   SpEd   Other/None

QUALITY STANDARDS CHECKLIST

No Program

RESOURCES

Total state Pre-K spending - - - - - - - - - - - - - - - - - $0
Local match required? - - - - - - - - - - - - - - - - - - - NA
State spending per child enrolled - - - - - - - - - - - - - $0
State spending per 3-year-old - - - - - - - - - - - - - - - $0
State spending per 4-year-old - - - - - - - - - - - - - - - $0

SPENDING PER CHILD ENROLLED

PRE-K* $0
HDST $7,228
K–12** $8,084

0   2   4   6   8   10   12   14
$ thousands

State Contribution   Local Contribution   Federal Contribution

* Pre-K programs may receive additional funds from federal or local sources that are not included in this figure.
** K–12 expenditures include capital spending as well as current operating expenditures.
Data are for the '02–'03 school year, unless otherwise noted.

Georgia

'02–'03 ENROLLMENT   54% of 4-year-olds in state Pre-K

'03–'04 ENROLLMENT   56% of 4-year-olds in state Pre-K

QUALITY STANDARDS   6 of 10

'02–'03 RESOURCES $3,824 per child

'03–'04 RESOURCES $3,830 per child

↑ Up from '01–'02   ↓ Down from '01–'02   = No change from '01–'02

Started in 1993 and opened for unrestricted voluntary enrollment in 1995, the Georgia Prekindergarten Program was the United States' first preschool program open to all 4-year-olds statewide. Because programs are found in a variety of community-based settings—in both public schools and private child care centers, including those run by Head Start and faith-based organizations—Georgia is able to provide universal access to children in each of the state's school districts. Consistent quality standards are maintained across all types of program settings. The program, which is funded through the state lottery, served 65,900 4-year-olds in 2002–2003, with an additional 10,755 (9 percent) of Georgia's 4-year-olds served in the federal Head Start program. In 2002–2003, the Office of School Readiness awarded an additional $18,453,447 in Resource Coordination grants, which allowed 309 providers to expand services offered for at-risk families.

Teacher qualifications, type of program, and program location all factor into the reimbursement rate structure for Georgia's prekindergarten programs. For example, in 2003–2004, a private prekindergarten program in a metropolitan area was reimbursed at the rate of $3,566 per pupil if the teacher was certified, $3,177 per pupil if the teacher had a 4-year degree, and $2,951 per pupil if the teacher had a vocational degree.

Funding for the Georgia Prekindergarten Program was $261 million in 2003–2004, and 68,155 4-year-olds were served.

ACCESS RANKING—4s	ACCESS RANKING—3s	RESOURCES RANKING
2	None Served	12

ACCESS

Total state program enrollment - - - - - - - - - - - - - - 65,900

School districts that offer state program - - - - - - - - - 100% [1]

Income requirement - - - - - - - - - - - - - - - - - - - None

Hours of operation - - - - - - - - - - - - - - Full-day, full-week

Operating schedule - - - - - - - - - - - - - - - Academic year

Special education enrollment - - - - - - - - - - - - - - 9,178

Federally funded Head Start enrollment - - - - - - - - 21,879

State-funded Head Start enrollment - - - - - - - - - - - - - 0

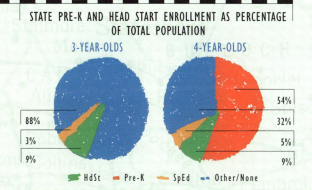

STATE PRE-K AND HEAD START ENROLLMENT AS PERCENTAGE OF TOTAL POPULATION

3-YEAR-OLDS

88%
3%
9%

4-YEAR-OLDS

54%
32%
5%
9%

■ HdSt ■ Pre-K ■ SpEd ⋯ Other/None

QUALITY STANDARDS CHECKLIST

POLICY	STATE PRE-K REQUIREMENT	BENCHMARK	DOES REQUIREMENT MEET BENCHMARK?
Curriculum standards - - - - - - - - - - - -	Not comprehensive	Comprehensive	☐
Teacher degree requirement - - - - - -	AA or Montessori diploma	BA	☐
Teacher specialized training requirement - -	Degree in ECE or meet Montessori requirements [2]	Specializing in Pre-K	☑
Assistant teacher degree req. - - -	HSD or equivalent + experience	CDA or equivalent	☐
Teacher in-service requirement - - - - - - - - -	12 clock hours [3]	At least 15 hours/year	☐
Maximum class size		20 or lower	☑
3-year-olds -	NA		
4-year-olds -	20		
Staff-child ratio		1:10 or better	☑
3-year-olds -	NA		
4-year-olds -	1:10		
Screening/referral requirements - - - -	Vision, hearing, and health	Vision, hearing, and health	☑
Required support services - - - - - - - - -	2 parent conferences and support services [4]	At least 1 service	☑
Meal requirement - - - - - - - - - - - - -	Lunch and snack	At least 1/day	☑

TOTAL:

6

of 10

RESOURCES

Total state Pre-K spending - - - - - - - - - - - - $252,000,000

Local match required? - - - - - - - - - - - - - - - - - - - No

State spending per child enrolled - - - - - - - - - - - - $3,824

State spending per 3-year-old - - - - - - - - - - - - - - - $0

State spending per 4-year-old - - - - - - - - - - - - - $2,075

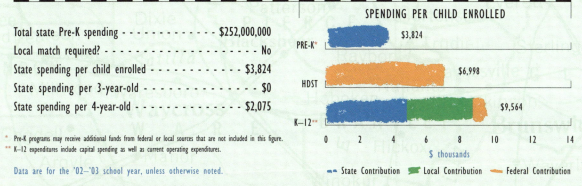

SPENDING PER CHILD ENROLLED

PRE-K* $3,824

HDST $6,998

K–12** $9,564

0   2   4   6   8   10   12   14
$ thousands

⋯ State Contribution   ■ Local Contribution   ■ Federal Contribution

* Pre-K programs may receive additional funds from federal or local sources that are not included in this figure.

** K–12 expenditures include capital spending as well as current operating expenditures.

Data are for the '02–'03 school year, unless otherwise noted.

1 Pre-K is offered in all districts through a combination of public and private providers.

2 The state-level public school certification covers preschool through grade 5. Local school system policies typically require that Pre-K teachers be certified.

3 Pre-K teachers are required to undergo 12 hours of training per year, for which they receive 10 hours' worth of Staff Development Unit (SDU) credits.

4 Support services include parenting support or training, parent involvement activities, health services for children, information about nutrition, and transition to kindergarten activities.

Hawaii

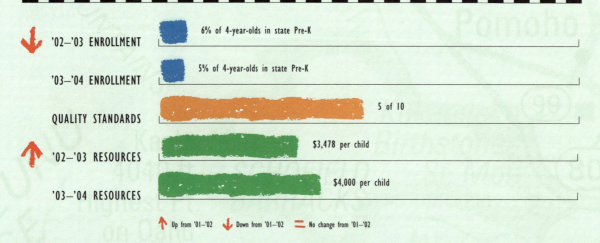

↓ '02–'03 ENROLLMENT   ▪ 6% of 4-year-olds in state Pre-K

'03–'04 ENROLLMENT   ▪ 5% of 4-year-olds in state Pre-K

QUALITY STANDARDS   5 of 10

↑ '02–'03 RESOURCES $3,478 per child

'03–'04 RESOURCES $4,000 per child

↑ Up from '01–'02   ↓ Down from '01–'02   ═ No change from '01–'02

Hawaii's Preschool Open Doors Project provides low-income parents with subsidies to purchase preschool for their 4-year-olds or, in a few cases, 3-year-olds with special needs. Families with incomes under 85 percent of the state median income ($44,136 a year for a family of three) are eligible. Among children whose families meet the income requirement, those with special needs are given first priority to enroll. The Preschool Open Doors Project uses the same income eligibility criteria as the child care subsidy program, but unlike that program does not require parents to be working or engaged in other work-related activities in order for their children to participate.

The Preschool Open Doors Project served fewer children in 2002–2003 than the previous year as monthly reimbursement rates paid to programs for each child enrolled rose, while overall state funding declined slightly. With less total funding available, and more spent on each child, the number of children able to participate decreased. In 2003–2004, about 800 4-year-olds were enrolled in the program, and state funding was $3.2 million.

In 2002, the new Hawaii Pre-Plus program received an appropriation of $5 million over two years for the construction of prekindergarten facilities at public elementary school sites. Thirteen sites were originally designated and, as of the 2003–2004 school year, eight sites were operating through Head Start agencies and private providers. The initiative does not fund direct services, so tuition for children enrolled at these facilities is covered by parent fees or other existing resources such as Preschool Open Doors funds.

Hawaii is working to ensure that children receive comprehensive services, beginning in prekindergarten, by initiating collaboration among different state agencies and focusing on health, safety, and school readiness.

ACCESS RANKING—4s	ACCESS RANKING—3s	RESOURCES RANKING
25	None Served	15

ACCESS

Total state program enrollment - - - - - - - - - - - - - - - - 934
School districts that offer state program - - - - - 100% (counties)
Income requirement - - - - - - - - - - - - - - - - - - 85% SMI [1]
Hours of operation - - - - - - - - - - - - Determined locally [2]
Operating schedule - - - - - - - - - - - - - - - Calendar year
Special education enrollment - - - - - - - - - - - - - 1,236
Federally funded Head Start enrollment - - - - - - - - - 2,638
State-funded Head Start enrollment - - - - - - - - - - - - 0

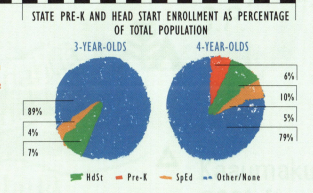

STATE PRE-K AND HEAD START ENROLLMENT AS PERCENTAGE OF TOTAL POPULATION

3-YEAR-OLDS
89%
4%
7%

4-YEAR-OLDS
6%
10%
5%
79%

■ HdSt ■ Pre-K ■ SpEd ■ Other/None

QUALITY STANDARDS CHECKLIST

POLICY	STATE PRE-K REQUIREMENT	BENCHMARK	DOES REQUIREMENT MEET BENCHMARK?
Curriculum standards	Comprehensive	Comprehensive	☑
Teacher degree requirement	CDA	BA	☐
Teacher specialized training requirement	CDA + 1 year exp.	Specializing in Pre-K	☑
Assistant teacher degree requirement	CDA + 6 mos. exp.	CDA or equivalent	☑
Teacher in-service requirement	None	At least 15 hours/year	☐
Maximum class size		20 or lower	☐
3-year-olds	No limit		
4-year-olds	No limit		
Staff-child ratio		1:10 or better	☐
3-year-olds	1:12		
4-year-olds	1:16		
Screening/referral requirements	None	Vision, hearing, and health	☐
Required support services	Support services [3]	At least 1 service	☑
Meal requirement	Lunch and snack	At least 1/day	☑

TOTAL:
5
of 10

RESOURCES

Total state Pre-K spending - - - - - - - - - - - - - $3,248,748
Local match required? - - - - - - - - - - - - - - - - - - - No
State spending per child enrolled - - - - - - - - - - - $3,478
State spending per 3-year-old - - - - - - - - - - - - - NA [4]
State spending per 4-year-old - - - - - - - - - - - - - $215 [4]

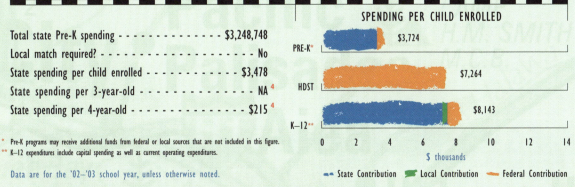

SPENDING PER CHILD ENROLLED

PRE-K* — $3,724
HDST — $7,264
K–12** — $8,143

0 2 4 6 8 10 12 14
$ thousands

■ State Contribution ■ Local Contribution ■ Federal Contribution

* Pre-K programs may receive additional funds from federal or local sources that are not included in this figure.
** K–12 expenditures include capital spending as well as current operating expenditures.

Data are for the '02–'03 school year, unless otherwise noted.

[1] Although the income requirement is 85% of SMI, most families served have incomes much lower than this eligibility cutoff.
[2] Parents may select either a half-day or full-day program. All programs operate 5 days per week.
[3] Support services include referral to social services and transition to kindergarten activities.
[4] For the purpose of these calculations all spending was considered to be directed toward 4-year-olds, because nearly all enrollees are age 4.

Idaho

NO PROGRAM

ACCESS RANKING—4s	ACCESS RANKING—3s	RESOURCES RANKING

No Program

ACCESS

Total state program enrollment - - - - - - - - - - - - - - - 0
School districts that offer state program - - - - - - - - - - NA
Income requirement - NA
Hours of operation - NA
Operating schedule - NA
Special education enrollment - - - - - - - - - - - - - - - 2,189
Federally funded Head Start enrollment - - - - - - - - 3,081
State-funded Head Start enrollment - - - - - - - - - - - - 151 [1]

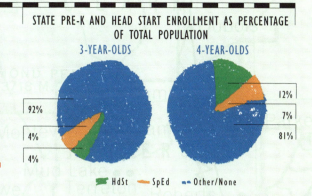

STATE PRE-K AND HEAD START ENROLLMENT AS PERCENTAGE OF TOTAL POPULATION

3-YEAR-OLDS: 92%, 4%, 4%
4-YEAR-OLDS: 12%, 7%, 81%

■ HdSt   ■ SpEd   ■ Other/None

QUALITY STANDARDS CHECKLIST

No Program

RESOURCES

Total state Pre-K spending - - - - - - - - - - - - - - - - - $0
Local match required? - NA
State spending per child enrolled - - - - - - - - - - - - - $0
State Head Start spending - - - - - - - - - - - - - $1,500,000
State spending per 3-year-old - - - - - - - - - - - - - - - $0
State spending per 4-year-old - - - - - - - - - - - - - - - $0

SPENDING PER CHILD ENROLLED

PRE-K* $0
HDST $7,424
K-12** $6,841

0 2 4 6 8 10 12 14
$ thousands

■■ State Contribution   ■ Local Contribution   ■ Federal Contribution

* Pre-K programs may receive additional funds from federal or local sources that are not included in this figure.
** K–12 expenditures include capital spending as well as current operating expenditures.
Data are for the '02–'03 school year, unless otherwise noted.

1 Idaho was not able to break its state-funded Head Start enrollment down by single year of age. As a result, this figure is an estimate based on the percentage of federal Head Start enrollees in Idaho who were 3 or 4 years old.

Illinois

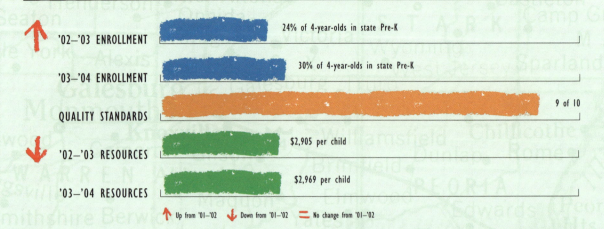

'02–'03 ENROLLMENT — 24% of 4-year-olds in state Pre-K

'03–'04 ENROLLMENT — 30% of 4-year-olds in state Pre-K

QUALITY STANDARDS — 9 of 10

'02–'03 RESOURCES — $2,905 per child

'03–'04 RESOURCES — $2,969 per child

↑ Up from '01–'02   ↓ Down from '01–'02   ═ No change from '01–'02

In 1985, education reform legislation led to the establishment of the Prekindergarten Program for At-Risk Children, and funding for the program has grown relatively steadily since then. Since 1998, funds for this initiative have been provided through the Early Childhood Block Grant (ECBG). Separate components of the block grant support a parent training initiative and prevention efforts for first-time and teen parents. In order to reach children considered to be the most at risk early in life, 11 percent of the total block grant must be used for children from birth to age 3.

Until 2003, funding for the Prekindergarten Program for At-Risk Children was distributed by the Illinois State Board of Education (ISBE) directly to school districts demonstrating the greatest need. Districts could then subcontract with nonpublic programs in order to provide services. As of 2003–2004, school districts as well as child care centers and Head Start programs are eligible to compete directly for funds distributed by the ISBE. All teachers in the Prekindergarten Program for At-Risk Children must hold an ISBE Early Childhood Teaching Certificate and are paid according to the public school salary scale.

Eligibility criteria are determined locally and based on community needs. Children between the ages of 3 and 5 who are considered at risk are eligible for the program, and targeted populations may include children from households with low parental education or children in poverty. Children are identified for enrollment based on individual screening and assessment.

In 2003–2004, the state significantly increased its appropriation for the Prekindergarten Program for At-Risk Children, bringing total state funding to $190,015,000. As a result, enrollment increased to an estimated 64,000 students.

ACCESS RANKING—4s	ACCESS RANKING—3s	RESOURCES RANKING
10	5	23

ACCESS

Total state program enrollment - - - - - - - - - - - - - 55,984

School districts that offer state program - - - - - - - - - 81%

Income requirement - - - - - - - - - - - - - - - - - - None [1]

Hours of operation - - - - - - - - - - - - - Determined locally [2]

Operating schedule - - - - - - - - - - - - - - Academic year

Special education enrollment - - - - - - - - - - - - 17,597

Federally funded Head Start enrollment - - - - - - - 32,592

State-funded Head Start enrollment - - - - - - - - - - - - 0

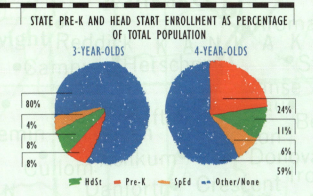

STATE PRE-K AND HEAD START ENROLLMENT AS PERCENTAGE OF TOTAL POPULATION

3-YEAR-OLDS
80%
4%
8%
8%

4-YEAR-OLDS
24%
11%
6%
59%

■ HdSt   ■ Pre-K   ■ SpEd   - Other/None

QUALITY STANDARDS CHECKLIST

POLICY	STATE PRE-K REQUIREMENT	BENCHMARK	DOES REQUIREMENT MEET BENCHMARK?
Curriculum standards - - - - - - - - - - - - - -	Comprehensive	Comprehensive	✓
Teacher degree requirement - - - - - - - - - - - - - -	BA	BA	✓
Teacher specialized training requirement - -	EC teaching certificate [3]	Specializing in Pre-K	✓
Assistant teacher degree requirement - - - - - - - - - -	AA	CDA or equivalent	✓
Teacher in-service requirement - - - - -	120 clock hours/5 years or 8 credit hours/5 years [4]	At least 15 hours/year	✓
Maximum class size		20 or lower	✓
3-year-olds - - - - - - - - - - - - - - - - - -	20		
4-year-olds - - - - - - - - - - - - - - - - - -	20		
Staff-child ratio		1:10 or better	✓
3-year-olds - - - - - - - - - - - - - - - - - -	1:10		
4-year-olds - - - - - - - - - - - - - - - - - -	1:10		
Screening/referral requirements - - - - - - -	Vision, hearing, health, developmental screening, and parent interview	Vision, hearing, and health	✓
Required support services - - - - - - - - - -	Support services [5]	At least 1 service	✓
Meal requirement - - - - - - - - - - - - - - - -	Snack [6]	At least 1/day	☐

TOTAL:

9

of 10

RESOURCES

Total state Pre-K spending - - - - - - - - - - - - - $162,618,616 [7]

Local match required? - - - - - - - - - - - - - - - - - No

State spending per child enrolled - - - - - - - - - - $2,905

State spending per 3-year-old - - - - - - - - - - $231 [8]

State spending per 4-year-old - - - - - - - - - - $708 [8]

SPENDING PER CHILD ENROLLED

PRE-K* — $2,905

HDST — $6,636

K–12** — $11,315

0   2   4   6   8   10   12   14
$ thousands

- State Contribution   ■ Local Contribution   ■ Federal Contribution

* Pre-K programs may receive additional funds from federal or local sources that are not included in this figure.

** K–12 expenditures include capital spending as well as current operating expenditures.

Data are for the '02–'03 school year, unless otherwise noted.

1 Eligibility criteria are determined locally, but low-income status may be considered as one of the risk factors that qualify a child to participate.

2 Most programs operate for a half day, 5 days per week. Districts request funds for the program type that they choose to operate.

3 The early childhood certificate covers birth through grade 3.

4 The in-service requirement can be met with 24 continuing education units over 5 years or by attaining a National Board for Professional Teaching Standards certification.

5 Support services include education services or job training for parents, parenting support or training, parent involvement activities, referral to social services, and transition to kindergarten activities.

6 Children in full-day programs generally receive lunch and a snack. Some programs use federal funds to provide breakfast as well.

7 This amount only includes funding for the prekindergarten component, and not the entire Early Childhood Block Grant.

8 Illinois did not break its total enrollment figure into specific numbers of 3- or 4-year-olds. As a result, these calculations are estimates, based on proportions of enrollees who were ages 3 and 4 in states that served 3-year-olds and provided age breakdowns for 2002–2003.

Indiana

NO PROGRAM

ACCESS RANKING—4s	ACCESS RANKING—3s	RESOURCES RANKING

No Program

ACCESS

Total state program enrollment - - - - - - - - - - - - - - - - 0

School districts that offer state program - - - - - - - - - - NA

Income requirement - NA

Hours of operation - NA

Operating schedule - NA

Special education enrollment - - - - - - - - - - - - - - 9,993

Federally funded Head Start enrollment - - - - - - - - - 11,415

State-funded Head Start enrollment - - - - - - - - - - - - - 0

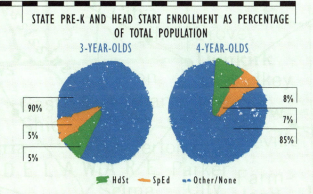

STATE PRE-K AND HEAD START ENROLLMENT AS PERCENTAGE OF TOTAL POPULATION

3-YEAR-OLDS   4-YEAR-OLDS

90%   8%
5%   7%
5%   85%

■ HdSt   ■ SpEd   ■ Other/None

QUALITY STANDARDS CHECKLIST

No Program

RESOURCES

Total state Pre-K spending - - - - - - - - - - - - - - - - $0

Local match required? - - - - - - - - - - - - - - - - - - NA

State spending per child enrolled - - - - - - - - - - - - - $0

State spending per 3-year-old - - - - - - - - - - - - - - $0

State spending per 4-year-old - - - - - - - - - - - - - - $0

SPENDING PER CHILD ENROLLED

PRE-K* $0

HDST $6,610

K–12** $10,073

0   2   4   6   8   10   12   14
$ thousands

■- State Contribution   ■ Local Contribution   ■ Federal Contribution

* Pre-K programs may receive additional funds from federal or local sources that are not included in this figure.

** K–12 expenditures include capital spending as well as current operating expenditures.

Data are for the '02–'03 school year, unless otherwise noted.

Iowa

↑	'02–'03 ENROLLMENT	5% of 4-year-olds in state Pre-K
	'03–'04 ENROLLMENT	Not available at press time
	QUALITY STANDARDS	5 of 10
↓	'02–'03 RESOURCES	$2,925 per child
	'03–'04 RESOURCES	Not available at press time

↑ Up from '01–'02   ↓ Down from '01–'02   ═ No change from '01–'02

I n 1989, Iowa established *Shared Visions*, a comprehensive child development program that serves children between the ages of 3 and 5. Children from families with incomes below 130 percent of the federal poverty level must fill at least 80 percent of the available program slots. The remaining 20 percent of these slots may be filled based on secondary risk factors, with parents paying a fee based on a sliding scale. Low birth weight, developmental delay, homelessness, or having a parent who is a substance abuser or incarcerated are some of the risk factors considered for eligibility. Programs may operate from 3 to 10 hours per day, because agencies that receive competitive grants structure programs to meet community needs. Since 2000, a 10 percent reduction in state funds has resulted in shorter hours of operation for some programs. Grantees—public schools, Head Start centers, child care centers, and other nonprofit agencies—increasingly rely on in-kind services and local funds for support.

State funding for *Shared Visions* was $6,868,353 in 2003–2004.

Grantee accreditation by the National Association for the Education of Young Children, development of Early Learning Standards, and training on the ECERS-R have all contributed to Iowa's efforts to enhance the quality of services for children and their families.

ACCESS RANKING–4s	ACCESS RANKING–3s	RESOURCES RANKING
30	20	22

ACCESS

Total state program enrollment - - - - - - - - - - - - - - 2,355

School districts that offer state program - - - - - 52% (counties)

Income requirement - - 80% of children must be below 130% FPL

Hours of operation - - - - - - - - - - - - - - Determined locally [1]

Operating schedule - - - - - - - - - - - - - Determined locally [2]

Special education enrollment - - - - - - - - - - - - - - - - 3,241

Federally funded Head Start enrollment - - - - - - - - - 6,437

State-funded Head Start enrollment - - - - - - - - - - - - - - 0

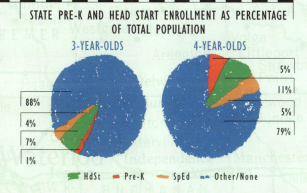

STATE PRE-K AND HEAD START ENROLLMENT AS PERCENTAGE OF TOTAL POPULATION

3-YEAR-OLDS: 88%, 4%, 7%, 1%

4-YEAR-OLDS: 5%, 11%, 5%, 79%

■ HdSt   ■ Pre-K   ■ SpEd   ■ Other/None

QUALITY STANDARDS CHECKLIST

POLICY	STATE PRE-K REQUIREMENT	BENCHMARK	DOES REQUIREMENT MEET BENCHMARK?
Curriculum standards	Not comprehensive	Comprehensive	☐
Teacher degree requirement	BA (public); AA for HdSt, None for child care (nonpublic)	BA	☐
Teacher specialized training req.	Licensing in EE with EC endorsement (public),[3] None (nonpublic) [4]	Specializing in Pre-K	☐
Assistant teacher degree requirement	None	CDA or equivalent	☐
Teacher in-service requirement	None [5]	At least 15 hours/year	☐
Maximum class size		20 or lower	☑
3-year-olds	16		
4-year-olds	16		
Staff-child ratio		1:10 or better	☑
3-year-olds	1:8		
4-year-olds	1:8		
Screening/referral requirements	Vision, hearing, and health [6]	Vision, hearing, and health	☑
Required support services	Support services [7]	At least 1 service	☑
Meal requirement	1 meal and snack [8]	At least 1/day	☑

TOTAL:

5

of 10

RESOURCES

Total state Pre-K spending - - - - - - - - - - - - - - $6,887,531

Local match required? - - - - - - Yes, 20% of total grant amount

State spending per child enrolled - - - - - - - - - - - $2,925

State spending per 3-year-old - - - - - - - - - - - - - - - $39

State spending per 4-year-old - - - - - - - - - - - - - - - $133

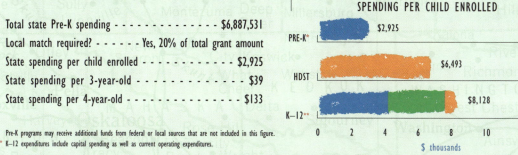

SPENDING PER CHILD ENROLLED

PRE-K*: $2,925

HDST: $6,493

K–12**: $8,128

$ thousands

■ State Contribution   ■ Local Contribution   ■ Federal Contribution

* Pre-K programs may receive additional funds from federal or local sources that are not included in this figure.

** K–12 expenditures include capital spending as well as current operating expenditures.

Data are for the '02–'03 school year, unless otherwise noted.

1 Grantees operate at least 3 but not more than 10 hours per day based on local need and the original grant submitted. Grantees operate an average of 4.74 days per week, and all operate at least 4 days per week.

2 Grantees operate an average of 181 days per year.

3 The early childhood teaching endorsement became a requirement in the 2002–2003 school year.

4 Teachers in nonpublic schools are required to have a state license for child care.

5 Although there is no specific amount of annual in-service professional development required, most grantees provide at least 15 hours per year, consistent with NAEYC recommendations.

6 Although *Shared Visions* does not have specific requirements for screening and referral, applicants are required to address the types of screening and referral that will be provided. All *Shared Visions* programs provide screening and referral for vision, hearing, and health. LEAs also decide which developmental, dental, and nutrition services to provide.

7 Support services include parenting support or training, at least two family nights, health services for children, information about nutrition, and referral to social services.

8 The specific meal (breakfast or lunch) depends on the time of day during which children are present. All applicants for *Shared Visions* funding must address meal requirements in their grant applications.

Kansas

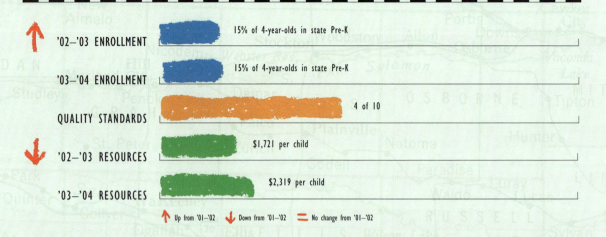

↑ '02–'03 ENROLLMENT	15% of 4-year-olds in state Pre-K
'03–'04 ENROLLMENT	15% of 4-year-olds in state Pre-K
QUALITY STANDARDS	4 of 10
↓ '02–'03 RESOURCES	$1,721 per child
'03–'04 RESOURCES	$2,319 per child

↑ Up from '01–'02   ↓ Down from '01–'02   = No change from '01–'02

I n order to serve at-risk children who were not eligible for Head Start, as well as those who were eligible but not enrolled, Kansas began the At-Risk Four-Year-Old Children Preschool Program in 1998. Eligibility criteria for the program include risk factors such as developmental delay, having a single or teen parent, English Language Learner or migrant status, free lunch eligibility, or referral from another agency. This program has grown quickly, and served more than twice as many children during 2002–2003 as during the previous year. Programs receive a base of $1,800 per student in state funding, and are operated exclusively by public schools.

For families with children from birth to age 3, the state provides a separate Parents as Teachers (PAT) program. With an emphasis on collaboration, all Kansas agencies serving young children share resources and space and have worked together to develop sets of standards, as well as core competencies for staff.

In 2003–2004, the At-Risk Four-Year-Old Children Preschool Program served 4,959 4-year-olds and received approximately $11.5 million in state general revenue funds. This amount includes tobacco settlement money, which provides some of the funding for the program.

ACCESS RANKING—4s	ACCESS RANKING—3s	RESOURCES RANKING
14	None Served	34

ACCESS

Total state program enrollment - - - - - - - - - - - - - 5,433
School districts that offer state program - - - - - - - - - 35%
Income requirement - - - - - - - - - - - - - - - 130% FPL [1]
Hours of operation - - - - - - - - - - - Determined locally [2]
Operating schedule - - - - - - - - - - - - - - - Academic year
Special education enrollment - - - - - - - - - - - - - 5,191
Federally funded Head Start enrollment - - - - - - - - 6,310
State-funded Head Start enrollment - - - - - - - - - - - - 0

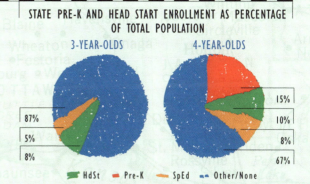

STATE PRE-K AND HEAD START ENROLLMENT AS PERCENTAGE OF TOTAL POPULATION

3-YEAR-OLDS
87%
5%
8%

4-YEAR-OLDS
15%
10%
8%
67%

HdSt   Pre-K   SpEd   Other/None

QUALITY STANDARDS CHECKLIST

POLICY	STATE PRE-K REQUIREMENT	BENCHMARK	DOES REQUIREMENT MEET BENCHMARK?
Curriculum standards	None	Comprehensive	☐
Teacher degree requirement	BA	BA	☑
Teacher specialized training requirement	4-year elementary teaching certificate	Specializing in Pre-K	☐
Assistant teacher degree requirement	2-year degree	CDA or equivalent	☑
Teacher in-service requirement	None [3]	At least 15 hours/year	☐
Maximum class size			
3-year-olds	NA	20 or lower	
4-year-olds	No limit [4]		☐
Staff-child ratio			
3-year-olds	NA	1:10 or better	
4-year-olds	No limit [4]		☐
Screening/referral requirements	Vision, hearing, general health, dental, and developmental [5]	Vision, hearing, and health	☑
Required support services	2 parent conferences and support services [6]	At least 1 service	☑
Meal requirement	Snack	At least 1/day	☐

TOTAL:
4
of 10

RESOURCES

Total state Pre-K spending - - - - - - - - - - - - $9,352,323
Local match required? - - - - - - - - - - - - - - - - - - No
State spending per child enrolled - - - - - - - - - - - $1,721
State spending per 3-year-old - - - - - - - - - - - - - - $0
State spending per 4-year-old - - - - - - - - - - - - - $253

SPENDING PER CHILD ENROLLED

PRE-K* $1,721
HDST $6,247
K-12** $8,576

0   2   4   6   8   10   12   14
$ thousands

State Contribution   Local Contribution   Federal Contribution

* Pre-K programs may receive additional funds from federal or local sources that are not included in this figure.
** K–12 expenditures include capital spending as well as current operating expenditures.

Data are for the '02–'03 school year, unless otherwise noted.

[1] Eligibility for free lunch (130% of poverty) is one of several risk factors considered sufficient to qualify a child for enrollment. This represents an income of $19,525 or below for a family of three during fiscal year 2002.
[2] Programs are required to operate at least 2.5 hours per day and a total of 465 hours per school year. All programs operate 5 days per week.
[3] Due to insufficient funding, workshops for professional development are offered but not required. Teachers participate on a voluntary basis.
[4] Although not mandated by the state, programs are encouraged to follow NAEYC recommendations and limit class size to 15 students with two teachers present. Many programs that combine special education and Pre-K children in the same classrooms require lower teacher-to-student ratios.
[5] Vision, hearing, and other general health screenings and referrals are not explicitly required, but must be included as part of the grant proposal. The schools must explain in their proposals how they will provide comprehensive health services in order to receive funding.
[6] Support services include parenting support or training, parent involvement activities, transportation, and transition to kindergarten activities.

Kentucky

↑	'02–'03 ENROLLMENT	28% of 4-year-olds in state Pre-K
	'03–'04 ENROLLMENT	Not available at press time
	QUALITY STANDARDS	7 of 10
↓	'02–'03 RESOURCES	$2,484 per child
	'03–'04 RESOURCES	Not available at press time

↑ Up from '01–'02   ↓ Down from '01–'02   ⚊ No change from '01–'02

The Kentucky Preschool Program was created as a result of the Kentucky Education Reform Act of 1990 and is offered to 4-year-olds who are eligible for free lunch, as well as all 3- and 4-year-olds with disabilities. Most of Kentucky's preschoolers with special needs are served within the program, and 63 percent of all participants had special needs in 2002–2003. All school districts in the state receive funding, although some contract with Head Start, private child care centers, and special education facilities to provide services. Many districts contribute additional funds when state funds are not sufficient. Federal funds from Head Start and IDEA are sometimes blended with state and local funds to support the Kentucky Preschool Program.

State funding for the program has decreased by $2.2 million since 2001, while the number of eligible preschool children has increased annually by 1,000. In some districts, this has led to cuts in the quality and duration of services offered.

Kentucky continues to strive toward improving education for preschoolers at risk and with disabilities. As of the 2004–2005 school year, the Kentucky Early Childhood teaching certificate will be required for all new teachers. The Kentucky Early Childhood Standards, released in 2003, are aligned with Head Start outcomes and the Kentucky Program of Studies K–12 content. The standards promote a learning continuum across all domains, including social and emotional development, for children from birth to age 4. Recently, the state-funded preschool program, the Head Start Collaboration Office, and the state child care initiative joined to form a new Division of Early Childhood Development within the Kentucky Department of Education.

ACCESS RANKING—4s	ACCESS RANKING—3s	RESOURCES RANKING
7	3	27

ACCESS

Total state program enrollment - - - - - - - - - - - - - - - 18,882

School districts that offer state program - - - - - - - - - - 100%

Income requirement - - - - - - - - - - - - - - - - - - - 130% FPL [1]

Hours of operation - - - - - - - - - - - - - - - Determined locally [2]

Operating schedule - - - - - - - - - - - - - - - - - Academic year

Special education enrollment - - - - - - - - - - - - - - - 11,128 [3]

Federally funded Head Start enrollment - - - - - - - - - 14,624

State-funded Head Start enrollment - - - - - - - - - - - - - 0

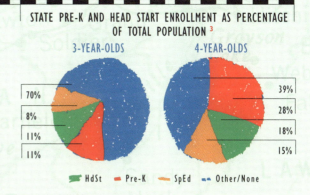

STATE PRE-K AND HEAD START ENROLLMENT AS PERCENTAGE OF TOTAL POPULATION [3]

3-YEAR-OLDS: 70%, 8%, 11%, 11%

4-YEAR-OLDS: 39%, 28%, 18%, 15%

HdSt ■ Pre-K ■ SpEd ■ Other/None

QUALITY STANDARDS CHECKLIST

POLICY	STATE PRE-K REQUIREMENT	BENCHMARK	DOES REQUIREMENT MEET BENCHMARK?
Curriculum standards	None [4]	Comprehensive	☐
Teacher degree requirement	CDA [5]	BA	☐
Teacher specialized training requirement	Meets CDA requirements [5]	Specializing in Pre-K	☑
Assistant teacher degree requirement	HSD	CDA or equivalent	☐
Teacher in-service requirement	4 days for certified teachers, 18 clock hours for CDAs or AAs	At least 15 hours/year	☑
Maximum class size			
3-year-olds	20		
4-year-olds	20	20 or lower	☑
Staff-child ratio			
3-year-olds	1:10		
4-year-olds	1:10	1:10 or better	☑
Screening/referral requirements	Vision, hearing, health, and developmental	Vision, hearing, and health	☑
Required support services	2 parent conferences and support services [6]	At least 1 service	☑
Meal requirement	Breakfast or lunch	At least 1/day	☑

TOTAL: 7 of 10

RESOURCES

Total state Pre-K spending - - - - - - - - - - - - - $46,900,000

Local match required? - - - - - - - - - - - - - - - - - - - No

State spending per child enrolled - - - - - - - - - - - $2,484

State spending per 3-year-old - - - - - - - - - - - - - - $261

State spending per 4-year-old - - - - - - - - - - - - - - $688

SPENDING PER CHILD ENROLLED

PRE-K* — $3,916

HDST — $6,515

K–12** — $7,922

$ thousands (0 2 4 6 8 10 12 14)

■ State Contribution ■ Local Contribution ■ Federal Contribution

* Pre-K programs may receive additional funds from federal or local sources that are not included in this figure.

** K–12 expenditures include capital spending as well as current operating expenditures.

Data are for the '02–'03 school year, unless otherwise noted.

1 Children with disabilities are not required to meet an income requirement.

2 Programs are required to operate for a minimum of 2.5 hours daily plus mealtime.

3 Because the state Pre-K program is inter-related with the state special education program, it is not possible to provide a unique special education enrollment count for Kentucky. The estimates for special education enrollment include some children also counted in the totals for state Pre-K.

4 The Kentucky Early Childhood Standards are not intended to serve as a curriculum guide. The document is designed to assist parents and professionals in planning experiences that promote student progress.

5 As of the 2004–2005 program year, all new teachers must have a BA and early childhood certification.

6 Services offered include education services or job training for parents, parenting support or training, health services for parents and children, information about nutrition, referral to social services, and other services based on local need.

Louisiana

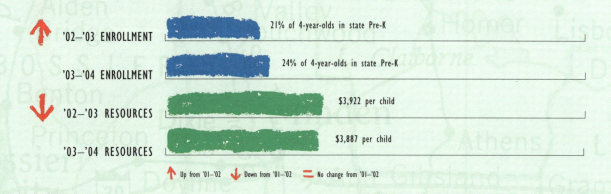

↑	'02–'03 ENROLLMENT	21% of 4-year-olds in state Pre-K
	'03–'04 ENROLLMENT	24% of 4-year-olds in state Pre-K
↓	'02–'03 RESOURCES	$3,922 per child
	'03–'04 RESOURCES	$3,887 per child

↑ Up from '01–'02   ↓ Down from '01–'02   ═ No change from '01–'02

I n 1988, Louisiana began funding and providing technical assistance for prekindergarten programs, using annual state appropriations to support the Model Early Childhood program through the 1992–1993 school year. Once general funds were no longer available, local public school systems began using funds from the 8(g) Student Enhancement Block Grant Program to support prekindergarten classes. All 8(g) programs are operated in public schools. Four-year-olds who are identified as at risk of being "insufficiently ready for school" are eligible for the 8(g) program, with priority given to low-income families. A total of $9,076,960 in state funds supported approximately 5,136 4-year-olds enrolled in 8(g) during 2003–2004.

A second state prekindergarten initiative, the LA4 program, is largely supported by TANF funds and serves 4-year-olds who qualify for free or reduced-price lunch. LA4 was established in 2001 and is administered by the Department of Education. Only schools can receive direct funding to operate programs, and most children are served in public school settings. However, a few districts subcontract with Head Start programs, private child care centers, and faith-based centers to provide services. LA4 programs provide 6 hours of instruction along with up to 4 hours of before- and after-school programming per day. During the 2003–2004 year, LA4 received $35,470,137 in TANF funds and served 6,912 children. A third state initiative, Starting Points, was established in 1992 and is similar to LA4 although it offers a shorter program day (6 hours) and provides a lower level of funding per child than LA4. During the 2003–2004 program year, Starting Points served 1,489 children, using $5,019,000 in TANF and tobacco settlement funds.

Louisiana provides a fourth prekindergarten initiative, known as the Nonpublic Schools Early Childhood Development Program (NSECD) and run by the Governor's office. The NSECD began in the 2001–2002 school year and provides tuition reimbursements to parents who wish to send their children to state-approved nonpublic preschools. The initiative is open to families with incomes below 200 percent of poverty. Programs are required to offer at least 6 hours of instruction along with up to 4 hours of before- and after-school programming per day. In 2003–2004, $8,500,000 in TANF funds was used to serve 1,400 4-year-olds.

In addition to the initiatives profiled in this report, Louisiana directed approximately $28 million in Title I funds to support preschool services for more than 9,000 4-year-olds.

Although most states have a single state-financed prekindergarten initiative, Louisiana makes significant contributions to prekindergarten through four initiatives: the 8(g) program, LA4, Starting Points, and NSECD. As a result, in the first two pages of this profile we present summary information reflecting the state's overall commitment to prekindergarten. Enrollment and state spending for all four initiatives are taken into account. Next, we present additional details about each initiative. Due to similarities between the LA4 and Starting Points programs, data from these programs are combined, with differences between the two programs noted.

STATE OVERVIEW

Total state program enrollment- - - - - - - - - - - - 12,968 [1]

Total state spending - - - - - - - - - - - - - - - - $50,858,905

State spending per child enrolled - - - - - - - - - - - $3,922

State spending per 3-year-old - - - - - - - - - - - - - $0

State spending per 4-year-old - - - - - - - - - - - - - $820

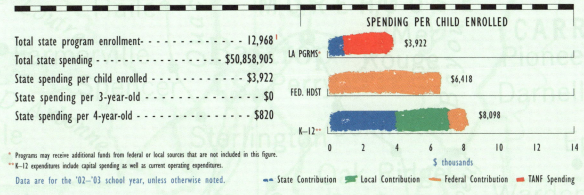

SPENDING PER CHILD ENROLLED

LA PGRMS* $3,922

FED. HDST $6,418

K–12** $8,098

0   2   4   6   8   10   12   14

$ thousands

■ State Contribution   ■ Local Contribution   ■ Federal Contribution   ■ TANF Spending

* Programs may receive additional funds from federal or local sources that are not included in this figure.

** K–12 expenditures include capital spending as well as current operating expenditures.

Data are for the '02–'03 school year, unless otherwise noted.

[1] This figure is a sum of the enrollment in each of the state's prekindergarten initiatives. There is duplication in this count, as some children are served by more than one program.

ACCESS RANKING—4s	ACCESS RANKING—3s	RESOURCES RANKING
12	None Served	10

99

LOUISIANA 8(g) STUDENT ENHANCEMENT BLOCK GRANT PROGRAM

ACCESS

Total state program enrollment - - - - - - - - - - - 4,721

School districts that offer state program - - - - - 98% (parishes)

Income requirement - - - - - - - - - - - - - - - - - None [1]

Hours of operation - - - - - - - - - - - - - Full-day, full-week

Operating schedule - - - - - - - - - - - - - - Academic year

Special education enrollment - - - - - - - - - - - - 5,558

Federally funded Head Start enrollment - - - - - - - - 18,831

State-funded Head Start enrollment - - - - - - - - - - - 0

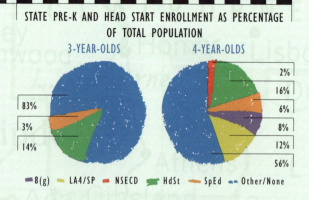

STATE PRE-K AND HEAD START ENROLLMENT AS PERCENTAGE OF TOTAL POPULATION

3-YEAR-OLDS
- 83%
- 3%
- 14%

4-YEAR-OLDS
- 2%
- 16%
- 6%
- 8%
- 12%
- 56%

■ 8(g)   ■ LA4/SP   ■ NSECD   ■ HdSt   ■ SpEd   ■ Other/None

QUALITY STANDARDS CHECKLIST

POLICY	STATE PRE-K REQUIREMENT	BENCHMARK	DOES REQUIREMENT MEET BENCHMARK?
Curriculum standards	Comprehensive	Comprehensive	✓
Teacher degree requirement	BA	BA	✓
Teacher specialized training req.	Certification in N or K	Specializing in Pre-K	☐
Assistant teacher degree requirement	Determined locally	CDA or equivalent	☐
Teacher in-service requirement	150 clock hours/5 years	At least 15 hours/year	✓
Maximum class size		20 or lower	✓
3-year-olds	NA		
4-year-olds	20		
Staff-child ratio		1:10 or better	✓
3-year-olds	NA		
4-year-olds	1:10 [2]		
Screening/referral requirements	Developmental screening [3]	Vision, hearing, and health	☐
Required support services	Support services [4]	At least 1 service	✓
Meal requirement	Breakfast, lunch, and snack	At least 1/day	✓

TOTAL:

7

of 10

RESOURCES

Total state Pre-K spending - - - - - - - - - - - - $9,358,905

Local match required? - - - - - - - - - - - - - - - - - - No

State spending per child enrolled - - - - - - - - - - $1,982

State spending per 3-year-old - - - - - - - - - - - - - - $0

State spending per 4-year-old - - - - - - - - - - - - - $151

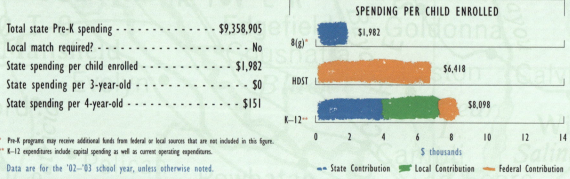

SPENDING PER CHILD ENROLLED

- 8(g)* — $1,982
- HDST — $6,418
- K–12** — $8,098

$ thousands (0 2 4 6 8 10 12 14)

■ State Contribution   ■ Local Contribution   ■ Federal Contribution

* Pre-K programs may receive additional funds from federal or local sources that are not included in this figure.

** K–12 expenditures include capital spending as well as current operating expenditures.

Data are for the '02–'03 school year, unless otherwise noted.

[1] The state does not set specific income eligibility criteria, but priority is given to children from low-income families.

[2] The staff-child ratio requirement changed from 1:15 to 1:10 effective with the 2002–2003 program year.

[3] Screening is conducted to determine which children are potentially eligible and to plan an appropriate program. The 8(g) program does not specifically require referrals, but programs refer children for services if any needs are identified.

[4] Support services include parenting support or training, parent involvement activities, referral to social services, transition to kindergarten activities, and other locally determined services. The number of required annual parent conferences and/or home visits is also determined locally.

ACCESS

Total state program enrollment	7,222 [1]
School districts that offer state program	82% [2]
Income requirement	185% FPL [3]
Hours of operation	Full-day, full-week
Operating schedule	Academic year
Special education enrollment	5,558
Federally funded Head Start enrollment	18,831
State-funded Head Start enrollment	0

STATE PRE-K AND HEAD START ENROLLMENT AS PERCENTAGE OF TOTAL POPULATION

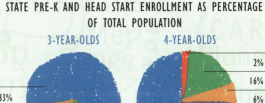
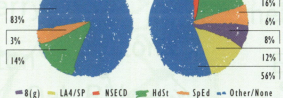

3-YEAR-OLDS: 83%, 3%, 14%

4-YEAR-OLDS: 2%, 16%, 6%, 8%, 12%, 56%

Legend: ■ 8(g) ■ LA4/SP ■ NSECD ■ HdSt ■ SpEd ■ Other/None

QUALITY STANDARDS CHECKLIST

POLICY	STATE PRE-K REQUIREMENT	BENCHMARK	DOES REQUIREMENT MEET BENCHMARK?
Curriculum standards	Comprehensive	Comprehensive	✓
Teacher degree requirement	BA	BA	✓
Teacher specialized training requirement	Certificate in N, K, or Early Intervention [4]	Specializing in Pre-K	☐
Assistant teacher degree requirement	HSD or equivalent (public), None (nonpublic)	CDA or equivalent	☐
Teacher in-service requirement	18 clock hours	At least 15 hours/year	✓
Maximum class size		20 or lower	✓
3-year-olds	NA		
4-year-olds	20		
Staff-child ratio		1:10 or better	✓
3-year-olds	NA		
4-year-olds	1:10		
Screening/referral requirements	Vision, hearing, and health	Vision, hearing, and health	✓
Required support services	2 parent conferences and support services [5]	At least 1 service	✓
Meal requirement	Lunch and snack	At least 1/day	✓

TOTAL: **8** of 10

RESOURCES

Total state Pre-K spending	$35,500,000 [6]
Local match required?	No
State spending per child enrolled	$4,916 [7, 8]
State spending per 3-year-old	$0
State spending per 4-year-old	$572 [7]

SPENDING PER CHILD ENROLLED

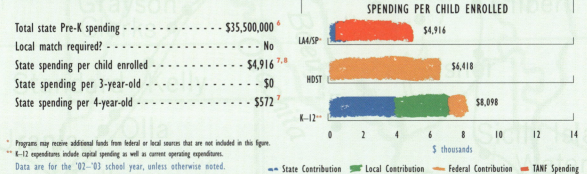

LA4/SP*: $4,916
HDST: $6,418
K–12**: $8,098

$ thousands

Legend: State Contribution · Local Contribution · Federal Contribution · TANF Spending

* Programs may receive additional funds from federal or local sources that are not included in this figure.

** K–12 expenditures include capital spending as well as current operating expenditures.

Data are for the '02–'03 school year, unless otherwise noted.

1 This total represents an enrollment of 5,717 children in LA4 and 1,505 children in Starting Points. Before- and/or after-school programming was provided to 2,075 children in LA4, approximately 717 of whom were not enrolled during regular operating hours.

2 LA4 programs were offered in 19 school districts, while Starting Points was offered in 55 districts. Some districts offer both LA4 and Starting Points programs.

3 Some families with incomes above this limit are able to pay tuition and enroll their children.

4 Teachers may also qualify with any of the following: an elementary certificate and an Out-of-Field Authorization to Teach, a BA and a Temporary Authority to Teach, Temporary Employment Permit, or an Out-of-State Provisional Certificate. Teachers qualifying under these conditions must be working toward obtaining a Louisiana teaching certificate specified in program requirements.

5 Support services include education services or job training for parents, parenting support or training, relevant parent workshops, referral to social services, transportation, and referral for mental health issues.

6 LA4 and Starting Points were supported with a total of $1.5 million in state funds, representing tobacco settlement money, as well as $34 million in federal TANF funds that the state chose to direct toward prekindergarten.

7 These estimates include both state and TANF funds.

8 This figure represents the average spending per child enrolled across Starting Points and LA4. While specific data are not available, LA4 spending per child is higher than spending per child in Starting Points.

LOUISIANA NONPUBLIC SCHOOLS EARLY CHILDHOOD DEVELOPMENT PROGRAM (NSECD)

ACCESS

Total state program enrollment - - - - - - - - - - - - 1,025

School districts that offer state program - - - - - 9% (parishes)

Income requirement - - - - - - - - - - - - - - - - 200% FPL

Hours of operation - - - - - - - - - - - - - Full-day, full-week

Operating schedule - - - - - - - - - - - - - - - Academic year

Special education enrollment - - - - - - - - - - - - 5,558

Federally funded Head Start enrollment - - - - - - - - - 18,831

State-funded Head Start enrollment - - - - - - - - - - - - 0

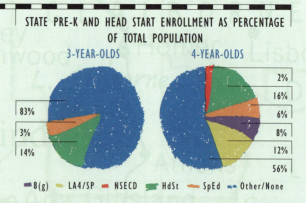

STATE PRE-K AND HEAD START ENROLLMENT AS PERCENTAGE OF TOTAL POPULATION

3-YEAR-OLDS: 83%, 3%, 14%

4-YEAR-OLDS: 2%, 16%, 6%, 8%, 12%, 56%

■ 8(g) ■ LA4/SP ■ NSECD ■ HdSt ■ SpEd ■ Other/None

QUALITY STANDARDS CHECKLIST

POLICY	STATE PRE-K REQUIREMENT	BENCHMARK	DOES REQUIREMENT MEET BENCHMARK?
Curriculum standards	Comprehensive	Comprehensive	✓
Teacher degree requirement	BA	BA	✓
Teacher specialized training requirement	Degree in EE, K, or N; or 12 credits in CD	Specializing in Pre-K	☐
Assistant teacher degree requirement	None	CDA or equivalent	☐
Teacher in-service requirement	None	At least 15 hours/year	☐
Maximum class size		20 or lower	✓
3-year-olds	NA		
4-year-olds	20		
Staff-child ratio		1:10 or better	✓
3-year-olds	NA		
4-year-olds	1:10		
Screening/referral requirements	Vision and hearing	Vision, hearing, and health	☐
Required support services	2 parent conferences and transition to K activities [1]	At least 1 service	✓
Meal requirement	Breakfast, lunch, and snack	At least 1/day	✓

TOTAL:

6

of 10

RESOURCES

Total state Pre-K spending - - - - - - - - - - - - $6,000,000 [2]

Local match required? - - - - - - - - - - - - - - - - - No

State spending per child enrolled - - - - - - - - - - - $5,854 [3]

State spending per 3-year-old - - - - - - - - - - - - - $0

State spending per 4-year-old - - - - - - - - - - - - - $97 [3]

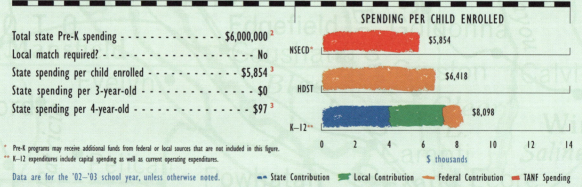

SPENDING PER CHILD ENROLLED

NSECD*: $5,854
HDST: $6,418
K–12**: $8,098

$ thousands

■ ■ State Contribution ■ Local Contribution ■ Federal Contribution ■ TANF Spending

* Pre-K programs may receive additional funds from federal or local sources that are not included in this figure.

** K–12 expenditures include capital spending as well as current operating expenditures.

Data are for the '02–'03 school year, unless otherwise noted.

1 Other specific services are locally determined.

2 This funding total consists of federal TANF funds that the state has chosen to direct toward prekindergarten. There are no additional state funds.

3 These estimates are based on the state's use of federal TANF funds for the NSECD program.

Marion

Bayou de Louisa

Haile

Farmerville

Spencer

D'Arbonne

wnsville

N

udrant

Calhoun Monroe

Cheniere Brake

Eros

OUACHITA

SON

tham

Casso Cr.

Sikes

udson

ul

N

oyce

Urania

Tullos

Zenoria

orgetown

Trout

Jena

Sicard

W

Monroe

Richwood

Riverton

Columbia

CALDWELL

Grayson

Clarks

Standard Kelly

Olla

LA SALLE

Ouachita

MOREHOUSE

Bastrop

Perryville

Sterlington

Swartz

Girard

Rayville

Alto

RICH

Hebert Winnsboro

FRANKLIN

Fort Necessity

Jigger

Boeuf

Enterprise

Harrisonburg

Manifest

Bonita

Mer Rouge

Collinston

Oak Ridge

Boeuf

Big Cr.

Mangham

Baskin

Crowville

Wisner

Joner

Oak Grove

WEST CARROLL

Pioneer

Darnell

Epps

Warden

N

Delhi

Holly Ridge

Tend

Bayou Macon

Ne T

Gilbert

St.

Sicily Island

Waterproof

Clayton

Spokad

Perry

103

Maine

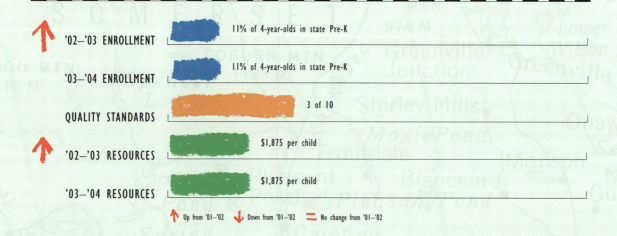

↑ '02–'03 ENROLLMENT	11% of 4-year-olds in state Pre-K
'03–'04 ENROLLMENT	11% of 4-year-olds in state Pre-K
QUALITY STANDARDS	3 of 10
↑ '02–'03 RESOURCES	$1,875 per child
'03–'04 RESOURCES	$1,875 per child

↑ Up from '01–'02   ↓ Down from '01–'02   = No change from '01–'02

Initiated by the state Legislature in 1983, Maine's Two-Year Kindergarten Program allows all 4-year-olds in the state to enter the public schools. However, school districts are not mandated to provide kindergarten to 4-year-olds and are only partially reimbursed for it, so the program has remained small. Over the past several years, though, the program has doubled in size with the encouragement of the State Department of Education. As there are no income requirements or other risk factors tied to eligibility, access depends upon the willingness of individual school districts to provide the program. Districts providing prekindergarten are reimbursed through the state aid formula based on the average daily attendance. Prekindergarten programs are all offered within public schools, and schools cannot contract with outside agencies to provide services.

The state continues to encourage districts to develop programs for 4-year-old children, and provided $5.9 million in combined state and local funds during 2003–2004 to serve an estimated minimum of 1,440 children.

In addition to funding for the Two-Year Kindergarten Program, Maine also provided $3,581,018 through a combination of state money and tobacco funds to supplement federal Head Start funding during fiscal year 2003.

ACCESS RANKING–4s	ACCESS RANKING–3s	RESOURCES RANKING
16	None Served	32

ACCESS

Total state program enrollment - - - - - - - - - - - - - - 1,440

School districts that offer state program - - - - - - - - 21%

Income requirement - - - - - - - - - - - - - - - - - - - None

Hours of operation - - - - - - - - - - - - Determined locally [1]

Operating schedule - - - - - - - - - - - Determined locally [2]

Special education enrollment - - - - - - - - - - - - - 3,005

Federally funded Head Start enrollment - - - - - - - - 2,889

State-funded Head Start enrollment - - - - - - - - - - - 199 [3]

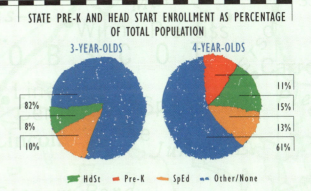

STATE PRE-K AND HEAD START ENROLLMENT AS PERCENTAGE OF TOTAL POPULATION

3-YEAR-OLDS
- 82%
- 8%
- 10%

4-YEAR-OLDS
- 11%
- 15%
- 13%
- 61%

■ HdSt ■ Pre-K ■ SpEd ⌁ Other/None

QUALITY STANDARDS CHECKLIST

POLICY	STATE PRE-K REQUIREMENT	BENCHMARK	DOES REQUIREMENT MEET BENCHMARK?
Curriculum standards	None	Comprehensive	☐
Teacher degree requirement	BA	BA	☑
Teacher specialized training requirement	EC or elem. certification	Specializing in Pre-K	☐
Assistant teacher degree requirement	30 credit hours	CDA or equivalent	☑
Teacher in-service requirement	90 clock hours/5 years	At least 15 hours/year	☑
Maximum class size		20 or lower	☐
3-year-olds	NA		
4-year-olds	No limit		
Staff-child ratio		1:10 or better	☐
3-year-olds	NA		
4-year-olds	1:18		
Screening/referral requirements	Vision and hearing	Vision, hearing, and health	☐
Required support services	None	At least 1 service	☐
Meal requirement	None	At least 1/day	☐

TOTAL:

3

of 10

RESOURCES

Total state Pre-K spending - - - - - - - - - - - - $2,700,000

Local match required? - - - - - - - - - - - - - - - - - - No

State spending per child enrolled - - - - - - - - - - $1,875

State Head Start spending - - - - - - - - - - - - $3,581,018

State spending per 3-year-old - - - - - - - - - - - - - - $0

State spending per 4-year-old - - - - - - - - - - - - - $203

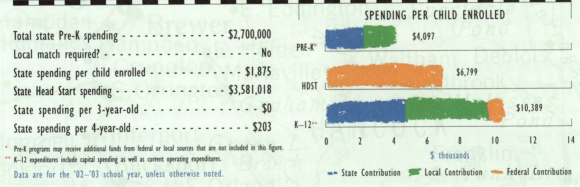

SPENDING PER CHILD ENROLLED

PRE-K* — $4,097

HDST — $6,799

K–12** — $10,389

0 2 4 6 8 10 12 14
$ thousands

⌁ State Contribution ■ Local Contribution ■ Federal Contribution

* Pre-K programs may receive additional funds from federal or local sources that are not included in this figure.

** K–12 expenditures include capital spending as well as current operating expenditures.

Data are for the '02–'03 school year, unless otherwise noted.

1 Most programs operate for 2.5 hours per day, and many are moving toward a 4-day-per-week schedule with Fridays used for parent outreach.

2 Most programs operate for the academic year.

3 The state did not track the number of additional children served through its Head Start supplement. This figure is an estimate based on the number of non-federally funded children in Maine reported in Head Start's 2002–2003 Program Information Report and proportions of Maine's federal Head Start enrollees who were 3 or 4 years old.

Maryland

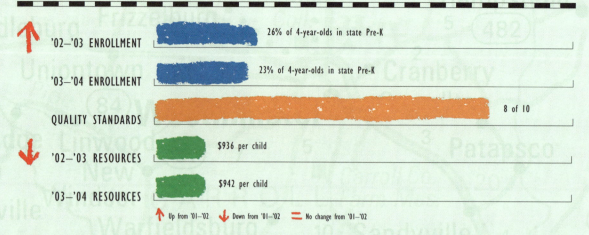

↑ '02–'03 ENROLLMENT	26% of 4-year-olds in state Pre-K
'03–'04 ENROLLMENT	23% of 4-year-olds in state Pre-K
QUALITY STANDARDS	8 of 10
↓ '02–'03 RESOURCES	$936 per child
'03–'04 RESOURCES	$942 per child

↑ Up from '01–'02   ↓ Down from '01–'02   ═ No change from '01–'02

Started in 1979 as a pilot program in Baltimore City and Prince George's County, the Extended Elementary Education Program (EEEP) grew into a state prekindergarten initiative serving Maryland's at-risk 4-year-olds. Since 2002, the initiative has been referred to as the Prekindergarten Program. A state report on school readiness found that those who had participated in the state prekindergarten program—children considered at risk who generally start school with lesser skills than more advantaged children—perform as well as their peers upon entering kindergarten.

As of 2002–2003, children automatically qualified for the program if they had limited English proficiency, were homeless, had special health care needs, or were previously enrolled in Head Start or Even Start. The Bridge to Excellence in Public Schools Act revised the eligibility criteria for 2003–2004 and laid out a timetable for expanding prekindergarten. All local school systems are now required to provide prekindergarten to all 4-year-old applicants who are homeless or from economically disadvantaged families (defined by eligibility for free or reduced-price lunch). Once these children are served, districts may enroll other children based on secondary factors such as developmental delay in social, academic, health, language, or other areas. Local boards of education are expected to gradually expand the availability of prekindergarten sites and will be required to accommodate all eligible 4-year-olds seeking enrollment by 2007–2008.

Although most programs operate in public schools, some districts subcontract with Head Start and child care centers to provide services that meet Prekindergarten Program standards. The state expects to make greater use of settings outside of public schools as the program expands.

In 2003–2004, the Prekindergarten Program received $19,262,500 in state funding, and enrolled 4,008 3-year-olds and 16,450 4-year-olds. The state places an emphasis on coordinating funding streams from various sources in support of prekindergarten. Districts blend state prekindergarten funds with other federal, state, and local sources to meet operating costs and to provide a coherent program that expands available services. The state intends to fund universal Pre-K by significantly increasing state aid money available to districts by 2007–2008, at which time EEEP funds will be phased out.

Maryland also supplements the federal Head Start program. In fiscal year 2003, $3 million in state funding was used for extended-year and extended-day services as well as quality improvement. In addition, the Judith P. Hoyer Early Care and Education Enhancement Program earmarks about $8 million to support comprehensive early childhood centers that are based in or linked to schools.

Maryland promotes quality in its early education programs by providing professional development opportunities and establishing quality standards for prekindergarten, kindergarten, Head Start, and center-based programs that voluntarily allow state validation/accreditation.

ACCESS RANKING–4s	ACCESS RANKING–3s	RESOURCES RANKING
8	14	37

ACCESS

Total state program enrollment - - - - - - - - - 20,569 [1]

School districts that offer state program - - - - - - - - 100%

Income requirement - - - - - - - - - - - - - - - - - - None

Hours of operation - - - - - - - - - - - Half-day[2], full-week

Operating schedule - - - - - - - - - - - - - Academic year

Special education enrollment - - - - - - - - - - - - 6,762

Federally funded Head Start enrollment - - - - - - - 9,535

State-funded Head Start enrollment - - - - - - - - - - 26 [3]

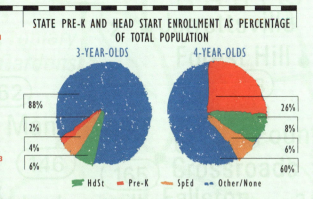

STATE PRE-K AND HEAD START ENROLLMENT AS PERCENTAGE OF TOTAL POPULATION

3-YEAR-OLDS: 88%, 2%, 4%, 6%

4-YEAR-OLDS: 26%, 8%, 6%, 60%

HdSt   Pre-K   SpEd   Other/None

QUALITY STANDARDS CHECKLIST

POLICY	STATE PRE-K REQUIREMENT	BENCHMARK	DOES REQUIREMENT MEET BENCHMARK?
Curriculum standards	Comprehensive	Comprehensive	✓
Teacher degree requirement	BA	BA	✓
Teacher specialized training requirement	Degree in EC + certification in N—3, —6, or —8, and must be licensed	Specializing in Pre-K	✓
Assistant teacher degree requirement	HSD or equivalent	CDA or equivalent	☐
Teacher in-service requirement	6 credit hours/5 years [4]	At least 15 hours/year	✓
Maximum class size		20 or lower	✓
3-year-olds	NA [5]		
4-year-olds	20		
Staff-child ratio		1:10 or better	✓
3-year-olds	NA [5]		
4-year-olds	1:10		
Screening/referral requirements	Vision, hearing, health, immunization, and lead screening [6]	Vision, hearing, and health	✓
Required support services	2 parent conferences and support services [7]	At least 1 service	✓
Meal requirement	Determined locally [8]	At least 1/day	☐

TOTAL: **8** of 10

RESOURCES

Total state Pre-K spending - - - - - - - - - - - $19,262,500 [9]

Local match required? - - - - - - - - - - - - - - - - - No

State spending per child enrolled - - - - - - - - - $936 [9]

State Head Start spending - - - - - - - - - - $3,000,000

State spending per 3-year-old - - - - - - - - - - - - $19

State spending per 4-year-old - - - - - - - - - - - - $246

SPENDING PER CHILD ENROLLED

PRE-K* — $4,067

HDST — $7,411

K–12** — $9,180

$ thousands (0 2 4 6 8 10 12 14)

State Contribution   Local Contribution   Federal Contribution

* Pre-K programs may receive additional funds from federal or local sources that are not included in this figure.

** K–12 expenditures include capital spending as well as current operating expenditures.

Data are for the '02–'03 school year, unless otherwise noted.

1 The enrollment total includes children served by public school districts through a combination of funds derived from EEEP as well as other federal, state, and local sources. Because districts blend these funding sources, a specific number of children supported by state Pre-K funds is not available. Additionally, 1,426 3-year-olds served in public school Pre-K programs are included in this enrollment total. These children were supported by sources other than EEEP funds, which can only be used to serve 4-year-olds.

2 Programs must operate for a minimum of 2.5 hours per day, and 450 children attend for more than 6 hours per day.

3 Maryland's state Head Start funds were also used to expand services or extend the program day for 484 children. Additionally, programs used state funds for professional development, parent education, mental health services, expanded transition services, and literacy projects. The state did not track the number of additional children served through its Head Start supplement. This figure is an estimate based on the number of non-federally funded children in Maryland reported in Head Start's 2002–2003 Program Information Report and proportions of Maryland's federal Head Start enrollees who were 3 or 4 years old.

4 Some in-service requirements may be imposed locally. Also, all schools involved in the Prekindergarten Program have adopted the Maryland Model for School Readiness, which entails 5 days of training in teachers' first year, 4 days of training in their second, and 2-day institutes in their school-system-selected focus area in subsequent years. There are new professional development standards as of 2003–2004. In addition, teachers must meet the requirements for "highly qualified" teachers under NCLB.

5 By policy, 3-year-olds are not eligible for the Prekindergarten Program, but the state reported the maximum class size and staff-child ratio requirement for 3-year-olds under child care regulations as 24 and 1:12, respectively.

6 Vision and health screening and referral are the responsibility of the school health services program in conjunction with the health department. These services are not all required by the Prekindergarten Program, but they are required under Title I, which applies to all children enrolled.

7 Support services include parenting support or training, parent involvement activities, health services for children, transition to kindergarten activities, and specific locally determined services. Many of these services are offered in accordance with Title I requirements.

8 Children in full-day programs are offered breakfast and lunch. In school-based half-day programs, nutrition requirements for preschool children are determined locally and are consistent with meal programs available to older children in each school.

9 This figure reflects EEEP funds only. Districts may use other sources of state money, such as state-aid funds, to support Pre-K.

Massachusetts

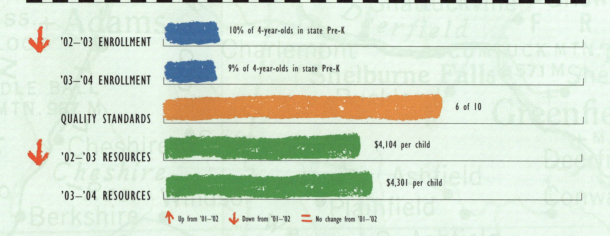

'02–'03 ENROLLMENT		10% of 4-year-olds in state Pre-K
'03–'04 ENROLLMENT		9% of 4-year-olds in state Pre-K
QUALITY STANDARDS		6 of 10
'02–'03 RESOURCES		$4,104 per child
'03–'04 RESOURCES		$4,301 per child

↑ Up from '01–'02   ↓ Down from '01–'02   = No change from '01–'02

The Massachusetts School Improvement Act of 1985 established a state-funded public school early childhood program for children at risk. This Act gave rise to the Community Partnerships for Children (CPC) initiative, which was expanded in 1993 to coordinate the services offered by all early care and education programs within a community. In 1996, a focus on services for 3- and 4-year-olds from working families was introduced. Children are eligible from the age of 2 years, 9 months until the locally determined kindergarten-entrance age. Parent fees are based on a sliding scale and scholarships are available to families with incomes up to 100 percent of the state median income (SMI). Once all children from these families are served, the community may then offer services to children from families earning up to 125 percent of SMI. Children in families with higher incomes are also eligible to be served if they have other risk factors such as low birth weight or a parent with a disability. The CPC preschool programs must be inclusive and serve children with and without disabilities.

The CPC initiative emphasizes community collaboration. The state distributes funds to local CPC councils, which are made up of parents; representatives of Head Start, public school, child care, and family child care programs; and other community representatives. Working together, they plan the expansion and coordination of preschool services based on community needs and resources. Local councils, in turn, allocate funds to private and public agencies to provide services. Annual proposals must address specific funding priorities, such as increasing the affordability and quality of early childhood programs. In April 2003, the state Board of Education adopted the Early Childhood Program Standards and Guidelines for Preschool Learning Experiences for the CPC programs.

Since fiscal year 2001, state funding for the initiative has been cut by $35.4 million, affecting the quality, quantity, and comprehensiveness of services that communities are able to offer. In 2003–2004, the state appropriated $68.6 million for the CPC program, which provided direct services for 15,950 children, as well as program quality assistance and comprehensive services benefiting thousands more.

Recent developments in Massachusetts include a superior court judge recommendation that calls preschool a "necessity" for children at risk and legislative action that serves as an initial step toward expanding high-quality early education across the state. The state created an independent board and a consolidated Office of Early Education and Care as part of this effort. Massachusetts also supplements federal funding for Head Start as a separate initiative, and in 2002–2003 provided $6.1 million to enhance quality and provide for 400 additional Head Start slots.

ACCESS RANKING–4s	ACCESS RANKING–3s	RESOURCES RANKING
17	2	9

ACCESS

Total state program enrollment - - - - - - - - - - - - 17,837 [1]

School districts that offer state program - - - - - - - 95% (towns)

Income requirement - - - - - - - - - - - - - - - 125% SMI

Hours of operation - - - - - - - - - - - - Determined locally [2]

Operating schedule - - - - - - - - - - - - Determined locally [3]

Special education enrollment - - - - - - - - - - - - 8,455

Federally funded Head Start enrollment - - - - - - - - 10,498

State-funded Head Start enrollment - - - - - - - - - - 335 [4]

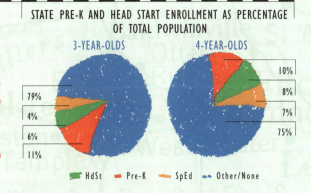

STATE PRE-K AND HEAD START ENROLLMENT AS PERCENTAGE OF TOTAL POPULATION

3-YEAR-OLDS: 79%, 4%, 6%, 11%

4-YEAR-OLDS: 10%, 8%, 7%, 75%

HdSt   Pre-K   SpEd   Other/None

QUALITY STANDARDS CHECKLIST

POLICY	STATE PRE-K REQUIREMENT	BENCHMARK	DOES REQUIREMENT MEET BENCHMARK?
Curriculum standards - - - - - - - - - - - - - - - -	Comprehensive	Comprehensive	☑
Teacher degree requirement - - - -	BA (public), None (nonpublic) [5]	BA	☐
Teacher specialized training requirement - - - -	EC license (public), [6] 1 ECE class + 9 mos. exp. (nonpublic)	Specializing in Pre-K	☐
Assistant teacher degree requirement -	HSD (public), 16 yrs. old + constant supervision (nonpublic)	CDA or equivalent	☐
Teacher in-service requirement - - - - - - - - -	20 clock hours [7]	At least 15 hours/year	☑
Maximum class size		20 or lower	☑
3-year-olds - - - - - - - - - - - - - - - - -	20		
4-year-olds - - - - - - - - - - - - - - - - -	20		
Staff-child ratio		1:10 or better	☑
3-year-olds - - - - - - - - - - - - - - - - -	1:10		
4-year-olds - - - - - - - - - - - - - - - - -	1:10		
Screening/referral requirements -	Vision, hearing, health, and dental	Vision, hearing, and health	☑
Required support services - - - - - - - - -	2 parent conferences and support services [8]	At least 1 service	☑
Meal requirement - - - - - - - - - - - - - - - - -	Varies [9]	At least 1/day	☐

TOTAL: 6 of 10

RESOURCES

Total state Pre-K spending - - - - - - - - - - - - - $73,200,000 [10]

Local match required? - - - - - - - - - - - - - - - - - No

State spending per child enrolled - - - - - - - - - - - $4,104 [11]

State Head Start spending - - - - - - - - - - - - - $6,100,000

State spending per 3-year-old - - - - - - - - - - - - $436 [11]

State spending per 4-year-old - - - - - - - - - - - - $430 [11]

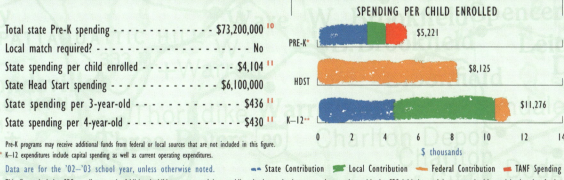

SPENDING PER CHILD ENROLLED

PRE-K* $5,221

HDST $8,125

K–12** $11,276

$ thousands: 0 2 4 6 8 10 12 14

State Contribution   Local Contribution   Federal Contribution   TANF Spending

* Pre-K programs may receive additional funds from federal or local sources that are not included in this figure.

** K–12 expenditures include capital spending as well as current operating expenditures.

Data are for the '02–'03 school year, unless otherwise noted.

1   This figure includes CPC enrollment only. Additional children are served in a public school preschool program that overlaps with the CPC initiative and is supported with special education funds, federal Title I dollars, local fees and other resources. Classroom composition in the public school program is highly inclusive—in classes of 20, no more than 30% of the children have special needs, and in classes of 15 or smaller, no more than 50% of the children have special needs.

2   Program operating schedules are determined by family needs and preferences. CPC programs operate between 2.5 and 10 hours per day, 2 to 5 days per week.

3   An estimated 60% of programs operate for the calendar year.

4   Massachusetts did not break its state Head Start enrollment figure into specific numbers of 3- or 4-year-olds. As a result, this figure is estimated using proportions of federal Head Start enrollees in each age category.

5   All teachers must be at least 21 years old. Furthermore, standards passed in 2003 require all newly hired teachers to attain at least an AA by 2010 and a BA by 2017.

6   Public school teachers must have an Early Childhood Teacher of Students With and Without Disabilities (Pre-K-Grade 2) license.

7   Public school teachers must meet additional union-negotiated local requirements.

8   Support services include parenting support or training, parent involvement activities, health services for children, information about nutrition, referral to social services, transition to kindergarten activities and other services that are determined locally and based on need.

9   Meal requirements depend on the length of the program day.

10 This figure includes $21 million in TANF funds.

11 These estimates include both state and TANF funds.

Michigan

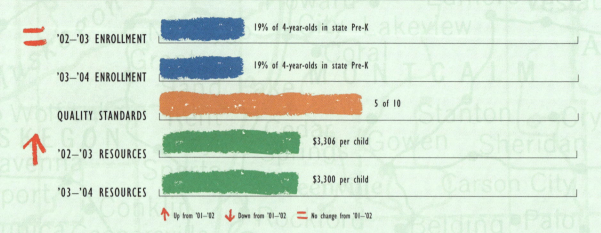

'02–'03 ENROLLMENT		19% of 4-year-olds in state Pre-K
'03–'04 ENROLLMENT		19% of 4-year-olds in state Pre-K
QUALITY STANDARDS		5 of 10
'02–'03 RESOURCES		$3,306 per child
'03–'04 RESOURCES		$3,300 per child

↑ Up from '01–'02   ↓ Down from '01–'02   = No change from '01–'02

The Michigan School Readiness Program, started as a pilot program in 1985, serves at-risk 4-year-old children. Public schools, Head Start, private child care centers, and health and social service agencies may receive state funds through competitive grants. However, most of the funding is provided to public schools, based on a formula that takes into account factors such as the size of the school district and the number of children eligible for free lunch. A minimum of 50 percent of the children in this program must meet the income eligibility criteria (having a family income below 185 percent of the federal poverty level), as well as at least one other risk factor from a list of 25 possible factors. Children who do not meet the income eligibility criteria must exhibit at least 2 of the 25 risk factors.

Reorganization efforts are underway to integrate the delivery of early childhood special education services with the services provided by the Michigan School Readiness Program. The state Standards of Quality are currently being revised, and an accountability system has been developed and implemented to assess program quality.

During the 2003–2004 school year, the Michigan School Readiness Program provided 25,712 slots for 4-year-olds with a state budget of approximately $84.85 million.

ACCESS RANKING—4s	ACCESS RANKING—3s	RESOURCES RANKING
13	None Served	19

ACCESS

Total state program enrollment - - - - - - - - - - - - - - 25,712

School districts that offer state program - - - - - - - - - 85%

Income requirement - - - - - - - - - - - - - - - 50% of children
must be eligible for free or reduced-priced lunch

Hours of operation - - - - - - - - - - - - - Half-day, part-week [1]

Operating schedule - - - - - - - - - At least 30 weeks per year

Special education enrollment - - - - - - - - - - - - - 12,411

Federally funded Head Start enrollment - - - - - - - - 32,101

State-funded Head Start enrollment - - - - - - - - - - - - - 0

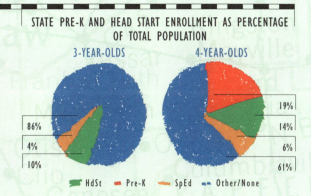

STATE PRE-K AND HEAD START ENROLLMENT AS PERCENTAGE OF TOTAL POPULATION

3-YEAR-OLDS
86%
4%
10%

4-YEAR-OLDS
19%
14%
6%
61%

HdSt Pre-K SpEd Other/None

QUALITY STANDARDS CHECKLIST

POLICY	STATE PRE-K REQUIREMENT	BENCHMARK	DOES REQUIREMENT MEET BENCHMARK?
Curriculum standards - - - - - - - - - -	Not comprehensive	Comprehensive	☐
Teacher degree requirement - -	BA (public), AA + CDA (nonpublic) [2]	BA	☐
Teacher specialized training req. - - -	Teaching certification with EC endorsement (public), meets CDA requirement (nonpublic)	Specializing in Pre-K	☑
Assistant teacher degree requirement - - -	CDA or 120 clock hrs [3]	CDA or equivalent	☑
Teacher in-service requirement - - - - - - - - - - - - -	None	At least 15 hours/year	☐
Maximum class size		20 or lower	☑
3-year-olds - - - - - - - - - - - - - - - -	NA		
4-year-olds - - - - - - - - - - - - - - - -	18		
Staff-child ratio		1:10 or better	☑
3-year-olds - - - - - - - - - - - - - - - -	NA		
4-year-olds - - - - - - - - - - - - - - - -	1:8 [4]		
Screening/referral requirements - - - - - - - - - - - -	None [5]	Vision, hearing, and health	☐
Required support services - - - - - - - -	4 parent conferences and support services [6]	At least 1 service	☑
Meal requirement -	Snack	At least 1/day	☐

TOTAL:
5
of 10

RESOURCES

Total state Pre-K spending - - - - - - - - - - - - $85,000,000

Local match required? - - - - - - - - - - - - - - - - - - - No

State spending per child enrolled - - - - - - - - - - $3,306

State spending per 3-year-old - - - - - - - - - - - - - - $0

State spending per 4-year-old - - - - - - - - - - - - - $636

SPENDING PER CHILD ENROLLED

PRE-K* — $3,306

HDST — $6,497

K-12** — $10,481

0 2 4 6 8 10 12 14
$ thousands

State Contribution Local Contribution Federal Contribution

* Pre-K programs may receive additional funds from federal or local sources that are not included in this figure.

** K–12 expenditures include capital spending as well as current operating expenditures.

Data are for the '02–'03 school year, unless otherwise noted.

1 Providers may charge tuition if offering a fifth day. Most programs operate for 4 half days, though some offer 2 full days.

2 Most teachers in a nonpublic setting have a BA.

3 Associate (assistant) teachers are given 2 years to meet the requirements of their position.

4 A qualified teacher must be present, plus an associate teacher in rooms with 9 to 16 children. If more than 16 students are in a class, then a third adult (who does not have to meet any specified qualifications) must be present.

5 Programs must make referrals, but are not required to conduct screenings. Screening is required before kindergarten entry.

6 Two of the required parent conferences ideally take place in the home. Support services offered include parent involvement activities and referral to social services.

Minnesota

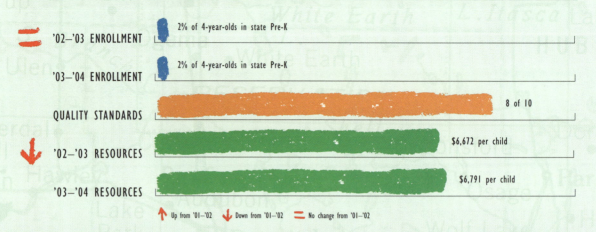

=	'02–'03 ENROLLMENT	2% of 4-year-olds in state Pre-K
	'03–'04 ENROLLMENT	2% of 4-year-olds in state Pre-K
	QUALITY STANDARDS	8 of 10
↓	'02–'03 RESOURCES	$6,672 per child
	'03–'04 RESOURCES	$6,791 per child

↑ Up from '01–'02   ↓ Down from '01–'02   = No change from '01–'02

Minnesota supplements federal Head Start and Early Head Start spending through a state-funded Head Start model. During 2002–2003, this initiative received $17.62 million in state funds to support 2,446 Head Start slots for 3- to 5-year-olds and Early Head Start services for 195 infants and toddlers. Funds were appropriated to 27 private, nonprofit agencies; seven Tribal Governments; and one public school district. Only federal Head Start grantees that existed prior to 1989 are eligible to receive state funds. Programs supported through this initiative are required to follow standards and provide comprehensive services as specified in the federal Head Start Program Performance Standards.

Funding for state Head Start has declined in each of the last three fiscal years. The state Legislature originally appropriated $18,375,000 for fiscal year 2003, but programs were only authorized to spend $17.62 million. The reduction in available funds reduced per-child spending, and included the "unallotment" of innovative grants that had already been awarded on a competitive basis. Further, budget cuts in fiscal years 2004 and 2005 reduced state Head Start funding by a total of $3.2 million, resulting in fewer available slots. The statute passed for 2004 eliminated innovative grants as well as set-aside grants that had supported services for children under 3 years of age. Funding in fiscal year 2004 was $16,475,000, providing 2,026 slots designated for 3- and 4-year olds.

Though not the focus of data in this profile, Minnesota's School Readiness Program is a separate initiative supporting more than 22 types of services for preschool-age children and their families. In addition to preschool education, other services include parent education through the Early Childhood Family Education program, home visits, and supplementary services for children with special needs. In 2002–2003, 99 percent of Minnesota's school districts offered services funded by the School Readiness Program. Individual school districts determine how they will use their funds and what types of services will be offered. If School Readiness funds are used in support of prekindergarten, programs are expected to follow standards specified at the state level, including maximum class sizes of 20, staff-child ratios of 1:10 or better, and several family support services. Children are prioritized for services based on needs identified through a comprehensive Early Childhood Health and Development Screening.

In this report, the School Readiness Program is viewed as a funding stream supporting a variety of locally selected services for preschoolers rather than as a separate, statewide preschool education initiative. During 2002–2003, a total of $9,543,469 in state funds was used to support all components of the School Readiness Program. The state is not able to provide an unduplicated count of the number of children attending center-based preschool education programs or specific information about the amount of School Readiness funds used for such programs.

Though funding for early childhood programs has declined, Minnesota has also seen some recent positive developments, including the alignment of its Early Learning Standards (Early Childhood Indicators of Progress) with Minnesota Kindergarten Standards and Head Start Outcomes.

ACCESS RANKING—4s	ACCESS RANKING—3s	RESOURCES RANKING
36	19	2

ACCESS

Total state program enrollment - - - - - - - - - - - - - - 2,641 [1]

School districts that offer state program - - - - - [see footnotes] [2]

Income req. - - - 90% of children must be at or below 100% FPL

Hours of operation - - - - - - - - - - - - - Determined locally [3]

Operating schedule - - - - - - - - - - - - - Determined locally [3]

Special education enrollment - - - - - - - - - - - - 7,294

Federally funded Head Start enrollment - - - - - - - - 10,015

State-funded Head Start enrollment - - - - - - - - - - 2,206

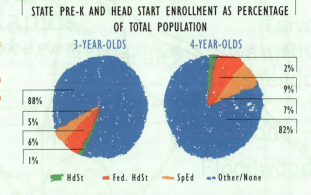

STATE PRE-K AND HEAD START ENROLLMENT AS PERCENTAGE OF TOTAL POPULATION

3-YEAR-OLDS 88% / 5% / 6% / 1%

4-YEAR-OLDS 2% / 9% / 7% / 82%

HdSt ■ Fed. HdSt ■ SpEd ■ Other/None

QUALITY STANDARDS CHECKLIST

POLICY	STATE PRE-K REQUIREMENT	BENCHMARK	DOES REQUIREMENT MEET BENCHMARK?
Curriculum standards - - - - - - - - - - - - - -	Comprehensive	Comprehensive	☑
Teacher degree requirement - - - - - - - - - - - - -	CDA	BA	☐
Teacher specialized training req. - - - - -	Meets CDA requirements	Specializing in Pre-K	☑
Assistant teacher degree requirement - - - - -	Meets child care regs. [5]	CDA or equivalent	☑
Teacher in-service requirement - -	1.5% or 2% of total work hours [6]	At least 15 hours/year	☐
Maximum class size		20 or lower	☑
3-year-olds - - - - - - - - - - - - - - -	17		
4-year-olds - - - - - - - - - - - - - - -	20		
Staff-child ratio		1:10 or better	☑
3-year-olds - - - - - - - - - - - - - - -	2:17		
4-year-olds - - - - - - - - - - - - - - -	1:10		
Screening/referral requirements -	Vision, hearing, health and dental	Vision, hearing, and health	☑
Required support services - - - - - - - - - -	2 home visits and support services [7]	At least 1 service	☑
Meal requirement - - - - - - - - - - - -	Lunch and/or breakfast [8]	At least 1/day	☑

TOTAL: **8** of 10

RESOURCES

Total state Pre-K spending - - - - - - - - - - - - - $17,620,000 [9]

Local match required? - - - - - - - - - - - - - - - - No

State spending per child enrolled - - - - - - - - - - - $6,672

State Head Start spending - - - - - - - - - - - $17,620,000 [10]

State spending per 3-year-old - - - - - - - - - - - - $89

State spending per 4-year-old - - - - - - - - - - - - $138

SPENDING PER CHILD ENROLLED

PRE-K* $6,672

FED. HDST $6,811

K–12** $10,941

$ thousands

▬■ State Contribution ■ Local Contribution ■ Federal Contribution

* Programs may receive additional funds from federal or local sources that are not included in this figure.

** K–12 expenditures include capital spending as well as current operating expenditures.

Data are for the '02–'03 school year, unless otherwise noted.

1 This enrollment total includes 195 children under age 3 and 240 5-year-olds.

2 In 2002–2003, state Head Start funding went to one school district; seven Tribal Governments; and 27 private, nonprofit agencies, each serving one or more counties. State Head Start grantees include all federally designated Head Start programs in Minnesota as of 1989.

3 Minimum operating hours must be consistent with the requirements of the federal Head Start Program Performance Standards. Programs must operate at least 3.5 hours per day, 4 days per week, and 32 weeks per year.

4 Minnesota's School Readiness Program (MSRP) supports a range of services, including part-day prekindergarten programs as well as services such as summer programs, story hours, transportation assistance, and other activities. The state did not provide unduplicated counts of children by type of service received, or information regarding the amounts of MSRP funds devoted to specific services. As a result, children who received any type of service as part of the School Readiness Program are included in the Other/None category on the Access pie graph.

5 Assistant teachers in settings subject to child care regulations must work under the supervision of a teacher, be at least 18 years old, and meet one of nine combined credential, educational, and experience requirements, such as a high school diploma, 12 quarter credits in early childhood or a related field, and 2,080 hours of experience.

6 Non-degreed staff are required to complete 2% of their total working hours for in-service training (full-time employment requires 40 hours of in-service) and degreed staff are required to complete 1.5% of total working hours for in-service.

7 Support services include education services or job training for parents, parenting support or training, parent involvement activities, health services for parents and children, information about nutrition, referral to social services, and transition to kindergarten activities. Programs are required to provide all activities specified in the federal Head Start Program Performance Standards.

8 Part-day programs are required to provide children with at least one-third of their daily nutritional needs, as determined by the USDA. Full-day programs must provide one-half to two-thirds of daily nutritional needs, depending on length of the program day.

9 This includes $1 million in state Head Start funds that was set aside in 2002–2003 to serve children birth to age 3. The set-aside was eliminated for fiscal year 2004 so that grantees now serve children birth to age 5 with state Head Start funds.

10 All spending through this initiative is directed toward Head Start programs.

Mississippi

NO PROGRAM

ACCESS RANKING—4s	ACCESS RANKING—3s	RESOURCES RANKING
No Program		

ACCESS

Total state program enrollment - - - - - - - - - - - - - - - 0

School districts that offer state program - - - - - - - - - NA

Income requirement - NA

Hours of operation - NA

Operating schedule - NA

Special education enrollment - - - - - - - - - - - - - 3,121

Federally funded Head Start enrollment - - - - - - - - 25,685

State-funded Head Start enrollment - - - - - - - - - - - - 0

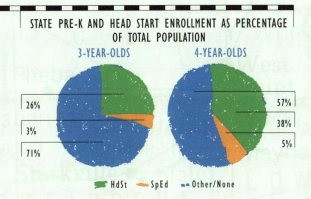

STATE PRE-K AND HEAD START ENROLLMENT AS PERCENTAGE
OF TOTAL POPULATION

3-YEAR-OLDS

26%
3%
71%

4-YEAR-OLDS

57%
38%
5%

■ HdSt ■ SpEd ■ Other/None

QUALITY STANDARDS CHECKLIST

No Program

RESOURCES

Total state Pre-K spending - - - - - - - - - - - - - - - - $0

Local match required? - - - - - - - - - - - - - - - - - - NA

State spending per child enrolled - - - - - - - - - - - - - $0

State spending per 3-year-old - - - - - - - - - - - - - - - $0

State spending per 4-year-old - - - - - - - - - - - - - - - $0

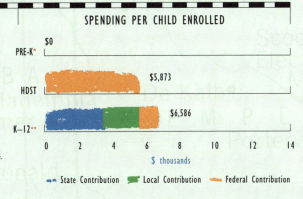

SPENDING PER CHILD ENROLLED

PRE-K* $0

HDST $5,873

K–12** $6,586

0   2   4   6   8   10   12   14
$ thousands

■- State Contribution   ■ Local Contribution   ■ Federal Contribution

* Pre-K programs may receive additional funds from federal or local sources that are not included in this figure.

** K–12 expenditures include capital spending as well as current operating expenditures.

Data are for the '02–'03 school year, unless otherwise noted.

Missouri

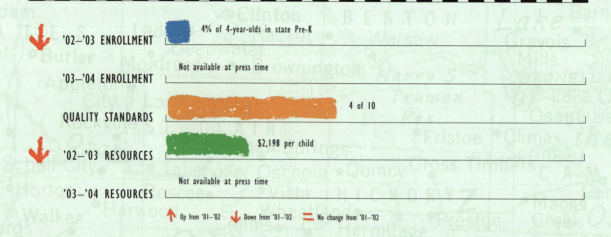

↓	'02–'03 ENROLLMENT	4% of 4-year-olds in state Pre-K
	'03–'04 ENROLLMENT	Not available at press time
	QUALITY STANDARDS	4 of 10
↓	'02–'03 RESOURCES	$2,198 per child
	'03–'04 RESOURCES	Not available at press time

↑ Up from '01–'02   ↓ Down from '01–'02   = No change from '01–'02

The Missouri Preschool Project (MPP) was established in 1998 as part of the Early Child Development Education and Care fund, which is supported by gaming revenues. The program serves children who will be 3 or 4 years of age by August 1 of the program year. Since 1999, MPP funds have been available to public schools, Head Start centers, private child care centers, and family child care homes through a competitive grant process. Programs are required to operate for five days per week and for a minimum of nine months per year. All children are eligible to enroll, but programs receive priority funding if they provide services for children from low-income families or with special needs.

In an effort to increase the quality of preschool programs, MPP requires each program to reserve a minimum of 10 percent of its grant to provide professional development opportunities for teachers in other licensed programs within the same community. Programs awarded in the past three years receive on-site technical assistance, and teachers in these programs have the opportunity to attend full-day training programs four times per year.

ACCESS RANKING—4s	ACCESS RANKING—3s	RESOURCES RANKING
31	11	30

ACCESS

Total state program enrollment - - - - - - - - - - - - - - - 4,888

School districts that offer state program - - - - - - - - - - 39%

Income requirement - - - - - - - - - - - - - - - - - - - None [1]

Hours of operation - - - - - - - - - - - - - Determined locally [2]

Operating schedule - - - - - - - - - - - - - Determined locally [3]

Special education enrollment - - - - - - - - - - - - - - - - 8,014

Federally funded Head Start enrollment - - - - - - - - - - 15,016

State-funded Head Start enrollment - - - - - - - - - - - - - 0

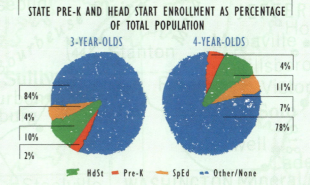

STATE PRE-K AND HEAD START ENROLLMENT AS PERCENTAGE OF TOTAL POPULATION

3-YEAR-OLDS
84%
4%
10%
2%

4-YEAR-OLDS
4%
11%
7%
78%

HdSt   Pre-K   SpEd   Other/None

QUALITY STANDARDS CHECKLIST

POLICY	STATE PRE-K REQUIREMENT	BENCHMARK	DOES REQUIREMENT MEET BENCHMARK?
Curriculum standards - - - - - - - - - - -	Not comprehensive	Comprehensive	☐
Teacher degree requirement - - - - -	BA (public), CDA (nonpublic)	BA	☐
Teacher specialized training req. - - - - - -	License and certificate in EC or ECSE, or 4-yr CD degree (public); Meets CDA requirements (nonpublic)	Specializing in Pre-K	☑
Assistant teacher degree requirement - - - - - - -	HSD + voc. cert. in ECE (public); HSD (nonpublic)	CDA or equivalent	☐
Teacher in-service req. - 12 clock hours and 2 full-day trainings [4]		At least 15 hours/year	☑
Maximum class size		20 or lower	☑
3-year-olds -	20		
4-year-olds -	20		
Staff-child ratio		1:10 or better	☑
3-year-olds -	1:10		
4-year-olds -	1:10		
Screening/referral requirements - - - - - - - - - - -	None	Vision, hearing, and health	☐
Required support services - - - - - - - - - - - - - - -	None [5]	At least 1 service	☐
Meal requirement - - - - - - - - - - - - - - - - - - -	Varies [6]	At least 1/day	☐

TOTAL:
4
of 10

RESOURCES

Total state Pre-K spending - - - - - - - - - - - - - - $10,744,988

Local match required? - No

State spending per child enrolled - - - - - - - - - - - - $2,198

State spending per 3-year-old - - - - - - - - - - - - - - $52

State spending per 4-year-old - - - - - - - - - - - - - - $95

SPENDING PER CHILD ENROLLED

PRE-K* $2,198

HDST $6,582

K–12** $8,334

0   2   4   6   8   10   12   14
$ thousands

State Contribution   Local Contribution   Federal Contribution

* Pre-K programs may receive additional funds from federal or local sources that are not included in this figure.

** K–12 expenditures include capital spending as well as current operating expenditures.

Data are for the '02–'03 school year, unless otherwise noted.

1 Programs are funded through a competitive process and receive extra points in the scoring system for serving children with special needs or from low-income families.

2 Each program may choose to apply as either a full-day program (6.5 hours) or a half-day program (3 hours). Programs awarded in 1998–1999 had the option to operate 4 days per week with the fifth day for home visiting. This practice is being phased out and most programs now operate 5 days per week.

3 Programs must operate a minimum of 9 months, but may choose to operate for up to 12 months.

4 Teachers are required to attend two full-day training programs at minimum, and receive on-site technical assistance. All professional development opportunities paid for through MPP funds are additional hours beyond the 12 clock hours required for licensure.

5 Parent conferences are optional. Two hundred MPP programs involved a total of 4,109 families in some type of conference. In addition, MPP programs offered 1,579 parent involvement activities in which 3,613 families participated, although the provision of such services is optional.

6 Child care licensing requires full-day programs to offer lunch and two snacks. Half-day programs must offer either a morning or afternoon snack.

Montana

NO PROGRAM

ACCESS RANKING—4s	ACCESS RANKING—3s	RESOURCES RANKING
No Program		

ACCESS

Total state program enrollment - - - - - - - - - - - - - - - 0

School districts that offer state program - - - - - - - - - - NA

Income requirement - NA

Hours of operation - NA

Operating schedule - NA

Special education enrollment - - - - - - - - - - - - - 875

Federally funded Head Start enrollment - - - - - - - - - 3,767

State-funded Head Start enrollment - - - - - - - - - - - - 0

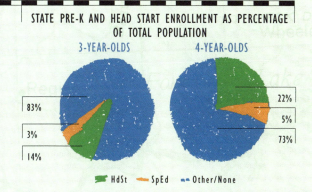

STATE PRE-K AND HEAD START ENROLLMENT AS PERCENTAGE OF TOTAL POPULATION

3-YEAR-OLDS

83%
3%
14%

4-YEAR-OLDS

22%
5%
73%

■ HdSt   ■ SpEd   ▪▪ Other/None

QUALITY STANDARDS CHECKLIST

No Program

RESOURCES

Total state Pre-K spending - - - - - - - - - - - - - - - - $0

Local match required? - - - - - - - - - - - - - - - - - - NA

State spending per child enrolled - - - - - - - - - - - - $0

State spending per 3-year-old - - - - - - - - - - - - - - $0

State spending per 4-year-old - - - - - - - - - - - - - - $0

SPENDING PER CHILD ENROLLED

PRE-K* $0

HDST $6,899

K–12** $7,818

0   2   4   6   8   10   12   14

$ thousands

■ State Contribution   ■ Local Contribution   ■ Federal Contribution

* Pre-K programs may receive additional funds from federal or local sources that are not included in this figure.

** K–12 expenditures include capital spending as well as current operating expenditures.

Data are for the '02–'03 school year, unless otherwise noted.

Nebraska

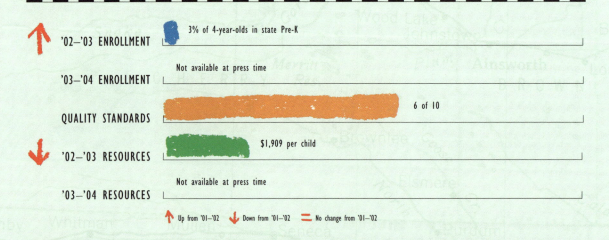

↑ '02–'03 ENROLLMENT	3% of 4-year-olds in state Pre-K
'03–'04 ENROLLMENT	Not available at press time
QUALITY STANDARDS	6 of 10
↓ '02–'03 RESOURCES	$1,909 per child
'03–'04 RESOURCES	Not available at press time

↑ Up from '01–'02   ↓ Down from '01–'02   ═ No change from '01–'02

Nebraska's Early Childhood Grant Program has its basis in a pilot project that was established in 1990 and implemented in 1992 with total funding of $500,000. Legislation in 2001 expanded the initiative and made funds available for additional classrooms. The state provides grants to public schools and educational service units, which must collaborate with community initiatives and may also subcontract with other public schools and community programs, such as private child care centers or Head Start providers. Early Childhood Grant funding from the state represents an average of 34 percent, and is not allowed to exceed 50 percent, of each program's budget. Grants are intended to support collaboration, and all grantees are required to supplement grant funds with additional funding derived from federal, state, or local sources.

Most participants are 3 or 4 years old, but in programs designed to serve children of teen parents, children may enter the Early Childhood Grant Program as early as 6 weeks of age. Programs are required to designate at least 70 percent of their budgets to provide for children who meet one of four priority areas identified by the state. Priority areas include: children eligible for free or reduced-price lunch, children born prematurely or with low birth weights, children of teen parents who have not completed high school, and English Language Learners. Revisions to state regulations in 2002 require that programs operated by schools and educational service units increase staff qualifications and expectations for program quality. For example, Early Childhood Grant Programs in these settings must be accredited by NAEYC within 3 years of receiving state funding.

Although enrollment more than doubled between 2001–2002 and 2002–2003, a 10 percent reduction in state funds in 2003–2004 led to cuts in training and technical assistance and reduced funding for five programs.

ACCESS RANKING—4s	ACCESS RANKING—3s	RESOURCES RANKING
33	17	31

ACCESS

Total state program enrollment - - - - - - - - - - - - - - 1,100 [1]

School districts that offer state program - - - - - - - - - - 5% [2]

Income requirement - - - - - - - - - - - - - - - - - - - None [3]

Hours of operation - - - - - - - - - - - - - Determined locally [4]

Operating schedule - - - - - - - - - - - - - Determined locally [5]

Special education enrollment - - - - - - - - - - - - - - 2,584

Federally funded Head Start enrollment - - - - - - - - 4,406

State-funded Head Start enrollment - - - - - - - - - - - - 0

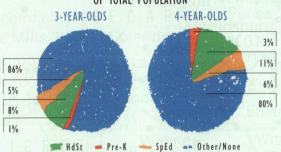

STATE PRE-K AND HEAD START ENROLLMENT AS PERCENTAGE OF TOTAL POPULATION

3-YEAR-OLDS
- 86%
- 5%
- 8%
- 1%

4-YEAR-OLDS
- 3%
- 11%
- 6%
- 80%

HdSt — Pre-K — SpEd — Other/None

QUALITY STANDARDS CHECKLIST

POLICY	STATE PRE-K REQUIREMENT	BENCHMARK	DOES REQUIREMENT MEET BENCHMARK?
Curriculum standards	Not comprehensive	Comprehensive	☐
Teacher degree requirement	BA	BA	☑
Teacher specialized training req.	Certification and EC endorsement	Specializing in Pre-K	☑
Assistant teacher degree req.	12 cr. hours in EC or equivalent	CDA or equivalent	☑
Teacher in-service requirement	12 clock hours	At least 15 hours/year	☐
Maximum class size		20 or lower	☑
3-year-olds	20		
4-year-olds	20		
Staff-child ratio		1:10 or better	☑
3-year-olds	1:10		
4-year-olds	1:10		
Screening/referral requirements	Determined locally	Vision, hearing, and health	☐
Required support services	2 parent conferences and support services [6]	At least 1 service	☑
Meal requirement	Varies [7]	At least 1/day	☐

TOTAL:

6

of 10

RESOURCES

Total state Pre-K spending - - - - - - - - - - - - - $2,100,000

Local match required? - - - - - - - - - - - - - - - - - - Yes [8]

State spending per child enrolled - - - - - - - - - - - $1,909

State spending per 3-year-old - - - - - - - - - - - - - - $28

State spending per 4-year-old - - - - - - - - - - - - - - $49

SPENDING PER CHILD ENROLLED

PRE-K*	$5,455
HDST	$6,729
K-12**	$8,098

0 2 4 6 8 10 12 14

$ thousands

— State Contribution — Local Contribution — Federal Contribution

* Pre-K programs may receive additional funds from federal or local sources that are not included in this figure.

** K–12 expenditures include capital spending as well as current operating expenditures.

Data are for the '02–'03 school year, unless otherwise noted.

[1] There were 176 children younger than 3 years old enrolled in the program.

[2] Programs are also offered in 3 out of 19 Educational Service Units.

[3] Grants are competitive with priority given to districts with large English Language Learner or low-income populations. In addition, districts offer priority enrollment to children born prematurely or with low birth rates. Up to 30% of funds can be used to serve children without these risk factors.

[4] Programs operate at least 12 to 15 hours per week, and approximately half run full-day, five days per week.

[5] Grants can be either for the academic or the calendar year.

[6] Support services include parenting support or training, parent involvement activities, and transition to kindergarten activities.

[7] Meal requirements depend on hours during which children attend the program. All programs provide snacks, most offer lunch, and some provide breakfast as well.

[8] The state funds up to 50% of the total cost per child, and districts supplement the remainder with local resources and other funds from sources such as Special Education, Head Start, and Title I.

Nevada

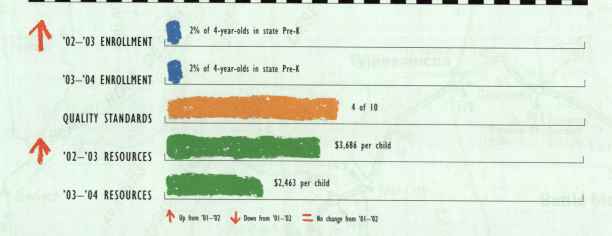

'02–'03 ENROLLMENT — 2% of 4-year-olds in state Pre-K

'03–'04 ENROLLMENT — 2% of 4-year-olds in state Pre-K

QUALITY STANDARDS — 4 of 10

'02–'03 RESOURCES — $3,686 per child

'03–'04 RESOURCES — $2,463 per child

↑ Up from '01–'02   ↓ Down from '01–'02   = No change from '01–'02

In operation since early 2002, the Nevada Early Childhood Education Comprehensive Plan (ECE) was established to fund new prekindergarten education programs in the state and to expand existing programs. Funding is available to school districts and community-based organizations—including family child care homes, private child care centers, and Head Start agencies—on a competitive grant basis. In order to receive funding, each provider must tailor a program to meet demonstrated needs of the host community and develop detailed eligibility criteria. All ECE programs are required to provide additional services to parents, including parenting education and opportunities for parent involvement. Program quality is controlled primarily through the competitive grant process rather than through explicit policy.

The ECE program provides services to children from birth to age 5 and most programs give priority to children from low-income families. All teachers must be licensed and are paid on the public school salary scale, regardless of program location.

Due to state budget constraints, 2003–2004 funding was decreased to $2,595,583, which supported services for 1,054 children. However, Nevada ECE showed a commitment to improving classroom quality by recommending programs follow NAEYC guidelines and pursue accreditation. The state will also implement new content standards for prekindergarten.

Nevada also provides funding for a separate program known as Classroom on Wheels (COW), which offers preschool opportunities for 3- and 4-year-olds through the use of buses refurbished as classrooms. Initially a grassroots effort to provide early childhood services to children from low-income families, COW has grown into a statewide program and is in the process of raising its standards to meet the same requirements as other state-funded preschools. All data in this report are specific to the Nevada Early Childhood Education Comprehensive Plan.

ACCESS RANKING—4s	ACCESS RANKING—3s	RESOURCES RANKING
38	24	13

ACCESS

Total state program enrollment - - - - - - - - - - - - - - - - 814 [1]

School districts that offer state program - - - - - 65% (counties)

Income requirement - None [2]

Hours of operation - - - - - - - - - - - - - - Determined locally [3]

Operating schedule - - - - - - - - - - - - Determined locally [4]

Special education enrollment - - - - - - - - - - - - - - - 2,486

Federally funded Head Start enrollment - - - - - - - - - 2,329

State-funded Head Start enrollment - - - - - - - - - - - - - 0

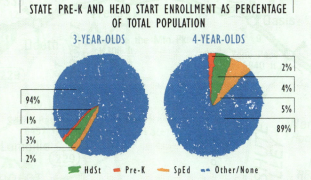

STATE PRE-K AND HEAD START ENROLLMENT AS PERCENTAGE OF TOTAL POPULATION

3-YEAR-OLDS

94%
1%
3%
2%

4-YEAR-OLDS

2%
4%
5%
89%

■ HdSt   ■ Pre-K   ■ SpEd   ■ Other/None

QUALITY STANDARDS CHECKLIST

POLICY	STATE PRE-K REQUIREMENT	BENCHMARK	DOES REQUIREMENT MEET BENCHMARK?
Curriculum standards	None	Comprehensive	☐
Teacher degree requirement	BA	BA	☑
Teacher specialized training requirement	ECE teacher license	Specializing in Pre-K	☑
Assistant teacher degree requirement	GED or HSD [5]	CDA or equivalent	☐
Teacher in-service requirement	5 credit hours/5 years	At least 15 hours/year	☑
Maximum class size		20 or lower	☐
3-year-olds	No limit [6]		
4-year-olds	No limit [6]		
Staff-child ratio		1:10 or better	☐
3-year-olds	No limit [6]		
4-year-olds	No limit [6]		
Screening/referral requirements	Determined locally	Vision, hearing, and health	☐
Required support services	Support services [7]	At least 1 service	☑
Meal requirement	None	At least 1/day	☐

TOTAL:
4
of 10

RESOURCES

Total state Pre-K spending - - - - - - - - - - - - - $3,000,000

Local match required? - No

State spending per child enrolled - - - - - - - - - - - $3,686

State spending per 3-year-old - - - - - - - - - - - - - $25

State spending per 4-year-old - - - - - - - - - - - - - $57

SPENDING PER CHILD ENROLLED

PRE-K* : $3,686

HDST : $8,466

K–12** : $8,505

0   2   4   6   8   10   12   14
$ thousands

→ State Contribution   ■ Local Contribution   ■ Federal Contribution

* Pre-K programs may receive additional funds from federal or local sources that are not included in this figure.

** K–12 expenditures include capital spending as well as current operating expenditures.

Data are for the '02–'03 school year, unless otherwise noted.

1 Total enrollment includes an estimated 88 children younger than 3 years of age who were enrolled during 2002–2003.

2 However, all programs give enrollment priority to students from low-income families, and specify detailed eligibility criteria that align with individual program needs. Many programs offer priority enrollment to children with limited English proficiency.

3 Most programs operate 2.5 hours per day and 4 days per week.

4 The yearly Pre-K schedule is need based. Most programs operate for the academic year. Children in center-based programs were served an average of 38.8 hours per month for 7.3 months out of the year.

5 Teachers in Title I schools must fulfill degree requirements set forth by Title I.

6 Programs must provide a rationale for class size and staff-child ratio. The state recommends that they follow NAEYC guidelines, and in 2002–2003 all sites maintained a staff-child ratio of 1:8 or better.

7 Support services include parenting support or training and parent involvement activities. Additionally, each program is required to have a parent involvement component that is sensitive to individual needs. A prescribed number of parent conferences is therefore deemed unnecessary. In 2002–2003, most programs provided home visits and parent conferences to the majority of families served.

New Hampshire

NO PROGRAM

ACCESS RANKING—4s	ACCESS RANKING—3s	RESOURCES RANKING
No Program		

ACCESS

Total state program enrollment - - - - - - - - - - - - - - - 0
School districts that offer state program - - - - - - - - - - NA
Income requirement - - - - - - - - - - - - - - - - - - - NA
Hours of operation - - - - - - - - - - - - - - - - - - - NA
Operating schedule - - - - - - - - - - - - - - - - - - - NA
Special education enrollment - - - - - - - - - - - - - 1,505
Federally funded Head Start enrollment - - - - - - - - - 1,306
State-funded Head Start enrollment - - - - - - - - - - - - 0

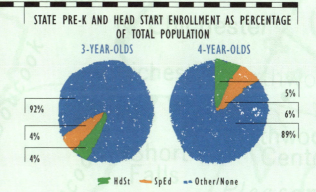

STATE PRE-K AND HEAD START ENROLLMENT AS PERCENTAGE OF TOTAL POPULATION

3-YEAR-OLDS
92%
4%
4%

4-YEAR-OLDS
5%
6%
89%

● HdSt ● SpEd ● Other/None

QUALITY STANDARDS CHECKLIST

No Program

RESOURCES

Total state Pre-K spending - - - - - - - - - - - - - - - $0
Local match required? - - - - - - - - - - - - - - - - - NA
State spending per child enrolled - - - - - - - - - - - - $0
State Head Start spending - - - - - - - - - - - - $241,337
State spending per 3-year-old - - - - - - - - - - - - - $0
State spending per 4-year-old - - - - - - - - - - - - - $0

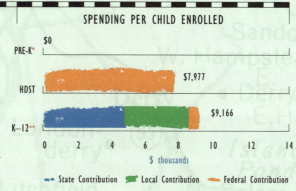

SPENDING PER CHILD ENROLLED

PRE-K* $0
HDST $7,977
K–12** $9,166

0 2 4 6 8 10 12 14
$ thousands

●- State Contribution ● Local Contribution ● Federal Contribution

* Pre-K programs may receive additional funds from federal or local sources that are not included in this figure.
** K–12 expenditures include capital spending as well as current operating expenditures.

Data are for the '02–'03 school year, unless otherwise noted.

New Jersey

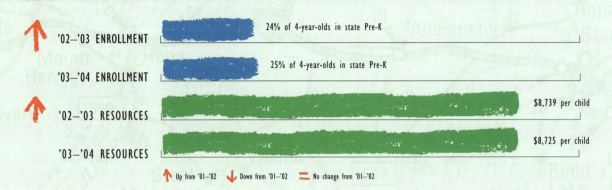

'02–'03 ENROLLMENT — 24% of 4-year-olds in state Pre-K

'03–'04 ENROLLMENT — 25% of 4-year-olds in state Pre-K

'02–'03 RESOURCES — $8,739 per child

'03–'04 RESOURCES — $8,725 per child

↑ Up from '01–'02   ↓ Down from '01–'02   ═ No change from '01–'02

I n 1998, the New Jersey Supreme Court mandated that all children in the state's 30 highest poverty districts—known as Abbott districts—be provided with a high-quality preschool education to prepare them with the skills and abilities necessary for success in elementary school. The result of this ruling is that quality preschool programs are offered to all 3- and 4-year-old children in districts where at least 40 percent of the children qualify for free or reduced-price lunch. Funds from the Department of Education are used by public schools, Head Start programs, and private child care centers to provide full-day services (6 hours per day). Additional money from the Department of Human Services funds extended-day services. The school districts are responsible for ensuring that individual programs meet the standards set out by the state Supreme Court. These standards include requirements regarding teacher certification, curriculum, class size, facilities, and comprehensive services. The Abbott program now supplies full funding for teacher salaries, providing qualified teachers in private centers with salaries comparable to the public schools. The program was expanded to include one additional district in summer 2004.

In addition to the Abbott prekindergarten initiative, state funds are provided for Non-Abbott Early Childhood Program Aid (ECPA), which allow an additional 102 districts to offer half-day preschool mostly to 4-year-olds. Funds through this initiative are available to districts in which 20 to 40 percent of the children qualify for free or reduced-price lunch. The majority of programs are in public schools, but some operate in Head Start or private child care centers. Districts that receive ECPA funds are also required to provide full-day kindergarten. While primarily used to provide preschool and full-day kindergarten services, some ECPA funds are used for grades 1 to 3.

New Jersey is working toward improving quality in the ECPA districts by aligning standards with the high-quality program standards for the Abbott districts. The development of Abbott and Non-Abbott versions of the Preschool Program Implementation Guidelines provides districts with guidance for implementing state expectations and the enhancement of quality preschool programs. In addition, revisions to state code regulating the ECPA program were presented to the State Board of Education in September 2004.

In 2003–2004, Abbott programs received $365 million in state funds from the Department of Education to serve 37,765 children (supplemented by $114.5 million from the Department of Human Services). ECPA received an estimated $30 million to serve 7,509 children. Also, New Jersey is seeking to expand access to preschool for 4-year-olds through the new Early Launch to Learning Initiative (ELLI). The state has set aside $15 million to potentially serve another 4,000 low-income preschoolers throughout the state in fiscal year 2005.

Although most states have a single state-financed prekindergarten initiative, New Jersey makes significant contributions to prekindergarten through two separate initiatives—the Abbott program and ECPA. As a result, in the first two pages of this profile we present summary information reflecting the state's overall commitment to prekindergarten. Enrollment and state spending for both the Abbott and ECPA initiatives are taken into account. Next, we present specific details about each initiative in the state. The third page of this profile focuses exclusively on the Abbott program, while the final page focuses exclusively on the ECPA program.

STATE OVERVIEW

Total state program enrollment- - - - - - - - - - - - - 43,678

Total state spending - - - - - - - - - - - - - - - $381,704,925

State spending per child enrolled - - - - - - - - - - - $8,739

State spending per 3-year-old - - - - - - - - - - - - $1,373

State spending per 4-year-old - - - - - - - - - - - - $2,009

SPENDING PER CHILD ENROLLED

NJ PGRMS* — $8,739

HDST — $8,392

K–12** — $11,616

0   2   4   6   8   10   12   14
$ thousands

-- State Contribution   Local Contribution   -- Federal Contribution

* Pre-K programs may receive additional funds from federal or local sources that are not included in this figure.

** K–12 expenditures include capital spending as well as current operating expenditures.

Data are for the '02–'03 school year, unless otherwise noted.

ACCESS RANKING—4s	ACCESS RANKING—3s	RESOURCES RANKING

NEW JERSEY ABBOTT PRESCHOOL PROGRAM

ACCESS

Total state program enrollment - - - - - - - - - - - - - - 36,465
School districts that offer state program - - - - - - - - - 6%
Income requirement - - - - - - - - - - - - - - - - - - - None [1]
Hours of operation - - - - - - - - - - - - - - - Full-day, full-week
Operating schedule - - - - - - - - - - - - Determined locally [2]
Special education enrollment - - - - - - - - - - - - - 9,304
Federally funded Head Start enrollment - - - - - - - - - 13,141
State-funded Head Start enrollment - - - - - - - - - - - - 0

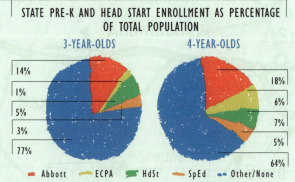

STATE PRE-K AND HEAD START ENROLLMENT AS PERCENTAGE OF TOTAL POPULATION

3-YEAR-OLDS: 14%, 1%, 5%, 3%, 77%
4-YEAR-OLDS: 18%, 6%, 7%, 5%, 64%

■ Abbott ■ ECPA ■ HdSt ■ SpEd ■ Other/None

QUALITY STANDARDS CHECKLIST

POLICY	STATE PRE-K REQUIREMENT	BENCHMARK	DOES REQUIREMENT MEET BENCHMARK?
Curriculum standards	Comprehensive	Comprehensive	✓
Teacher degree requirement	BA [3]	BA	✓
Teacher specialized training requirement	EC certificate [3]	Specializing in Pre-K	✓
Assistant teacher degree requirement	HSD	CDA or equivalent	☐
Teacher in-service requirement	100 clock hours/5 years	At least 15 hours/year	✓
Maximum class size		20 or lower	✓
3-year-olds	15		
4-year-olds	15		
Staff-child ratio		1:10 or better	✓
3-year-olds	2:15		
4-year-olds	2:15		
Screening/referral requirements	Vision, hearing, health, and developmental	Vision, hearing, and health	✓
Required support services	Support services [4]	At least 1 service	✓
Meal requirement	Breakfast, lunch, and snack	At least 1/day	✓

TOTAL: 9 of 10

RESOURCES

Total state Pre-K spending - - - - - - - - - - - - $351,704,925 [5]
Local match required? - - - - - - - - - - - - - - - - - - No
State spending per child enrolled - - - - - - - - - - - - $9,645
State spending per 3-year-old - - - - - - - - - - - - - $1,349
State spending per 4-year-old - - - - - - - - - - - - - $1,768

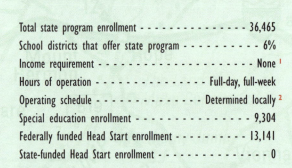

SPENDING PER CHILD ENROLLED

ABBOTT* — $9,645
HDST — $8,392
K–12** — $11,616

$ thousands

■ State Contribution ■ Local Contribution ■ Federal Contribution

* Pre-K programs may receive additional funds from federal or local sources that are not included in this figure.
** K–12 expenditures include capital spending as well as current operating expenditures.

Data are for the '02–'03 school year, unless otherwise noted.

1 While there are no income eligibility criteria for individual children, only districts where at least 40 percent of children qualify for free or reduced-price lunch receive funding through this initiative. All 3- and 4-year-old children within those districts are eligible to participate.
2 Programs are required to operate for a minimum of 6 hours per day, 180 days per year. Funds from the Department of Human Services are combined with Department of Education funds to operate year-round programs that provide services for up to 10 hours per day.
3 Teachers who worked in center-based programs before the degree requirement was implemented and have made sufficient progress toward the BA must meet the degree requirement by September 2006.
4 Support services include parent involvement activities, health services for children, information about nutrition, referral to social services, and transition to kindergarten activities. All programs conduct parent conferences, although the required number of annual conferences is not specified.
5 This total does not include $121 million from the Department of Human Services used to fund extended-day services.

NEW JERSEY NON-ABBOTT EARLY CHILDHOOD PROGRAM AID

ACCESS

Total state program enrollment - - - - - - - - - - - - - 7,213
School districts that offer state program - - - - - - - - - - 19%
Income requirement - - - - - - - - - - - - - - - - - - None [1]
Hours of operation - - - - - - - - - - - - - Half-day, full-week [2]
Operating schedule - - - - - - - - - - - - - - - Academic year
Special education enrollment - - - - - - - - - - - - - 9,304
Federally funded Head Start enrollment - - - - - - - - 13,141
State-funded Head Start enrollment - - - - - - - - - - - - 0

STATE PRE-K AND HEAD START ENROLLMENT AS PERCENTAGE OF TOTAL POPULATION

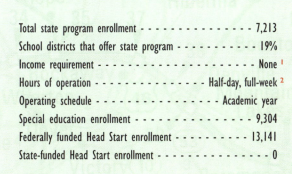

3-YEAR-OLDS

14%
1%
5%
3%
77%

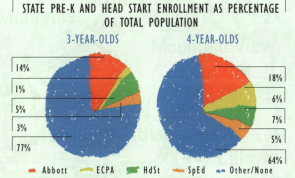

4-YEAR-OLDS

18%
6%
7%
5%
64%

● Abbott ● ECPA ● HdSt ● SpEd ● Other/None

QUALITY STANDARDS CHECKLIST

POLICY	STATE PRE-K REQUIREMENT	BENCHMARK	DOES REQUIREMENT MEET BENCHMARK?
Curriculum standards	Comprehensive	Comprehensive	✓
Teacher degree requirement	BA	BA	✓
Teacher specialized training requirement	Certification in EC or EE	Specializing in Pre-K	☐
Assistant teacher degree requirement	HSD	CDA or equivalent	☐
Teacher in-service requirement	100 clock hours/5 years	At least 15 hours/year	✓
Maximum class size		20 or lower	☐
3-year-olds	No limit		
4-year-olds	No limit		
Staff-child ratio		1:10 or better	☐
3-year-olds	No limit		
4-year-olds	No limit		
Screening/referral requirements	Vision, hearing, and health	Vision, hearing, and health	✓
Required support services	Support services [3]	At least 1 service	✓
Meal requirement	None	At least 1/day	☐

TOTAL:

5

of 10

RESOURCES

Total state Pre-K spending - - - - - - - - - - - - $30,000,000 [4]
Local match required? - - - - - - - - - - - - - - - - - - No
State spending per child enrolled - - - - - - - - - - - $4,159
State spending per 3-year-old - - - - - - - - - - - - $24
State spending per 4-year-old - - - - - - - - - - - - $241

SPENDING PER CHILD ENROLLED

ECPA* $4,159

HDST $8,392

K–12** $11,616

0   2   4   6   8   10   12   14
$ thousands

▬ State Contribution   ▬ Local Contribution   ▬ Federal Contribution

* Pre-K programs may receive additional funds from federal or local sources that are not included in this figure.
** K–12 expenditures include capital spending as well as current operating expenditures.

Data are for the '02–'03 school year, unless otherwise noted.

1 While there are no income eligibility criteria for individual children, only districts where 20 to 40 percent of children qualify for free or reduced-price lunch receive funding through this initiative. All 3- and 4-year-old children within those districts are eligible to participate.
2 Programs must operate a minimum of 3 hours per day.
3 Support services include education services or job training for parents, transition to kindergarten activities, and other services that are determined locally.
4 This figure is an estimate of state funds directed to services for preschool-age children.

New Mexico

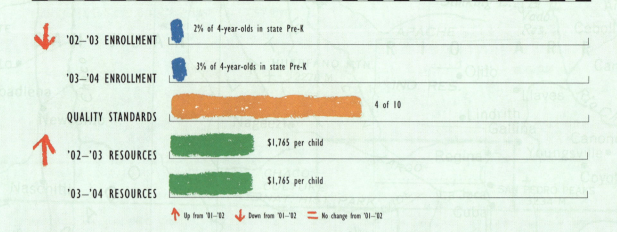

↓ '02–'03 ENROLLMENT	2% of 4-year-olds in state Pre-K
'03–'04 ENROLLMENT	3% of 4-year-olds in state Pre-K
QUALITY STANDARDS	4 of 10
↑ '02–'03 RESOURCES	$1,765 per child
'03–'04 RESOURCES	$1,765 per child

↑ Up from '01–'02   ↓ Down from '01–'02   ▬ No change from '01–'02

New Mexico began appropriating funds for the Child Development Program in 1991. These funds support prekindergarten as well as home visits, family support services, and other types of services for children from birth to age 5. The Child Development Program does not have specific income criteria but instead aims to serve children at risk who do not qualify for other eligibility-based programs. This allows for local flexibility, with enrollment priorities based on local needs. Groups that communities choose to target include children of teen parents, homeless families, families in poverty, or children with special emotional or mental health needs.

Prekindergarten classes funded by the program can be operated by public schools, private child care centers, or institutions of higher education. Programs are required to offer comprehensive services and work toward accreditation. The Child Development Program also funds home-based services such as Parents as Teachers programs and hospital-based services for high-risk infants.

All programs that children attend on a regular basis are required to use the Focused Portfolio System, which assists teachers in observing and documenting children's cognitive, social, emotional, and physical development, and in planning appropriate activities.

In 2003–2004, state funding of $1,499,900 provided for an enrollment of 850 children.

New Mexico also dedicates funds to enhance services in federal Head Start classrooms. During fiscal year 2003, the state supplement to Head Start totaled $1.65 million.

ACCESS RANKING—4s	ACCESS RANKING—3s	RESOURCES RANKING
34	23	33

ACCESS

Total state program enrollment - - - - - - - - - - - - - - - 850 [1]

School districts that offer state program - - - - - - - - - - 17%

Income requirement - None

Hours of operation - - - - - - - - - - - - - Determined locally

Operating schedule - - - - - - - - - - - - Determined locally [2]

Special education enrollment - - - - - - - - - - - - - - 3,116

Federally funded Head Start enrollment - - - - - - - - - 7,031

State-funded Head Start enrollment - - - - - - - - - - - - - 0

STATE PRE-K AND HEAD START ENROLLMENT AS PERCENTAGE OF TOTAL POPULATION

3-YEAR-OLDS

86%
4%
9%
1%

4-YEAR-OLDS

2%
18%
8%
72%

HdSt   Pre-K   SpEd   Other/None

QUALITY STANDARDS CHECKLIST

POLICY	STATE PRE-K REQUIREMENT	BENCHMARK	DOES REQUIREMENT MEET BENCHMARK?
Curriculum standards - - - - - - - - - - -	Not comprehensive	Comprehensive	☐
Teacher degree requirement - - - - - - - - - - - - - - -	None	BA	☐
Teacher specialized training requirement - - - - - - - - -	None	Specializing in Pre-K	☐
Assistant teacher degree requirement - - - - - - - - -	None	CDA or equivalent	☐
Teacher in-service requirement - - - - - - - -	24 clock hours	At least 15 hours/year	☑
Maximum class size		20 or lower	☐
3-year-olds - - - - - - - - - - - - - - - - - - -	24 [3]		
4-year-olds - - - - - - - - - - - - - - - - - - -	24 [3]		
Staff-child ratio		1:10 or better	☐
3-year-olds - - - - - - - - - - - - - - - - - - -	1:12 [3]		
4-year-olds - - - - - - - - - - - - - - - - - - -	1:12 [3]		
Screening/referral requirements - - - -	Vision, hearing, and health	Vision, hearing, and health	☑
Required support services - - - - - - - - -	2 parent conferences and support services [4]	At least 1 service	☑
Meal requirement - - - - - - - - - - - - - -	At least 1 meal [5]	At least 1/day	☑

TOTAL:

4

of 10

RESOURCES

Total state Pre-K spending - - - - - - - - - - - - - - $1,499,900

Local match required? - No

State spending per child enrolled - - - - - - - - - - - - $1,765

State Head Start spending - - - - - - - - - - - - - - $1,650,000

State spending per 3-year-old - - - - - - - - - - - - - $14 [6]

State spending per 4-year-old - - - - - - - - - - - - - $44 [6]

SPENDING PER CHILD ENROLLED

PRE-K* $1,765

HDST $6,646

K–12** $8,712

0   2   4   6   8   10   12   14
$ thousands

State Contribution   Local Contribution   Federal Contribution

* Pre-K programs may receive additional funds from federal or local sources that are not included in this figure.

** K–12 expenditures include capital spending as well as current operating expenditures.

Data are for the '02–'03 school year, unless otherwise noted.

[1] This enrollment total includes children from birth to age 5. Some of the infants and toddlers received home-visiting or hospital-based services rather than attending center-based programs.

[2] Most programs operate year-round.

[3] These figures represent state child care licensing regulations. Child Development programs are required by contract to be accredited or working toward accreditation. Out of the 18 center-based programs in operation during 2002–2003, 10 are either accredited or awaiting validation. These 10 programs maintain lower class sizes and child-staff ratios than licensing regulations require.

[4] Support services include parenting support or training, parent involvement activities, referral to social services, transition to kindergarten activities, and child assessments.

[5] Center-based programs that meet for at least a half-day session must provide meals. The home-visiting and hospital-based programs funded by this initiative are not required to offer meals.

[6] New Mexico did not break its total enrollment figure into specific numbers of 3- or 4-year-olds. As a result, these calculations are estimates, based on proportions of enrollees who were ages 3 and 4 in states that served 3-year-olds and provided age breakdowns for 2002–2003. Although New Mexico's Pre-K program served children younger than age 3, for the purposes of these calculations we considered all children to be ages 3 or 4. This likely results in overestimates of spending per 3-year-old and spending per 4-year-old.

New York

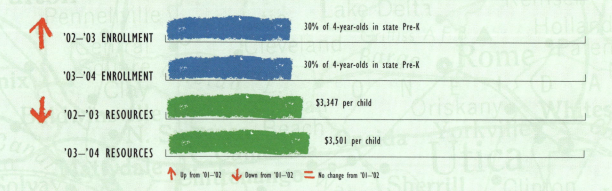

↑ '02–'03 ENROLLMENT	30% of 4-year-olds in state Pre-K
'03–'04 ENROLLMENT	30% of 4-year-olds in state Pre-K
↓ '02–'03 RESOURCES	$3,347 per child
'03–'04 RESOURCES	$3,501 per child

↑ Up from '01–'02   ↓ Down from '01–'02   ═ No change from '01–'02

I n 1966, the New York state Legislature created and began funding the Experimental Prekindergarten program (EPK), a half-day preschool program similar to Head Start. This program serves 4-year-olds living in one of 97 districts that were selected to be phased in as the program was implemented. Priority is given to children from economically disadvantaged families, including families eligible for free or reduced-price lunch, TANF, food stamps, or one of several additional federal programs supporting low-income families. EPK seeks to provide comprehensive services such as social services, nutritional information and family involvement opportunities. All programs are operated by public schools, and teachers are required to have a Master's degree (unless they had a Bachelor's degree prior to 1978). Teachers must also have certification in Nursery–Grade 6 or, if certified after February 2004, Birth–Grade 2. State funding for EPK peaked at $54 million in fiscal year 1995, but the program has experienced flat or reduced funding in subsequent years. Effective with the 2003–2004 budget, the EPK initiative has been renamed the Targeted Prekindergarten Program. For the corresponding program year, $50.2 million was appropriated to support a projected enrollment of 1,336 3-year-olds and 12,482 4-year-olds.

A second state-funded prekindergarten initiative—the Universal Prekindergarten program (UPK)—was established in 1997 with the goal of making prekindergarten accessible to all 4-year-olds in New York state. School districts were to give priority to economically disadvantaged children during the initial stages of implementation and then gradually increase access so that by 2002 the program would be available to all 4-year-olds whose families wanted to participate. However, planned program expansion has not occurred, as in recent years UPK state funding has been level. To date, the program reaches only about one-quarter of the state's 4-year-olds, primarily serving children from low-income families.

UPK funds flow through public schools, although at least 10 percent of funds must go to subcontracts with Head Start, private child care providers, or other community-based organizations. In practice, more than half of UPK funds are subcontracted to these agencies. All public school teachers in the UPK program must meet the same degree and certification requirements that apply to teachers in the EPK program. As of September 2004, teachers in community-based UPK programs will be required to have these same credentials as well.

During the 2003–2004 year, the state appropriated $204.7 million for UPK, with a projected enrollment of 58,984 4-year-olds.

Although most states have a single state-financed prekindergarten initiative, New York makes significant contributions to prekindergarten through two separate initiatives—EPK and UPK. As a result, in the first two pages of this profile we present summary information reflecting the state's overall commitment to prekindergarten. Enrollment and state spending for both the EPK and UPK initiatives are taken into account. Next, we present specific details about each initiative in the state. The third page of this profile focuses exclusively on the UPK program, while the final page focuses exclusively on the EPK program.

STATE OVERVIEW

Total state program enrollment- - - - - - - - - - - - - - 72,652

Total state spending - - - - - - - - - - - - - - - - - - $243,200,000

State spending per child enrolled - - - - - - - - - - - - $3,347

State spending per 3-year-old - - - - - - - - - - - - $20

State spending per 4-year-old - - - - - - - - - - - - - $996

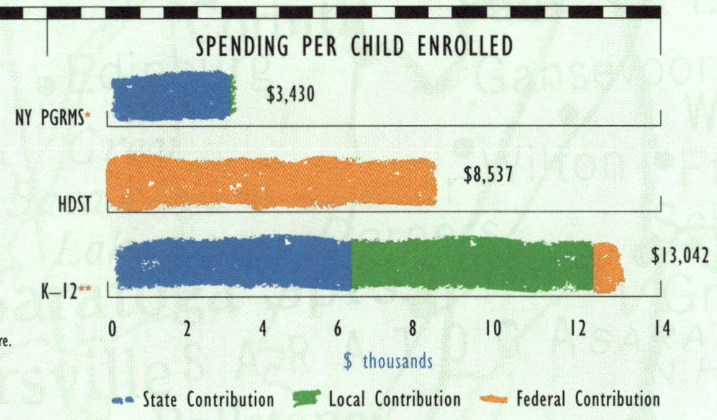

* Pre-K programs may receive additional funds from federal or local sources that are not included in this figure.

** K–12 expenditures include capital spending as well as current operating expenditures.

Data are for the '02–'03 school year, unless otherwise noted.

SPENDING PER CHILD ENROLLED

NY PGRMS* — $3,430

HDST — $8,537

K–12** — $13,042

$ thousands

0   2   4   6   8   10   12   14

■– State Contribution   ■ Local Contribution   ■– Federal Contribution

ACCESS RANKING—4s	ACCESS RANKING—3s	RESOURCES RANKING
5	25	16

ACCESS

Total state program enrollment - - - - - - - - - - - - - - - 58,460

School districts that offer state program - - - - - - - - - 28%

Income requirement - None

Hours of operation - - - - - - - - - - - - Determined locally [1]

Operating schedule - - - - - - - - - - - - - - Academic year

Special education enrollment - - - - - - - - - - - - - - 53,735

Federally funded Head Start enrollment - - - - - - - - - 41,496

State-funded Head Start enrollment - - - - - - - - - - - - 0

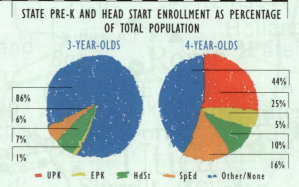

STATE PRE-K AND HEAD START ENROLLMENT AS PERCENTAGE OF TOTAL POPULATION

3-YEAR-OLDS
86%
6%
7%
1%

4-YEAR-OLDS
44%
25%
5%
10%
16%

■ UPK ■ EPK ■ HdSt ■ SpEd ■ Other/None

QUALITY STANDARDS CHECKLIST

POLICY	STATE PRE-K REQUIREMENT	BENCHMARK	DOES REQUIREMENT MEET BENCHMARK?
Curriculum standards	Comprehensive	Comprehensive	✓
Teacher degree requirement	BA prior to 1978, MA after (public); None (nonpublic) [2]	BA	☐ [2]
Teacher specialized training req.	Certification in N–6 (public), 9 credits toward CDA (nonpublic) [2,3]	Specializing in Pre-K	☐ [2]
Assistant teacher degree requirement	HSD + 6 credits in EC or related field (public)[4], HSD (nonpublic)	CDA or equivalent	☐
Teacher in-service requirement	175 clock hours/5 years	At least 15 hours/year	✓
Maximum class size		20 or lower	✓
3-year-olds	NA		
4-year-olds	20		
Staff-child ratio		1:10 or better	✓
3-year-olds	NA		
4-year-olds	1:9 or 3:20		
Screening/referral requirements	None [5]	Vision, hearing, and health	☐
Required support services	Support services [6]	At least 1 service	✓
Meal requirement	Varies [7]	At least 1/day	☐

TOTAL:

5

of 10

RESOURCES

Total state Pre-K spending - - - - - - - - - - - - - $195,300,000

Local match required? - - - - - - - - - - - - - - - - - - - No

State spending per child enrolled - - - - - - - - - - - - $3,341

State spending per 3-year-old - - - - - - - - - - - - - - $0

State spending per 4-year-old - - - - - - - - - - - - - - $816

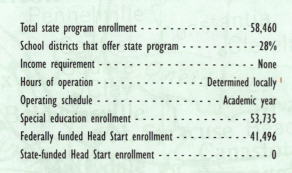

SPENDING PER CHILD ENROLLED

UPK* — $3,341

HDST — $8,537

K–12** — $13,042

0 2 4 6 8 10 12 14
$ thousands

■ State Contribution ■ Local Contribution ■ Federal Contribution

* Pre-K programs may receive additional funds from federal or local sources that are not included in this figure.

** K–12 expenditures include capital spending as well as current operating expenditures.

Data are for the '02–'03 school year, unless otherwise noted.

1 Programs may be full-day (5 hours) or half-day (2.5 hours). About 83% of enrollees attend a half-day program. All programs operate 5 days per week.
2 Effective in September 2005, UPK teachers in nonpublic school settings must meet the same degree and certification requirements as teachers in public school settings. When this requirement goes into effect, the UPK program will meet the NIEER benchmarks for teacher degree requirements and teacher specialized training requirements.
3 For the 2002–2003 school year, districts reported 80% of all UPK teachers to be state certified. In February 2004, the required certification changed to cover Birth–Grade 2.
4 Effective February 2004, assistant teachers in public schools must have a Level 1 certification (one year non-renewable), which requires a high school diploma or equivalent and passing of the Assessment of Teaching Assistant Skills Test.
5 UPK policy requires every child to have a signed medical statement stating that the child is free from contagious or communicable diseases and has been immunized in accordance with Public Health Law. If a child does not meet this requirement the family will be referred to resources in the community. The district does not directly provide the exam or immunizations.
6 Support services include parent involvement activities, referral to social services, transition to kindergarten activities, and other services determined by family needs. The number of required annual parent conferences or home visits is determined locally.
7 UPK programs operating less than 3 hours must provide a nutritional meal and/or snack. Programs operating more than 3 hours must provide appropriate meals and snacks to ensure that nutritional needs of children are met.

NEW YORK EXPERIMENTAL PREKINDERGARTEN

ACCESS

Total state program enrollment - - - - - - - - - - - - - - - 14,192

School districts that offer state program - - - - - - - - - - 14%

Income requirement - - - - - - - - - Economically disadvantaged [1]

Hours of operation - - - - - - - - - - - - - - Determined locally [2]

Operating schedule - - - - - - - - - - - - - - - - Academic year

Special education enrollment - - - - - - - - - - - - - - - 53,735

Federally funded Head Start enrollment - - - - - - - - - 41,496

State-funded Head Start enrollment - - - - - - - - - - - - - 0

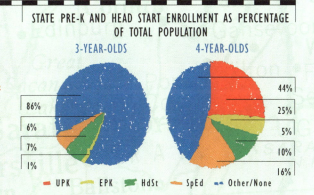

STATE PRE-K AND HEAD START ENROLLMENT AS PERCENTAGE OF TOTAL POPULATION

3-YEAR-OLDS

86%
6%
7%
1%

4-YEAR-OLDS

44%
25%
5%
10%
16%

■ UPK   ■ EPK   ■ HdSt   ■ SpEd   ■ Other/None

QUALITY STANDARDS CHECKLIST

POLICY	STATE PRE-K REQUIREMENT	BENCHMARK	DOES REQUIREMENT MEET BENCHMARK?
Curriculum standards	Comprehensive	Comprehensive	✓
Teacher degree requirement	BA prior to 1978, MA after	BA	✓
Teacher specialized training requirement	Certification in N–6 [3]	Specializing in Pre-K	✓
Assistant teacher degree requirement	HSD + 6 credits in EC or related field [4]	CDA or equivalent	☐
Teacher in-service requirement	175 clock hours/5 years	At least 15 hours/year	✓
Maximum class size		20 or lower	✓
3-year-olds	20		
4-year-olds	20		
Staff-child ratio		1:10 or better	✓
3-year-olds	1:9 or 3:20		
4-year-olds	1:9 or 3:20		
Screening/referral requirements	None	Vision, hearing, and health	☐
Required support services	Support services [5]	At least 1 service	✓
Meal requirement	At least 1 meal	At least 1/day	✓

TOTAL:

8

of 10

RESOURCES

Total state Pre-K spending - - - - - - - - - - - - - $47,900,000

Local match required? - Yes—at least 11% of funding must be local

State spending per child enrolled - - - - - - - - - - - $3,375

State spending per 3-year-old - - - - - - - - - - - - - - $20

State spending per 4-year-old - - - - - - - - - - - - - - $180

SPENDING PER CHILD ENROLLED

EPK* $3,798

HDST $8,537

K–12** $13,042

0   2   4   6   8   10   12   14

$ thousands

■ State Contribution   ■ Local Contribution   ■ Federal Contribution

* Pre-K programs may receive additional funds from federal or local sources that are not included in this figure.

** K–12 expenditures include capital spending as well as current operating expenditures.

Data are for the '02–'03 school year, unless otherwise noted.

[1] Economically disadvantaged is defined as applying to children whose families are eligible for some form of assistance such as free or reduced-price lunch, food stamps, Medicaid, unemployment compensation, or disability compensation.

[2] Programs may be full- or half-day, and operate 4 or 5 days per week.

[3] In February 2004, the required certification changed to cover Birth–Grade 2.

[4] Effective February 2004, assistant teachers must have a Level 1 certification (one year non-renewable), which requires a high school diploma or equivalent and passing the Assessment of Teaching Assistant Skills Test.

[5] Support services include parenting support or training, parent involvement activities, health services for children, and other services determined by family needs. The number of required annual parent conferences or home visits is determined locally.

North Carolina

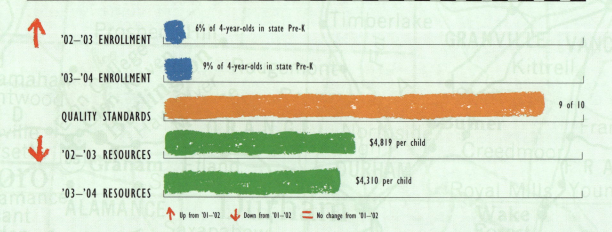

↑ '02–'03 ENROLLMENT	▮	6% of 4-year-olds in state Pre-K
'03–'04 ENROLLMENT	▮	9% of 4-year-olds in state Pre-K
QUALITY STANDARDS		9 of 10
↓ '02–'03 RESOURCES		$4,819 per child
'03–'04 RESOURCES		$4,310 per child

↑ Up from '01–'02　↓ Down from '01–'02　= No change from '01–'02

Established in 2001, *More at Four* provides prekindergarten for 4-year-olds considered at risk for future school failure. The program has grown rapidly over the past three years, offering an estimated 10,000 available slots in 2003–2004. Individual programs determine eligibility for services, but are required to consider family income and risk factors related to child health status, disability, parent education, family composition, parent employment, housing stability, and English proficiency. Programs may also offer enrollment to children based on minority status. First priority for enrollment is given to children who present risk factors but have not previously participated in an early childhood program. By the year 2004–2005, at least 80 percent of participants will be required to come from families at or below 75 percent of the state median income. The remaining 20 percent of enrollees may come from families with incomes up to 300 percent of the federal poverty level. To be eligible, children from these families must have one of the following risk factors: an identified disability, a chronic health condition, limited English proficiency, or an educational or developmental need.

School districts, child care centers, and Head Start agencies may receive funding to operate *More at Four* programs if they have a four- or five-star license—the top quality ratings under North Carolina's child care licensing system—or if they currently have three stars and are working toward four. All teachers must have a bachelor's degree with a Birth–K license, and programs are evaluated annually using assessments of both program quality and child developmental outcomes.

Funding for *More at Four* has increased to $43.1 million in 2003–2004, and will increase to approximately $50 million in 2004–2005, at which time the program is expected to serve 12,000 children.

Although *More at Four* is the focus of data in this report, North Carolina also funds Smart Start, a separate initiative begun in 1993, which supports local planning and collaboration to provide comprehensive early childhood services. Based on the needs of each county, Smart Start serves children from birth to age 5 and provides funds that may be used to increase child care quality, improve child health outcomes, provide family support services, or support prekindergarten programs. Funding for Smart Start in 2002–2003 was $198.6 million. After several budget cuts in preceding years, funding further decreased to $190.7 million in 2003–2004, and will remain level in 2004–2005.

ACCESS RANKING—4s	ACCESS RANKING—3s	RESOURCES RANKING
28	None Served	6

ACCESS

Total state program enrollment - - - - - - - - - - - - - - 6,271

School districts that offer state program - - - - - 91% (counties)

Income requirement - None [1]

Hours of operation - - - - - - - - - - - - - - Full-day, full-week

Operating schedule - - - - - - - - - - - - - - - Academic year

Special education enrollment - - - - - - - - - - - - - - 10,487

Federally funded Head Start enrollment - - - - - - - - 17,684

State-funded Head Start enrollment - - - - - - - - - - - - - 0

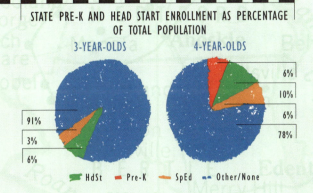

STATE PRE-K AND HEAD START ENROLLMENT AS PERCENTAGE OF TOTAL POPULATION

3-YEAR-OLDS   4-YEAR-OLDS

91%
3%
6%

6%
10%
6%
78%

HdSt   Pre-K   SpEd   Other/None

QUALITY STANDARDS CHECKLIST

POLICY	STATE PRE-K REQUIREMENT	BENCHMARK	DOES REQUIREMENT MEET BENCHMARK?
Curriculum standards	None	Comprehensive	☐
Teacher degree requirement	BA [2]	BA	☑
Teacher specialized training requirement	Birth–K license [2]	Specializing in Pre-K	☑
Assistant teacher degree requirement	CDA or meets NCLB regs. (public), CDA (nonpublic) [3]	CDA or equivalent	☑
Teacher in-service requirement	150 clock hours/5 years or 15 credit hours/5 years [4]	At least 15 hours/year	☑
Maximum class size			
3-year-olds	NA		
4-year-olds	18	20 or lower	☑
Staff-child ratio			
3-year-olds	NA		
4-year-olds	1:9	1:10 or better	☑
Screening/referral requirements	Vision, hearing, health, and dental	Vision, hearing, and health	☑
Required support services	Support services [5]	At least 1 service	☑
Meal requirement	Lunch and either breakfast or snack	At least 1/day	☑

TOTAL:

9

of 10

RESOURCES

Total state Pre-K spending - - - - - - - - - - - - - $30,217,723

Local match required? - - - - - - - - - - - - - - - - - - Yes [6]

State spending per child enrolled - - - - - - - - - - - - $4,819

State spending per 3-year-old - - - - - - - - - - - - - - - - $0

State spending per 4-year-old - - - - - - - - - - - - - - - $271

* Pre-K programs may receive additional funds from federal or local sources that are not included in this figure.

** K–12 expenditures include capital spending as well as current operating expenditures.

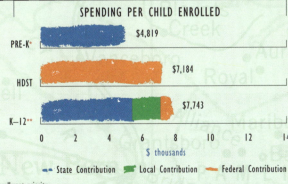

SPENDING PER CHILD ENROLLED

PRE-K* $4,819

HDST $7,184

K–12** $7,743

0   2   4   6   8   10   12   14
$ thousands

State Contribution   Local Contribution   Federal Contribution

Data are for the '02–'03 school year, unless otherwise noted.

1 In 2002–2003, low family income was one of the risk factors that could be considered for enrollment priority.

2 Providers are given 4 years to phase in the degree requirement after being recognized as a *More at Four* program. Teachers with degrees in other fields may be given provisional licenses, but must work toward a Birth–K license.

3 An AA in early childhood or child development is encouraged for assistant teachers in both public and private settings. Teachers in public schools must meet the employment provisions of the No Child Left Behind law, which generally requires that assistant teachers have at least a 2-year degree. Assistant teachers in public schools who meet NCLB employment provisions (with a BA or AA) but do not hold a CDA must also have 6 semesters of coursework in early childhood or 2 years in an early childhood classroom setting.

4 All licensed Pre-K teachers have a continuing education requirement to renew their licenses every 5 years. If they do not hold a Birth–K license, they must be working toward one at the rate of a minimum of 6 semester hours per year.

5 Support services include parent involvement activities and transition to kindergarten activities. Parent conferences are recommended but not required.

6 Legislation requires that local districts access resources other than state funding to support the program, but does not specify an amount of federal or local funds that must be used.

North Dakota

NO PROGRAM

ACCESS RANKING—4s	ACCESS RANKING—3s	RESOURCES RANKING
No Program		

ACCESS

Total state program enrollment - - - - - - - - - - - - - - - - 0

School districts that offer state program - - - - - - - - - - NA

Income requirement - NA

Hours of operation - NA

Operating schedule - NA

Special education enrollment - - - - - - - - - - - - - - - 788

Federally funded Head Start enrollment - - - - - - - - - 2,799

State-funded Head Start enrollment - - - - - - - - - - - - - - 0

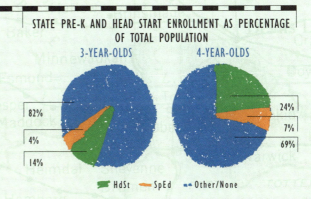

STATE PRE-K AND HEAD START ENROLLMENT AS PERCENTAGE OF TOTAL POPULATION

3-YEAR-OLDS

82%
4%
14%

4-YEAR-OLDS

24%
7%
69%

■ HdSt ■ SpEd -■- Other/None

QUALITY STANDARDS CHECKLIST

No Program

RESOURCES

Total state Pre-K spending - - - - - - - - - - - - - - - - $0

Local match required? - - - - - - - - - - - - - - - - - - - NA

State spending per child enrolled - - - - - - - - - - - - - $0

State spending per 3-year-old - - - - - - - - - - - - - - $0

State spending per 4-year-old - - - - - - - - - - - - - - $0

SPENDING PER CHILD ENROLLED

PRE-K* $0

HDST $7,084

K–12** $7,757

0   2   4   6   8   10   12   14

$ thousands

-■- State Contribution   ■ Local Contribution   -■- Federal Contribution

* Pre-K programs may receive additional funds from federal or local sources that are not included in this figure.

** K–12 expenditures include capital spending as well as current operating expenditures.

Data are for the '02–'03 school year, unless otherwise noted.

Ohio

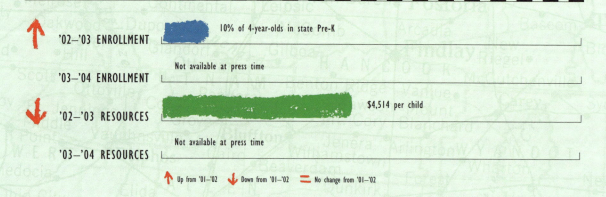

↑ '02–'03 ENROLLMENT	10% of 4-year-olds in state Pre-K
'03–'04 ENROLLMENT	Not available at press time
↓ '02–'03 RESOURCES	$4,514 per child
'03–'04 RESOURCES	Not available at press time

↑ Up from '01–'02   ↓ Down from '01–'02   ▬ No change from '01–'02

Following the success of pilot preschool programs initiated in 1986, Ohio's Public School Preschool Program was started in 1990. Only public schools, Joint Vocational Schools, and County Educational Service Centers can receive direct funding to operate programs. These entities are permitted to subcontract with Head Start and private child care centers, but few children enrolled are served in settings other than public schools. The program is open to 3- and 4-year-olds from families with incomes below 185 percent of the federal poverty level, with families between 100 and 185 percent of the poverty level paying fees on a sliding scale. Schools may also offer enrollment to children from families above the income cutoff, but generally support these slots using parent tuition and district funds.

In 2003–2004, the Public School Preschool Program served 8,543 children and received $18,638,180 in state funding.

Through a separate initiative, Ohio began supplementing the federal Head Start program with state funds in 1990. Recent years have seen most of these state funds replaced with federal welfare dollars, as well as cuts in overall spending and numbers of children served. With a combination of $69,229,403 in TANF and $18,402,753 in state general revenue funds, 17,284 children were served during fiscal year 2003. State Head Start funds are used to serve 3- and 4-year-olds in poverty and are provided to all but two of Ohio's federally funded Head Start programs. One Head Start program is completely funded through the state Head Start initiative.

The state recently developed a new initiative called Head Start Plus. This program is intended to meet the needs of working families and improve the school readiness of children in poverty by providing full-day, full-year services to 10,000 children through Head Start programs and Head Start partnerships with child care. Information about the impact of the Head Start Plus initiative will be available from the state at the conclusion of the 2004 fiscal year.

Although most states have a single state-financed prekindergarten initiative, Ohio makes significant contributions to prekindergarten through two separate initiatives—Public School Preschool and the state-funded Head Start model. As a result, in the first two pages of this profile we present summary information reflecting the state's overall commitment to prekindergarten. Enrollment and state spending for both the Public School Preschool and state-financed Head Start initiatives are taken into account. Next, we present specific details about each initiative in the state. The third page of this profile focuses exclusively on the Public School Preschool program, while the final page focuses exclusively on the state-funded Head Start program.

STATE OVERVIEW

Total state program enrollment - - - - - - - - - - - - - 23,543

Total state spending - - - - - - - - - - - - - - - - $106,270,336

State spending per child enrolled - - - - - - - - - - - $4,514

State Head Start spending - - - - - - - - - - - - - $87,632,156

State spending per 3-year-old - - - - - - - - - - - - $292

State spending per 4-year-old - - - - - - - - - - - - - $416

* Programs may receive additional funds from federal or local sources that are not included in this figure.

** K–12 expenditures include capital spending as well as current operating expenditures.

Data are for the '02–'03 school year, unless otherwise noted.

SPENDING PER CHILD ENROLLED

OH PGRMS* $4,514

FED. HDST $6,307

K–12** $9,988

0 2 4 6 8 10 12 14

$ thousands

State Contribution   Local Contribution   Federal Contribution   TANF Spending

ACCESS RANKING—4s	ACCESS RANKING—3s	RESOURCES RANKING
20	7	8

OHIO PUBLIC SCHOOL PRESCHOOL PROGRAM

ACCESS

Total state program enrollment - - - - - - - - - - - - 6,259 [1]

School districts that offer state program - - - - - 61% (counties)

Income requirement - - - - - - - - - - - - - - - - 185% FPL

Hours of operation - - - - - - - - - - - - - Determined locally [2]

Operating schedule - - - - - - - - - - - - Determined locally [2]

Special education enrollment - - - - - - - - - - - 10,526

Federally funded Head Start enrollment - - - - - - - - 34,347

State-funded Head Start enrollment - - - - - - - - - - 17,284 [3]

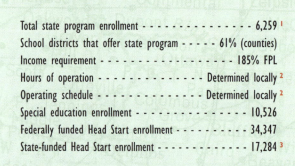
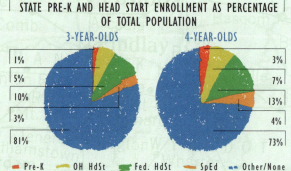

STATE PRE-K AND HEAD START ENROLLMENT AS PERCENTAGE OF TOTAL POPULATION

3-YEAR-OLDS

1%
5%
10%
3%
81%

4-YEAR-OLDS

3%
7%
13%
4%
73%

■ Pre-K ■ OH HdSt ■ Fed. HdSt ■ SpEd ■ Other/None

QUALITY STANDARDS CHECKLIST

POLICY	STATE PRE-K REQUIREMENT	BENCHMARK	DOES REQUIREMENT MEET BENCHMARK?
Curriculum standards - - - - - - - - - - - - -	Not comprehensive	Comprehensive	☐
Teacher degree requirement - -	AA + Pre-K Assoc. Level teaching cert. (public), CDA (nonpublic) [4]	BA	☐
Teacher specialized training requirement - - - -	Pre-K certification [5]	Specializing in Pre-K	☑
Assistant teacher degree requirement - - - - - - - - - - - - -	HSD	CDA or equivalent	☐
Teacher in-service requirement - - - - - - - - - - -	15 clock hours [6]	At least 15 hours/year	☑
Maximum class size		20 or lower	☐
3-year-olds - - - - - - - - - - - - - - - -	24		
4-year-olds - - - - - - - - - - - - - - - -	28		
Staff-child ratio		1:10 or better	☐
3-year-olds - - - - - - - - - - - - - - - -	1:12		
4-year-olds - - - - - - - - - - - - - - - -	1:14		
Screening/referral requirements - - - -	Vision, hearing, and health	Vision, hearing, and health	☑
Required support services - - - - - - - - - - - - -	2 home visits and support services [7]	At least 1 service	☑
Meal requirement - - - - - - - - - - - - - - -	Breakfast or lunch	At least 1/day	☑

TOTAL:

5

of 10

RESOURCES

Total state Pre-K spending - - - - - - - - - - - $18,638,180

Local match required? - - - - - - - - - - - - - - - - - No

State spending per child enrolled - - - - - - - - - - - $2,978 [8]

State Head Start spending - - - - - - - - - - - $87,632,156 [9]

State spending per 3-year-old - - - - - - - - - - - $31 [10]

State spending per 4-year-old - - - - - - - - - - - $93 [10]

SPENDING PER CHILD ENROLLED

PRE-K* $2,978

FED. HDST $6,307

K–12** $9,988

0 2 4 6 8 10 12 14
$ thousands

■ State Contribution ■ Local Contribution ■ Federal Contribution

* Pre-K programs may receive additional funds from federal or local sources that are not included in this figure.

** K–12 expenditures include capital spending as well as current operating expenditures.

Data are for the '02–'03 school year, unless otherwise noted.

1 An additional 2,284 children from families who exceed the income requirement are served in the Public School Preschool Program using parent fees and/or district funds.
2 Public School Preschool programs follow federal Head Start Performance Standards for minimum hours of operation and yearly operating schedule. Programs must operate for at least 3.5 hours per day, 4 days per week, and 32 weeks per year.
3 Ohio's state Head Start program did not break its enrollment figure into specific numbers of 3- and 4-year-olds. As a result, age breakdowns used in the Access table and pie chart were estimated, using proportions of federal Head Start enrollees in each age category.
4 Teachers in nonpublic schools were required to have or be working toward an AA by 2003. By 2007, all teachers must have obtained this degree.
5 License types offered include: Pre-K Associate (2-year level), Pre-K (4-year level), Kindergarten (with early childhood coursework), and the Early Childhood License (age 3–grade 3). Teachers can also qualify with a BA including 20 credits in early childhood plus a supervised practicum with preschoolers.
6 In-service requirements associated with renewal of licenses or certificates take precedence. In these circumstances, the specific requirements depend upon the type of license or certificate.
7 Support services include parenting support or training, parent involvement activities, health services for children, information about nutrition, referral to social services, transportation, and transition to kindergarten activities.
8 This calculation is based on a state-funded enrollment of 6,259.
9 This figure includes $69,229,403 in TANF funds.
10 The Public School Preschool Program did not break its total enrollment figure into specific numbers of 3- or 4-year-olds. These calculations are estimates, based on the proportions of enrollees who were ages 3 and 4 in states that served 3-year-olds and provided age breakdowns for 2002–2003.

OHIO STATE-FUNDED HEAD START MODEL

ACCESS

Total state program enrollment - - - - - - - - - - - - - 17,284 [1]

School districts that offer state program - - - - - 97% (counties)

Income req. - - - 90% of children must be at or below 185% FPL

Hours of operation - - - - - - - - - - - - - Determined locally [2]

Operating schedule - - - - - - - - - - - - - Determined locally [2]

Special education enrollment - - - - - - - - - - - - - 10,526

Federally funded Head Start enrollment - - - - - - - - 34,347

State-funded Head Start enrollment - - - - - - - - - - 17,284 [1]

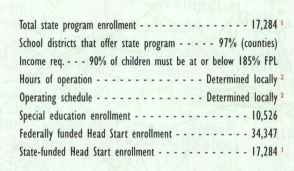
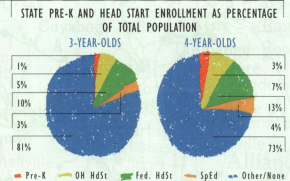

STATE PRE-K AND HEAD START ENROLLMENT AS PERCENTAGE OF TOTAL POPULATION

3-YEAR-OLDS: 1%, 5%, 10%, 3%, 81%

4-YEAR-OLDS: 3%, 7%, 13%, 4%, 73%

■ Pre-K ■ OH HdSt ■ Fed. HdSt ■ SpEd ■ Other/None

QUALITY STANDARDS CHECKLIST

POLICY	STATE PRE-K REQUIREMENT	BENCHMARK	DOES REQUIREMENT MEET BENCHMARK?
Curriculum standards	Not comprehensive	Comprehensive	☐
Teacher degree requirement	CDA [3]	BA	☐
Teacher specialized training req.	Meets CDA requirements	Specializing in Pre-K	☑
Assistant teacher degree requirement	HSD	CDA or equivalent	☐
Teacher in-service requirement	15 clock hours [4]	At least 15 hours/year	☑
Maximum class size		20 or lower	☑
3-year-olds	17		
4-year-olds	20		
Staff-child ratio		1:10 or better	☑
3-year-olds	2:17		
4-year-olds	1:10		
Screening/referral requirements	Vision, hearing, and health	Vision, hearing, and health	☑
Required support services	2 home visits and support services [5]	At least 1 service	☑
Meal requirement	Lunch and/or breakfast [6]	At least 1/day	☑

TOTAL:

7

of 10

RESOURCES

Total state Pre-K spending - - - - - - - - - - - - - $87,632,156 [7]

Local match required? - - - - - - - - - - - - - - - - - No

State spending per child enrolled - - - - - - - - - - - $5,070

State Head Start spending - - - - - - - - - - - - - $87,632,156 [8]

State spending per 3-year-old - - - - - - - - - - - - $261 [1]

State spending per 4-year-old - - - - - - - - - - - - $323 [1]

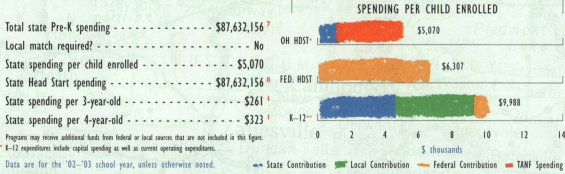

SPENDING PER CHILD ENROLLED

OH HDST* — $5,070

FED. HDST — $6,307

K–12** — $9,988

$ thousands (0, 2, 4, 6, 8, 10, 12, 14)

■◄ State Contribution   ■ Local Contribution   ■ Federal Contribution   ■ TANF Spending

* Programs may receive additional funds from federal or local sources that are not included in this figure.

** K–12 expenditures include capital spending as well as current operating expenditures.

Data are for the '02–'03 school year, unless otherwise noted.

[1] All state-funded Head Start enrollment is through Ohio's Head Start Model prekindergarten program. The state did not break program enrollment into specific numbers of 3- and 4-year-olds. As a result, age breakdowns used in the Access pie chart and Resources section were estimated, using proportions of federal Head Start enrollees in each age category. Estimates in the Resources section include TANF Funds.

[2] Ohio Head Start programs follow federal Head Start Performance Standards, which require center-based programs to operate for at least 3.5 hours per day, 4 days per week, and for 32 weeks per year.

[3] As of 2003, the Ohio DOE requires all classroom teachers to be working toward obtaining an AA. All teachers are required to have obtained degrees by 2007.

[4] In-service requirements associated with renewal of licenses or certificates take precedence. In these circumstances, the specific requirements depend upon the type of license or certificate.

[5] Support services include parenting support or training, parent involvement activities, health services for children, information about nutrition, referral to social services, transportation, and transition to kindergarten activities.

[6] Federal Head Start Performance Standards require that part-day programs provide children with at least one-third of their daily nutritional needs, as determined by the USDA. Full-day programs must provide one-half to two-thirds of daily nutritional needs, depending upon program length. All children in morning center-based settings must be given the opportunity to eat a nutritious breakfast.

[7] This figure includes $69,229,403 in TANF funds.

[8] All spending through this initiative is directed toward Head Start programs.

Oklahoma

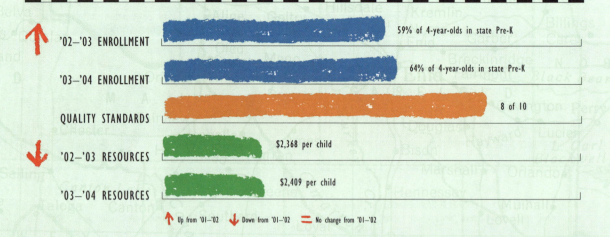

↑ '02–'03 ENROLLMENT	59% of 4-year-olds in state Pre-K
'03–'04 ENROLLMENT	64% of 4-year-olds in state Pre-K
QUALITY STANDARDS	8 of 10
↓ '02–'03 RESOURCES	$2,368 per child
'03–'04 RESOURCES	$2,409 per child

↑ Up from '01–'02   ↓ Down from '01–'02   ▬ No change from '01–'02

Oklahoma has been providing prekindergarten for 4-year-olds since 1980 when the state Legislature appropriated funds for a pilot program. This initiative continued until 1990 when additional legislation broadened the program to include 4-year-olds eligible for Head Start. Since 1998, the Early Childhood Four-Year-Old program has further expanded eligibility criteria to include all 4-year-old children whose parents wish them to attend. The number of districts offering prekindergarten and the number of children participating have steadily increased, and in 2002–2003 Oklahoma ranked first in the nation for the percentage of 4-year-olds enrolled.

Districts that choose to provide prekindergarten are reimbursed through the school funding formula for each child enrolled. The funding amount varies depending on whether schools offer a half-day program or a full-day program. The large majority of participating children are served in public schools, but some local districts collaborate with child care centers, Head Start programs and other community-based organizations to provide services.

All prekindergarten teachers, regardless of the setting in which prekindergarten is offered, are required to have a bachelor's degree with certification in early childhood education and are paid on the same salary scale as other public school teachers in higher grades.

The Early Childhood Four-Year-Old Program was funded at $72,703,361 and served 30,180 children during the 2003–2004 school year.

Oklahoma also provides state supplement funds to some federal Head Start grantees. In fiscal year 2003, $3.3 million was appropriated to Head Start programs to support additional enrollment, expanded services, and extended program hours.

ACCESS RANKING—4s	ACCESS RANKING—3s	RESOURCES RANKING
1	None Served	29

ACCESS

Total state program enrollment - - - - - - - - - - - - - - - 28,060
School districts that offer state program - - - - - - - - - - - 91%
Income requirement - - - - - - - - - - - - - - - - - - - None
Hours of operation - - - - - - - - - - - - - Determined locally [1]
Operating schedule - - - - - - - - - - - - - - - Academic year
Special education enrollment - - - - - - - - - - - - - - - 3,952
Federally funded Head Start enrollment - - - - - - - - - 14,543
State-funded Head Start enrollment - - - - - - - - - - - - 105 [2]

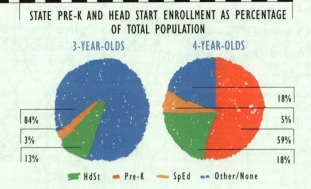

STATE PRE-K AND HEAD START ENROLLMENT AS PERCENTAGE OF TOTAL POPULATION

3-YEAR-OLDS
84%
3%
13%

4-YEAR-OLDS
18%
5%
59%
18%

■ HdSt   ■ Pre-K   ■ SpEd   ■ Other/None

QUALITY STANDARDS CHECKLIST

POLICY	STATE PRE-K REQUIREMENT	BENCHMARK	DOES REQUIREMENT MEET BENCHMARK?
Curriculum standards - - - - - - - - - - - - - -	Comprehensive	Comprehensive	✓
Teacher degree requirement - - - - - - - - - - - - -	BA	BA	✓
Teacher specialized training requirement - - - - - -	EC certificate	Specializing in Pre-K	✓
Assistant teacher degree requirement - - - - - - - -	GED or HSD	CDA or equivalent	☐
Teacher in-service requirement - - - - - - - - -	15 clock hours	At least 15 hours/year	✓
Maximum class size		20 or lower	✓
3-year-olds -	NA		
4-year-olds - - - - - - - - - - - - - - - - - - -	20		
Staff-child ratio		1:10 or better	✓
3-year-olds -	NA		
4-year-olds - - - - - - - - - - - - - - - - - - -	1:10		
Screening/referral requirements - - - - - - -	Determined locally	Vision, hearing, and health	☐
Required support services - - - - - - - - - - -	Support services [3]	At least 1 service	✓
Meal requirement - - - - - - - - - -	Breakfast, lunch, and snack [4]	At least 1/day	✓

TOTAL:
8
of 10

RESOURCES

Total state Pre-K spending - - - - - - - - - - - - - $66,439,166
Local match required? - - - - - - - - - - - - - - - - - - No
State spending per child enrolled - - - - - - - - - - - $2,368
State Head Start spending - - - - - - - - - - - - - $3,300,000
State spending per 3-year-old - - - - - - - - - - - - - - $0
State spending per 4-year-old - - - - - - - - - - - - - $1,406

* Pre-K programs may receive additional funds from federal or local sources that are not included in this figure.
** K–12 expenditures include capital spending as well as current operating expenditures.

Data are for the '02–'03 school year, unless otherwise noted.

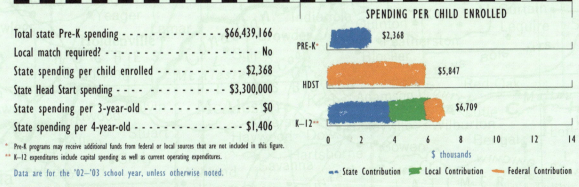

SPENDING PER CHILD ENROLLED

PRE-K* $2,368
HDST $5,847
K–12** $6,709

0   2   4   6   8   10   12   14
$ thousands

■■ State Contribution   ■■ Local Contribution   ■■ Federal Contribution

1 Half-day programs operate for 2.5 hours, while full-day programs operate for 6 hours. Many districts offer both full- and half-day programs. All programs must operate 5 days per week. Statewide, 15,746 children attend half-day programs, and 12,314 attend full-day programs.

2 Funds from Oklahoma's Head Start supplement were used mostly to enhance services. Some funds were also used to increase enrollment, although the state did not track the number of additional children served through its Head Start supplement. This figure is an estimate based on the number of non-ACYF funded children in Oklahoma reported in Head Start's 2002–2003 Program Information Report, and proportions of Oklahoma's federal Head Start enrollees who were 3 or 4 years old.

3 Support services include health services for children, transportation, and other services determined locally. Parent conferences are encouraged but not required; most programs offer two per year.

4 Pre-K programs are part of public school districts where breakfast and lunch are required to be made available for all children.

Oregon

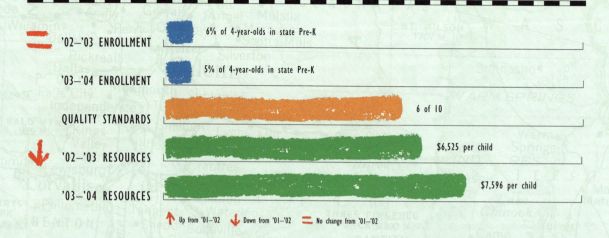

'02–'03 ENROLLMENT	6% of 4-year-olds in state Pre-K
'03–'04 ENROLLMENT	5% of 4-year-olds in state Pre-K
QUALITY STANDARDS	6 of 10
↓ **'02–'03 RESOURCES**	$6,525 per child
'03–'04 RESOURCES	$7,596 per child

↑ Up from '01–'02   ↓ Down from '01–'02   ═ No change from '01–'02

The Oregon Head Start Prekindergarten program, established in 1987, is modeled after the federal Head Start program and provides comprehensive child development services to the state's lowest income and highest need children. The state prekindergarten program has adopted the federal Head Start Performance Standards into state law in order to provide quality services for 3- and 4-year-olds from families with incomes below 100 percent of the federal poverty level. State funding is provided to all federal Head Start grantees, as well as some private, nonprofit organizations that do not receive federal Head Start funds but meet the required standards.

Although Oregon's vision is to eventually serve all preschool children in the Head Start Prekindergarten program, state funding was reduced by 8 percent for the 2003–2005 biennium, decreasing the number of slots available. Funding for 2003–2004 was estimated at $26.6 million, providing for 1,191 3-year-olds and 2,311 4-year-olds.

ACCESS RANKING—4s	ACCESS RANKING—3s	RESOURCES RANKING
27	10	3

ACCESS

Total state program enrollment - - - - - - - - - - - - - - 4,000

School districts that offer state program - - - - 100% (counties)

Income requirement - - 80% of children must be below 100% FPL [1]

Hours of operation - - - - - - - - - - - - - - Determined locally [2]

Operating schedule - - - - - - - - - - - - - Determined locally [2]

Special education enrollment - - - - - - - - - - - - - 4,513

Federally funded Head Start enrollment - - - - - - - - - 7,844

State-funded Head Start enrollment - - - - - - - - - - 4,000 [3]

STATE PRE-K AND HEAD START ENROLLMENT AS PERCENTAGE OF TOTAL POPULATION

3-YEAR-OLDS

87%
4%
6%
3%

4-YEAR-OLDS

6%
11%
6%
77%

■ HdSt   ■ Pre-K   ■ SpEd   ■ Other/None

QUALITY STANDARDS CHECKLIST

POLICY	STATE PRE-K REQUIREMENT	BENCHMARK	DOES REQUIREMENT MEET BENCHMARK?
Curriculum standards - - - - - - - - - - - - - - - - - - - None		Comprehensive	☐
Teacher degree requirement - - - - - BA (public), CDA (nonpublic) [4]		BA	☐
Teacher specialized training requirement - - - EC certificate (public), Meets CDA requirements (nonpublic) [4]		Specializing in Pre-K	☑
Assistant teacher degree requirement - - - - - - - HSD or GED [5]		CDA or equivalent	☐
Teacher in-service requirement - - - - - - - - - - - - - - None [6]		At least 15 hours/year	☐
Maximum class size		20 or lower	☑
3-year-olds - 17			
4-year-olds - 20			
Staff-child ratio		1:10 or better	☑
3-year-olds - 2:17			
4-year-olds - 1:10			
Screening/referral requirements - - - Hearing, vision, general health, dental, and immunization		Vision, hearing, and health	☑
Required support services - - - - - - - - - 4 parent conferences and support services [7]		At least 1 service	☑
Meal requirement - - - - - - Lunch and either breakfast or snack		At least 1/day	☑

TOTAL:

6

of 10

RESOURCES

Total state Pre-K spending - - - - - - - - - - - - - $26,100,000 [8]

Local match required? - - - - - - - - - - - - - - - - - - - No

State spending per child enrolled - - - - - - - - - - - $6,525

State Head Start spending - - - - - - - - - - - - $26,100,000 [8]

State spending per 3-year-old - - - - - - - - - - - - - $197

State spending per 4-year-old - - - - - - - - - - - - - $379

SPENDING PER CHILD ENROLLED

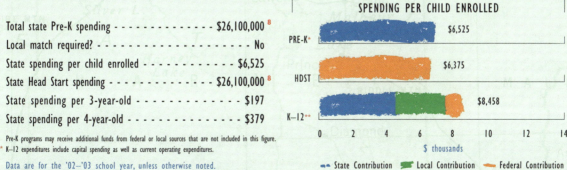

PRE-K* — $6,525

HDST — $6,375

K–12** — $8,458

0   2   4   6   8   10   12   14
$ thousands

■ State Contribution   ■ Local Contribution   ■ Federal Contribution

* Pre-K programs may receive additional funds from federal or local sources that are not included in this figure.

** K–12 expenditures include capital spending as well as current operating expenditures.

Data are for the '02–'03 school year, unless otherwise noted.

1 The federal poverty line is $15,020 for a family of three according to the DHHS (February 2002). This guideline was used for 2002–2003 enrollment. Although state law allows up to 20% of families enrolled to have incomes above the FPL, only 6% of enrolled children were from such families. These children generally had disabilities or were from isolated, rural areas.

2 Programs must be offered at least 3.5 hours per day, but are not funded to operate more than 6 hours per day. Most programs operate 3 to 4 days per week for the duration of the academic year.

3 This number represents enrollment in the Oregon Head Start Prekindergarten program. All state-funded Head Start enrollment is through this program.

4 In nonpublic schools, half of grantee teachers must have an AA or higher degree either in ECE or with a minimum of 15 ECE college credits. Teachers in classrooms run by agencies other than the public schools, even if located in public schools through a collaborative partnership, are not required to meet public school standards.

5 An assistant teacher paid through Title I funds must meet the Title I paraprofessional requirements, which include an AA degree or local district qualifying procedures.

6 Each program allocates 2.5% of its budget for training; these funds are used for professional development of staff.

7 Support services include parenting support or training, health services for children, information about nutrition, referral to social services, transition to kindergarten activities, mental health, and community partnerships. In addition, programs must follow all federal Head Start Performance Standards for comprehensive services including parent involvement activities.

8 This is the estimated state contribution to the Oregon Head Start Prekindergarten program, which is a state-funded Head Start model. All state Pre-K spending is therefore directed toward Head Start programs.

Pennsylvania

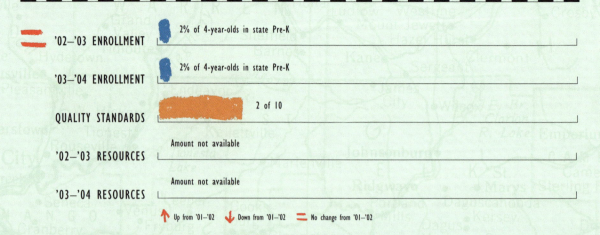

'02–'03 ENROLLMENT	2% of 4-year-olds in state Pre-K
'03–'04 ENROLLMENT	2% of 4-year-olds in state Pre-K
QUALITY STANDARDS	2 of 10
'02–'03 RESOURCES	Amount not available
'03–'04 RESOURCES	Amount not available

↑ Up from '01–'02   ↓ Down from '01–'02   ═ No change from '01–'02

Although Pennsylvania does not have a state-funded prekindergarten program, 6 percent of the state's school districts voluntarily provide a preschool education to 4-year-olds through a public school program known as Kindergarten for Four-Year-Olds. State law does not consider this program to be a distinct preschool initiative and the program does not require any specific early childhood standards.

In districts offering Kindergarten for Four-Year-Olds programs, the participants are included in the districts' daily membership counts and are partially funded through the state's basic instructional subsidy formula. Most districts provide additional funding for their programs through local taxes, Title I, or Head Start partnerships. In 2003–2004, districts served 2,438 children through this initiative.

Pennsylvania has taken steps to begin expanding prekindergarten opportunities and providing state funding for preschool. In 2004, the state Legislature approved a new Education Accountability Block Grant totaling $200 million, two-thirds of which will be dedicated to improving early childhood programs. Individual school districts determine how to target these funds and can use them for a range of purposes, including full-day kindergarten and reduced class sizes in grades K through 3, as well as prekindergarten.

This block grant will provide over $9 million to 40 school districts, allowing them to serve approximately 3,426 prekindergarten students. Thirteen districts will establish new prekindergarten programs using these funds.

Through a separate initiative, the state provided $2 million in fiscal year 2003 to support extended-day child care for Head Start participants. As a result of new funding initiatives, $15 million in state funds has been allocated for 2004–2005 to support Head Start programs. These funds are distributed through a competitive grant process and provide for increases in Head Start enrollment and extended program hours.

ACCESS RANKING—4s	ACCESS RANKING—3s	RESOURCES RANKING
37	None Served	NA

ACCESS

Total state program enrollment - - - - - - - - - - - - - - 2,609

School districts that offer state program - - - - - - - - - - 6%

Income requirement - None

Hours of operation - - - - - - - - - - - - - - Determined locally [1]

Operating schedule - - - - - - - - - - - - - - - - Academic year

Special education enrollment - - - - - - - - - - - - - - 14,947

Federally funded Head Start enrollment - - - - - - - - 26,101

State-funded Head Start enrollment - - - - - - - - - - - - 0 [2]

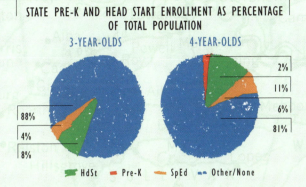

STATE PRE-K AND HEAD START ENROLLMENT AS PERCENTAGE OF TOTAL POPULATION

3-YEAR-OLDS

88%
4%
8%

4-YEAR-OLDS

2%
11%
6%
81%

■ HdSt ■ Pre-K ■ SpEd ▪▪ Other/None

QUALITY STANDARDS CHECKLIST

POLICY	STATE PRE-K REQUIREMENT	BENCHMARK	DOES REQUIREMENT MEET BENCHMARK?
Curriculum standards	Not comprehensive [3]	Comprehensive	☐
Teacher degree requirement	BA	BA	☑
Teacher specialized training requirement	Teaching license and certificate in ECE (Pre-K–3) or EE (K–6)	Specializing in Pre-K	☐
Assistant teacher degree requirement	NA [4]	CDA or equivalent	☐
Teacher in-service requirement	6 credit hours/5 years	At least 15 hours/year	☑
Maximum class size		20 or lower	☐
3-year-olds	NA		
4-year-olds	No limit		
Staff-child ratio		1:10 or better	☐
3-year-olds	NA		
4-year-olds	No limit		
Screening/referral requirements	Determined locally	Vision, hearing, and health	☐
Required support services	Determined locally [5]	At least 1 service	☐
Meal requirement	None	At least 1/day	☐

TOTAL:

2

of 10

RESOURCES

Total state Pre-K spending - - - - - - - - - - - Not available [6]

Local match required? - - - - - - - - - - - - - - - - - - - No

State spending per child enrolled - - - - - - - - Not available

State Head Start spending - - - - - - - - - - - - $2,000,000 [2]

State spending per 3-year-old - - - - - - - - - Not available

State spending per 4-year-old - - - - - - - - - Not available

* Data are not available.

** K–12 expenditures include capital spending as well as current operating expenditures.

Data are for the '02–'03 school year, unless otherwise noted.

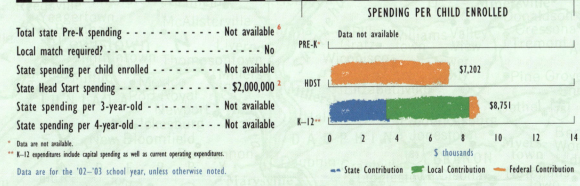

SPENDING PER CHILD ENROLLED

PRE-K* Data not available

HDST $7,202

K–12** $8,751

0 2 4 6 8 10 12 14

$ thousands

▪▪ State Contribution ■ Local Contribution ▪▪ Federal Contribution

1 Programs using basic education funding must operate at least 2.5 hours per day, but there is no maximum number of hours per day that a program may operate. Programs must operate at least 180 days per year.

2 In fiscal year 2003, the state provided $2,000,000 in federal TANF funds to extend the Head Start day, but data on the number of children served are not available. For 2003–2004, the state has allocated $15,000,000 for Head Start programs so they can offer extended-day services as well as serve additional children.

3 Comprehensive program standards were developed and offered to school districts as guidance in designing Pre-K programs under the state's new Education Accountability Block Grant.

4 Assistant teachers are not required in classrooms.

5 Districts design and manage their own support services, but there is no program-wide requirement.

6 For fiscal year 2003, money was available through the basic education formula to support prekindergarten programs, but the specific amount used for this purpose is not available.

Rhode Island

NO PROGRAM

Rhode Island does not have a standard state prekindergarten initiative that fits the definition used in this report. However, the state does support prekindergarten through several initiatives that aim to build on existing programs and resources.

The Early Childhood Investment Fund provides school districts with resources for a variety of purposes, including prekindergarten, before- and after-school care, extended-day kindergarten, class size reduction in elementary school, and parent education and family support programs. Districts determine how to use the funds, and in 2002–2003, six districts reported using a portion of these funds, in coordination with other resources, to finance preschool programs. These programs give priority to serving children with disabilities, children from disadvantaged backgrounds, and/or those whose first language is not English.

The state does not have specific standards for this particular initiative, but it does have standards that apply to all early childhood programs and meet most of the 10 benchmarks on NIEER's quality checklist. For example, the state requires head teachers to have bachelor's degrees with early childhood certification and staff–child ratios to be 1:9 for 3-year-olds and 1:10 for 4-year-olds.

A separate initiative, supported with CCDF quality funds, serves children ages 3 and 4 from low-income families. Rhode Island's Comprehensive Child Care Services Program (CCCSP) aims to promote high-quality, comprehensive early education services—modeled on Head Start—in community-based centers and family child care homes. There are 1,100 children receiving full-day, full-year services and 60 children receiving part-day, full-year services.

ACCESS RANKING—4s	ACCESS RANKING—3s	RESOURCES RANKING
	No Program	

ACCESS

Total state program enrollment - - - - - - - - - - - - - - - 0

School districts that offer state program - - - - - - - - - - NA

Income requirement - - - - - - - - - - - - - - - - - - - NA

Hours of operation - - - - - - - - - - - - - - - - - - - NA

Operating schedule - - - - - - - - - - - - - - - - - - - NA

Special education enrollment - - - - - - - - - - - - - 1,580

Federally funded Head Start enrollment - - - - - - - - 2,389

State-funded Head Start enrollment - - - - - - - - - - - 339 [1]

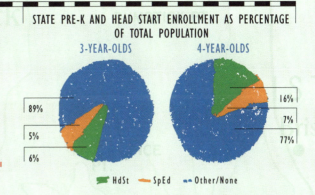

STATE PRE-K AND HEAD START ENROLLMENT AS PERCENTAGE OF TOTAL POPULATION

3-YEAR-OLDS   4-YEAR-OLDS

89%   16%
5%   7%
6%   77%

■ HdSt   ■ SpEd   ■ Other/None

QUALITY STANDARDS CHECKLIST

No Program

RESOURCES

Total state Pre-K spending - - - - - - - - - - - - - - - $0

Local match required? - - - - - - - - - - - - - - - - - NA

State spending per child enrolled - - - - - - - - - - - - $0

State Head Start spending - - - - - - - - - - - - $1,800,000

State spending per 3-year-old - - - - - - - - - - - - - $0

State spending per 4-year-old - - - - - - - - - - - - - $0

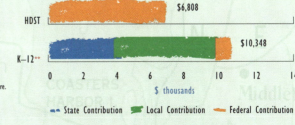

SPENDING PER CHILD ENROLLED

PRE-K* $0

HDST $6,808

K–12** $10,348

0   2   4   6   8   10   12   14
$ thousands

■- State Contribution   ■ Local Contribution   ■ Federal Contribution

* Pre-K programs may receive additional funds from federal or local sources that are not included in this figure.

** K–12 expenditures include capital spending as well as current operating expenditures.

Data are for the '02–'03 school year, unless otherwise noted.

1 Rhode Island was not able to break its state-funded Head Start enrollment down by single year of age. As a result, this figure is an estimate based on the percentage of federal Head Start enrollees in Rhode Island who were 3 or 4 years old.

South Carolina

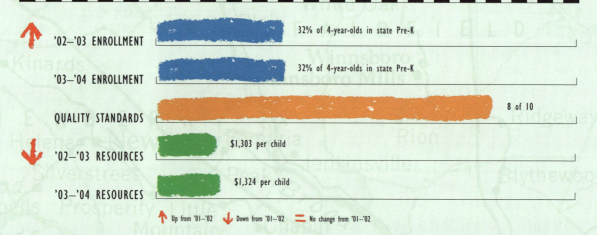

↑ '02–'03 ENROLLMENT		32% of 4-year-olds in state Pre-K
'03–'04 ENROLLMENT		32% of 4-year-olds in state Pre-K
QUALITY STANDARDS		8 of 10
↓ '02–'03 RESOURCES		$1,303 per child
'03–'04 RESOURCES		$1,324 per child

↑ Up from '01–'02   ↓ Down from '01–'02   ═ No change from '01–'02

S outh Carolina's Half-Day Child Development Program (4K) was established under the 1984 Education Improvement Act as part of efforts to better prepare the state's 4-year-olds for kindergarten and first grade. Each district is required to provide at least one prekindergarten class, with funding allocated based on the number of kindergarten children eligible for free or reduced-price lunch. Most districts offer only half-day classes, but some offer full-school-day classes using state, Title I, or local funds to extend the program day.

Children's eligibility for the prekindergarten program is determined by factors such as the presence of disabilities, parent education level, and socioeconomic status. Local districts determine how many risk factors children must have to qualify for participation. Most children are served in public schools, but some are served in other locations through public-private partnerships. Only schools can receive direct funding, but they may subcontract with other agencies, including Head Start programs, private child care centers, faith-based programs, and family child care homes.

In the spring of 2004, the state began monitoring program quality using the Early Childhood Environment Rating Scale (ECERS). Legislation now requires an annual evaluation to be submitted to the Education Oversight Committee, the Governor's Office, and the state Legislature.

As the state has dealt with budget crises, the 4K program has experienced some funding cuts over the past two years, although it has not been cut as deeply as some other state Department of Education programs. In 2003–2004, 17,279 children were enrolled in 4K programs, which received $22,870,783 in state funding.

Although not the focus of data in this report, the state also has a separate early childhood initiative known as First Steps to School Readiness. This initiative helps support various programs and services to meet the needs of young children and their families through public-private collaborations. First Steps County Partnerships decide how to distribute funds at the local level, with some guidance from the state. These funds can be used to supplement the 4K program by extending services to full-day programs, adding new full-day classes, or serving additional children in half-day classes. In 2002–2003, approximately 320 children were served in 16 First Steps public-private partnership sites.

Districts reported over 3,900 children on waiting lists during 2003–2004 as a result of cuts in 4K funding. A collaborative effort is underway to make about 1,000 available slots in Head Start programs accessible to children on school district waiting lists. Some districts are seeking other sources of funding to allow them to continue providing the full range of 4K services without reducing the number of slots available.

ACCESS RANKING—4s	ACCESS RANKING—3s	RESOURCES RANKING
4	15	35

ACCESS

Total state program enrollment - - - - - - - - - - - - - 17,279
School districts that offer state program - - - - - - - - - 100%
Income requirement - - - - - - - - - - - - - - - - - - None
Hours of operation - - - - - - - - - - - Half-day, full-week [1,2]
Operating schedule - - - - - - - - - - - - - - - Academic year [3]
Special education enrollment - - - - - - - - - - - - - - 5,520
Federally funded Head Start enrollment - - - - - - - - - 11,343
State-funded Head Start enrollment - - - - - - - - - - - - 0

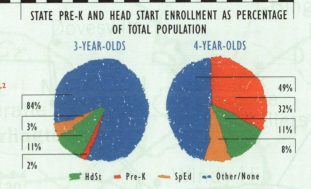

STATE PRE-K AND HEAD START ENROLLMENT AS PERCENTAGE OF TOTAL POPULATION

3-YEAR-OLDS: 84%, 3%, 11%, 2%
4-YEAR-OLDS: 49%, 32%, 11%, 8%

HdSt · Pre-K · SpEd · Other/None

QUALITY STANDARDS CHECKLIST

POLICY	STATE PRE-K REQUIREMENT	BENCHMARK	DOES REQUIREMENT MEET BENCHMARK?
Curriculum standards - - - - - - - - - - -	Not comprehensive	Comprehensive	☐
Teacher degree requirement - - - - - - - - - - - - -	BA	BA	☑
Teacher specialized training req. - -	EC certification and licensure	Specializing in Pre-K	☑
Assistant teacher degree req. - - -	HSD (public), None (nonpublic) [4]	CDA or equivalent	☐
Teacher in-service requirement - - - - -	12 clock hours/year and 6 credit hours/5 years	At least 15 hours/year	☑
Maximum class size		20 or lower	☑
3-year-olds - - - - - - - - - - - - - - - - - -	20		
4-year-olds - - - - - - - - - - - - - - - - - -	20		
Staff-child ratio		1:10 or better	☑
3-year-olds - - - - - - - - - - - - - - - - - -	1:10		
4-year-olds - - - - - - - - - - - - - - - - - -	1:10		
Screening/referral requirements - - - -	Vision, hearing, and health	Vision, hearing, and health	☑
Required support services - - - - - - - - -	4 parent conferences and support services [5]	At least 1 service	☑
Meal requirement - - - - - - - - - - - - - - -	1 meal and snack [6]	At least 1/day	☑

TOTAL: 8 of 10

RESOURCES

Total state Pre-K spending - - - - - - - - - - - - - $22,514,278
Local match required? - - - - - - - - - - - - - - - - - - No
State spending per child enrolled - - - - - - - - - - - $1,303
State spending per 3-year-old - - - - - - - - - - - - - - $25
State spending per 4-year-old - - - - - - - - - - - - - $421

SPENDING PER CHILD ENROLLED

PRE-K*: $1,467
HDST: $6,550
K–12**: $9,544

$ thousands: 0 2 4 6 8 10 12 14

State Contribution · Local Contribution · Federal Contribution

* Pre-K programs may receive additional funds from federal or local sources that are not included in this figure.
** K–12 expenditures include capital spending as well as current operating expenditures.

Data are for the '02–'03 school year, unless otherwise noted.

1 Full-day classes are offered in 18 districts using Title I or local funding, and in 3 districts using state Education Improvement Act funds.
2 Three districts use one day each week for in-home visits with children and families who most need home services.
3 Two districts that serve a total of 80 children operate for the 12-month calendar year.
4 It is recommended that assistant teachers complete an early childhood class within one year of their hiring date.
5 Two parent conferences are required to be held in a setting other than the school. Support services include education services or job training for parents, parenting support or training, parent involvement activities, health services for children (if health problems are found), transportation, and transition to kindergarten activities.
6 At least one meal and one snack are provided to all children. Children enrolled in half-day programs receive either breakfast or lunch plus a snack, and children in full-day programs receive breakfast and lunch plus a snack, as required by the Office of Food Service.

South Dakota

NO PROGRAM

ACCESS RANKING—4s	ACCESS RANKING—3s	RESOURCES RANKING
No Program		

ACCESS

Total state program enrollment - - - - - - - - - - - - - - - - 0

School districts that offer state program - - - - - - - - - - NA

Income requirement - NA

Hours of operation - NA

Operating schedule - NA

Special education enrollment - - - - - - - - - - - - - - 1,320

Federally funded Head Start enrollment - - - - - - - - - 3,347

State-funded Head Start enrollment - - - - - - - - - - - - - 0

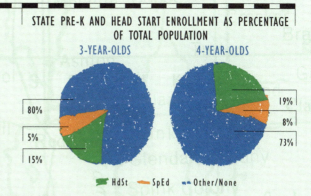

STATE PRE-K AND HEAD START ENROLLMENT AS PERCENTAGE OF TOTAL POPULATION

3-YEAR-OLDS: 80%, 5%, 15%

4-YEAR-OLDS: 19%, 8%, 73%

HdSt   SpEd   Other/None

QUALITY STANDARDS CHECKLIST

No Program

RESOURCES

Total state Pre-K spending - - - - - - - - - - - - - - - - - $0

Local match required? - NA

State spending per child enrolled - - - - - - - - - - - - - $0

State spending per 3-year-old - - - - - - - - - - - - - - - $0

State spending per 4-year-old - - - - - - - - - - - - - - - $0

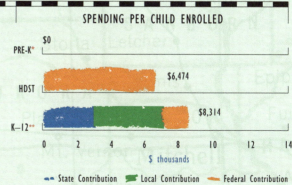

SPENDING PER CHILD ENROLLED

PRE-K* $0

HDST $6,474

K–12** $8,314

$ thousands

State Contribution   Local Contribution   Federal Contribution

* Pre-K programs may receive additional funds from federal or local sources that are not included in this figure.

** K–12 expenditures include capital spending as well as current operating expenditures.

Data are for the '02–'03 school year, unless otherwise noted.

Tennessee

↑ '02–'03 ENROLLMENT	3% of 4-year-olds in state Pre-K
'03–'04 ENROLLMENT	3% of 4-year-olds in state Pre-K
QUALITY STANDARDS	8 of 10
↓ '02–'03 RESOURCES	$4,573 per child
'03–'04 RESOURCES	$3,534 per child

↑ Up from '01–'02   ↓ Down from '01–'02   ⚌ No change from '01–'02

State funding for the Early Childhood Education (ECE) Pilot Program started in 1998 and was supplemented with significant federal TANF funds in the 2002 and 2003 fiscal years. ECE funds are distributed through a competitive grant process, and programs are operated by public schools, Head Start, private child care providers, and institutes of higher education. First priority for enrollment is given to children whose family income falls below 185 percent of the federal poverty level; children are also eligible for the program if they are at risk for abuse or neglect, in state custody, or have Individualized Education Plans where community placement is the least restrictive environment. The state requires all programs to operate at least 5.5 hours per day, and all teachers must be licensed with a Pre-K endorsement, regardless of program location.

Although state funding increased for the 2003–2004 program year, the elimination of TANF funding has resulted in a loss of $30,000 per classroom. This has led to a reduction in the number of classrooms and the number of children served, but quality standards have not been reduced. During the 2003–2004 school year, 2,830 children were served with $10 million in state funding. Tennessee began a state lottery in 2004—although proceeds will primarily fund college scholarships, excess funds will benefit early childhood programs.

ACCESS RANKING—4s	ACCESS RANKING—3s	RESOURCES RANKING
32	21	7

ACCESS

Total state program enrollment - - - - - - - - - - - - - - - 3,280

School districts that offer state program - - - - - - - - - - 46%

Income requirement - - - - - - - - - - - - - - - - - - - 185% FPL [1]

Hours of operation - - - - - - - - - 5.5 hours per day, full-week

Operating schedule - - - - - - - - - - - - - - - - - Academic year

Special education enrollment - - - - - - - - - - - - - - 5,262

Federally funded Head Start enrollment - - - - - - - - - 15,564

State-funded Head Start enrollment - - - - - - - - - - - 0

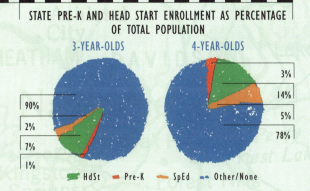

STATE PRE-K AND HEAD START ENROLLMENT AS PERCENTAGE OF TOTAL POPULATION

3-YEAR-OLDS: 90%, 2%, 7%, 1%
4-YEAR-OLDS: 3%, 14%, 5%, 78%

HdSt ■ Pre-K ■ SpEd ■ Other/None

QUALITY STANDARDS CHECKLIST

POLICY	STATE PRE-K REQUIREMENT	BENCHMARK	DOES REQUIREMENT MEET BENCHMARK?
Curriculum standards	None	Comprehensive	☐
Teacher degree requirement	BA	BA	✓
Teacher specialized training requirement	Teacher license with Pre-K endorsement	Specializing in Pre-K	✓
Assistant teacher degree requirement	CDA	CDA or equivalent	✓
Teacher in-service requirement	18 clock hours	At least 15 hours/year	✓
Maximum class size		20 or lower	✓
3-year-olds	16		
4-year-olds	20		
Staff-child ratio		1:10 or better	✓
3-year-olds	1:8		
4-year-olds	1:10		
Screening/referral requirements	Health [2]	Vision, hearing, and health	☐
Required support services	2 parent conferences and support services [3]	At least 1 service	✓
Meal requirement	Lunch and snack	At least 1/day	✓

TOTAL:
8
of 10

RESOURCES

Total state Pre-K spending - - - - - - - - - - - - $15,000,000 [4]

Local match required? - - - - - - - - - - - - - - - - - - No

State spending per child enrolled - - - - - - - - - - - $4,573 [5]

State spending per 3-year-old - - - - - - - - - - - - - $49 [5]

State spending per 4-year-old - - - - - - - - - - - - - $147 [5]

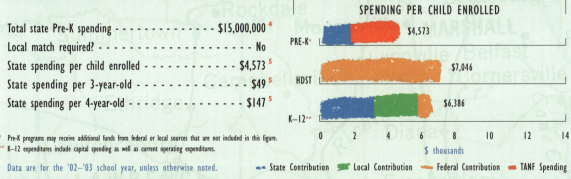

SPENDING PER CHILD ENROLLED

PRE-K*: $4,573
HDST: $7,046
K–12**: $6,386

$ thousands

■ State Contribution ■ Local Contribution ■ Federal Contribution ■ TANF Spending

* Pre-K programs may receive additional funds from federal or local sources that are not included in this figure.

** K–12 expenditures include capital spending as well as current operating expenditures.

Data are for the '02–'03 school year, unless otherwise noted.

1 Children eligible for free or reduced-price lunch receive highest priority for enrollment.

2 Screening and referral requirements for vision and hearing are determined locally.

3 Services offered include parent involvement activities, transition to Pre-K, and transition to kindergarten activities.

4 This figure includes $9 million in TANF funds.

5 These estimates include both state and TANF funds.

Texas

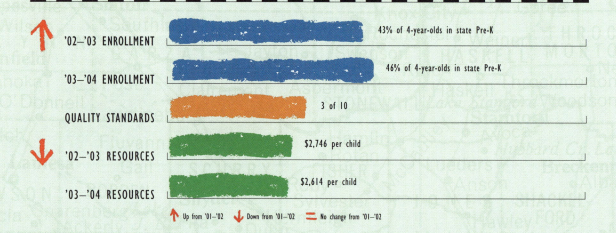

↑	'02–'03 ENROLLMENT	43% of 4-year-olds in state Pre-K
	'03–'04 ENROLLMENT	46% of 4-year-olds in state Pre-K
	QUALITY STANDARDS	3 of 10
↓	'02–'03 RESOURCES	$2,746 per child
	'03–'04 RESOURCES	$2,614 per child

↑ Up from '01–'02   ↓ Down from '01–'02   ═ No change from '01–'02

Established in 1984, Texas' Public School Prekindergarten initiative provides half-day preschool primarily for 4-year-olds from low-income families. Children qualify for the program if they are eligible for free or reduced-price lunch, unable to speak and understand the English language, or homeless. Public School Prekindergarten programs are part of the K–12 system, and are thus supported by a combination of state and local funds. Individual school districts are responsible for operating prekindergarten programs but are encouraged to consider using existing Head Start or local child care providers as program sites. All districts with 15 or more eligible children who are at least 4 years old are required to offer the prekindergarten program. Although not required, full-day programs and access for 3-year-olds are provided in some locations with the use of additional district and state funding. Services for children who do not meet eligibility criteria are largely paid for by parent tuition.

Annual grants that have allowed some districts to provide full-day services have been reduced by the Legislature for the 2003–2004 and 2004–2005 school years from $100 million to $92.5 million. These expansion grants are awarded on a competitive basis, with priority going to districts with low third-grade reading scores. Including these grants, the Public School Prekindergarten Program was funded with a total of $435,500,000 during the 2003–2004 school year, enrolling 14,283 3-year-olds and 151,620 4-year-olds.

ACCESS RANKING—4s	ACCESS RANKING—3s	RESOURCES RANKING
3	8	26

ACCESS

Total state program enrollment - - - - - - - - - - - - - - 157,498

School districts that offer state program - - - - - - - - - - 74%

Income requirement - - - - - - Free or reduced-price lunch eligible [1]

Hours of operation - - - - - - - - - - - - - - Half-day, full-week [2]

Operating schedule - - - - - - - - - - - - - - - Academic year [3]

Special education enrollment - - - - - - - - - - - - - - 20,046

Federally funded Head Start enrollment - - - - - - - - - 63,949

State-funded Head Start enrollment - - - - - - - - - - - - - - 0

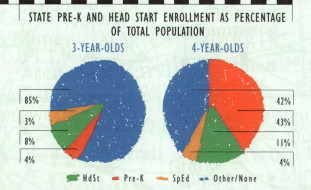

STATE PRE-K AND HEAD START ENROLLMENT AS PERCENTAGE OF TOTAL POPULATION

3-YEAR-OLDS
- 85%
- 3%
- 8%
- 4%

4-YEAR-OLDS
- 42%
- 43%
- 11%
- 4%

■ HdSt ■ Pre-K ■ SpEd ┅ Other/None

QUALITY STANDARDS CHECKLIST

POLICY	STATE PRE-K REQUIREMENT	BENCHMARK	DOES REQUIREMENT MEET BENCHMARK?
Curriculum standards - - - - - - - - - - - - - - -	Comprehensive	Comprehensive	✓
Teacher degree requirement - - - - - - - - - - - - - -	BA	BA	✓
Teacher specialized training req. - - - -	Endorsement in EC or K [4]	Specializing in Pre-K	☐
Assistant teacher degree requirement - - - -	Determined locally	CDA or equivalent	☐
Teacher in-service requirement - - - - - - - - -	Not specified	At least 15 hours/year	☐
Maximum class size		20 or lower	☐
3-year-olds - - - - - - - - - - - - - - - - - - -	No limit [5]		
4-year-olds - - - - - - - - - - - - - - - - - - -	No limit [5]		
Staff-child ratio		1:10 or better	☐
3-year-olds - - - - - - - - - - - - - - - - - - -	No limit [5]		
4-year-olds - - - - - - - - - - - - - - - - - - -	No limit [5]		
Screening/referral requirements - - - - - -	Vision and hearing	Vision, hearing, and health	☐
Required support services - - - - - - - - -	Support services [6]	At least 1 service	✓
Meal requirement - - - - - - - - - - - - - - - - - -	Varies [7]	At least 1/day	☐

TOTAL: 3 of 10

RESOURCES

Total state Pre-K spending - - - - - - - - - - - - $432,436,912 [8]

Local match required? - - - - - - - - - - - - - - - - - - - No

State spending per child enrolled - - - - - - - - - - - $2,746

State spending per 3-year-old - - - - - - - - - - - - - $112

State spending per 4-year-old - - - - - - - - - - - - - $1,192

SPENDING PER CHILD ENROLLED

PRE-K* — $2,746

HDST — $6,868

K–12** — $8,621

$ thousands (0 2 4 6 8 10 12 14)

┅ State Contribution ■ Local Contribution ■ Federal Contribution

* Pre-K programs may receive additional funds from federal or local sources that are not included in this figure.

** K–12 expenditures include capital spending as well as current operating expenditures.

Data are for the '02–'03 school year, unless otherwise noted.

1 Children may also qualify if they are homeless or are unable to speak or comprehend the English language. During 2002–2003, 72% of attendees were eligible for free or reduced-price lunch.

2 Public School Prekindergarten funds can only be used to support a 3-hour day, but districts can provide 6-hour-a-day programs using Prekindergarten Expansion Grant funds, tuition, local revenue, or other funds.

3 The prekindergarten program follows an academic year schedule. In addition, each school district that is required to offer a bilingual education or special language program must offer a voluntary program for children of limited English proficiency who will be eligible for admission to kindergarten or the first grade at the beginning of the next school year.

4 Teachers assigned to a bilingual education program must be appropriately certified for bilingual education. Teachers assigned to an English as a Second Language or other special language program must also be appropriately certified.

5 There is no class size or staff-child ratio requirement for prekindergarten. Most classes do not exceed 18 children. A teacher and an aide are present in most classrooms, although the aide is optional.

6 Some support services are required, but specific services are determined locally.

7 Most school districts serve either breakfast or lunch and some serve both meals. School districts that offer a full-day program always provide lunch and often provide breakfast.

8 This figure includes $100 million in expansion grants provided by the state to support full-day services.

Utah

NO PROGRAM

ACCESS RANKING—4s	ACCESS RANKING—3s	RESOURCES RANKING

No Program

ACCESS

Total state program enrollment - - - - - - - - - - - - - - - 0
School districts that offer state program - - - - - - - - - - - NA
Income requirement - NA
Hours of operation - NA
Operating schedule - NA
Special education enrollment - - - - - - - - - - - - - - 3,904
Federally funded Head Start enrollment - - - - - - - - - 5,218
State-funded Head Start enrollment - - - - - - - - - - - - - 0

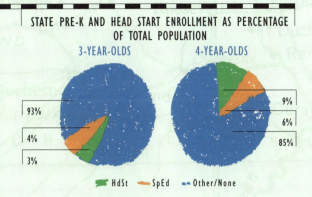

STATE PRE-K AND HEAD START ENROLLMENT AS PERCENTAGE OF TOTAL POPULATION

3-YEAR-OLDS
93%
4%
3%

4-YEAR-OLDS
9%
6%
85%

HdSt   SpEd   Other/None

QUALITY STANDARDS CHECKLIST

No Program

RESOURCES

Total state Pre-K spending - - - - - - - - - - - - - - - - - $0
Local match required? - - - - - - - - - - - - - - - - - - - NA
State spending per child enrolled - - - - - - - - - - - - - - $0
State spending per 3-year-old - - - - - - - - - - - - - - - - $0
State spending per 4-year-old - - - - - - - - - - - - - - - - $0

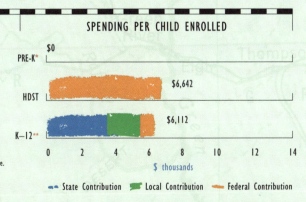

SPENDING PER CHILD ENROLLED

PRE-K* $0
HDST $6,642
K–12** $6,112

0   2   4   6   8   10   12   14
$ thousands

State Contribution   Local Contribution   Federal Contribution

* Pre-K programs may receive additional funds from federal or local sources that are not included in this figure.
** K–12 expenditures include capital spending as well as current operating expenditures.

Data are for the '02–'03 school year, unless otherwise noted.

Vermont

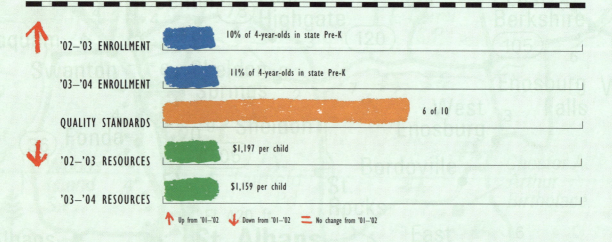

↑ '02–'03 ENROLLMENT	10% of 4-year-olds in state Pre-K
'03–'04 ENROLLMENT	11% of 4-year-olds in state Pre-K
QUALITY STANDARDS	6 of 10
↓ '02–'03 RESOURCES	$1,197 per child
'03–'04 RESOURCES	$1,159 per child

↑ Up from '01–'02   ↓ Down from '01–'02   = No change from '01–'02

Started in 1987, Vermont's Early Education Initiative (EEI) provides grants to increase the accessibility of preschool programs in the state's communities. Public schools, Parent-Child Centers, private child care programs, and Head Start agencies receive direct funding from the state. Collaborative planning is an EEI requirement, and state prekindergarten funds must be coordinated with other resources and programs. The EEI program provides preschool access for 3- and 4-year-old children who are at risk. At least half of the enrollees must come from families with incomes below 185 percent of the federal poverty level. Children are also eligible to enroll if they possess risk factors such as exposure to violence, neglect or substance abuse, low parental education levels, social isolation, limited English proficiency, or developmental delay.

The Vermont Early Learning Standards have recently become a curricular requirement for EEI programs, and professional development programs for Pre-K and kindergarten teachers have been aligned with these standards.

State funding for EEI has remained level for the past 5 years. Due to inflation, this has diminished the value of the grants received by programs, resulting in reductions in enrollment and intensity of services. In 2003–2004, the state provided $1,328,785 in funding for the EEI program to support 440 3-year-olds and 692 4-year-olds.

ACCESS RANKING—4s	ACCESS RANKING—3s	RESOURCES RANKING
19	6	36

ACCESS

Total state program enrollment - - - - - - - - - - - - - 1,110
School districts that offer state program - - - - - - 57% (towns)
Income requirement - - 50% of children must be below 185% FPL
Hours of operation - - - - - - - - - - - - - - Determined locally [1]
Operating schedule - - - - - - - - - - - - - Determined locally [2]
Special education enrollment - - - - - - - - - - - - - 838
Federally funded Head Start enrollment - - - - - - - - - 1,109
State-funded Head Start enrollment - - - - - - - - - - - - 0

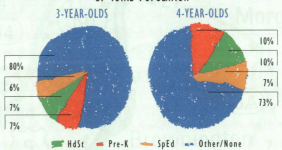

STATE PRE-K AND HEAD START ENROLLMENT AS PERCENTAGE OF TOTAL POPULATION

3-YEAR-OLDS
80%
6%
7%
7%

4-YEAR-OLDS
10%
10%
7%
73%

■ HdSt ■ Pre-K ■ SpEd ■ Other/None

QUALITY STANDARDS CHECKLIST

POLICY	STATE PRE-K REQUIREMENT	BENCHMARK	DOES REQUIREMENT MEET BENCHMARK?
Curriculum standards	None	Comprehensive	☐
Teacher degree requirement	BA	BA	☑
Teacher specialized training requirement	Degree in EC [3]	Specializing in Pre-K	☑
Assistant teacher degree requirement	BA (public), Determined locally (nonpublic)	CDA or equivalent	☐
Teacher in-service requirement	9 cr. hours/7 years (public), 9 clock hours/year (nonpublic)	At least 15 hours/year	☐
Maximum class size		20 or lower	☑
3-year-olds	16		
4-year-olds	16		
Staff-child ratio		1:10 or better	☑
3-year-olds	1:8		
4-year-olds	1:8		
Screening/referral requirements	Vision, hearing, health, and developmental [4]	Vision, hearing, and health	☑
Required support services	2 parent conferences and support services [5]	At least 1 service	☑
Meal requirement	Varies [6]	At least 1/day	☐

TOTAL:

6

of 10

RESOURCES

Total state Pre-K spending - - - - - - - - - - - - - $1,328,785
Local match required? - - - - - - - - - - - - - - - - - - No
State spending per child enrolled - - - - - - - - - - - $1,197
State spending per 3-year-old - - - - - - - - - - - - - $84
State spending per 4-year-old - - - - - - - - - - - - - $117

SPENDING PER CHILD ENROLLED

PRE-K* ▮ $1,197
HDST $8,381
K–12** $11,346

0   2   4   6   8   10   12   14
$ thousands

■ State Contribution ■ Local Contribution ■ Federal Contribution

* Pre-K programs may receive additional funds from federal or local sources that are not included in this figure.
** K–12 expenditures include capital spending as well as current operating expenditures.

Data are for the '02–'03 school year, unless otherwise noted.

1 Programs operate for an average of 10.5 hours per week.
2 Public school and Head Start programs generally follow the academic year, while programs in child care centers usually operate throughout the calendar year.
3 Additionally, public school teachers are required to have an EC license/endorsement that covers children age 3–Grade 3, and an ECSE license that covers ages 3 to 6.
4 All districts conduct vision, hearing and general health screenings for 3- to 5-year-olds in conjunction with a district-wide developmental screening. As children participate in general preschool screenings to determine eligibility, they receive services (e.g., vision, health, etc.). Therefore, all children benefit from screening and referrals, even those not found to be eligible for EEI. General eligibility screenings are mandatory for participation in EEI.
5 Year-round programs are required to offer three parent conferences. Additional support services include education services or job training for parents, parenting support or training, parent involvement activities, health services for children, information about nutrition, referral to social services, and transition to kindergarten activities.
6 The meal requirement depends on length of the program day. A snack is required per 3-hour program; a meal plus a snack is required for any program running over 4 hours.

Virginia

=	'02–'03 ENROLLMENT	6% of 4-year-olds in state Pre-K
	'03–'04 ENROLLMENT	6% of 4-year-olds in state Pre-K
	QUALITY STANDARDS	5 of 10
↓	'02–'03 RESOURCES	$3,090 per child
	'03–'04 RESOURCES	$3,102 per child

↑ Up from '01–'02   ↓ Down from '01–'02   = No change from '01–'02

Established in 1995, the Virginia Preschool Initiative was developed to meet the needs of 4-year-old children not being served by existing preschool education programs. Public schools receive allocations sufficient to fund services for 60 percent of the at-risk 4-year-olds in a community who are not being served by federal programs, including Head Start and Title I. Public schools may subcontract with Head Start or YMCA programs to operate prekindergarten classes. Although all children who participate must be at risk, the specific risk factors used to determine eligibility are chosen and identified at the local level. Some risk factors that are frequently used include poverty, homelessness, parents who have dropped out of school or who have limited education, family underemployment or incarceration, and limited English proficiency.

The Virginia Preschool Initiative has a required local match, based on a composite index that reflects local districts' abilities to contribute additional funds. In general, this index is designed to promote equity across communities, such that wealthy communities are required to contribute more funds than less wealthy communities.

The 2002–2003 school year saw the publication of Virginia's Foundation Blocks for early literacy and mathematics, which have become a required a part of the curriculum.

Major program changes were approved in a special session of the state General Assembly in 2004. Districts will be given the opportunity to choose whether to provide half-day or full-day services; currently, full-day programs are mandated. In addition, the state will make funding available for districts to serve 90 percent of at-risk 4-year-olds not already being served by Head Start.

The Virginia Preschool Initiative served 5,895 4-year-olds in 2003–2004 and received $18,285,745 in state funding.

ACCESS RANKING—4s	ACCESS RANKING—3s	RESOURCES RANKING
24	None Served	20

ACCESS

Total state program enrollment - - - - - - - - - - - - - - - - 5,886
School districts that offer state program - - - - - - - - - 55%
Income requirement - None
Hours of operation - - - - - - - - - - - - - Full-day, full-week
Operating schedule - - - - - - - - - - - - - - - - Academic year
Special education enrollment - - - - - - - - - - - - - - - 8,710
Federally funded Head Start enrollment - - - - - - - - - 11,682
State-funded Head Start enrollment - - - - - - - - - - - - - 0

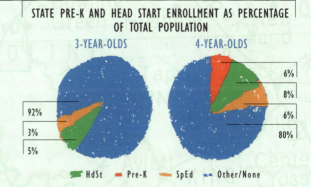

STATE PRE-K AND HEAD START ENROLLMENT AS PERCENTAGE OF TOTAL POPULATION

3-YEAR-OLDS
92%
3%
5%

4-YEAR-OLDS
6%
8%
6%
80%

■ HdSt ■ Pre-K ■ SpEd ■ Other/None

QUALITY STANDARDS CHECKLIST

POLICY	STATE PRE-K REQUIREMENT	BENCHMARK	DOES REQUIREMENT MEET BENCHMARK?
Curriculum standards - - - - - - - - - - -	Not comprehensive	Comprehensive	☐
Teacher degree requirement - - - - -	BA (public), None (nonpublic) [1]	BA	☐
Teacher specialized training requirement -	Certification in Pre-K–3 or –6 (public), None (nonpublic) [1]	Specializing in Pre-K	☐
Assistant teacher degree requirement - - - - - - - - -	HSD or GED	CDA or equivalent	☐
Teacher in-service requirement - - - - - -	Determined locally	At least 15 hours/year	☐
Maximum class size		20 or lower	☑
3-year-olds - - - - - - - - - - - - - - - - -	NA		
4-year-olds - - - - - - - - - - - - - - - - -	16		
Staff-child ratio		1:10 or better	☑
3-year-olds - - - - - - - - - - - - - - - - -	NA		
4-year-olds - - - - - - - - - - - - - - - - -	1:8		
Screening/referral requirements - - - -	Vision, hearing, and health	Vision, hearing, and health	☑
Required support services - - - - - - - - - - - -	Support services [2]	At least 1 service	☑
Meal requirement - - - - - - - - - - - - - -	Lunch and snack	At least 1/day	☑

TOTAL:
5
of 10

RESOURCES

Total state Pre-K spending - - - - - - - - - - - - - $18,189,075
Local match required? - - - - - - - - Yes—based on composite index of local ability to pay [3]
State spending per child enrolled - - - - - - - - - - - $3,090
State spending per 3-year-old - - - - - - - - - - - - - - $0
State spending per 4-year-old - - - - - - - - - - - - - $195

SPENDING PER CHILD ENROLLED

PRE-K* $3,090
HDST $6,988
K–12** $7,089

0 2 4 6 8 10 12 14
$ thousands

■ State Contribution ■ Local Contribution ■ Federal Contribution

* Pre-K programs may receive additional funds from federal or local sources that are not included in this figure.
** K–12 expenditures include capital spending as well as current operating expenditures.

Data are for the '02–'03 school year, unless otherwise noted.

1 All staff must have some training in early childhood development. Minimum teacher qualifications depend on the location of the program: public school teachers must be certified, Head Start teachers must hold a CDA, and there is no minimum degree requirement for teachers in child care settings.

2 Support services include parent involvement activities, health services for children, referral to social services, and transportation. The annual number of required parent conferences and/or home visits is determined locally.

3 In general, the composite index is designed so that counties with large low-income populations are required to contribute less of a local match than wealthier communities. The percentage of costs covered by matching funds varies by community, but more specific information could not be reported.

Washington

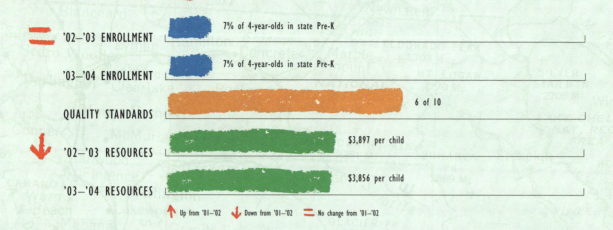

'02–'03 ENROLLMENT		7% of 4-year-olds in state Pre-K
'03–'04 ENROLLMENT		7% of 4-year-olds in state Pre-K
QUALITY STANDARDS		6 of 10
'02–'03 RESOURCES		$3,897 per child
'03–'04 RESOURCES		$3,856 per child

↑ Up from '01–'02   ↓ Down from '01–'02   = No change from '01–'02

The Early Childhood Education and Assistance Program (ECEAP) was initiated in 1985 in response to calls for early childhood education reform. The program primarily targets 4-year-olds from families at or below 110 percent of the federal poverty level, but can be extended to 3-year-olds after eligible 4-year-olds have been served. Additionally, space is reserved to meet the needs of preschool children of migrant workers or Native Americans, as well as children with environmental or developmental risk factors. Funding is provided through a competitive grant process to contractors from public schools, child care centers, and nonprofit organizations, which can then subcontract with a range of agencies to deliver services. The state strongly encourages contractors to use the Devereux Early Childhood Assessment Program (DECA) to identify children's social and emotional strengths and use that information in tailoring classroom strategies and working with parents.

In recent years, state budget decisions have reduced funding for ECEAP, which has resulted in the loss of slots and services. In 2003–2004, the state provided $26,537,328 to serve 5,436 4-year-olds and 1,446 3-year-olds.

ACCESS RANKING–4s	ACCESS RANKING–3s	RESOURCES RANKING
23	16	11

ACCESS

Total state program enrollment - - - - - - - - - - - - - 6,918

School districts that offer state program - - - - - - - - - 41%

Income req. - - - 90% of children must be at or below 110% FPL [1]

Hours of operation - - - - - - - - - - - - - - Determined locally [2]

Operating schedule - - - - - - - - - - - - - Determined locally [3]

Special education enrollment - - - - - - - - - - - - - 7,039

Federally funded Head Start enrollment - - - - - - - - 11,339

State-funded Head Start enrollment - - - - - - - - - - - - 0

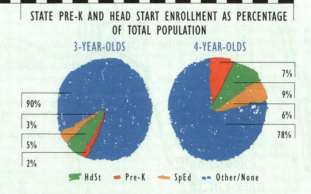

STATE PRE-K AND HEAD START ENROLLMENT AS PERCENTAGE OF TOTAL POPULATION

3-YEAR-OLDS
90%
3%
5%
2%

4-YEAR-OLDS
7%
9%
6%
78%

HdSt   Pre-K   SpEd   Other/None

QUALITY STANDARDS CHECKLIST

POLICY	STATE PRE-K REQUIREMENT	BENCHMARK	DOES REQUIREMENT MEET BENCHMARK?
Curriculum standards	Not comprehensive	Comprehensive	☐
Teacher degree requirement	BA (public), AA (nonpublic)	BA	☐
Teacher specialized training req.	Pre-K–3 endorsement or SpEd certification with EC endorsement (public), 30 quarter units in ECE (nonpublic)	Specializing in Pre-K	☑
Assistant teacher degree requirement	CDA or passing proficiency test (public), CDA (nonpublic)	CDA or equivalent	☑
Teacher in-service requirement	Determined locally [4]	At least 15 hours/year	☐
Maximum class size		20 or lower	☐
3-year-olds	24 [5]		
4-year-olds	24		
Staff-child ratio		1:10 or better	☑
3-year-olds	1:9 [5]		
4-year-olds	1:9		
Screening/referral requirements	Vision, hearing, health, and developmental	Vision, hearing, and health	☑
Required support services	3 hours of education planning time with parents and support services [6]	At least 1 service	☑
Meal requirement	Breakfast, lunch, and snack	At least 1/day	☑

TOTAL:
6
of 10

RESOURCES

Total state Pre-K spending - - - - - - - - - - - - $26,957,519 [7]

Local match required? - - - - - - - - - - - - - - - - - - No

State spending per child enrolled - - - - - - - - - - $3,897

State spending per 3-year-old - - - - - - - - - - - - - $69

State spending per 4-year-old - - - - - - - - - - - - $270

SPENDING PER CHILD ENROLLED

PRE-K* $4,640

HDST $8,910

K–12** $9,040

0 2 4 6 8 10 12 14
$ thousands

State Contribution   Local Contribution   Federal Contribution

* Pre-K programs may receive additional funds from federal or local sources that are not included in this figure.

** K–12 expenditures include capital spending as well as current operating expenditures.

Data are for the '02–'03 school year, unless otherwise noted.

1 This income cutoff would be equivalent to $16,522 a year for a family of three in 2002–2003.

2 Providers design initiatives based on community needs. All programs operate at least 2.5 hours per session. The majority of programs operate for 3 to 4 days per week.

3 Most programs operate for the academic year.

4 ECEAP requires in-service training, but does not specify the number of hours required.

5 Program standards are targeted to 4-year-olds, but since 3-year-olds are in blended classrooms, ECEAP standards apply to the educational setting for both ages. In classes of 24 students, the staff-child ratio must be 1:6.

6 Support services include education services or job training for parents, parenting support or training, parent involvement activities, health services for children, information about nutrition, referral to social services, and transition to kindergarten activities.

7 The ECEAP program also received $5,141,990 from CCDF during both 2002–2003 and 2003–2004.

167

West Virginia

↑ | '02–'03 ENROLLMENT | 29% of 4-year-olds in state Pre-K
| '03–'04 ENROLLMENT | 32% of 4-year-olds in state Pre-K
| QUALITY STANDARDS | 5 of 10
↑ | '02–'03 RESOURCES | $3,309 per child
| '03–'04 RESOURCES | $4,543 per child

↑ Up from '01–'02   ↓ Down from '01–'02   = No change from '01–'02

West Virginia has provided funding for prekindergarten since 1983, when a revision of the state school code allowed preschool programs to be created by local school boards. The state's financial contribution to the Public School Early Childhood Education program is supplemented by significant federal Title I and IDEA funds. This program currently serves both 3- and 4-year-olds. In 2002–2003, various models were used across the state to determine eligibility for the Public School Early Childhood Education program. In many counties, all children were eligible as long as they met the age requirements and lived in participating districts. In a smaller subset of counties, eligibility was based on at-risk status, using criteria such as family income levels.

The state is focused on increasing accessibility to all families desiring preschool for their 4-year-olds. Recent legislation requires that universal prekindergarten be made available for all of West Virginia's 4-year-olds by the 2012–2013 school year, and that 50 percent of the programs be in collaborative settings with Head Start, child care, or private prekindergarten programs. However, effective July 2004, access for 3-year-olds is limited to those who have Individualized Education Plans for special needs.

The recently adopted West Virginia Early Learning Standards Framework promotes learning standards across all domains, including social and emotional development, and provides guidelines for assessment.

With state funding of $36,000,000, the Public School Early Childhood Education program enrolled 7,924 children during the 2003–2004 school year.

ACCESS RANKING—4s	ACCESS RANKING—3s	RESOURCES RANKING
6	4	18

ACCESS

Total state program enrollment - - - - - - - - - - - - - - 7,727

School districts that offer state program - - - - - 80% (counties)

Income requirement - None

Hours of operation - - - - - - - - - - - - - - Determined locally [1]

Operating schedule - - - - - - - - - - - - - - - - Academic year

Special education enrollment - - - - - - - - - - - - - 2,678

Federally funded Head Start enrollment - - - - - - - - 6,767

State-funded Head Start enrollment - - - - - - - - - - - - 0

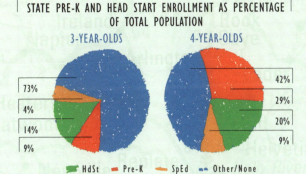

STATE PRE-K AND HEAD START ENROLLMENT AS PERCENTAGE OF TOTAL POPULATION

3-YEAR-OLDS: 73%, 4%, 14%, 9%

4-YEAR-OLDS: 42%, 29%, 20%, 9%

HdSt Pre-K SpEd Other/None

QUALITY STANDARDS CHECKLIST

POLICY	STATE PRE-K REQUIREMENT	BENCHMARK	DOES REQUIREMENT MEET BENCHMARK?
Curriculum standards	None	Comprehensive	☐
Teacher degree requirement	BA	BA	☑
Teacher specialized training req.	Certified in Birth–5, EC, or Preschool Special Needs; or Pre-K/K endorsement on EE cert.	Specializing in Pre-K	☑
Assistant teacher degree requirement	HSD or equivalent	CDA or equivalent	☐
Teacher in-service requirement	18 clock hours	At least 15 hours/year	☑
Maximum class size		20 or lower	☑
3-year-olds	20		
4-year-olds	20		
Staff-child ratio		1:10 or better	☐
3-year-olds	No limit [2]		
4-year-olds	No limit [2]		
Screening/referral requirements	Vision, hearing, and health [3]	Vision, hearing, and health	☑
Required support services	None [4]	At least 1 service	☐
Meal requirement	Varies [5]	At least 1/day	☐

TOTAL:

5

of 10

RESOURCES

Total state Pre-K spending - - - - - - - - - - - - - $25,571,000

Local match required? - - - - - - - - - - - - - - - - - - - No

State spending per child enrolled - - - - - - - - - - - $3,309

State spending per 3-year-old - - - - - - - - - - - - - $313 [6]

State spending per 4-year-old - - - - - - - - - - - - - $957 [6]

SPENDING PER CHILD ENROLLED

PRE-K* — $5,032

HDST — $6,435

K–12** — $9,910

0   2   4   6   8   10   12   14

$ thousands

State Contribution   Local Contribution   Federal Contribution

* Pre-K programs may receive additional funds from federal or local sources that are not included in this figure.

** K–12 expenditures include capital spending as well as current operating expenditures.

Data are for the '02–'03 school year, unless otherwise noted.

1 There are two prevailing models: one option provides 2 full-day classes each week, and the other model offers 4 full days, with Friday reserved for activities such as home visits or planning.

2 As of the 2003–2004 program year, the staff-child ratio requirement is 1:10 with a certified teacher present at all times.

3 Dental and developmental screening and referral were added for the 2003–2004 year.

4 West Virginia Board of Education Policy 2525 went into effect February 12, 2003, requiring two face-to-face visits with parents, including one in the home. Many school systems did not institute full compliance with this policy until the 2003–2004 school year.

5 Programs that received state funding in 2002 primarily used the National School Lunch Program (NSLP) to support nutritional services in Pre-K. Meals and snacks were determined by NSLP guidelines based on the length of the program day.

6 West Virginia did not break its total enrollment figure into specific numbers of 3- or 4-year-olds. As a result, these calculations are estimates, based on proportions of enrollees who were ages 3 and 4 in states that served 3-year-olds and provided age breakdowns for 2002–2003.

Wisconsin

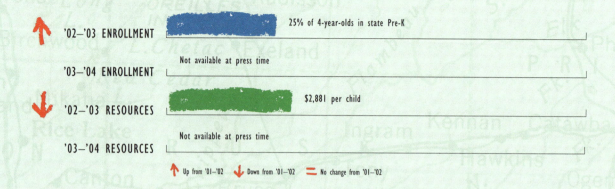

↑ '02–'03 ENROLLMENT		25% of 4-year-olds in state Pre-K
'03–'04 ENROLLMENT	Not available at press time	
↓ '02–'03 RESOURCES		$2,881 per child
'03–'04 RESOURCES	Not available at press time	

↑ Up from '01–'02   ↓ Down from '01–'02   ═ No change from '01–'02

Wisconsin's constitution has included a commitment to free education for 4-year-olds since 1848. The current Four-Year-Old Kindergarten (4K) program dates back to 1873, although state aid was suspended from 1957 to 1984. Through the 4K program, local school districts that choose to provide half-day classes for 4-year-olds receive 50 percent of the standard state per-pupil contribution provided for K–12, or 60 percent if the school also offers parent support. Most prekindergarten classes are offered in public schools, but the state is encouraging more subcontracting with local Head Start and child care centers for services.

The state promotes the expansion of the 4K program by urging districts that do not offer prekindergarten to take advantage of the option to do so, and by encouraging districts that already offer prekindergarten to serve more children. Other recent efforts to improve the program include the development of Model Early Learning Standards through collaborative work among state agencies. During the 2003–2004 school year, 4K programs received a total of $43 million in state funds (plus $22 million in local funds) and served 16,968 children.

In addition to supporting the 4K program, Wisconsin also reserves funding to supplement federal Head Start grantees. These programs follow the federal Head Start Performance Standards and provide comprehensive early education for 3- and 4-year-old children who are from low-income families or who have disabilities. The state supplement to Head Start was reduced during the 2003–2004 year.

Although most states have a single state-financed prekindergarten initiative, Wisconsin makes significant contributions to prekindergarten through two separate initiatives—4K and the state-funded Head Start model. As a result, in the first two pages of this profile we present summary information reflecting the state's overall commitment to prekindergarten. Enrollment and state spending for both the 4K and state-financed Head Start initiatives are taken into account. Next, we present specific details about each initiative in the state. The third page of this profile focuses exclusively on the 4K program, while the final page focuses exclusively on the state-funded Head Start program.

STATE OVERVIEW

Total state program enrollment - - - - - - - - - - - - 17,500

Total state spending - - - - - - - - - - - - - - - - $50,425,000

State spending per child enrolled - - - - - - - - - - $2,881

State Head Start spending - - - - - - - - - - - - - $7,425,000

State spending per 3-year-old - - - - - - - - - - - - $44

State spending per 4-year-old - - - - - - - - - - - - $700

* Programs may receive additional funds from federal or local sources that are not included in this figure.

** K–12 expenditures include capital spending as well as current operating expenditures.

Data are for the '02–'03 school year, unless otherwise noted.

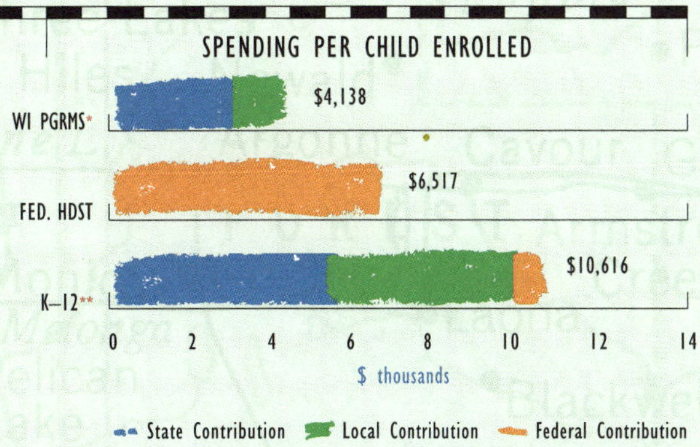

SPENDING PER CHILD ENROLLED

WI PGRMS* $4,138

FED. HDST $6,517

K–12** $10,616

0   2   4   6   8   10   12   14

$ thousands

➤➤ State Contribution   ■ Local Contribution   ➤ Federal Contribution

ACCESS RANKING—4s	ACCESS RANKING—3s	RESOURCES RANKING
9	22	24

ACCESS

Total state program enrollment - - - - - - - - - - - - - - - 16,051

School districts that offer state program - - - - - - - - - 45%

Income requirement - None

Hours of operation - - - - - - - - - - - - - Determined locally [1]

Operating schedule - - - - - - - - - - - - - - - Academic year [1]

Special education enrollment - - - - - - - - - - - - - - 8,696

Federally funded Head Start enrollment - - - - - - - - - 12,901

State-funded Head Start enrollment - - - - - - - - - - - - 1,449 [2]

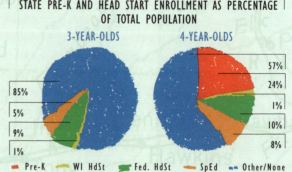

STATE PRE-K AND HEAD START ENROLLMENT AS PERCENTAGE OF TOTAL POPULATION

3-YEAR-OLDS: 85%, 5%, 9%, 1%

4-YEAR-OLDS: 57%, 24%, 1%, 10%, 8%

■ Pre-K   ■ WI HdSt   ■ Fed. HdSt   ■ SpEd   ■ Other/None

QUALITY STANDARDS CHECKLIST

POLICY	STATE PRE-K REQUIREMENT	BENCHMARK	DOES REQUIREMENT MEET BENCHMARK?
Curriculum standards	None	Comprehensive	☐
Teacher degree requirement	BA	BA	☑
Teacher specialized training requirement	Teaching license in Pre-K–K, Pre-K–3, Pre-K–6, or K [3]	Specializing in Pre-K	☐
Assistant teacher degree requirement	Teacher asst. license or AA (public), 18 yrs old + 1 course in EC (nonpublic) [4]	CDA or equivalent	☐
Teacher in-service requirement	6 credit hours or 180 DPI clock hours/5 years [5]	At least 15 hours/year	☑
Maximum class size		20 or lower	☐
3-year-olds	NA		
4-year-olds	Determined locally		
Staff-child ratio		1:10 or better	☐
3-year-olds	NA		
4-year-olds	Determined locally		
Screening/referral requirements	Determined locally [6]	Vision, hearing, and health	☐
Required support services	Support services [7]	At least 1 service	☑
Meal requirement	None	At least 1/day	☐

TOTAL:

3

of 10

RESOURCES

Total state Pre-K spending - - - - - - - - - - - - - $43,000,000

Local match required? - - - - Yes—local share of school revenue

State spending per child enrolled - - - - - - - - - - - - $2,679

State Head Start spending - - - - - - - - - - - - - - $7,425,000

State spending per 3-year-old - - - - - - - - - - - - - - - $0

State spending per 4-year-old - - - - - - - - - - - - - - $635

SPENDING PER CHILD ENROLLED

PRE-K*: $4,050

FED. HDST: $6,517

K–12**: $10,616

$ thousands

■ State Contribution   ■ Local Contribution   ■ Federal Contribution

* Pre-K programs may receive additional funds from federal or local sources that are not included in this figure.

** K–12 expenditures include capital spending as well as current operating expenditures.

Data are for the '02–'03 school year, unless otherwise noted.

1 Programs must operate for a minimum of 437 hours per year and may add 87.5 hours for parent outreach. Most programs operate 2.5 hours per day, 5 days per week for 180 days per year. Some programs operate 4 days per week with parent outreach on the fifth day. Several school districts operate programs for the full calendar year, but they receive the same funding as academic year programs.

2 Wisconsin did not break this figure into specific numbers of 3- or 4-year-olds. As a result, age breakdowns used in the Access pie chart were also estimated, using proportions of federal Head Start enrollees in each age category.

3 New licensing standards take effect in 2004 creating early-childhood-level licenses.

4 Assistant teachers in Title I schools are required to have an AA. The requirements for assistant teachers in nonpublic schools reflect child care licensing standards.

5 As of 2004, new teachers will be required to have professional development plans, mentors, and team support. Teachers hired before 2004 may use either the old system of credits (rather than clock hours) or the new system of professional development planning.

6 Vision, hearing, and general health screenings are required at kindergarten entrance for all children. Typically they are provided by family physicians or through the state Women, Infants, and Children (WIC) program. LEAs follow up with children who do not receive these services. Referrals, however, are not mandatory.

7 Support services include parent involvement activities, health services for children, referral to social services, transportation, and school counseling. The number of required annual parent conferences or home visits is determined locally.

WISCONSIN STATE-FUNDED HEAD START MODEL

ACCESS

Total state program enrollment - - - - - - - - - - - - - - 1,449 [1]

School districts that offer state program - - - - - - 94% (federal Head Start grantees)

Income requirement - 90% of children must be at or below 100% FPL

Hours of operation - - - - - - - - - - - - - - - Determined locally [2]

Operating schedule - - - - - - - - - - - - - Determined locally [2]

Special education enrollment - - - - - - - - - - - - - - 8,696

Federally funded Head Start enrollment - - - - - - - - - 12,901

State-funded Head Start enrollment - - - - - - - - - - - 1,449 [1]

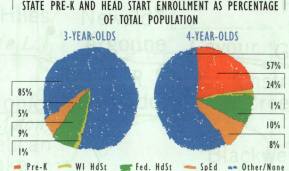

STATE PRE-K AND HEAD START ENROLLMENT AS PERCENTAGE OF TOTAL POPULATION

3-YEAR-OLDS
- 85%
- 5%
- 9%
- 1%

4-YEAR-OLDS
- 57%
- 24%
- 1%
- 10%
- 8%

■ Pre-K ■ WI HdSt ■ Fed. HdSt ■ SpEd ⚬ Other/None

QUALITY STANDARDS CHECKLIST

POLICY	STATE PRE-K REQUIREMENT	BENCHMARK	DOES REQUIREMENT MEET BENCHMARK?
Curriculum standards - - - - - - - - - - - - - - - - - -	None	Comprehensive	☐
Teacher degree requirement - - - - - - - - - - - - - -	CDA [3]	BA	☐
Teacher specialized training requirement - Meets CDA requirements		Specializing in Pre-K	☑
Assistant teacher degree requirement - Determined locally (public) [4], 18 yrs old + 1 course in EC (nonpublic)		CDA or equivalent	☐
Teacher in-service requirement - - - - - - - - Amount not specified		At least 15 hours/year	☐
Maximum class size		20 or lower	☑
3-year-olds -	17		
4-year-olds -	20		
Staff-child ratio		1:10 or better	☑
3-year-olds -	2:17		
4-year-olds -	1:10		
Screening/referral requirements - - - - - Vision, hearing, and health		Vision, hearing, and health	☑
Required support services - - - 2 home visits and support services [5]		At least 1 service	☑
Meal requirement - - - - - - - - - - - - - - Lunch and/or breakfast [6]		At least 1/day	☑

TOTAL: 6 of 10

RESOURCES

Total state Pre-K spending - - - - - - - - - - - - - - $7,425,000

Local match required? - - - - - - - - - - - - - - - - - - - No

State spending per child enrolled - - - - - - - - - - - $5,124

State Head Start spending - - - - - - - - - - - - - - $7,425,000 [7]

State spending per 3-year-old - - - - - - - - - - - - - $44 [1]

State spending per 4-year-old - - - - - - - - - - - - - $65 [1]

SPENDING PER CHILD ENROLLED

WI HDST*	$5,124
FED. HDST	$6,517
K–12**	$10,616

0 2 4 6 8 10 12 14
$ thousands

⚬ State Contribution ■ Local Contribution ■ Federal Contribution

* Programs may receive additional funds from federal or local sources that are not included in this figure.

** K–12 expenditures include capital spending as well as current operating expenditures.

Data are for the '02–'03 school year, unless otherwise noted.

[1] Wisconsin's state-funded Head Start program did not break its enrollment figure into specific numbers of 3- or 4-year-olds. As a result, age breakdowns used in the Access pie chart and Resources section were also estimated, using proportions of federal Head Start enrollees in each age category.

[2] Programs must operate a minimum of 3.5 hours per day, 4 days per week, and for 32 weeks per year, as required by federal Head Start Performance Standards.

[3] When a school district is the federal Head Start grantee, it may require a BA and appropriate licensure.

[4] When a school district is the federal Head Start grantee, it may require an AA degree and assistant license.

[5] Support services include education services or job training for parents, parenting support or training, parent involvement activities, health services for parents and children, referral to social services, transition to kindergarten activities, and other locally determined services.

[6] The federal Head Start Performance Standards require that part-day programs provide children with at least one-third of their daily nutritional needs, and full-day programs provide one-half to two-thirds of daily nutritional needs, depending on the length of the program day. All children in morning center-based settings must be given the opportunity to have a nutritious breakfast.

[7] All spending though this initiative is directed toward Head Start programs.

Wyoming

NO PROGRAM

ACCESS RANKING—4s	ACCESS RANKING—3s	RESOURCES RANKING
No Program		

ACCESS

Total state program enrollment - - - - - - - - - - - - - - - 0
School districts that offer state program - - - - - - - - - - NA
Income requirement - - - - - - - - - - - - - - - - - - - NA
Hours of operation - - - - - - - - - - - - - - - - - - - NA
Operating schedule - - - - - - - - - - - - - - - - - - - NA
Special education enrollment - - - - - - - - - - - - - - 1,340
Federally funded Head Start enrollment - - - - - - - - - 1,740
State-funded Head Start enrollment - - - - - - - - - - - - 0

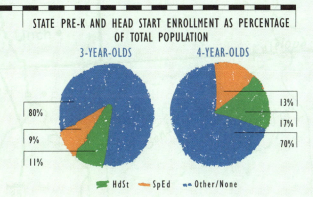

STATE PRE-K AND HEAD START ENROLLMENT AS PERCENTAGE OF TOTAL POPULATION

3-YEAR-OLDS
80%
9%
11%

4-YEAR-OLDS
13%
17%
70%

HdSt   SpEd   Other/None

QUALITY STANDARDS CHECKLIST

No Program

RESOURCES

Total state Pre-K spending - - - - - - - - - - - - - - - $0
Local match required? - - - - - - - - - - - - - - - - - NA
State spending per child enrolled - - - - - - - - - - - - $0
State spending per 3-year-old - - - - - - - - - - - - - - $0
State spending per 4-year-old - - - - - - - - - - - - - - $0

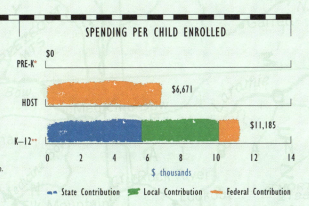

SPENDING PER CHILD ENROLLED

PRE-K* | $0
HDST | $6,671
K–12** | $11,185

0   2   4   6   8   10   12   14
$ thousands

State Contribution   Local Contribution   Federal Contribution

* Pre-K programs may receive additional funds from federal or local sources that are not included in this figure.
** K–12 expenditures include capital spending as well as current operating expenditures.

Data are for the '02–'03 school year, unless otherwise noted.

District of Columbia

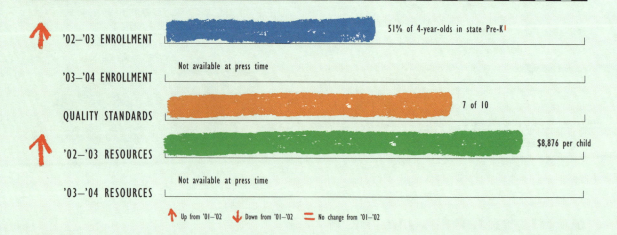

↑ '02–'03 ENROLLMENT		51% of 4-year-olds in state Pre-K
'03–'04 ENROLLMENT	Not available at press time	
QUALITY STANDARDS		7 of 10
↑ '02–'03 RESOURCES		$8,876 per child
'03–'04 RESOURCES	Not available at press time	

↑ Up from '01–'02   ↓ Down from '01–'02   ═ No change from '01–'02

The District of Columbia has funded prekindergarten since the 1960s. Most city schools offer the Public School Preschool program, though they are not required to do so. Funding is provided through the school funding formula with allocations made on a per pupil basis. All 4-year-olds are eligible for the program, although participation is limited by space and funds.

In addition to the preschool program, the District of Columbia Public School System (DCPS) also operates federally funded Head Start programs. These programs follow all federal Head Start Program Performance Standards and provide services for 3- and 4-year-old children from families with incomes below the federal poverty level. The program is available in communities that have large populations of low-income families who may benefit from the comprehensive services offered by Head Start.

In recent years, the DCPS prekindergarten program has experienced budget cuts, resulting in teacher layoffs, reduced funding for supplies and field trips, and schools being unable to accommodate all children whose families wish them to attend. However, there have also been some positive developments. The DCPS has reestablished an office for early childhood education and is collaborating with city agencies to align early childhood practice and policy. New instructional materials have been adopted for reading, math, social studies, and science in all prekindergarten classrooms. Additionally, citywide standards for all programs serving 4-year-olds are being developed, with the Creative Curriculum used to structure the preschool environment and The Letter People used to structure content. Finally, the Child Plus data management system is now applied to both preschool and Head Start.

Although this profile provides detailed information about access to prekindergarten programs within the District of Columbia in the same way as the state profiles, because it is a city the District is not ranked among the states according to resources or enrollment. Further complicating attempts to compare the District to states is the fact that the DCPS functions as both a state and a local education agency.

ACCESS

Total state program enrollment - - - - - - - - - - - - - - 4,281 [2]

School districts that offer state program - - - - - - - - - 71% [3]

Income requirement - - - - - - - - - - - - - - - - - - - None [4]

Hours of operation - - - - - - - - - - - - - - Full-day, full-week

Operating schedule - - - - - - - - - - - - - - - - Academic year

Special education enrollment - - - - - - - - - - - - - - - 188

Federally funded Head Start enrollment - - - - - - - - 2,753 [5]

State-funded Head Start enrollment - - - - - - - - - - - - 0

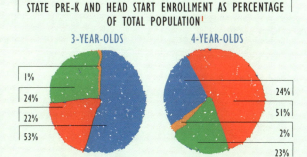

STATE PRE-K AND HEAD START ENROLLMENT AS PERCENTAGE OF TOTAL POPULATION[1]

3-YEAR-OLDS
- 1%
- 24%
- 22%
- 53%

4-YEAR-OLDS
- 24%
- 51%
- 2%
- 23%

■ HdSt   ■ Pre-K   ■ SpEd   ■ Other/None

QUALITY STANDARDS CHECKLIST

POLICY	STATE PRE-K REQUIREMENT	BENCHMARK	DOES REQUIREMENT MEET BENCHMARK?
Curriculum standards - - - - - - - - - - -	Not comprehensive	Comprehensive	☐
Teacher degree requirement - - - - - - - - - - - - - - -	BA	BA	☑
Teacher specialized training req. - - - -	Training and certification in EC (Pre-K–3)	Specializing in Pre-K	☑
Assistant teacher degree requirement - - - - - - - - - - -	HSD	CDA or equivalent	☐
Teacher in-service requirement - - - - - -	6 clock hours/year or 6 credit hours/5 years	At least 15 hours/year	☑
Maximum class size			
3-year-olds -	15	20 or lower	☑
4-year-olds -	20		
Staff-child ratio			
3-year-olds -	2:15	1:10 or better	☑
4-year-olds -	1:10		
Screening/referral requirements - - - - - - - - - - - - - -	None [6]	Vision, hearing, and health	☐
Required support services - - - - - - - - -	4 parent conferences and support services [7]	At least 1 service	☑
Meal requirement - - - - - - - - - - - - - -	Breakfast and lunch	At least 1/day	☑

TOTAL: **7** of 10

RESOURCES

Total state Pre-K spending - - - - - - - - - - - - - $38,000,000 [8]

Local match required? - - - - - - - - - - - - - - - - - - No [9]

State spending per child enrolled - - - - - - - - - - - $8,876

State spending per 3-year-old - - - - - - - - - - - $1,952

State spending per 4-year-old - - - - - - - - - - - $4,512

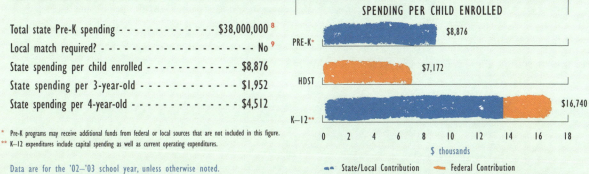

SPENDING PER CHILD ENROLLED

PRE-K* $8,876

HDST $7,172

K–12** $16,740

0 2 4 6 8 10 12 14 16 18
$ thousands

■- State/Local Contribution   ■ Federal Contribution

* Pre-K programs may receive additional funds from federal or local sources that are not included in this figure.

** K–12 expenditures include capital spending as well as current operating expenditures.

Data are for the '02–'03 school year, unless otherwise noted.

1. The increase in the percentage of 4-year-olds served in the District of Columbia's program is due to a declining population of 4-year-olds in the city rather than to an increase in the program's enrollment.
2. This enrollment count includes 1,782 children enrolled in the federally funded Head Start program operated by the DCPS system.
3. Programs are offered in all P–6 and P–8 schools, and in 104 out of 146 total schools in the District.
4. DCPS-operated Head Start programs follow guidelines for federal Head Start.
5. Some duplication may exist in the enrollment counts for city preschool and federal Head Start.
6. Children in DCPS-operated Head Start programs receive screenings and referrals as required by Head Start.
7. Support services include parent involvement activities, transition to kindergarten activities, and other locally determined services.
8. This spending figure includes $10 million in federal Head Start funds for DCPS-operated Head Start programs.
9. Head Start programs require a 20% match.

States That Do Not Invest in Prekindergarten Initiatives

Twelve states—Alaska, Florida, Idaho, Indiana, Mississippi, Montana, New Hampshire, North Dakota, Rhode Island, South Dakota, Utah, and Wyoming—do not invest in state prekindergarten initiatives. More than 900,000 children ages 3 and 4 live in these states, representing 12 percent of children this age in the United States. Including enrollment in federal Head Start, preschool special education, and state prekindergarten, only about 15 percent of 3- and 4-year-olds in these "dirty dozen" states are served—compared to almost 25 percent in the 38 states that fund preschool. Five of the six states that enroll the lowest percentage of preschool-age children in these three types of early childhood education programs do not fund a prekindergarten initiative.

While these states do not invest in their own prekindergarten initiatives, a few provide supplemental state funding for Head Start. For example, in 2002–2003, Alaska made $6,276,000 available to federal Head Start grantees to enhance services, improve quality, and (to the extent possible) serve additional children and families. Rhode Island gave $1.8 million in state funds as discretionary grants to fund an estimated 340 slots in Head Start. Idaho used $1.5 million of its TANF funds to support Head Start slots for 188 children, and New Hampshire provided $240,000 to federal Head Start programs to supplement teacher salaries.

The next few years represent a critical time during which policymakers should push for progress and turn these lagging states into national leaders in early education. Some states that do not fund prekindergarten have at least begun to look at investing in early childhood. In Idaho, the Boise School District launched a pilot preschool for low-income children using private and federal dollars. The state superintendent plans to build on this effort by offering a legislative proposal within the next few years for a comprehensive preschool plan. Although the state Legislature in Indiana did not adopt a plan for statewide full-day kindergarten, the governor used an executive order to create the Indiana Commission for Early Learning and School Readiness to continue promoting early childhood programs. The Wyoming Legislature has not addressed prekindergarten, but did approve $300,000 in 2003 to fund full-day kindergarten for an estimated 625 students in Title I schools. In Mississippi, the Stennis Institute published a report in January 2004 that included a recommendation for a full-day voluntary prekindergarten program by 2008 that would be coordinated with existing programs. Finally, an early learning task force in South Dakota will submit a report to the Legislature by December 2004.

This year we consider Florida and Rhode Island states that do not invest in preschool. The School Readiness Program in Florida coordinates a range of programs and services for children from birth to age 5, but uncertainty still surrounds the implementation of a voter mandate to make prekindergarten available to all 4-year-olds by 2005. In Rhode Island, money from the Early Childhood Investment Fund may be used to support preschool, but most districts opt to use these funds to provide a variety of other types of early childhood or elementary school services for children and families.

State Head Start Supplements

In 2002–2003, 17 states supplemented the federal Head Start program with state funds—Alaska, Connecticut, Delaware, Hawaii, Idaho, Maine, Maryland, Massachusetts, Minnesota, New Hampshire, New Mexico, Ohio, Oklahoma, Oregon, Pennsylvania, Rhode Island, and Wisconsin. Collectively, these states spent nearly $178 million on their Head Start supplements. The funds were used to support 28,000 slots in Head Start programs as well as wrap-around services and quality enhancements. In addition, Kansas provided $7.8 million for Early Head Start to serve infants and toddlers. To put this in context, total federal funding for Head Start was $6.67 billion in fiscal year 2003 for 909,608 slots.

State funding for Head Start is down from previous years. Overall, using inflation-adjusted figures for 2001–2002, state Head Start funding fell by $26 million, or 13 percent, from 2001–2002 to 2002–2003, with further decreases planned in a few states. Some states have had particularly large cuts to their Head Start supplements. New Mexico's funding for its state supplement decreased from $6 million in 2001–2002 to $1.65 million in 2002–2003. Connecticut reduced its funding for 2002–2003 by 14 percent while Oregon cut funding by 11 percent for the 2003–2005 biennium. In Ohio, most state funding has been replaced with TANF funds and overall funding has declined. State Head Start funding has also been reduced in Maine, Massachusetts, Minnesota, New Hampshire, and Wisconsin. Indiana and Washington eliminated state Head Start funding altogether after 2001–2002.

Although total state funding for Head Start has decreased, the number of children served by Head Start supplements has remained relatively constant. This fact suggests that states are providing less funding per child enrolled in the program or they are devoting fewer resources to enhancing services for children supported by federal funds.

All states providing Head Start supplements require that programs receiving funds comply with the comprehensive federal Head Start Program Performance Standards. However, states vary in their approaches to Head Start supplements with respect to the way the funds are used, the agencies eligible to receive funds, the role of the state in overseeing the funds, and other issues.

Although many states use their funds to support additional slots in the Head Start program, a number of states—including Connecticut, Maryland, Massachusetts, New Hampshire, New Mexico, Oklahoma, and Pennsylvania—target some or all of their Head Start funds toward enhancing services and/or providing extended-day/extended-year programming. For example, New Hampshire uses state funds to boost teacher salaries in order to attract and retain better-qualified staff. Connecticut supports additional slots as well as extended-day services and literacy initiatives with its funds. In Maryland, some of the funds are directed toward quality improvements and programs also use funds for professional development, parent education, mental health services, transition activities, and literacy projects.

States also differ as to which types of agencies they allow to receive state Head Start supplements. A state may provide funds to all federal Head Start grantees, a subset of the federal Head Start grantees, and, in a few cases, to "Head Start" agencies that receive no federal funds. For example, Oregon provides state Head Start funding to all federal Head Start grantees in the state (with the exception of Tribal Head Start programs, which are allowed to apply for funds but have not done so) as well as other non-federal grantees. In Ohio, all but two federal Head Start grantees receive state funds and one grantee receives only state funds and no federal dollars. Connecticut provides funds for quality enhancement to all federal Head Start grantees, but funds for additional slots and extended-day services are targeted to federal Head Start grantees in high-poverty urban school districts. Idaho funded some but not all federal grantees. In Alaska, Minnesota, New Hampshire, and Oklahoma, only federal Head Start grantees are allowed to receive funds, and most or all federal grantees do receive funds.

There is also variation in the extent to which states actively monitor state Head Start grantees. For example, Oklahoma state staff conducts on-site monitoring of every grantee annually. In Delaware, the state also conducts its own monitoring, which includes a site visit every three years. In Alaska, state staff members participate in federal reviews to the extent possible. Connecticut has a Memorandum of Understanding in place to include state participants in training of monitors and the monitoring process, but only federal staff is typically included on the monitoring teams. Idaho and New Hampshire reported that all monitoring is handled at the federal level.

In several states, TANF was the source of all or a portion of the funding for the state Head Start supplement. In Ohio, TANF funds accounted for $69.2 million out of $87.6 million in total funding for the state Head Start initiative in 2002–2003. In Alaska, about two-fifths of the funds for the Head Start supplement came from TANF dollars. TANF was the sole source of funding for the Head Start supplement in Idaho.

Most state Head Start supplements are relatively small and serve a relatively small number of children. Only a few states, Delaware, Minnesota, Ohio, Oregon, and Wisconsin, had supplements that were considered sufficiently large to be counted as full-fledged state prekindergarten initiatives and to merit their own pages in the state profile section. For other states, data on funding and enrollment for their Head Start supplements are incorporated into the tables and charts on access and resources shown on the state profile pages.

Appendices

- 🟢 Enrollment
- 🟠 Quality
- 🟠 Access
- 🔵 Standards
- 🟡 Resources

APPENDIX A: STATE SURVEY DATA

STATE	ACCESS		
	Availability of program	Are districts/towns/etc. required to offer program?	Program enrollment— Fall 2002, by age
Alabama	63 out of 67 counties (94%)	No, Optional/Competitive	1,260 4-year-olds
Arizona	45 out of 577 school districts and charter schools (8%)[1]	No, Optional/Competitive	4,092 total (mostly 4-year-olds)
Arkansas	194 out of 310 school districts (63%)[1]	No, Optional/Competitive	3,086 total[2]; 848 3-year-olds; 2,238 4-year-olds
California	320 out of 1,056 school districts (30%)[1]	No, Optional/Competitive	75,231 total[2]; 10,562 3-year-olds; 43,058 4-year-olds; 21,611 5-year-olds
Colorado	154 out of 178 school districts (87%)	No, Optional/Competitive	10,923 total; 906 3-year-olds; 8,459 4-year-olds; 1,494 5-year-olds; 64 younger than 3 years
Connecticut	43 out of 165 communities (26%)	Yes, Required for some	6,369 total
Delaware	3 out of 3 counties (100%)[1]	No, Optional/Competitive	843 4-year-olds
Georgia	159 out of 159 counties (100%)[1]	No, Optional/Competitive	65,900 4-year-olds
Hawaii	4 out of 4 counties (100%)	No, Optional/Competitive	934 4-year-olds
Illinois	642 out of 790 school districts (81%)	No, Optional/Competitive	55,984 total
Iowa	51 out of 99 counties (52%)	No, Optional/Competitive	2,355 total; 478 3-year-olds; 1,645 4-year-olds; 232 5-year-olds
Kansas	35% of school districts	No, Optional/Competitive	5,433 4-year-olds
Kentucky	176 out of 176 school districts (100%)	Yes	18,882 total; 5,207 3-year-olds; 13,675 4-year-olds
Louisiana 8(g)	65 out of 66 parishes (98%)	No, Optional	4,721 4-year-olds
LA4 & Starting Pts	56 out of 68 school districts (82%)[1]	No, Optional/Competitive	7,222 4-year-olds[2]
Louisiana NSECD	6 out of 64 parishes (9%)	No, Optional/Competitive	1,025 total
Maine	60 out of 285 school districts (21%)	No, Optional/Competitive	1,440 4-year-olds
Maryland	24 out of 24 school districts (100%)	Yes	20,569 total[1]; 1,426 3-year-olds; 18,605 4-year-olds
Massachusetts	335 out of 351 towns (95%)	No, Optional/Competitive	17,837 total[1,2]; 8,027 3-year-olds; 8,027 4-year-olds; 1,783 5-year-olds
Michigan	467 out of 550 school districts (85%)	No, Optional/Competitive	25,712 4-year-olds
Minnesota HdSt	[see footnotes][1]	NA	2,641 total; 862 3-year-olds; 1,344 4-year-olds; 240 5-year-olds[2]
Missouri	205 out of 524 school districts (39%)	No, Optional/Competitive	4,888 total; 1,714 3-year-olds; 3,174 4-year-olds
Nebraska	25 out of 517 school districts (5%)[1]	No, Optional/Competitive	1,100 total[2]; 341 3-year-olds; 583 4-year-olds
Nevada	11 out of 17 counties (65%)	No, Optional/Competitive	814 total; 218 3-year-olds; 492 4-year-olds; 16 5-year-olds[1]
New Jersey Abbott	30 out of 539 school districts (6%)	Yes, Required for 30 Abbott districts	36,465 total; 15,663 3-year-olds; 20,802 4-year-olds
New Jersey ECPA	102 out of 539 school districts (19%)	Yes, Required for some	7,213 total; 648 3-year-olds; 6,565 4-year-olds
New Mexico	15 out of 88 school districts (17%)	No, Optional/Competitive	850 total[1]
New York EPK	97 out of 680 school districts (14%)	No, Optional/Competitive	14,192 total; 1,430 3-year-olds; 12,762 4-year-olds
New York UPK	190 out of 680 school districts (28%)	No, Optional/Competitive	58,460 4-year-olds
North Carolina	91 out of 100 counties (91%)	No, Optional	6,271 4-year-olds
Ohio HdSt	85 out of 88 counties (97%)	No, Optional/Competitive	17,284 total
Ohio PSP	54 out of 88 counties (61%)	No, Optional/Competitive	6,259 total[1]
Oklahoma	494 out of 541 school districts (91%)	No, Optional	28,060 4-year-olds
Oregon	36 out of 36 counties (100%)	No, Optional/Competitive	4,000 total; 1,360 3-year-olds (estimate); 2,640 4-year-olds (estimate)
Pennsylvania	32 out of 501 school districts (6%)	No, Optional/Competitive	2,609 4-year-olds
South Carolina	85 out of 85 school districts (100%)	Yes[1]	17,279 total; 955 3-year-olds; 16,324 4-year-olds
Tennessee	63 out of 136 school districts (46%)[1]	No, Optional/Competitive	3,280 total; 800 3-year-olds; 2,400 4-year-olds; 70 5-year-olds (with IEPs)
Texas	933 out of 1256 school districts (74%)	No, Optional/Competitive[1]	157,498 total[2]; 13,662 3-year-olds; 143,074 4-year-olds; 654 5-year-olds
Vermont	144 out of 251 towns (57%)	No, Optional/Competitive	1,110 total; 456 3-year-olds; 644 4-year-olds
Virginia	75 out of 137 school districts (55%)	No, Optional/Competitive	5,886 4-year-olds
Washington	122 out of 295 school districts (41%)	No, Optional/Competitive	6,918 total; 1,389 3-year-olds; 5,529 4-year-olds
West Virginia	44 out of 55 counties (80%)	No, Optional/Competitive	7,727 total; age breakdown unknown
Wisconsin 4K	189 out of 416 elementary school districts (45%)	No, Optional[1]	16,051 4-year-olds
Wisconsin HdSt	32 out of 34 federal Head Start grantees (94%)	No, Optional/Competitive	1,449 total

STATE	Enrollment explanation, if not unduplicated Fall count	Number of children counted in enrollment supported using...
Alabama	NA	Local sources, 1,260; Fed. HdSt, 144[1]; TANF, 222
Arizona	NA	Local sources (number unknown)[2]
Arkansas	NA	Local sources[3], IDEA (numbers unknown)[4]
California	As of Apr. 2003[3]	IDEA, 2.9%
Colorado	Based on Oct. 1 count period, enrollment reflects number of children funded in CPP during FY 2002–2003	Local sources (number unknown); Fed. HdSt, almost 16%; CCDF, TANF (numbers unknown)[1]
Connecticut	Count from Oct. 2002 (children are not tracked by age)	Local sources (all children partially supported w/parent fees and/or child care certificates); Fed. HdSt, 730; IDEA, 211
Delaware	Funded slots	No additional funds
Georgia	NA	None
Hawaii	NA	Fed. HdSt (number unknown)[1]
Illinois	Year-end data	None
Iowa	NA	Local sources, 286[1]; Fed. HdSt (number unknown); IDEA, 379[2]
Kansas	NA	Local sources (number unknown)[1]
Kentucky	No enrollment cut-off date	Local sources[1], Fed. HdSt[2], IDEA[2]
Louisiana 8(g)	May include duplicated count[1]	Local sources, IDEA, and TANF may be used (numbers of children served with these sources unknown)
LA4 & Starting Pts	NA	IDEA, 405; TANF, 6,505
Louisiana NSECD	NA	TANF, 1,025
Maine	NA	Local sources, IDEA (numbers unknown); Fed. HdSt, CCDF, TANF (DK if used)
Maryland	NA	Local sources (number unknown); Fed. HdSt, 2,264[2]; IDEA (number unknown)[3]
Massachusetts	NA	Local sources[3], Fed. HdSt[4], IDEA (numbers unknown); TANF[5]
Michigan	Funded slots	None[1]
Minnesota HdSt	Funded slots	Required local match for Fed. HdSt funds (number unknown)[3]; IDEA, 271 (estimate); CCDF, 333 (estimate); TANF (number unknown)
Missouri	NA	Local sources, Fed. HdSt, IDEA, CCDF (numbers unknown)[1]
Nebraska	NA	Local sources[3]; Fed. HdSt, 21%; IDEA, 9%; CCDF Subsidy, 5%
Nevada	Enrollment count Dec. 15, 2002	IDEA (number unknown)[2]
New Jersey Abbott	As of Jan. 15, 2003	Fed. HdSt, 2,458 partially supported; IDEA, 1,130 self-contained, 577 inclusion
New Jersey ECPA	NA	Fed. HdSt, 42; IDEA, 980
New Mexico	Approximation of the number of children served; fluctuates depending on the time it is reported	Local sources, IDEA, state child development funds[2] (numbers unknown)
New York EPK	NA	Local sources, 14,192[1]; IDEA, 1,633
New York UPK	NA	Fed. HdSt, 5,588[1]; IDEA, 2,434[2]; CCDF, TANF, and local sources (numbers unknown)[3]
North Carolina	NA	Local sources, Fed. HdSt, IDEA, CCDF, TANF (numbers unknown)
Ohio HdSt	Enrollment as of Dec. 1, 2002	TANF (number unknown)
Ohio PSP	Enrollment as of Dec. 1, 2002	Local sources, 4,913[2]
Oklahoma	NA	Fed. HdSt[1], IDEA[2]
Oregon	Enrollment as of Jan. 2003	Local sources, 152
Pennsylvania	NA	Local sources, Fed. HdSt, IDEA (numbers unknown)
South Carolina	NA	Local sources, 2,348[2]; IDEA, 580[3]; Title I (number unknown)
Tennessee	Enrollment total represents data from end-of-year report	Fed. HdSt, 415[1]; IDEA, 399[2]; TANF, 1,836
Texas	NA	Local sources (number unknown)[3]
Vermont	10 children are classified as "other" age group	Local sources (number unknown); Fed. HdSt, 77[1]; IDEA, 139[2]; CCDF, 150; TANF (DK if used)
Virginia	NA	Not available
Washington	Count as of Jun. 30, 2003[1]	Local sources, IDEA (numbers unknown); CCDF, 6,918[2]
West Virginia	NA	Fed. HdSt (number unknown)[1]; IDEA, 2,400
Wisconsin 4K	NA	Local sources, 16,051[2]; IDEA[3] (number unknown); Fed. HdSt, CCDF, TANF (DK if used)
Wisconsin HdSt	Funded slots	Local sources[1], HdSt[1], IDEA[2], CCDF, TANF (numbers unknown)

STATE	ACCESS	
	Number of children not counted in enrollment supported using...	Program enrollment by type of school—Fall 2002
Alabama	None	Public, 558; HdSt, 144; Private CC, 378; Faith-based, 18; Other, 162[2]
Arizona	Local sources (number unknown)[3]; Fed. HdSt, 385; IDEA (number unknown)	Public, 3,598; HdSt, 205[4]; Private CC, 289[5]
Arkansas	None	Public, 1,447; HdSt, 366; Private CC, 303[5]
California	None	DK[4]
Colorado	Local sources, Fed. HdSt, IDEA, CCDF, TANF (numbers unknown)	Public, 5,983; HdSt, 1,492; Private CC, 1,954; Full-day kindergarten, 1,494[2]
Connecticut	DK	Public, 943; HdSt, 1,832; Private CC, 2,734; Faith-based, 860
Delaware	No additional funds	Public, 227; HdSt, 481; Private CC, 17; Community college CC, 17; Nonprofit organizations, 101
Georgia	None	Public, 28,445; HdSt, 782; Private CC, 36,137[2]
Hawaii	Fed. HdSt (number unknown)[1]	HdSt, Private CC, Faith-based (numbers unknown)[2]
Illinois	IDEA (number unknown)	Public, majority
Iowa	None	Public, 1,343; HdSt, 740; Private CC, 272
Kansas	Local sources (number unknown)[2,3]	Public, 5,433
Kentucky	Local sources	Public, >75%; HdSt, Private CC, and Faith-based (numbers unknown)[3]
Louisiana 8(g)	IDEA and TANF may be used (numbers unknown)	Public, 4,721
LA4 & Starting Pts	Local sources, 251[3]	Public, 6,446; Private CC, 40 (LA4); Faith-based, 19 (Starting Points)
Louisiana NSECD	None	Private CC, 26; Faith-based, 999
Maine	None	Public, 1,440
Maryland	IDEA, 2,723 3-year-olds, 4,039 4-year-olds	Public, 20,490[2]; Private CC, 79
Massachusetts	Local sources, Fed. HdSt, IDEA, CCDF, TANF (numbers unknown)	Public, 6,674; HdSt, 2,458; Private CC (including Faith-based), 8,013; Family CC, 1,248[6]
Michigan	Local sources, Fed. HdSt, CCDF, TANF (numbers unknown)	Public, 20,481; HdSt, 2,486; Private CC, 2,280; Faith-based, 149; Home-based, 316
Minnesota HdSt	Local sources, Fed. HdSt[4], IDEA, CCDF, TANF (numbers unknown)	DK[5]
Missouri	None	Public, 3,798; Private CC, 946; Nonprofit, 144
Nebraska	None	DK[4]
Nevada	None	Public, 822[3]; Other, 205[4,5]
New Jersey Abbott	None	Public, 11,387; HdSt, 2,458; Private CC, 22,620
New Jersey ECPA	None	Public, 6,426; HdSt, 42; Private CC, 745
New Mexico	None	Public, 123[3]; Private CC, 284 (includes 3 early intervention); Faith-based, 46; Higher Ed, 87[3]
New York EPK	None	Public, 14,192
New York UPK	Local sources, Fed. HdSt, IDEA[4], CCDF, TANF (numbers unknown)	Public, 21,524; HdSt, 5,588; Private CC, 17,530; Faith-based (number unknown); Family CC, 879; Other, 12,939
North Carolina	Local sources, Fed. HdSt, IDEA, CCDF, TANF (numbers unknown)	Public, 43%; HdSt, 10%; Private CC, 43%; Faith-based (number unknown)
Ohio HdSt	None	Public, 2,249; HdSt, 8,760; Private CC, 5,885; Family CC, 390
Ohio PSP	Local sources (number unknown)	Public, 8,003; HdSt, 540[3]
Oklahoma	None	Public, 23,134; HdSt, 4,004; Private CC, 266; Faith-based, 98 (estimated totals)
Oregon	None	Public, 835; HdSt, 2,993; Private CC, 69; Faith-based, 21; Family CC, 18; Community Pre-K, 46; Higher Ed, 18
Pennsylvania	None	Public, 2,609
South Carolina	None	Public, 17,279[4]
Tennessee	None	Public, 2,700; HdSt, 180; Private CC, 120; Faith-based, 180; Higher Ed, 100
Texas	None	Public, 157,498[4]
Vermont	None	Public, 621; HdSt, 77; Private CC, 122; Family CC, 14; Parent Child Centers, 266[3]
Virginia	Not available	Not available
Washington	Local sources, Fed. HdSt, IDEA, CCDF (numbers unknown)	Public, 3,950; Private CC, 1,345; Faith-based, 304; Family CC, 65; Other, 1,254[3]
West Virginia	None	Public, 7,727
Wisconsin 4K	None	Public, 16,051[4]
Wisconsin HdSt	None	HdSt, 1,449; Other (number unknown)[3]

STATE	ACCESS		
	Daily hours of operation	Weekly operating schedule	Yearly operating schedule
Alabama	At least 6 hours per day	5 days/week	Academic year
Arizona	Determined locally	Determined locally[6]	Determined locally[6]
Arkansas	At least 6 hours per day	5 days/week	Academic year
California	Determined locally	5 days/week	Academic year[5]
Colorado	At least 2.5 but not more than 4 hours per day	Less than 5 days/week[3]	Academic year
Connecticut	Determined by type of slot[1]	5 days/week	Determined by type of slot[1]
Delaware	At least 4 but not more than 6 hours per day	5 days/week	Academic year
Georgia	At least 6 hours per day	5 days/week	Academic year
Hawaii	Determined locally[3]	5 days/week	Calendar year
Illinois	Determined locally[1]	Determined locally[1]	Academic year
Iowa	Determined locally[3]	Determined locally[4]	Determined locally[4]
Kansas	Determined locally[4]	5 days/week	Academic year
Kentucky	At least 2.5 but not more than 4 hours per day	Determined locally (standard is 4 to 5 days/week)	Academic year
Louisiana 8(g)	At least 6 hours per day	5 days/week	Academic year
LA4 & Starting Pts	At least 6 hours per day	5 days/week	Academic year
Louisiana NSECD	10 hours per day	5 days/week	Academic year
Maine	Determined locally—most operate for 2.5 hours per day	Determined locally[1]	Determined locally[2]
Maryland	At least 2.5 hours per day (450 children attend more than 6 hours per day)	5 days/week	Academic year
Massachusetts	At least 2.5 but not more than 10 hours per day[7]	2 to 5 days/week[8]	Determined locally[8]
Michigan	At least 2 but not more than 4 hours per day	Less than 5 days/week[2]	Determined locally
Minnesota HdSt	Determined locally[6]	Determined locally[6]	Determined locally[6]
Missouri	Determined locally[2]	5 days/week[3]	Determined locally[4]
Nebraska	At least 12 hours per week for part-day programs	Determined locally[5]	Determined locally[6]
Nevada	At least 2 but not more than 4 hours per day	Determined locally[6]	Determined locally[7]
New Jersey Abbott	At least 6 hours per day	5 days/week	Determined locally[1]
New Jersey ECPA	At least 3 hours per day	5 days/week	Academic year
New Mexico	Determined locally	Determined locally[4]	Determined locally[4]
New York EPK	Determined locally	Determined locally[2]	Academic year
New York UPK	Determined locally[5]	5 days/week	Academic year
North Carolina	At least 6 hours per day	5 days/week	Academic year
Ohio HdSt	Determined locally[1]	Determined locally[1]	Determined locally[1]
Ohio PSP	Determined locally[4]	Determined locally[4]	Determined locally[4]
Oklahoma	Determined locally[3]	5 days/week	Academic year
Oregon	At least 3.5 but not more than 6 hours per day	Determined locally[1]	Determined locally[2]
Pennsylvania	Determined locally[1]	5 days/week	Academic year
South Carolina	At least 2 but not more than 4 hours per day[5]	5 days/week[6]	Academic year[7]
Tennessee	At least 4 but not more than 6 hours per day	5 days/week	Academic year
Texas	At least 2 but not more than 4 hours per day[5]	5 days/week	Academic year[6]
Vermont	Determined locally; average of 10.5 hours per week	Determined locally	Determined locally[4]
Virginia	At least 6 hours per day	5 days/week	Academic year
Washington	At least 2.5 hours per session	Determined locally[4]	Determined locally[5]
West Virginia	Determined locally[2]	Determined locally[2]	Academic year
Wisconsin 4K	Determined locally	Determined locally	Academic year[5]
Wisconsin HdSt	Determined locally	Determined locally	Determined locally

STATE	ACCESS		
	Minimum operating schedule	Does funding vary based on operating schedule?	Do any programs offer wrap-around services?
Alabama	6.5 hours/day, 175 days/year	No	No
Arizona	None[7]	No	No
Arkansas	7.5 hours/day, 178 days/year	No	Yes
California	3 hours/day, 175 days/year	Yes, varies by days of operation per year	Yes
Colorado	2.5 hours/day, 10 hours/week, 360 hours/year	No	Yes
Connecticut	Full-day: 10 hours/day, 5 days/week, 50 weeks/year; Part-day: 2.5 hours/day, 180 days/year[1]	Yes, full-day—$7,000; part-day—$4,500; extended-day—$2,500	Yes
Delaware	160 days/year	No	Yes
Georgia	6.5 hours/day, 5 days/week, 36 weeks/year	No	Yes
Hawaii	None	Yes, amount per child depends on center's tuition cost (up to a maximum) and number of months in operation	Yes
Illinois	180 days/year	Yes, full-day programs have higher cost per child, but not double	Yes
Iowa	None	No	Yes
Kansas	2.5 hours/day, 465 hours/academic year	No	No
Kentucky	2.5 hours/day, plus mealtime (breakfast or lunch)	No	Yes
Louisiana 8(g)	None	No	No[2]
LA4 & Starting Pts	360 instructional minutes/day, 177 instructional days/year	No	Yes
Louisiana NSECD	180 days/year	No	Yes
Maine	None	No	No
Maryland	2.5 hours/day, 5 days/week	No	Yes
Massachusetts	None	Yes, determined locally	Yes
Michigan	At least 30 weeks/year	No	Yes
Minnesota HdSt	3.5 hours/day, 4 days/week, 32 weeks/year[6]	No	Yes
Missouri	5 days/week, 9 months/year	Yes, per-child funding is less for half-day programs	Yes
Nebraska	12 hours/week, academic year	Yes, based on length of program day	No[7]
Nevada	None	Yes, based on total program delivery needs	Not directly; several partner with other programs in order to provide full-day service
New Jersey Abbott	6 hours/day, 180 days/year	Yes, per-pupil amounts vary due to factors unique to each district, such as teacher salaries and facilities costs	Yes
New Jersey ECPA	3 hours/day, 180 days/year	No	Yes
New Mexico	None	No	Yes
New York EPK	12 hours/week, at least 4 days/week	No[3]	No
New York UPK	2.5 hours/day, 5 days/week, 180 days/year	No	Yes[6]
North Carolina	180 days/year	No	No[1]
Ohio HdSt	3.5 hours/day, 4 days/week, 32 weeks/year[1]	No	No
Ohio PSP	3.5 hours/day, 4 days/week, 32 weeks/year[4]	No	No
Oklahoma	At least 2.5 hours/day, 5 days/week, 175 teaching days/year	Yes[4]	Yes
Oregon	474 hours/year (including classroom and home visit time)	Yes, reasonable cost based on program design and local costs	Yes
Pennsylvania	Programs using basic education funding must operate 2.5 hours/day, 180 days/year	No	DK
South Carolina	2.5 hours/day, 180 days/year	No[8]	Yes[9]
Tennessee	5.5 hours/day (excluding naptime), 5 days/week, 180 days/year	No	Yes
Texas	3 hours/day (half-day), 6 hours/day (full-day); 180 days/year	Yes[5]	Yes
Vermont	10 hours/week, 32 weeks/year	No	Yes
Virginia	None	No	No
Washington	240 hours of direct child services over 30 weeks[6]	No	No
West Virginia	None	Yes, hours per week determine percentage of FTE	Yes
Wisconsin 4K	437 hours/year[6]	Yes[7]	Yes
Wisconsin HdSt	3.5 hours/day, 4 days/week, 32 weeks/year	No	Yes

STATE	ACCESS			
	Number of children receiving wrap-around services	Funding sources for wrap-around services	Does program have home-based option?	Number of children in home-based option
Alabama	NA	NA	No	NA
Arizona	NA	NA	No	NA
Arkansas	Approx. 40%	CCDF, private pay (parent fees)	Yes	4,719 (not counted in enrollment total)
California	3,536[6]	General Child Care (state funds)	No	NA
Colorado	DK	State Pre-K, CCDF, parent tuition, HdSt, private grants[4]	No	NA
Connecticut	730	State Pre-K	No	NA
Delaware	DK	CCDF, private pay	No	NA
Georgia	DK	State Pre-K, CCDF[3], parent fees, local funds	No	NA
Hawaii	90% (estimate)	State Pre-K, CCDF	No	NA
Illinois	DK	CCDF	No	NA
Iowa	DK	CCDF, HdSt	No	NA
Kansas	NA	NA	No	NA
Kentucky	DK[4]	CCDF, Family Resource Centers	Yes	112
Louisiana 8(g)	NA	NA	No	NA
LA4 & Starting Pts	2,705 (LA4)[4]	TANF, tuition (for families above 185% FPL)	No	NA
Louisiana NSECD	DK	TANF	No	NA
Maine	NA	NA	No	NA
Maryland	5%	State Pre-K, CCDF, Judith P. Hoyer Early Care and Education Enhancement Program funds[4]	No	NA
Massachusetts	DK[9]	TANF, State Pre-K	Yes	1,169 (not counted in enrollment total)
Michigan	DK	CCDF, tuition, local sources	Yes	316 (counted in enrollment total)
Minnesota HdSt	12%	CCDF, other sources	Yes	220 (counted in enrollment total)
Missouri	DK	CCDF, local funds, parent fees	No	NA
Nebraska	NA	NA	No	NA
Nevada	DK	Child care subsidy funds, other sources	Yes[8]	171[9]
New Jersey Abbott	28,378 (78%)	DHS funds	No	NA
New Jersey ECPA	DK	DK	No	NA
New Mexico	15%	State Pre-K	Yes	213[5]
New York EPK	NA	NA	No	NA
New York UPK	DK[7]	CCDF, parent fees, TANF, other local sources (United Way)	No	NA
North Carolina	NA	NA	No	NA
Ohio HdSt	NA	CCDF	Yes	625 (counted in enrollment total)
Ohio PSP	NA	NA	No	NA
Oklahoma	Determined locally	CCDF, parent fees, HdSt	No	NA
Oregon	13% of all federally- and state-funded HdSt	State Pre-K, CCDF, HdSt	Yes	209 (estimate; counted in enrollment total)
Pennsylvania	NA	NA	No	NA
South Carolina	DK	CCDF	No	NA
Tennessee	38%	Child care certificate dollars by private party	No	NA
Texas	DK[7]	Local sources	No	NA
Vermont	488	CCDF, parent fees	No	NA
Virginia	NA	NA	No	NA
Washington	NA	NA	Yes	20 (counted in enrollment total)
West Virginia	DK	CCDF, 21st Century (federal program)	No	NA
Wisconsin 4K	DK	CCDF, HdSt, local school revenue	Yes[8]	DK
Wisconsin HdSt	DK	State Pre-K, CCDF	Yes, if the federal grantee has such a model	DK

STATE	ELIGIBILITY REQUIREMENTS		
	Minimum age for eligibility	Maximum age for eligibility	Kindergarten-eligibility age
Alabama	4 by Sept. 1	5	5 by Sept. 1
Arizona	Children are eligible for Pre-K if they are not eligible for K	5 by Sept. 1	5 by Sept. 1
Arkansas	Birth	5 by Sept. 15	5 by Sept. 15
California	3 by Dec. 2	5 by Dec. 2	5 by Dec. 2
Colorado	3 by Oct. 1[5]	6[6]	5 by Oct. 1 (some school districts may have earlier eligibility dates)
Connecticut	3	5	5 by Jan. 1
Delaware	4 by Aug. 31	5 by Aug. 31	5 by Aug. 31
Georgia	4 by Sept. 1	5 by Sept. 1[4]	5 by Sept. 1
Hawaii	3 by Dec. 31[4]	5 by Dec. 31	5 by Dec. 31
Illinois	3 by Sept. 1	5 by Aug. 31	5 by Sept. 1
Iowa	3 by Sept. 15	5 by Sept. 15	5 by Sept. 15
Kansas	4 by Aug. 31	5 by Aug. 31	5 by Aug. 31
Kentucky	3[5]	5 by Oct. 1[6]	5 by Oct. 1
Louisiana 8(g)	4 by Sept. 30	5 by Sept. 30	5 by Sept. 30
LA4 & Starting Pts	4 by Sept. 30	5 by Sept. 30	5 by Sept. 30
Louisiana NSECD	4 by Sept. 30	5 by Sept. 30	5 by Sept. 30
Maine	4 by Oct. 15	No limit	5 by Oct. 15
Maryland	4 by Nov. 30	5 by Jan. 1	5 by Dec. 31
Massachusetts	2 years, 9 months	Sept. of K-eligibility year	Determined locally
Michigan	4 by Dec. 1	5 by Dec. 1	5 by Dec. 1
Minnesota HdSt	Birth[7]	May participate until slot in K or elementary school is available	5 by Sept. 1
Missouri	3 by Aug. 1	5 by Aug. 1	5 by Aug. 1
Nebraska	6 weeks	5 by Oct. 15	5 by Oct. 15
Nevada	Birth	5 by Oct. 1	5 by Sept. 30
New Jersey Abbott	3 by locally determined date	5 by locally determined date	Determined locally
New Jersey ECPA	3 by locally determined date	5 by locally determined date	Determined locally
New Mexico	Birth	5 by Aug. 31	5 by Sept. 1
New York EPK	3 by Dec. 1	5 by Dec. 1	5 by Dec. 1[4]
New York UPK	4 by Dec. 1	5 by Dec. 1	5 by Dec. 1[8]
North Carolina	4 by Oct. 16	5 by Oct. 16	5 by Oct. 17
Ohio HdSt	3	5	5 by Aug. 1 or Sept. 30 (determined locally)
Ohio PSP	3 by locally determined date	5 by Aug. 1 or Sept. 30 (determined locally)	5 by Aug. 1 or Sept. 30 (determined locally)
Oklahoma	4 by Sept. 1	5	5 by Sept. 1
Oregon	3 by Sept. 1	5 by Sept. 1	5 by Sept. 1
Pennsylvania	4 by locally determined date	5 by locally determined date	Determined locally
South Carolina	4 by Sept. 1	5 by Sept. 1	5 by Sept. 1
Tennessee	3 by Sept. 30	5 by Sept. 30	5 by Sept. 30
Texas	3 by Sept. 1	5 by Sept. 1	5 by Sept. 1
Vermont	3 by Sept. 1–Dec. 31, depending on locally determined K-eligibility date	5 by Sept. 1–Dec. 31, depending on locally determined K-eligibility date	5 by Sept. 1–Dec. 31, depending on locally determined K-eligibility date
Virginia	4 by Sept. 30	5 by Sept. 30	5 by Sept. 30
Washington	3 by Aug. 31	5 by Aug. 31	5 by Aug. 31
West Virginia	3 by Sept. 1	5 by Sept. 1	5 by Sept. 1
Wisconsin 4K	4 by Sept. 1	No limit	5 by Sept. 1
Wisconsin HdSt	3 by Sept. 1	5 by Sept. 1	5 by Sept. 1

State	Number of years attendance allowed	Income requirement?	Are other risk factors tied to eligibility?	Number of risk factors tied to eligibility
Alabama	2[3]	No	No[4]	NA
Arizona	1[8]	Yes; all families at or below 185% FPL ($27,787 for family of 3)	No	NA
Arkansas	5	Yes; 156% FPL ($23,523 for family of 3)	Yes[6]	1
California	2	Yes; 230% FPL ($34,632 for family of 3)[7]	Yes[8]	1
Colorado	1	No	Yes[7]	1[8]
Connecticut	2	Yes; each participating community must ensure that at least 60% of children enrolled are from families with an income at or below 75% SMI	No	NA
Delaware	1	Yes; 90% of children must be below 100% FPL	No[2]	NA
Georgia	1	No	No	NA
Hawaii	2[4]	Yes; 85% SMI ($44,136 for family of 3)[5]	Yes, special needs	1
Illinois	2	No[2]	Yes[3]	Determined locally[4]
Iowa	2	Yes; 80% of children must be from families below 130% FPL	Yes[5]	1
Kansas	1	Yes; eligibility for free lunch (130% FPL)[5]	Yes[6]	1
Kentucky	2[7]	Yes; 4-year-olds w/o disability must be eligible for free lunch ($19,977 for family of 3)	Yes, disability	1
Louisiana 8(g)	1	No[3]	Yes[4]	2
LA4 & Starting Pts	1	Yes; 185% FPL[5]	No	NA
Louisiana NSECD	1	Yes; 200% FPL	No	NA
Maine	1	No	No	NA
Maryland	1	No	Yes[5]	1
Massachusetts	2	Yes; up to 125% SMI (after families up to 100% SMI are served)	Yes[10]	1[11]
Michigan	1	Yes; 50% of children must be eligible for free or reduced-price lunch ($27,787 for family of 3)	Yes[3]	2
Minnesota HdSt	2	Yes; 90% of children must be at or below 100% FPL	Yes[8]	1
Missouri	2	No[5]	No	NA
Nebraska	5	No[8]	Yes[8]	1
Nevada	5[10]	No[11]	No[11]	NA
New Jersey Abbott	2	No[2]	No	NA
New Jersey ECPA	2	No[1]	No	NA
New Mexico	5	No	No[6]	NA
New York EPK	2[5]	Yes; economically disadvantaged[6]	No[7]	NA
New York UPK	1	No	No	NA
North Carolina	1	No[2]	Yes[3]	Determined locally[4]
Ohio HdSt	2	Yes; 90% of children must be from families at or below 185% FPL[2]	Yes, at least 10% of students must be identified with disability	1
Ohio PSP	2	Yes; 185% FPL—applies to all children funded by Public Preschool grant	No	NA
Oklahoma	1[5]	No	No	NA
Oregon	2	Yes; at least 80% of children must be from families with incomes below 100% FPL[3]	Yes[4]	1
Pennsylvania	1	No	No	NA
South Carolina	1[10]	No	Yes[11]	Determined locally—based on local need
Tennessee	2[3]	Yes[4]; 185% of HHS poverty guidelines	Yes[5]	1
Texas	2	Yes[8]	Yes[1]	1
Vermont	2	Yes; at least 50% of children must be below 185% FPL ($27,787 for family of 3)	Yes[5]	1
Virginia	1	No	Determined locally[1]	Determined locally[1]
Washington	1[7]	Yes; 90% of children must be at or below 110% FPL[8]	Yes[9]	1
West Virginia	2	No	No	NA
Wisconsin 4K	1[9]	No	No	NA
Wisconsin HdSt	2	Yes; 90% of children must be at or below 100% FPL	Yes[4]	1

STATE	ELIGIBILITY REQUIREMENTS	
	How do risk factors relate to income criteria?	Is there a sliding payment scale based on income?
Alabama	NA	No
Arizona	NA	No
Arkansas	Meeting the income criteria can count as one of the risk factors	No
California	Children must have one risk factor in addition to meeting the income criteria, except for those with CPS referrals	No
Colorado	Meeting the income criteria can count as one of the risk factors	No
Connecticut	NA	Yes, the School Readiness Sliding Fee Scale sets parent fees based on family size and income. The scale applies to all participants unless a fee is determined by certificates from Care 4 Kids.[2]
Delaware	NA	No
Georgia	NA	NA
Hawaii	Children must meet the income criteria, but a child with identified special needs is given higher priority	Yes, applies to children in families with incomes above 100% of poverty[6]
Illinois	NA—though low income may be considered locally as a risk factor	No
Iowa	Meeting the income criteria can count as one of the risk factors	Yes, applies to children over the income guideline who have other risk factors
Kansas	Meeting the income criteria can count as one of the risk factors[7]	No
Kentucky	4-year-olds must meet income criteria or have a disability; 3-year-olds must have a disability	No[8]
Louisiana 8(g)	NA	No
LA4 & Starting Pts	NA	Yes, applies to children who do not meet the income criteria
Louisiana NSECD	NA	No
Maine	NA	No
Maryland	NA	No
Massachusetts	Income criteria apply to all children except those in legal custody of grandparents or other family members, foster children, and children served with funding streams targeted to at-risk families	Yes[12]
Michigan	Meeting the income criteria can count as one of the risk factors[4]	No
Minnesota HdSt	Meeting the income criteria can count as one of the risk factors	No
Missouri	NA	Yes[6]
Nebraska	Meeting the income criteria can count as one of the risk factors	Yes, applies to children who do not meet any risk factors
Nevada	NA	No
New Jersey Abbott	NA	No
New Jersey ECPA	NA	No
New Mexico	NA	No
New York EPK	NA	No
New York UPK	NA	No
North Carolina	Income is considered to be the primary risk factor	No
Ohio HdSt	Meeting the income criteria can count as one of the risk factors	No
Ohio PSP	NA	Yes, families between 100% and 185% FPL pay on a sliding scale. Families above 185% FPL pay full tuition.
Oklahoma	NA	No
Oregon	Meeting the income criteria can count as one of the risk factors[5]	No
Pennsylvania	NA	No
South Carolina	NA	No
Tennessee	Children who qualify based on other risk factors do not need to meet income guidelines	No[6]
Texas	Meeting the income criteria can count as one of the risk factors	No
Vermont	Meeting the income criteria can count as one of the risk factors	No
Virginia	NA	No
Washington	Meeting the income criteria can count as one of the risk factors	No
West Virginia	NA	No
Wisconsin 4K	NA	No
Wisconsin HdSt	Meeting the income criteria can count as one of the risk factors	No

ACCESS FOR CHILDREN WITH SPECIAL NEEDS

	Number/percentage of children enrolled who have an IEP/IFSP	How are services for preschoolers with special needs provided?
Alabama	DK	Children are served in state Pre-K classrooms or in other locations, and are funded by a combination of state Pre-K funds and funds from other sources, or entirely by other sources.
Arizona	Minimal[9]	Children are served in state Pre-K classrooms but are funded by other sources such as IDEA; or are served through, and funded by, sources other than the state Pre-K program.
Arkansas	26%	Children are served in state Pre-K classrooms or in other locations, and are funded by state Pre-K, by other sources such as IDEA, or by a combination of funds.
California	2.9% (estimated)	Children are served in state Pre-K classrooms and are funded by a combination of state Pre-K funds and funds from other sources.
Colorado	None[9]	Children are served in state Pre-K classrooms or in other locations, but are funded by other sources such as IDEA and state early childhood special education funds.
Connecticut	313[3]	Children are served in state Pre-K classrooms or in other locations, but are funded by other sources such as IDEA.
Delaware	10%	Children are served in state Pre-K classrooms or in other locations, and are funded by a combination of state Pre-K and other sources, or supported entirely by other sources.
Georgia	NA	Children are served through, and funded by, sources other than the state Pre-K program.[5]
Hawaii	DK	Children are served in state Pre-K classrooms funded either by state Pre-K sources or by other sources such as IDEA.[7]
Illinois	DK	Children are served in state Pre-K classrooms or in other locations, and are funded either entirely by other sources such as IDEA, or by a combination of funds from State Pre-K and other sources.
Iowa	379	Children are served in state Pre-K classrooms or in other locations, but are entirely funded by other sources such as IDEA.
Kansas	None[8]	Children are served in state Pre-K classrooms or in other locations, and are funded by sources other than the state Pre-K program.
Kentucky	63%	Kentucky Pre-K is completely inter-related with the special education program. Children are funded by state Pre-K, or by a combination of state and federal sources, and either attend Pre-K classrooms or are served in other locations.[9]
Louisiana 8(g)	DK	Children are served in state Pre-K classrooms and funded by the state Pre-K program, by other sources such as IDEA, or by a combination of funds.
LA4 & Starting Pts	4%	Children are served in state Pre-K classrooms or other locations, and may be funded by the state Pre-K program, through other sources such as IDEA, or through a combination of funds.
Louisiana NSECD	DK	Private schools decide whether children with special needs will be served in Pre-K classrooms and what funds will be used to pay for services. Schools are allowed to use state Pre-K funds.
Maine	DK	Children are served in state Pre-K classrooms and are funded by a combination of state Pre-K funds and funds from other sources; or are served through, and funded by, sources other than the state Pre-K program.
Maryland	8%	Children are served in state Pre-K classrooms or in other locations, and are funded by the state Pre-K program, by other sources such as IDEA, or by a combination of funds.
Massachusetts	1,107 (6%)	Children are served in state Pre-K classrooms and in other locations, and are funded by the state Pre-K program, other sources such as IDEA, or by a combination of funds.[13]
Michigan	DK[5]	Children are served in state Pre-K classrooms or in other locations, and are funded by state Pre-K, other sources, or a combination of funds.[6]
Minnesota HdSt	13.85%	Children are served in state Pre-K classrooms and are funded by the state Pre-K program or by a combination of state Pre-K funds and funds from other sources.
Missouri	1,136	Children are served in state Pre-K classrooms or in other locations, and are funded by a combination of state Pre-K and other sources, or supported entirely by other sources.
Nebraska	Approx. 99 (9%)	Children are served in state Pre-K classrooms but are funded by IDEA.
Nevada	DK	Children are served in state Pre-K classrooms as an inclusive environment, or in other locations, and are funded by a combination of state Pre-K funds and other sources such as IDEA, or entirely by other sources.
New Jersey Abbott	1,707 (4.7%)	Children are served in state Pre-K classrooms or in other locations, but are funded by other sources such as IDEA.
New Jersey ECPA	980	Children are served in state Pre-K classrooms or in other locations, and are funded by state Pre-K funds, other sources, or by a combination of funds.
New Mexico	DK	Children are served in state Pre-K classrooms or in other locations, and are funded by state Pre-K sources, by other sources such as IDEA, or by a combination of funds.
New York EPK	11.5%	Children are served in state Pre-K classrooms or in other locations, and are funded by state Pre-K funds, other sources such as IDEA, or by a combination of funds.
New York UPK	4.2%	Children are served in state Pre-K classrooms or in other locations, and are funded by the state Pre-K program, by other sources such as IDEA, or by a combination of funds.
North Carolina	11%	Children are served in state Pre-K classrooms or in other locations, and are funded by state Pre-K sources, other sources such as IDEA, or by a combination of funds.
Ohio HdSt	At least 10%	Children are served in state Pre-K classrooms or in other locations, and are funded by state Pre-K, other sources such as IDEA, or by a combination of funds.
Ohio PSP	Approx. 5%	Children are served in state Pre-K classrooms or in other locations, and are funded by state Pre-K, other sources such as IDEA, or by a combination of funds.
Oklahoma	2,551	Children are served in state Pre-K classrooms and are funded by state Pre-K sources, by other sources such as IDEA, or by a combination of funds; or children are served through, and funded by, sources other than state Pre-K.
Oregon	16%	Children are served in state Pre-K classrooms but are funded by other sources such as IDEA.
Pennsylvania	DK	Children are served in Pre-K classrooms or in other locations, but are funded through sources other than state Pre-K such as IDEA.[2]
South Carolina	580 (3%)	DK
Tennessee	399 (12%)	Children are served in state Pre-K classrooms and funded by a combination of state Pre-K funds and funds from other sources; or are served through, and funded by, sources other than the state Pre-K program.[7]
Texas	DK	Children are served in state Pre-K classrooms or in other locations, and are funded by state Pre-K funds, other sources such as IDEA, or by a combination of funds.[9]
Vermont	139	Children are served in state Pre-K classrooms or in other locations, and are funded by the state Pre-K program, other sources, or by a combination of funds.
Virginia	Not available	Children are served through, and funded by, sources other than the state Pre-K program.
Washington	288	Children are served in state Pre-K classrooms or in other locations, and are funded by the state Pre-K program, other sources such as IDEA, or by a combination of funds.
West Virginia	33%	Children are served in state Pre-K classrooms and are funded by other sources such as IDEA, or by a combination of state Pre-K dollars and other sources.[3]
Wisconsin 4K	DK[10]	Children are served in state Pre-K classrooms or in other locations, and are funded by state Pre-K funds, other sources such as IDEA, or by a combination of funds.
Wisconsin HdSt	DK[5]	Children are served in state Pre-K classrooms or in other locations, and are supported by state Pre-K funds, other sources such as IDEA, or by a combination of funds.

STATE	PROGRAM STANDARDS		
	Maximum class size	Staff-child ratio requirement	Meal requirement
Alabama	3-year-olds, NA; 4-year-olds, 18	3-year-olds, NA; 4-year-olds, 1:9	Lunch and snack
Arizona	3- and 4-year-olds, 20[10]	3- and 4-year-olds, 1:10[10]	Varies[11]
Arkansas	3- and 4-year-olds, 20	3- and 4-year-olds; 1:10	Lunch and snack
California	3- and 4-year-olds, No limit[9]	3- and 4-year-olds, 1:8	Depends on length of program day[10]
Colorado	3- and 4-year-olds, 15	3- and 4-year-olds, 1:8	Depends on length of program day[10]
Connecticut	3- and 4-year-olds, 20	3- and 4-year-olds, 1:10	Varies[4]
Delaware	3-year-olds, NA; 4-year-olds, 20	3-year-olds, NA; 4-year-olds, 1:10	Breakfast and lunch
Georgia	3-year-olds, NA; 4-year-olds, 20	3-year-olds, NA; 4-year-olds, 1:10	Lunch and snack
Hawaii	3- and 4-year-olds, No limit	3-year-olds, 1:12; 4-year-olds, 1:16	Lunch and snack
Illinois	3- and 4-year-olds, 20	3- and 4-year-olds, 1:10	Snack[5]
Iowa	3- and 4-year-olds, 16	3- and 4-year-olds, 1:8	1 meal and snack[6]
Kansas	3-year-olds, NA; 4-year-olds, No limit[9]	3-year-olds, NA; 4-year-olds, No limit[9]	Snack
Kentucky	3- and 4-year-olds, 20	3- and 4-year-olds, 1:10	At least 1 meal (breakfast or lunch)
Louisiana 8(g)	3-year-olds, NA; 4-year-olds, 20	3-year-olds, NA; 4-year-olds, 1:10[5]	Breakfast, lunch, and snack
LA4 & Starting Pts	3-year-olds, NA; 4-year-olds, 20	3-year-olds, NA; 4-year-olds, 1:10	Lunch and snack
Louisiana NSECD	3-year-olds, NA; 4-year-olds, 20	3-year-olds, NA; 4-year-olds, 1:10	Breakfast, lunch, and snack
Maine	3-year-olds, NA; 4-year-olds, No limit	3-year-olds, NA; 4-year-olds, 1:18	None
Maryland	3-year-olds, NA[6]; 4-year-olds, 20	3-year-olds, NA[6]; 4-year-olds, 1:10	Breakfast and lunch (full-day); Determined locally (half-day)
Massachusetts	3- and 4-year-olds, 20	3- and 4-year-olds, 1:10	Depends on length of program day
Michigan	3-year-olds, NA; 4-year-olds, 18	3-year-olds, NA; 4-year-olds, 1:8[7]	Snack
Minnesota HdSt	3-year-olds, 17; 4-year-olds, 20	3-year-olds, 2:17; 4-year-olds, 1:10	Lunch and/or breakfast[9]
Missouri	3- and 4-year-olds, 20	3- and 4-year-olds, 1:10	Varies[7]
Nebraska	3- and 4-year-olds, 20	3- and 4-year-olds, 1:10	Depends on length of program day[9]
Nevada	3- and 4-year-olds, No limit[12]	3- and 4-year-olds, No limit[12]	None
New Jersey Abbott	3- and 4-year-olds, 15	3- and 4-year-olds, 2:15	Breakfast, lunch, and snack
New Jersey ECPA	3- and 4-year-olds, No limit	3- and 4-year-olds, No limit	None
New Mexico	3-and 4-year-olds, 24[7]	3- and 4-year-olds, 1:12[7]	At least 1 meal[8]
New York EPK	3- and 4-year-olds, 20	3- and 4-year-olds, 1:9 or 3:20	At least 1 meal[8]
New York UPK	3-year-olds, NA; 4-year-olds, 20	3-year-olds, NA; 4-year-olds, 1:9 or 3:20	Varies[9]
North Carolina	3-year-olds, NA; 4-year-olds, 18	3-year-olds, NA; 4-year-olds, 1:9	Lunch and either breakfast or snack
Ohio HdSt	3-year-olds, 17; 4-year-olds, 20	3-year-olds, 2:17; 4-year-olds, 1:10	Lunch and/or breakfast[3]
Ohio PSP	3-year-olds, 24; 4-year-olds, 28	3-year-olds, 1:12; 4-year-olds, 1:14	Breakfast or lunch
Oklahoma	3-year-olds, NA; 4-year-olds, 20	3-year-olds, NA; 4-year-olds, 1:10	Breakfast, lunch, and snack[6]
Oregon	3-year-olds, 17; 4-year-olds, 20	3-year-olds, 2:17; 4-year-olds, 1:10	Lunch and either breakfast or snack
Pennsylvania	3-year-olds, NA; 4-year-olds, No limit	3-year-olds, NA; 4-year-olds, No limit	None
South Carolina	3- and 4-year-olds, 20	3- and 4-year-olds, 1:10	1 meal and snack[12]
Tennessee	3-year-olds, 16; 4-year-olds, 20	3-year-olds, 1:8; 4-year-olds, 1:10	Lunch and snack
Texas	3- and 4-year-olds, No limit[10]	3- and 4-year-olds, No limit[10]	Depends on length of program day[11]
Vermont	3- and 4-year-olds, 16	3- and 4-year-olds, 1:8	Depends on length of program day[6]
Virginia	3-year-olds, NA; 4-year-olds, 16	3-year-olds, NA; 4-year-olds, 1:8	Lunch and snack
Washington	3- and 4-year-olds, 24[10]	3- and 4-year-olds, 1:9[10]	Breakfast, lunch, and snack
West Virginia	3- and 4-year-olds, 20	3- and 4-year-olds, No limit[4]	Depends on length of program day[5]
Wisconsin 4K	3-year-olds, NA; 4-year-olds, Determined locally	3-year-olds, NA; 4-year-olds, Determined locally	None
Wisconsin HdSt	3-year-olds, 17; 4-year-olds, 20	3-year-olds, 2:17; 4-year-olds, 1:10	Lunch and/or breakfast[6]

STATE	Screening and referral requirements	Translator required?	Number of parent conferences or home visits required annually
Alabama	Vision, hearing, health, and dental	No	2
Arizona	None	No	None
Arkansas	Vision, hearing, and health	No	1[7]
California	None[11]	Yes	2
Colorado	Health; Vision and hearing are determined locally	No	1
Connecticut	Health[5]	No[6]	2
Delaware	Vision, hearing, health, developmental, and behavioral	Yes	4
Georgia	Vision, hearing, and health	No	2
Hawaii	None	No	None
Illinois	Vision, hearing, health, developmental screening, and parent interview	No[6]	None[7]
Iowa	Vision, hearing, and health[7]	No, determined locally	None[8]
Kansas	Vision, hearing, health, dental, and developmental[10]	No	2
Kentucky	Vision, hearing, health, and developmental	No	2
Louisiana 8(g)	Developmental screening required[6]	No[7]	Determined locally
LA4 & Starting Pts	Vision, hearing, and health	No	2
Louisiana NSECD	Vision and hearing	No	2
Maine	Vision and hearing	No	None
Maryland	Vision, hearing, health, immunization, and lead screening[7]	No	2
Massachusetts	Vision, hearing, health, and dental	No[14]	2
Michigan	None[8]	No	4 (2 of which are ideally home visits)
Minnesota HdSt	Vision, hearing, health, and dental	Yes, at least 1 staff member must speak language of majority	2 home visits
Missouri	None	No	None[8]
Nebraska	Determined locally	Yes[10]	2
Nevada	Determined locally	Determined locally	None[13]
New Jersey Abbott	Vision, hearing, health, and developmental	No	Not specified
New Jersey ECPA	Vision, hearing, and health	No	Not specified
New Mexico	Vision, hearing, and health	No	2
New York EPK	None	Yes, for bilingual classes	Determined locally
New York UPK	None[10]	Yes, for bilingual classes	Determined locally
North Carolina	Vision, hearing, health, and dental	No	None (but conferences are recommended)
Ohio HdSt	Vision, hearing, and health	Yes, at least 1 staff member must speak the language of the majority	2 home visits
Ohio PSP	Vision, hearing, and health	Yes, at least 1 staff member must speak the language of the majority	2 home visits
Oklahoma	Determined locally	No	None[7]
Oregon	Hearing, vision, health, dental, and immunization	Yes, if at least half of the class speaks a language other than English	4
Pennsylvania	Left to LEAs to decide	Yes	Determined locally
South Carolina	Vision, hearing, and health	No	4 (2 must take place outside the school)
Tennessee	Health; Vision and hearing left to LEAS to decide	No, although a translator is available as needed by the local school system	2
Texas	Vision and hearing	Yes[12]	None
Vermont	Vision, hearing, health, and developmental[7]	No	2 conferences for academic-year programs; 3 for year-round programs
Virginia	Vision, hearing, and health	No	Determined locally
Washington	Vision, hearing, health, and developmental	Yes[11]	3 hours of education planning time with parents, 3 hours of adult contact hours
West Virginia	Vision, hearing, and health[6]	No	None[7]
Wisconsin 4K	Left to LEAs to decide[11]	No	Determined locally
Wisconsin HdSt	Vision, hearing, and health	Yes, in some cases at least 1 staff member must speak language of majority.	2 home visits

STATE	PROGRAM STANDARDS
	Support services required for all programs
Alabama	Parenting support or training, parent involvement activities[5], health services for children, transition to K activities
Arizona	None
Arkansas	Education services or job training for parents, parenting support or training, parent involvement activities[8], health services for children, information about nutrition, referral to social services, transition to K activities
California	Parenting support or training, parent involvement activities[12], health services for children, referral to social services, transition to K activities
Colorado	Parenting support or training, parent involvement activities[11], health services for parents and children, information about nutrition, referral to social services, transition to K activities
Connecticut	Educational services or job training for parents, parenting support or training, relevant parent workshops[7], health services for children, information about nutrition, referral to social services, transition to K activities, other services[8]
Delaware	Parenting support or training, parent involvement activities[3], health services for children, information about nutrition, referral to social services, transition to K activities, medical and dental services
Georgia	Parenting support or training, parent involvement activities[6], health services for children, information about nutrition, transition to K activities
Hawaii	Referral to social services, transition to K activities
Illinois	Education services or job training for parents, parenting support or training, parent involvement activities, referral to social services, transition to K activities
Iowa	Parenting support or training, at least two family nights, health services for children, information about nutrition, referral to social services
Kansas	Parenting support or training, parent involvement activities[11], transportation, transition to K activities
Kentucky	Education services or job training for parents, parenting support or training, health services for parents and children, information about nutrition, referral to social services, other services based on local need
Louisiana 8(g)	Parenting support or training, parent involvement activities, referral to social services, transition to K activities, other locally determined services
LA4 & Starting Pts	Education services or job training for parents, parenting support or training, relevant parent workshops, referral to social services, transportation, referral for mental health issues
Louisiana NSECD	Transition to K activities, other specific locally determined services
Maine	None
Maryland	Parenting support or training, parent involvement activities[8], health services for children, transition to K activities, specific locally determined services
Massachusetts	Parenting support or training, parent involvement activities[15], health services for children, information about nutrition, referral to social services, transition to K activities
Michigan	Parent involvement activities, referral to social services
Minnesota HdSt	Education services or job training for parents, parenting support or training, parent involvement activities, health services for parents and children, information about nutrition, referral to social services, transition to K activities[10]
Missouri	None[9]
Nebraska	Parenting support or training, parent involvement activities[11], transition to K activities
Nevada	Parenting support or training, parent involvement activities[14]
New Jersey Abbott	Parent involvement activities[3], health services for children, information about nutrition, referral to social services, transition to K activities
New Jersey ECPA	Education services or job training for parents, transition to K activities, specific locally determined services
New Mexico	Parenting support or training, parent involvement activities[9], referral to social services, transition to K activities, child assessments
New York EPK	Parenting support or training, parent involvement activities[9], health services for children, other services[10]
New York UPK	Parent involvement activities[11], referral to social services, transition to K activities[12]
North Carolina	Parent involvement activities, transition to K activities
Ohio HdSt	Parenting support or training, parent involvement activities, health services for children, information about nutrition, referral to social services, transportation, transition to K activities
Ohio PSP	Parenting support or training, parent involvement activities, health services for children, information about nutrition, referral to social services, transportation, transition to K activities
Oklahoma	Health services for children, transportation, other services determined locally
Oregon	Parenting support or training, parent involvement activities, health services for children, information about nutrition, referral to social services, transition to K activities, mental health, community partnerships[6]
Pennsylvania	None[3]
South Carolina	Education services or job training for parents, parenting support or training, parent involvement activities[13], health services for children (if health problems are found), transportation, transition to K activities
Tennessee	Parent involvement activities[8], transition to Pre-K and K activities[9]
Texas	Some comprehensive services are required, but specific services are determined locally
Vermont	Education services or job training for parents, parenting support or training, parent involvement activities[8], health services for children, information about nutrition, referral to social services, transition to K activities
Virginia	Parent involvement activities, health services for children, referral to social services, transportation
Washington	Education services or job training for parents, parenting support or training, parent involvement activities, health services for children, information about nutrition, referral to social services, transition to K activities[12]
West Virginia	None
Wisconsin 4K	Parent involvement activities[12], health services for children, referral to social services, transportation, school counseling
Wisconsin HdSt	Education services or job training for parents, parenting support or training, parent involvement activities[7], health services for parents and children, referral to social services, transition to K activities

STATE	Minimum teacher degree requirement	Are teachers required to have certification/licensure/endorsement?
Alabama	BA in ECE, ECSE, EE, or CD	Yes, teacher specialization covers Pre-K–elementary age children
Arizona	CDA[10]	No
Arkansas	BA + P–4 teacher license	Yes, P–4 teacher license[9]
California	CDA[13]	Yes
Colorado	CDA[12]	No
Connecticut	BA or CDA + 9 credits in EC (public); CDA + 9 credits in EC (nonpublic)[9]	Yes, certificate in elementary with Pre-K endorsement, N–K, or SpEd with Pre-K–12 endorsement (public); No (nonpublic)[9]
Delaware	CDA	No
Georgia	AA in ECE or Montessori diploma	Yes[7]
Hawaii	CDA + 1 year experience	No
Illinois	BA	Yes, EC certificate in Birth–Grade 3
Iowa	EE teacher license (public); AA for HdSt (nonpublic)[9]	Yes, EC teaching endorsement (public)[10]; State license for child care (nonpublic)[9]
Kansas	4-year elementary teaching certificate	Yes, elementary certification
Kentucky	CDA[10]	Yes, Interdisciplinary Early Childhood Education certificate in birth-primary, general, or special education
Louisiana 8(g)	BA + certification in N or K	Yes, certification in N or K
LA4 & Starting Pts	BA + certification in N, K, or Early Intervention[6]	Yes, certificate in N, K, or Early Intervention[6]
Louisiana NSECD	BA in EE, K, or N; or BA (any field) + 12 credits in CD	No
Maine	BA + EC or Elementary certificate	Yes, licensure and EC or Elementary certificate
Maryland	BA in EC	Yes, certificate in N–3, –6, or –8, and teachers must be licensed
Massachusetts	BA + EC certificate (public); 1 ECE class + 9 months experience (nonpublic)[16]	Yes, Early Childhood Teacher of Students With and Without Disabilities (Pre-K–Grade 2) license (public); No (nonpublic)
Michigan	BA with teaching certificate and EC endorsement (public); AA + CDA (nonpublic)[9]	Yes, EC endorsement (Public); No (nonpublic)
Minnesota HdSt	CDA	No
Missouri	BA + EC or ECSE certificate, or 4-year CD degree (public); CDA (nonpublic)	Yes, must be licensed and certified in EC or ECSE, or have 4-year CD degree (public); No (nonpublic)
Nebraska	BA with EC endorsement	Yes, certification and EC endorsement
Nevada	BA	Yes, ECE license
New Jersey Abbott	BA + EC certificate[4]	Yes, EC certificate covers Pre-K–Grade 3
New Jersey ECPA	BA + certification in EC or EE	Yes, EC certificate covers Pre-K–Grade 3; EE covers K–8
New Mexico	None	No
New York EPK	BA prior to 1978; MA after 1978	Yes, certification in N–6[11]
New York UPK	BA prior to 1978, MA after (public); 9 credits toward CDA (nonpublic)[13]	Yes, certification in N–6 (public); No (nonpublic)[13, 14]
North Carolina	BA + Birth–K license[5]	Yes, Birth–K license[5]
Ohio HdSt	CDA[4]	No
Ohio PSP	AA + Pre-K certificate	No[5]
Oklahoma	BA + EC certification	Yes, EC certification
Oregon	BA + EC certificate (public); CDA (nonpublic)[7]	Yes, licensed with 15 hours of ECE college credits (public); No (nonpublic)[8]
Pennsylvania	BA + teaching license	Yes, certificate in ECE (Pre-K–3) or EE (K–6)
South Carolina	BA + EC certificate	Yes, certification in EC and licensure
Tennessee	BA + teacher license with Pre-K endorsement	Yes, endorsement must be in Pre-K
Texas	BA with endorsement in EC or K[13]	Yes, endorsement in EC or kindergarten[13]
Vermont	BA in early education	Yes, EC license/endorsement covers children age 3–Grade 3, and ECSE license includes ages 3–6 (public); No (nonpublic)
Virginia	BA + certification in Pre-K–3 or Pre-K–6 (public); None (nonpublic)[2]	Yes, public school teachers must be licensed and certified in Pre-K–3 or Pre-K–6[2]
Washington	BA (public); AA with 30 quarter units in ECE (nonpublic)	Yes, Pre-K–3 endorsement or certification in SpEd with EC endorsement (public); No (nonpublic)
West Virginia	BA in EC, Preschool Special Needs, or EE	Yes, certification in Birth–5, EC, or Preschool Special Needs, or a Pre-K–K endorsement on an EE certification
Wisconsin 4K	BA + license in Pre-K–K, –3, or –6, or K license[13]	Yes, license in Pre-K–K, –3, or –6, or K license
Wisconsin HdSt	CDA[8]	Determined locally (public)[9]; No (nonpublic)

STATE	PERSONNEL		
	Minimum assistant teacher degree requirement	Teacher in-service requirement	Are teachers req'd to be paid on public school salary scale?
Alabama	CDA + experience in Pre-K classroom	40 clock hours per year	Yes
Arizona	None	12 clock hours per year	No
Arkansas	CDA	30 clock hours per year	Yes
California	Child Development Assistant Teacher Permit[14]	105 clock hours per 5 years	No
Colorado	None	10 clock hours per year	No
Connecticut	None[10]	75 CEUs per 5 years (public); CC licensing—1% of hours worked (nonpublic)[11]	Yes (public)[12]; No (nonpublic)
Delaware	HSD	15 clock hours per year[4]	No
Georgia	HSD or equivalent, plus experience	12 clock hours per year[8]	No
Hawaii	CDA + 6 months experience	None	No[8]
Illinois	AA	120 clock hours or 8 credit hours per 5 years[8]	Yes
Iowa	None	None[11]	Yes (public); No (nonpublic)
Kansas	2-year degree	None[12]	Yes
Kentucky	HSD	4 days per year (certified teachers); 18 clock hours per year (CDAs or AAs)	Yes (public); No (nonpublic)[11]
Louisiana 8(g)	Determined locally	150 clock hours per 5 years	Yes
LA4 & Starting Pts	HSD or equivalent (public); None (nonpublic)	18 clock hours per year	Yes (public); No (nonpublic)
Louisiana NSECD	None	None	No
Maine	30 credit hours	90 clock hours per 5 years	No
Maryland	HSD or equivalent	6 credit hours per 5 years[9]	Yes
Massachusetts	At least 18 years old and HSD (public); At least 16 years old or HSD and constant supervision (nonpublic)	20 clock hours per year (all); additional union-negotiated local requirements (public)	Yes (public); No (nonpublic)
Michigan	CDA or 120 clock hours[10]	None	No
Minnesota HdSt	Meets child care regulations[11]	1.5% or 2% of total work hours[12]	No
Missouri	HSD + Voc. certification in ECE (public); HSD (nonpublic)	12 clock hours per year[10]	Yes (public); No (nonpublic)[11]
Nebraska	12 credit hours in EC or equivalent	12 clock hours per year	No
Nevada	GED or HSD[15]	5 credit hours per 5 years	Yes
New Jersey Abbott	HSD	100 clock hours per 5 years	Yes
New Jersey ECPA	HSD	100 clock hours per 5 years	Yes (public); No (nonpublic)
New Mexico	None	24 clock hours per year	No, unless directly employed by a public school district
New York EPK	HSD or equivalent + 6 credits in EC or related field[12]	175 clock hours per 5 years	Yes
New York UPK	HSD or equivalent + 6 credits in EC or related field (public)[15]; HSD (nonpublic)	175 clock hours per 5 years	Yes (public); No (nonpublic)
North Carolina	CDA or meets NCLB regulations (public); CDA (nonpublic)[6]	150 clock hours per 5 years[7] or 15 credit hours per 5 years	Yes (public); Yes, if they have Birth–K license (nonpublic)
Ohio HdSt	HSD	15 clock hours per year[5]	No
Ohio PSP	HSD	15 clock hours per year[6]	No
Oklahoma	GED or HSD	15 clock hours per year	Yes
Oregon	GED or HSD[9]	None[10]	Yes (public); No (nonpublic)
Pennsylvania	NA[4]	6 credit hours per 5 years	Determined locally
South Carolina	HSD (public); None (nonpublic)[14]	12 clock hours per year and 6 credit hours per 5 years	Yes[15]
Tennessee	CDA	18 clock hours per year	Yes (public); No (nonpublic)
Texas	Determined locally	Not specified	Yes
Vermont	BA (public); Determined locally (nonpublic)	9 credit hours per 7 years (public); 9 clock hours per year (nonpublic)	Yes (public); No (nonpublic)
Virginia	GED or HSD	Determined locally	Yes (public); No (nonpublic)
Washington	CDA or passing proficiency test (public); CDA (nonpublic)	Determined locally[13]	No
West Virginia	18 years old and HSD or equivalent	18 clock hours per year	Yes
Wisconsin 4K	Teacher assistant license, or, in Title I schools, AA (public); child care licensing standards: at least 18 years old + 1 course in EC (nonpublic)	180 DPI[14] or 6 credit hours per 5 years	Yes (public); No (nonpublic)
Wisconsin HdSt	Determined locally (public)[9]; 18 years old + 1 course in EC (nonpublic)	Some in-service activity is required, but amount not specified	No[10]

STATE	RESOURCES		
	Total 2002–2003 spending	How much of total spending came from…	Federal sources used
Alabama	$8,145,000	State, $3,584,500; Federal, $2,000,000; Local, $2,560,500	TANF, $1,000,000; HdSt (amount unknown); Appalachian Regional Commission, $1,000,000
Arizona	$9,953,752	State, $9,953,752	None
Arkansas	$15,417,142	State, $9,250,285; Local, $6,166,857	Title I, IDEA (amounts unknown)
California	$249,522,000[15]	State, $249,522,000	IDEA (amount unknown)
Colorado	$31,287,685	State, $31,287,685[13]	TANF, CCDF, Title I, IDEA, HdSt, Even Start (amounts unknown)
Connecticut	$46,928,387	State, $35,674,423; Local, $11,253,964	None
Delaware	$4,456,700	State, $4,456,700	None
Georgia	$252,000,000	State, $252,000,000	None
Hawaii	$3,478,863	State, $3,248,748; Federal, $230,115[9]	CCDF, $230,115[9]
Illinois	$162,618,616	State, $162,618,616	Title I, IDEA (amounts unknown)
Iowa	$6,887,531	State, $6,887,531	Title I, IDEA, HdSt (amounts unknown)
Kansas	$9,352,323	State, $9,352,323	None
Kentucky	$73,950,000	State, $46,900,000; Federal, $7,750,000; Local, $19,300,000	Title I, $2,425,000; IDEA, $5,325,000; HdSt, Even Start (amounts unknown)
Louisiana 8(g)	$9,358,905	State, $9,358,905	TANF, Title I, IDEA, Even Start (amounts unknown)
LA4 & Starting Pts	$35,500,000	State (tobacco settlement), $1,500,000; Federal, $34,000,000	TANF, $34,000,000; IDEA (amount unknown)
Louisiana NSECD	$6,000,000[1]	Federal, $6,000,000	TANF, $6,000,000
Maine	$5,900,000	State, $2,700,000; Local, $3,200,000	None
Maryland	$83,664,408[10]	State, $19,262,500; Federal, $15,348,496; Local, $49,053,412[11]	Title I, IDEA, HdSt, Even Start (amounts unknown)[12]
Massachusetts	$93,132,061	State, $52,200,000; Federal, $21,000,000; Local, $19,932,061[17]	TANF, $21,000,000[18, 19]
Michigan	$85,000,000	State, $85,000,000[11, 12]	Title I (amount unknown)[11]
Minnesota HdSt	$17,620,000[13]	State, $17,620,000	IDEA, Even Start (amounts unknown)
Missouri	$10,744,988[12]	State, $10,744,988	Title I, IDEA (amounts unknown); TANF, CCDBG/CCDF, HdSt, Even Start (DK if used)
Nebraska	Approx. $6,000,000	State, $2,100,000 (Approx.); Federal, $2,400,000 (Approx.); Local, $1,500,000 (Approx.)	CCDF Subsidy, $300,000 (Approx.); Title I, $240,000 (Approx.); IDEA, $540,000 (Approx.); HdSt, $1,260,000 (Approx.)[12]
Nevada	$3,000,000	State, $3,000,000	IDEA, Even Start (amounts unknown); TANF, CCDF, Title I, HdSt (DK if used)
New Jersey Abbott	$351,704,925[5]	State, $351,704,925[5]	IDEA, Fed. HdSt (amounts unknown)
New Jersey ECPA	Approx. $30,000,000	State, $30,000,000	None
New Mexico	$1,499,900	State, $1,499,900	None[10]
New York EPK	$53,900,000[13]	State, $47,900,000; Local, $6,000,000[14]	Title I, IDEA, Even Start (amounts unknown)
New York UPK	$195,300,000[16]	State, $195,300,000	Title I, IDEA, Fed. HdSt (amounts unknown)
North Carolina	$59,000,000 (estimate)[8]	State, $30,217,723[9]	Title I, IDEA, HdSt, Even Start, Other sources (amounts unknown)
Ohio HdSt	$87,632,156	State, $18,402,753; Federal, $69,229,403	TANF, $69,229,403
Ohio PSP	$18,638,180	State, $18,638,180	Not reported
Oklahoma	$66,439,166	State, $66,439,166	Title I, IDEA, Fed. HdSt, Even Start (amounts unknown)
Oregon	$26,100,000 (estimate)[11]	State, $26,100,000 (estimate)[12]	DK[13]
Pennsylvania	DK[5]	DK	DK[6]
South Carolina	$25,355,278	State, $22,514,278; Federal, $2,841,000	IDEA, $1,740,000; Title I, $1,101,000
Tennessee	$15,000,000[10]	State, $6,000,000; Federal, $9,000,000	TANF, $9,000,000; IDEA, HdSt, Even Start (amounts unknown)
Texas	$432,436,912[14]	State, $432,436,912	Title I, IDEA (amounts unknown)
Vermont	$1,328,785	State, $1,328,785	CCDF, Title I, IDEA, HdSt (amounts unknown)
Virginia	$18,189,075 (includes state funds only)	State, $18,189,075	None
Washington	$32,099,509	State, $26,957,519; Federal, $5,141,990	CCDF, $5,141,990; USDA (amount unknown)
West Virginia	$38,882,000	State, $25,571,000; Federal, $13,311,000	CCDF (amount unknown); Title I, $8,268,000; IDEA, $3,435,000; HdSt (amount unknown); Even Start, $1,608,000
Wisconsin 4K	$65,000,000	State, $43,000,000; Local, $22,000,000	Title I, CCDF, IDEA, HdSt (amounts unknown)[15]
Wisconsin HdSt	$7,425,000	State, $7,425,000	TANF, CCDF, HdSt (amounts unknown)

STATE	RESOURCES		
	Local sources used	Is there a required local match?	State estimate of cost per child
Alabama	Local matches (DK if used); In-kind (amount unknown)	Yes, 50% of granted amount	$6,464
Arizona	None	No	DK
Arkansas	Local matches, In-kind (amounts unknown)	Yes, must match 40% of total funding	$4,996[10]
California	DK if used[16]	No	$3,143
Colorado	Parent fees, Local matches, In-kind, School district general funds (amounts unknown)	No	$2,864[14]
Connecticut	Parent fees, $11,253,964; In-kind (amount unknown)	No	DK
Delaware	In-kind, Local funding (amounts unknown)	No	$5,200 (expenditure, not cost)
Georgia	In-kind (amount unknown)[9]	No	$3,855[10]
Hawaii	Parent fees (amount unknown)[10]	No	$4,512[11]
Illinois	Local matches, In-kind (amounts unknown)	No	$2,785, total; $2,650, half-day; $3,200, full-day (state appropriation only)
Iowa	Parent fees, Local matches, In-kind, Community empowerment funds (amounts unknown)	Yes, local entities must provide 20% of total grant amount to agency	DK
Kansas	District funds (amount unknown)	No	$1,800 in state funds
Kentucky	Local matches, $19,300,000; In-kind, Parent fees (amounts unknown)	No	$3,916 (includes state, IDEA, Title I, and district funds)
Louisiana 8(g)	DK if used	No	DK
LA4 & Starting Pts	Parent fees, In-kind, Local general funds (amounts unknown)	No	LA4, $5,000; Starting Points, $3,300[7]
Louisiana NSECD	None	No	DK
Maine	In-kind, Other (amounts unknown)	No	DK
Maryland	In-kind, Other (amounts unknown)	No	$4,068
Massachusetts	Parent fees, $12,900,000; In-kind, $7,032,061[20]	No	$4,104 (federal and state funding divided by enrollment)[21]
Michigan	Parent fees (for additional time), Local matches, In-kind, Other (amounts unknown)[12]	No	DK
Minnesota HdSt	In-kind (amount unknown)	No	$6,649
Missouri	Parent fees, Local matches, In-kind (amounts unknown)	No	DK
Nebraska	Parent fees, $420,000 (Approx.); Local matches, $540,000 (Approx., includes In-kind); Other, $660,000 (Approx.)	Yes[13]	DK[13]
Nevada	None	No	$3,686 (estimate based on state Pre-K funds only)
New Jersey Abbott	None	No	$9,645[6]
New Jersey ECPA	None	No	$4,813
New Mexico	Materials fees, In-kind (amounts unknown)	No	DK
New York EPK	Local matches, $6,000,000; In-kind, Local tax levy (amounts unknown)	Yes, 11% of funding must be local	DK
New York UPK	Local matches, In-kind (amounts unknown)	No	DK
North Carolina	Local matches, In-kind (amounts unknown)	Yes[10]	DK
Ohio HdSt	None	No	$4,825 (state sources, $1,013; federal sources, $3,812)
Ohio PSP	Parent fees, In-kind, Local budget (amounts unknown)	No	$3,836[7]
Oklahoma	HdSt, District general funds (amounts unknown)	No	$1,743, half-day; $3,238, full-day
Oregon	DK[14]	No	$7,716
Pennsylvania	Local matches, In-kind, Other (DK if used)[6]	No	DK
South Carolina	Parent fees, In-kind (amounts unknown)[16]	No	$1,400
Tennessee	In-kind (amount unknown)	No	$4,900 (including state and TANF dollars)
Texas	Parent fees (amount unknown)	No	$2,375 through Foundation School Program[15]
Vermont	Parent fees, Local matches, In-kind (amounts unknown)	No	$1,197
Virginia	Local matches, In-kind (amounts unknown)	Yes, based on composite index of local ability to pay[3]	Not available
Washington	In-kind, Other (amounts unknown)[14]	No	$4,127 (state and CCDF only)
West Virginia	In-kind (amount unknown)	No	DK
Wisconsin 4K	Local matches, $22,000,000	Yes, local share of school revenue generated through property tax	DK
Wisconsin HdSt	Local matches, In-kind (amounts unknown)	No	$5,150[11]

STATE	Agencies eligible to receive funding directly	Agencies with which subcontracting is permitted
Alabama	Public schools, HdSt centers, Private CC, Faith-based centers	None
Arizona	Public schools	Public schools, HdSt centers, Private CC, Faith-based centers
Arkansas	Public schools, HdSt centers, Private CC, Faith-based centers, Family CC, any licensed EC program meeting ABC standards and state accreditation	None
California	Public schools, HdSt centers, Private CC, Faith-based centers	Public schools, HdSt centers, Private CC, Faith-based centers
Colorado	Public schools	HdSt centers, Private CC, Faith-based centers (with some restrictions)
Connecticut	None[13]	Public schools, HdSt centers, Private CC, Faith-based centers
Delaware	Public schools, HdSt centers, Private CC, Faith-based centers, Family CC, Nonprofit agencies	None
Georgia	Public schools, HdSt centers, Private CC, Faith-based centers, Other[11]	None
Hawaii	Parents receive subsidies directly to cover tuition costs	Parents may use the subsidies to purchase services at any licensed child care center
Illinois	Public schools[9]	Public schools, HdSt centers, Private CC, Faith-based centers, Family CC[10]
Iowa	Public schools, HdSt centers, Private CC, Faith-based centers, Nonprofit agencies	Public schools, HdSt centers, Private CC, Faith-based centers, Family CC
Kansas	Public schools	None
Kentucky	Public schools	Public schools, HdSt centers, Private CC, Faith-based centers, SpEd facilities
Louisiana 8(g)	Public schools[8]	None
LA4 & Starting Pts	Public schools, Faith-based centers (Starting Points only)[8]	HdSt centers, Private CC, Faith-based centers[9]
Louisiana NSECD	Private CC, Faith-based centers	None
Maine	Public schools	None
Maryland	Public schools	Public schools, HdSt centers, Private CC, Faith-based centers
Massachusetts	Public schools, HdSt centers, Private CC, Faith-based centers	Public schools, HdSt centers, Private CC, Faith-based centers, Family CC homes, Family CC systems
Michigan	Public schools, HdSt centers, Private CC, Faith-based centers, Other[13]	Public schools, HdSt centers, Private CC, Faith-based centers
Minnesota HdSt	Federally designated HdSt grantees prior to 1989	Public schools, HdSt centers, Private CC, Faith-based centers, Family CC, Other
Missouri	Public schools, HdSt centers, Private CC, Family CC	Public schools, HdSt centers, Private CC, Family CC
Nebraska	Public schools, Other[14]	Public schools, HdSt centers, Private CC
Nevada	Public schools, HdSt centers, Private CC, Faith-based centers, Family CC	DK
New Jersey Abbott	Public schools	HdSt centers, Private CC, Faith-based centers, Family CC
New Jersey ECPA	Public schools	HdSt centers, Private CC, Faith-based centers
New Mexico	Public schools, Private CC, Faith-based centers	EC Consultant[11]
New York EPK	Public schools	None
New York UPK	Public schools	HdSt centers, Private CC, Faith-based centers, Family CC[17]
North Carolina	School systems, Government agencies, Nonprofit organizations such as Smart Start	Public schools, HdSt centers, Private CC, Faith-based centers[11]
Ohio HdSt	Public schools, HdSt centers, Private CC, Faith-based centers, Family CC, HdSt grantees	Public schools, HdSt centers, Private CC, Faith-based centers, Family CC
Ohio PSP	Public schools, Joint Vocational Schools, County Educational Service Centers	Public schools, HdSt centers, Private CC, Joint Vocational Schools, County Educational Service Centers
Oklahoma	Public schools, Other[8]	HdSt centers, Private CC, Faith-based centers
Oregon	Public schools, HdSt centers, Private CC, Higher Ed, Community Action Agencies, Other[15]	Public schools, HdSt centers, Private CC, Family CC, Higher Ed, Community Action Agencies, Other[16]
Pennsylvania	Public schools	None
South Carolina	Public schools	Public schools, HdSt centers, Private CC, Faith-based centers, Family CC
Tennessee	Public schools, Private CC, Faith-based centers, Institutes of Higher Ed, CAP agencies that administer HdSt	Public schools, HdSt centers, Private CC, Faith-based centers, Institutes of Higher Ed
Texas	Public schools	Public schools, HdSt centers, Private CC
Vermont	Public schools, HdSt centers, Private CC, Faith-based centers, Family CC, Social service agencies	Public schools, HdSt centers, Private CC, Faith-based centers, Family CC
Virginia	Public schools	HdSt centers, YMCA
Washington	Public schools, HdSt centers, Private CC, Faith-based centers, Community organization facilities, Colleges/Universities, Educational Service Districts, Local government, Tribal organizations, Business/Employment centers, Other	Same agencies eligible to receive direct funding
West Virginia	Public schools	HdSt centers, Private CC, Faith-based centers
Wisconsin 4K	Public schools	Public schools, HdSt centers, Private CC, Faith-based centers, Family CC
Wisconsin HdSt	Existing federal HdSt grantees	Public schools, HdSt centers, Private CC, Faith-based centers, Family CC, Other

STATE	MONITORING/EVALUATION	
	Frequency of monitoring requirements	Differences in monitoring requirements by location
Alabama	Site visits, 3/year; Review of records and financial review, 1/year	None
Arizona	None	None
Arkansas	Site visits, review of records, financial review, and teacher qualifications and training, 1/year	[see footnotes][11]
California	Site visits and review of records, every 4 years (LEAs), every 3 years (private); Financial review and self-evaluation process, 1/year (LEAs and private)	LEAs are subject to an audit of all education programs.[17] Private agencies are subject to a program-specific audit for the child development programs.
Colorado	Site visits, 2/year; Review of records and financial review, 1/year	None
Connecticut	Site visits, every 3 years[14]; Review of records, 2/year through RFP and annual program evaluation[15]; Financial review, 1/year	Public or independent school programs must be accredited/approved by NAEYC, HS, or NEASC.
Delaware	Site visits, every 3 years[5]; Financial review, 1/year	None
Georgia	Site visits, 2/year; Review of records and financial review, 1/year	None
Hawaii	None	None
Illinois	Site visits, vary according to need; Review of records, 1/year; Financial review, 4/year	Programs in nonpublic settings receive additional visits from ISBE auditors.
Iowa	Site visits, every 3 years by NAEYC; Review of records, according to NAEYC accreditation standards; Financial review, 1/year	None
Kansas	Review of records and financial review, 1/year	NA
Kentucky	Review of records, 1/year; Financial review, quarterly	None
Louisiana 8(g)	Site visits and financial review, 50–75% of projects visited each year; Review of records, 1/year	NA
LA4 & Starting Pts	Site visits, 1/3 of all classrooms each year; Review of records and financial review, 1/year	None
Louisiana NSECD	Site visits and review of records, 1/semester; Financial review, monthly	None
Maine	None	None
Maryland	Financial review, periodically; Programs provide semi-annual progress report	None
Massachusetts	Site visits, every 5 years; Financial review and review of quality compliance with standards and curriculum guidelines, 1/year; Ongoing technical assistance from assigned liaisons[22]	The monitoring requirements apply to local councils, not individual programs funded by the councils. The state visits selected individual programs across all program types.
Michigan	Financial review, 1/year[14]	None—lack of funds has limited monitoring capabilities
Minnesota HdSt	Site visits, review of compliance with quality standards, and financial review, 1/year[14]	None
Missouri	DK[13]	School districts review schools every 5 years using a monitoring checklist. Monitoring is not in place for private providers.
Nebraska	Site visits, 2/year; Review of records and financial review, 1/year; Fiscal narrative, 2/year	None
Nevada	Site visits, 1/year; Review of records, no minimum requirement; Financial review, 2/year	None
New Jersey Abbott	Site visits, 1/week; Review of records, 1/year[7]; Financial review, 4/year	Districts monitor nonpublic programs directly.
New Jersey ECPA	Site visits, every 7 years; Review of records and financial review, 1/year	None
New Mexico	Site visits, 2/year; Review of records, 4/year; Financial review, 1/year; Child assessment[12]	None
New York EPK	Review of records and financial review, 1/year	None
New York UPK	Review of records and financial review, 1/year	States monitor school districts while school districts monitor contracted agencies.
North Carolina	Site visits, 1/year	None
Ohio HdSt	Site visits, review of records, and financial review, 1/year	Not reported
Ohio PSP	Site visits, every 3 years; Review of records and financial review, 1/year	If districts sub-contract with HdSt programs, then HdSt monitoring rules and regulations apply.
Oklahoma	Site visits, review of records, and financial review, 3 or 4/year; District financial records are audited by an outside auditor	None
Oregon	Site visits to programs, review of quality compliance records, and financial review, every 3 years[17]	None
Pennsylvania	Financial review, 1/year	NA
South Carolina	Site visits, 1/year for randomly selected programs; Review of records, every 5 years for random selection; Financial review, 1/year; Other[17]	None
Tennessee	Site visits, 2/year; Review of records, 1/year; Attendance and staff updates, monthly	[see footnotes][11]
Texas	None	NA
Vermont	Site visits, review of records, and financial review, 1/year; Peer reviews, every 5 years	None
Virginia	Not available	Not available
Washington	Record reviews for programmatic quality and financial compliance, monthly; Site visits and comprehensive systems review, every 4 years[15]	None[16]
West Virginia	None	NA
Wisconsin 4K	Review of records and financial review, 1/year; School boards in each district oversee compliance with state statutes	[see footnotes][16]
Wisconsin HdSt	HdSt submits financial claims for reimbursement as per budget; Annual grant application[12]	None

Footnotes are grouped by state at the end of Appendix A.

STATE	Has there been an evaluation of program?	What information was collected for the evaluation?	What agency required, funded, or conducted the evaluation?
Alabama	No	NA	NA
Arizona	Yes	[see footnotes][12]	Required and funded by state; conducted by independent evaluator[12]
Arkansas	No	NA	NA
California	No[18]	NA	NA
Colorado	Yes	Program quality[15], child progress[16]	Required and conducted by state, but not funded by state
Connecticut	Yes	Program quality[16], child progress[17]	Required and funded by state; conducted by Teri Bond—Work and Family Institute
Delaware	Yes	Child and family progress[6]	Required and funded by state; conducted by state and independent evaluator
Georgia	Yes	Program quality, child progress	Not required, but funded by state; conducted by Georgia State University
Hawaii	No	NA	NA
Illinois	Yes	Child progress[11]	Required, funded, and conducted by state
Iowa	Yes	Program quality[12], child progress[13]	Required and funded by state; conducted by University of Northern Iowa Regent's Center for Early Developmental Education
Kansas	No	NA	NA[13]
Kentucky	Yes	Program quality, child progress	Required and funded by state; conducted by independent evaluator
Louisiana 8(g)	Yes	Child progress—cognitive, physical, and social-emotional development	Required and funded by state; conducted by independent evaluator
LA4 & Starting Pts	Yes	Program quality[10], child progress—math, language, and print concepts	Required and funded by state; conducted by the Civitan International Research Center in conjunction with Loyd B. Rockhold Center and LSU Health Sciences Center
Louisiana NSECD	Yes	Child progress—tests in math, language, and print	Not required, but funded by state; conducted by David Blouin and LSU, Department of Experimental Statistics
Maine	No	NA	NA
Maryland	Yes[13]	Program quality, child progress[14]	Required, funded, and conducted by state
Massachusetts	Yes	Program quality[23]	Required and funded by state; conducted by state and independent evaluators[24]
Michigan	Yes	Program quality[15], child progress[16]	Required and funded by state; conducted by High/Scope Educational Research Foundation
Minnesota HdSt	No	NA	NA
Missouri	Yes	Program quality, child progress[14]	Required and funded by state; conducted by the University of Missouri-Columbia
Nebraska	Yes	Program quality[15], child progress[16]	Required and funded by state; conducted by University of Nebraska Medical Center
Nevada	Yes	Program quality, child progress[16]	Required, but not funded by state[17]; conducted by Pacific Research Associates
New Jersey Abbott	Yes	Program quality[8], child progress[9]	Required, funded, and conducted by state[10]
New Jersey ECPA	No	NA	NA
New Mexico	No	NA	NA
New York EPK	No	NA	NA
New York UPK	No	NA	NA
North Carolina	Yes	Program quality[12], child progress[13]	Required and funded by state[14]; conducted by Frank Porter Graham Child Development Institute
Ohio HdSt	Yes	Child progress—literacy and math	Required and funded by state; conducted by state and University of Cincinnati
Ohio PSP	Yes	Child progress—literacy and math	Required and funded by state; conducted by state and University of Cincinnati
Oklahoma	Yes	Program quality[9], child progress	Neither required nor funded by state; conducted by Dr. William Gormley of Georgetown University
Oregon	No	NA	NA
Pennsylvania	No	NA	NA
South Carolina	Yes[18]	Child progress	Required, funded, and conducted by state[19]
Tennessee	Yes	Program quality[12], child progress[13]	Required and conducted by state, but not funded by state
Texas	Yes[16]	Program quality—developmentally appropriate practices; Child progress—SpEd services, retention rate, reading comprehension, and math skills	Neither required nor funded by state; conducted by state and the National INREAL Education Center of the University of Colorado
Vermont	Yes	Program quality—% of sites with national accreditation; Child progress—pre- and post-test developmental assessment results	Not required, but funded and conducted by state
Virginia	No	NA	NA
Washington	Yes	Program quality—indicators through contractor's self-assessment; Child progress—outcome indicators of health and social-emotional development[17]	Required and funded by state; conducted by state administrative agency
West Virginia	No	NA	NA
Wisconsin 4K	Yes	Program quality, child progress (indicators vary)	Neither required nor funded by state; conducted by independent evaluator[17]
Wisconsin HdSt	No	NA	NA

STATE	STATE-LEVEL SCHOLARSHIPS	
	Is scholarship/loan forgiveness program available?	How many scholarships granted or loans forgiven during 2002–2003?
Alabama	Yes	DK
Arizona	No	NA
Arkansas	Yes	597[12]
California	Yes	DK
Colorado	Yes[17]	275
Connecticut	Yes[18]	DK
Delaware	No	NA
Georgia	Yes	DK
Hawaii	Yes	DK
Illinois	Yes	DK
Iowa	Yes	1[14]
Kansas	Yes	DK
Kentucky	Yes[12]	49
Louisiana 8(g)	Yes	DK
LA4 & Starting Pts	No	NA
Louisiana NSECD	No	NA
Maine	No	NA
Maryland	No	NA
Massachusetts	Yes	2,400[25]
Michigan	No, available for CC only	NA
Minnesota HdSt	Yes	74
Missouri	Yes[15]	110
Nebraska	Yes[17]	7
Nevada	No	NA
New Jersey Abbott	Yes	DK
New Jersey ECPA	No	NA
New Mexico	Yes[13]	NA
New York EPK	No	NA
New York UPK	Yes[18]	DK
North Carolina	Yes	166
Ohio HdSt	No	NA
Ohio PSP	No	NA
Oklahoma	No	NA
Oregon	Yes, Oregon CARES is available in 5 counties	Between 2 and 4
Pennsylvania	Yes	DK
South Carolina	No[20]	NA
Tennessee	No	NA
Texas	DK[17]	DK
Vermont	No	NA
Virginia	No	NA
Washington	Yes	DK
West Virginia	No[8]	NA
Wisconsin 4K	Yes[18]	DK[19]
Wisconsin HdSt	Yes[13]	134[14]

STATE	Number of full-time professional staff at state level who administer EC programs	Breakdown of professional staff by program	Do all professional staff work as single agency?
Alabama	4	State Pre-K, 1; SpEd, 2; Even Start, 1	No
Arizona	9	ECBG, 2; Even Start/Migrant Even Start, 2; IDEA, 2; Admin, 3	Yes
Arkansas	3	Public Pre-K, 3	Yes
California	88[19]	DK	Yes
Colorado	7.5	CPP, 1; IDEA Part C, 4.5; EC SpEd, 2	No
Connecticut	4	SpEd Pre-K, 1; HdSt, 1; School Readiness in Priority School Districts, 1; Severe Needs Schools, 1	Yes
Delaware	1.5	Not reported	Yes
Georgia	DK[12]	DK[12]	Yes
Hawaii	DK	DK	NA
Illinois	10	DK	Yes
Iowa	3.3	State Pre-K, 1; SpEd, 1.5; EC birth-3rd grade, 0.8	Yes
Kansas	2	4-year-old at-risk programs, 1; SpEd/Parents as Teachers Consultant, 1	Yes
Kentucky	3	State Pre-K, 3	Yes
Louisiana 8(g)	DK	DK	No
LA4 & Starting Pts	21	LA 4 and SP, 8; Even Start, 1; HIPPY, 1; SpEd, 11[11]	No
Louisiana NSECD	DK	NSECD, 2	NA
Maine	2	SpEd, 1; Combined, 1	Yes
Maryland	13	Early Learning Office, 5; Preschool SpEd Specialists, 7; Even Start, 1	No
Massachusetts	26	DK	Yes
Michigan	14 (plus 4 school-age CC)	SpEd, 4; Even Start, 3; Pre-K, 5; Parent ed., 2[17]	Yes
Minnesota HdSt	4	State-funded HdSt, 1; State Pre-K, 1; EC SpEd, 1; Even Start, 1	Yes
Missouri	4	MPP, 4	No, but they do work together
Nebraska	6	EC Team, 4; SpEd, 1; HdSt Collaboration, 1	Yes
Nevada	2	State Pre-K, 1; SpEd, 1	Yes
New Jersey Abbott	18[11]	OECE, 14; SpEd, 4	Yes, different divisions of the DOE
New Jersey ECPA	18	OECE, 14; SpEd, 4	Yes, different divisions of the DOE
New Mexico	2	Not reported	Yes
New York EPK	20.25	Even Start, 2; Early Grade Class Size, 2; State Pre-K, 1; Reading Initiatives, 6; Nursery Schools, 1; SpEd, 8.25 FTE	Yes, separate units of DOE
New York UPK	20.25	Even Start, 2; Early Grade Class Size, 2; State Pre-K, 1; Reading Initiatives, 6; Nursery Schools, 1; SpEd, 8.25 FTE	Yes, separate units of DOE
North Carolina	10	State Pre-K, 6; SpEd, 1; Even Start, 1; EC, 2[15]	No
Ohio HdSt	10	Public Preschool, 2; HdSt, 3; Preschool SpEd, 4; Even Start, 1	Yes
Ohio PSP	10	Public Preschool, 2; HdSt, 3; Preschool SpEd, 3; Even Start, 1	Yes
Oklahoma	3[10]	State Pre-K Coordinators, 3 FTE	Yes
Oregon	6.5	Pre-K, 2.5; Even Start, 3.5; SpEd, 0.5	Yes
Pennsylvania	7	ECE, 1; SpEd/EI, 6	Yes
South Carolina	11	SpEd, 1; Even Start, 1; 4K, 8; First Steps, 1	No
Tennessee	8	State Pre-K, 2; Even Start, 2; SpEd, 4	Yes, all part of the DOE
Texas	2	Director of State Pre-K Program, Director of Preschool Program for Children with Disabilities	Yes
Vermont	4	Even Start, 1; EEI, 1; IDEA Part B, 1; IDEA Part C, 1	Yes
Virginia	2	ECSE, 1; Title I, Virginia Preschool Initiative, and Even Start, 1	Yes
Washington	DK	DK	No
West Virginia	2	IDEA Part B (619 Coordination), 1; Even Start/EC, 1	Yes
Wisconsin 4K	2	EC, 1; EC SpEd, 1	Yes
Wisconsin HdSt	2	EC, 1; EC SpEd, 1	Yes

ALABAMA — Alabama Pre-Kindergarten Pilot Program 2002–2003

1 The Office of School Readiness (OSR) gives all programs the same amount of funding to provide the same required services. However, Head Start programs often contribute additional funds so that OSR classrooms located in Head Start centers meet Head Start quality standards.
2 Children are also served in institutions such as child care management agencies, colleges and universities, authority housing, and community centers.
3 In order to enroll, a child must be 4 years old by September 1. If after one year of Pre-K a child is eligible but not ready for kindergarten, it is possible for that child to enroll in Pre-K again.
4 There are no eligibility criteria at the state or local level to prioritize children for services. All children who live in a particular host county are eligible to participate in the program.
5 Programs are required to provide a 6-hour Family Enrichment Workshop to facilitate parental involvement.

ARIZONA — Early Childhood Block Grant (ECBG)–Prekindergarten Component 2002–2003

1 There are 236 school districts and 341 charter schools in Arizona. Most charter schools do not participate in the Early Childhood Block Grant. Pre-K is offered in 47 of 329 districts and charter schools that participate in the ECBG.
2 Although local funds are used, parent fees are never used to supplement funds to provide program services to children who qualify for the Pre-K program.
3 The district-encouraged practice of inclusion, along with frequent "blending" and "braiding" of funds, allows children funded by the ECBG to be placed in classrooms with children funded by IDEA or in Head Start classrooms. Local districts reported using about $25 million from various federal sources to provide preschool services for children who may or may not have been in ECBG Pre-K classrooms. These children were not counted in ECBG Pre-K enrollment.
4 Head Start classrooms may be located on public school campuses. However, there is no delineation between Head Start classrooms located on public school campuses and those located outside public school campuses.
5 Faith-based centers, as well as programs without religious content, may be included in private child care.
6 The vast majority of programs operate 5 days per week for the academic year.
7 While there is no legal requirement, it is recommended that programs operate for a minimum of 12 hours per week.
8 Children may participate for two years if local need is met for all eligible children to participate for one year or if local need dictates more than one year of participation.
9 An increasing number of children with IEP's, usually funded through IDEA, are served in the same Pre-K classrooms with children funded through the ECBG. However, children funded with IDEA money are not enrolled in the ECBG program.
10 This requirement represents NAEYC standards. All programs must be accredited.
11 The state licensing agency requires licensed programs, including all ECBG Pre-K programs, to provide breakfast, lunch and snacks depending upon the length of time and the time of day that a child attends a program.
12 The Arizona Office of Auditor General conducted an independent evaluation. The evaluation was descriptive and focused on compliance issues.

ARKANSAS — Arkansas Better Chance (ABC) 2002–2003

1 Programs are offered in 68 out of 75 (91%) counties.
2 This figure reflects the number of children enrolled in the center-based component of the ABC program and does not include children served through a home-based option.
3 All 3,086 children in ABC are partially supported by a 40% local match.
4 IDEA special education funds were used in some areas as an addition to the required local match.
5 University-sponsored settings served 221 children, education cooperatives served 636 children, community mental health centers served 46 children, and developmental disabilities centers served 67 children.
6 Some of the risk factors tied to eligibility include: parent without high school diploma or GED, low birth weight, teen parents, substance abuse, Title I eligibility, IDEA eligibility, abuse or neglect, developmental delay and limited English proficiency.
7 Parent involvement is part of the ABC program. Funding specific to parent engagement is included in the Core Quality Component model for ABC programs. Home visits, however, are not required.
8 Schools are required to provide a parent involvement coordinator and offer extensive contacts to parents regarding kindergarten readiness, including activity calendars and workshops.
9 The P–4 teacher license covers birth to fourth grade.
10 This number is compiled by adding $2,998 in state funds and $1,998 from local match.
11 All center-based programs are monitored and evaluated annually using the Early Childhood Environment Rating Scale and must obtain a total score of at least 5.5 out of 7, with a minimum of 4.5 in every subscale.
12 This figure represents the total number of scholarships awarded to Pre-K teachers in Arkansas. Approximately 25% of those scholarships were awarded to ABC staff enrolled in CDA programs.

CALIFORNIA — State Preschool Program 2002–2003

1 There are a total of 476 contracts or agencies providing State Preschool services. The program is offered in 320 out of 1,165 (27%) Local Education Agencies, which include school districts, county offices of education, and community colleges.
2 A total of $303.8 million was provided for the State Preschool Program to fund 96,685 slots. However, some contractors were not able to spend all of the funding because they lacked staff or facilities, because working families opted for full-day instead of part-day programs, or due to other reasons. Reported enrollment reflects unallocated and under-earned contracts.
3 The enrollment figure represents a point-in-time count. A total of 152,700 children were served at some time during the 2002–2003 school year.
4 Of the 152,700 children served in the State Preschool Program for any time during fiscal year 2002–2003, 118,228 or 77.4% were served in LEAs (public school programs). The remaining children were served in Head Start, private child care, or faith-based agencies.
5 Children must be served for at least 175 days per year (equivalent to a school year), but an agency is permitted to operate for up to 250 days per year.
6 The total number of children served throughout the year in the wrap-around program was 6,870.
7 The income cutoff applies to all children except those who receive protective services, who are at risk for abuse or neglect, or who are identified as abused, neglected, or exploited.
8 Children are eligible if they have a CPS referral, LEP, or exceptional needs. Children are also eligible if family circumstances "may diminish opportunities for normal development."
9 Class size is not statutorily controlled but is typically limited to 24 in order to meet the staff-child ratio requirement of 1:8.
10 Each contractor must provide meals and snacks that meet nutritional requirements specified by the federal Child and Adult Care Food Program or the National School Lunch Program.
11 A physical exam is required for program entry. Health and social services referral and follow-up to meet family needs are required.
12 Parent involvement and education must include at least the following components: program orientation, at least two individual program conferences, parent meetings with program staff, and a Parent Advisory Committee.
13 The Associate Teacher permit requires 12 credits in early childhood education or child development and 50 days of work experience in an instructional capacity. A CDA credential issued in California may be substituted for this requirement. The associate level teacher may function as the lead teacher in a classroom and the permit may be renewed one time for a 5-year period. The full Child Development Teacher permit requires a minimum of 40 semester units of education of which a minimum of 24 units must be in early childhood education or child development. A CDA credential may be used as nine semester units toward the required 24.
14 The Child Development Assistant Teacher permit requires 6 credits in early childhood education or child development.
15 This figure represents actual spending on preschool. A total of $303.8 million was appropriated for the State Preschool Program to fund 96,685 slots, but not all of the funding was directed to State Preschool Program services.
16 While data are not collected on the sources of local funding that may be used to supplement the State Preschool Program or provide additional slots, many school districts subsidize their programs with school general fund money.
17 The audits and reviews of State Preschool Programs operated by LEAs are conducted as part of the monitoring of all LEA programs. However, child development consultants participate in the detailed program compliance reviews that are conducted every three years.
18 The state has not conducted an evaluation of the State Preschool Program, but each child's development progress is tracked using the Desired Results System. Results are used to plan curriculum and developmentally appropriate activities for children.
19 No staff members in the Special Education Division are devoted solely to early childhood education programs and are therefore not included in this total. Staff included in this figure deal with all age groups in administering Child Care and Development programs.

COLORADO – Colorado Preschool Program (CPP) 2002–2003

1 Blending of funds is encouraged by the CPP to serve three main purposes: 1) to extend the length of the school day for children, 2) to extend the types of services provided to children, 3) to allow children funded by different sources to attend the same classrooms. When children in a single classroom are funded by a variety of sources, it is recommended that each source pay a percentage of operating expenses based on the number of children supported by each source.

2 Children served in faith-based centers are included in the enrollment figure for children served in private child care centers. The Colorado Constitution prohibits public schools from paying public funds for sectarian purposes.

3 Most programs operate 4 days per week with the fifth day funded to provide home visits, teacher planning time, or staff training. Full-day programs have difficulty allocating time for home visits.

4 Selected pilot communities have the flexibility to serve one child using two slots to provide a full day of funding. Only 128 children were served in this way during fiscal year 2002–2003.

5 Three-year-olds with 3 or more significant risk factors may be served in CPP. Legislation passed in 2004 specifies that children served in CPP must reach the age of 3, 4, or 5 by October 1 to be eligible for the program.

6 Colorado Preschool Program funds may be used to extend kindergarten to a full day in selected school districts. Some children supported by these funds turn 6 years old during the kindergarten year.

7 Significant family risk factors that affect overall learning readiness must be present in a child's life. These risk factors are defined by the Legislature and include considerations such as: eligibility for free or reduced-price lunch, homelessness, exposure to domestic or substance abuse, age and education level of parents, frequent family relocation, and poor social skills of the child. Eligibility is also granted if children are in need of language development or receiving services from the state Department of Social Services as neglected or dependent children.

8 Three-year-olds must have at least 3 risk factors to be eligible. The average number of risk factors present for a child in CPP is 3.7.

9 Children who are eligible for state funding through special education are not funded through CPP.

10 Meals and nutritious snacks must be served at suitable intervals. Children who are in the program for more than 4 hours per day or during evenings must be offered a meal that meets at least one-third of the child's daily nutritional needs.

11 The Colorado Quality Standards for Early Childhood Care and Education Services specify requirements for establishing a family-staff partnership.

12 In the event that a teacher with a CDA is not available, an AA in early childhood education or child development becomes the minimum requirement.

13 The Colorado Preschool Program is funded by the School Finance Act. Funding for school districts is provided first by local sources, including revenues, property taxes and specific ownership taxes. State monies are then used to fund any shortfall. The state share is about 61% of total program funding.

14 This amount is an average and reflective of school finance money only. In FY 2002–2003, funding levels for CPP ranged from $2,587 to $6,000 per child, depending on the funding level for the school district.

15 All programs are required to follow the Colorado Quality Standards for Early Childhood Care and Education Services in monitoring for program quality. Furthermore, the Colorado Department of Education strongly encourages that all programs receiving funds under the Act be accredited by NAEYC. Selected programs are using the Educare rating system and others are using the ECERS to measure program quality.

16 Every district must report statewide third grade assessment scores for CPP graduates and results from CPP family surveys. Local programs decide how children will be evaluated during the preschool years, but every program is expected to use a portion of funding to assess child progress and evaluate program quality. Tools often used include the High/Scope Child Observation Record, Work Sampling, and Creative Curriculum Assessment.

17 Colorado funds the TEACH program primarily through the Child Care and Development Block Grant. There is also a loan forgiveness program for child care teachers.

CONNECTICUT – School Readiness 2002–2003

1 Each community chooses its own specific combination of slots. Types of slots include full-day, full-year (10 hours per day, 50 weeks per year); part-day, part-year (2.5 hours per day, 180 days per year); and extended-day (extends the hours, days and weeks of a non-School Readiness program to meet full-day requirements). At least 60% of slots in each community must be full-day, full-year. All programs operate 5 days per week and about 75% of programs are full-day.

2 TANF families and foster children are exempt from fees. Part-day and extended-day programs pay a lesser amount based on services offered. Communities can decide to exempt all part-day programs from charging fees.

3 Children with IEPs receive special education services paid for with special education funds but also participate in School Readiness programs.

4 Programs are required to serve one snack to children who attend less than 5 hours per day and one snack plus one meal to children in class for 5 to 8 hours per day. Children on the premises more than 8 hours per day must be provided one snack and two snacks and one meal. Either the program or the parent can provide food for all meals.

5 All children in the School Readiness program must have an annual well child checkup that conforms to EPSDT standards. Some communities provide vision, hearing, and dental check-ups.

6 However, programs are strongly encouraged to ensure that staff are employed who reflect the language and culture of the children being served.

7 Programs are required to offer parent education in nutrition, health, and literacy and to involve parents in activities that ensure they are partners in their children's education. All programs must have a Parent Advisory Board that involves parents in the policy-making decisions for the Pre-K program.

8 In addition, all programs must have written collaborative agreements with community agencies to serve family needs.

9 Programs operating in public schools are required to have a certified teacher present for at least 2.5 hours per day. Three types of certification are accepted: Elementary with a Pre-K endorsement, Nursery–K, or Special Education with an endorsement in Pre-K–12. For the remainder of the day, Pre-K teachers in public schools must meet the nonpublic requirements of a CDA plus 9 credits in early childhood.

10 Assistant teachers must meet teacher requirements if they act in the capacity of lead teacher for part of the day. In full-day programs, assistant teachers generally act in a lead capacity for half of the program day.

11 School Readiness program requirements also mandate that teachers take two courses or workshops in ECE and receive training on an annual basis in serving children with disabilities. They must also present documentation that they have attended at least one workshop on emerging pre-literacy skills and one on diversity.

12 Public School Readiness teacher salaries depend in part on job titles. An employee with the title of teacher must meet state certification requirements and be paid on the public school scale. Other job titles do not require certification nor that the employee be paid on the public school scale.

13 Allocations are awarded to the either the community or the board of education. The receiving agency is designated by the mayor and superintendent to be the fiscal agent. School Readiness Councils then advise the mayors and superintendents on the program applications and award funds to individual programs in their communities.

14 State site monitoring visits by the SDE program manager take place every 3 years. A community liaison conducts quarterly monitoring visits.

15 A community liaison reviews local programs and in combination with parents and the program director, completes the Connecticut School Readiness Preschool Program Evaluation System (CSRPPES) at the end of each fiscal year.

16 A 2-year evaluation and an Interim Evaluation Report examined if center quality, quality of care and education, and staff qualifications had improved. The Connecticut School Readiness Pre-K Program Evaluation System was used to evaluate the programs. This system has four components, which include the 10 quality components outlined in state legislation. In addition, compliance was reviewed by examining accreditation, credential requirements, and levels of parent satisfaction.

17 The evaluation examined whether child outcomes improved as measured by the Bracken Basic Concept Scale and the Child Observation Instrument.

18 Scholarships are available through Connecticut Charts a Course, which is funded by the Department of Social Services, the SDE, and other agencies and foundations.

DELAWARE – Early Childhood Assistance Program (ECAP) 2002–2003

1 The program is not targeted to particular school districts, communities, or towns, and is available in each of Delaware's 3 counties. In 2002–2003, at least 2 programs were available in each county.

2 At least 10% of children enrolled in the program must have an identified disability.

3 Parent involvement activities are required as per the federal Head Start Program Performance Standards. Examples include family literacy activities, involvement in parent governance, and participation in parent committees and policy groups.

4 This represents the requirement to meet state child care licensing standards. There is no specific ECAP requirement.

5 All programs must follow federal Head Start Program Performance Standards and are monitored every three years. The Delaware DOE conducts monitoring using the federal Head Start monitoring model, PRISM.

6 This children's outcome assessment is a separate state-required assessment process. State-funded Pre-K programs must assess each child's development (using some acceptable assessment instrument) on a pre/post schedule and report results to the DOE annually. Programs are using either the Creative Curriculum Continuum or the Work Sampling System.

GEORGIA — Georgia Prekindergarten Program 2002–2003

1   Pre-K is offered in all districts through a combination of public and private providers.
2   This enrollment breakdown is based on an estimated enrollment of 65,364. Faith-based organizations are counted as private child care centers in this estimate.
3   The state Pre-K funds are used as a state match for CCDF dollars and not used to fund specific children or services.
4   The majority of children exit the program in the spring after completing one year of Pre-K. In rare instances, a child is allowed to repeat the program. If a child is age eligible for kindergarten but has not attended Pre-K, he or she is allowed to enroll in Pre-K. Such instances are considered on a case-by-case basis.
5   Children with special needs may be served in Pre-K programs with services paid for by the local school system or other sources of funding. The Office of School Readiness (OSR) does not have data on the expenditures or numbers of children in such settings.
6   Providers are expected to encourage parents to volunteer in the classroom, offer parent meetings, conduct a minimum of two individual parent conferences, and share children's portfolios with their parents.
7   All Pre-K teachers must have a degree in an early childhood related field. The state-level public school certification covers preschool through grade 5. Local school system policies typically require that Pre-K teachers be certified.
8   Preschool teachers are required to undergo 12 hours of training per year, for which they receive 10 hours of SDU credits.
9   Parents may be charged fees for food, but relevant data regarding local funding are not available at the OSR.
10 This estimate was obtained by dividing the total budget by the number of children served.
11 State colleges, universities, and military bases are authorized to receive funding to operate Pre-K programs.
12 The OSR employs 23 full-time staff to administer Pre-K. One full-time position also exists at the Head Start Collaboration Office. Special education and Even Start staff are located at the state Department of Education.

HAWAII — Preschool Open Doors Project 2002–2003

1   For some children, Head Start funds are used to cover a half-day program while Preschool Open Doors supports wrap-around services.
2   Data are not available on the number of children served in each type of setting, but it is estimated that the majority of children are in private child care centers.
3   Parents may select either a half-day or full-day program.
4   Children with special needs are eligible at age 3, but nearly all enrolled children are 4 years old.
5   Most families served have incomes much lower than this eligibility cutoff.
6   Hawaii's sliding fee schedule has three income brackets: families at or below the federal poverty line have no copayment, families from 101% to 150% of the poverty line contribute 10% of the cost, and families above 151% of the poverty line contribute 20%.
7   Preschool Open Doors funds are used to serve children who have special needs but do not meet the state Department of Education's eligibility criteria for services funded by IDEA.
8   Teachers employed by the state DOE are paid according to the public school salary scale. However, private preschool or Head Start programs that occupy space on public school campuses are not required to follow the public school salary scale.
9   Federal funding covers the administrative costs of the Preschool Open Doors program.
10 Children funded by Preschool Open Doors are served in classrooms with children whose families pay full tuition.
11 This number represents state funding.

ILLINOIS — Prekindergarten Program for At-Risk Children 2002–2003

1   Most programs operate for a half-day, five days per week. Districts request funds for the program type that they choose to operate.
2   Eligibility criteria are determined locally, but low-income status may be considered as one of the risk factors that qualify a child to participate.
3   The state provides guidelines and districts specify eligibility criteria in their grant proposals. Criteria include low parental education, poverty, drug or alcohol abuse in the family, non-English speaking, and teen parents.
4   Multiple factors are required for eligibility. Children are identified for enrollment through individual screenings and assessments.
5   Children in full-day programs generally receive lunch and a snack. Some programs use federal funds to provide breakfast as well.
6   While programs are not required to provide a translator, communication with parents is part of the process of determining eligibility, so programs do offer a translating service.
7   Parent involvement is required, but there is no designated minimum number of conferences.
8   The in-service requirement can also be met with 24 continuing education units over 5 years or by attaining National Board for Professional Teaching Standards certification.
9   As of fiscal year 2004, agencies other than public schools are allowed to apply directly for state funds.
10 It is estimated that districts subcontracted with 350 programs statewide, most of which were located in Chicago.
11 Child progress is assessed using instruments such as Work Sampling or Creative Curriculum. All instruments used in these evaluations have been aligned with Illinois Early Learning Standards.

IOWA — Shared Visions 2002–2003

1   Families of children who are not at risk pay a fee.
2   Services for children with special needs are supported with IDEA funds. These funds are provided in addition to Shared Visions funds.
3   Grantees operate at least 3 but not more than 10 hours per day based on local need and the original grant submitted.
4   Grantees operate an average of 4.74 days per week and 181 days per year, and all operate at least 4 days per week.
5   Twenty percent of a program's enrollees may be children from families with incomes above the cut-off. These children must meet one or more risk factors such as: developmental delay, biological risk at birth, limited parental education, or exposure to substance abuse, mental illness, or physical abuse. Other special circumstances considered for eligibility include placement in foster care or being homeless.
6   The specific meal provided depends on the time of day during which children are present. All applicants for Shared Visions funding must address meal requirements in their grant applications.
7   Although Shared Visions does not have specific requirements for screening and referral, applicants are required to address the types of screening and referral that will be provided. All Shared Visions programs provide screening and referral for vision, hearing, and health. LEAs also decide which developmental, dental, and nutrition services to provide.
8   Although the number of required parent conferences is not specified in state regulations, programs are required to involve and work with parents by providing home visits, instruction on parenting skills, and other services.
9   Teachers in nonpublic schools are required to have a state license in child care. Head Start teachers are required to have an AA.
10 The early childhood teaching endorsement became a requirement in the 2002–2003 school year.
11 Although there is no specific amount of annual in-service professional development required, most grantees provide at least 15 hours per year, consistent with NAEYC recommendations.
12 External evaluators administered the ECERS-R to assess classroom environment.
13 External evaluators used a modified High Scope Child Observation Record to survey teachers.
14 Scholarships are only available to teachers in programs licensed as child care centers by the Department of Human Services.

KANSAS — At-Risk Four-Year-Old Children Preschool Program 2002–2003

1   State funds normally pay teacher salaries and may also provide for an aide. Districts typically pay for services such as bussing, teacher benefits, and in-kind contributions such as providing classroom space.
2   Districts request slots in the Pre-K program and are awarded grants to provide for a specified number of children. Some of these slots may be in special education or Head Start classrooms.
3   Funding sources are not blended to support children in the program, but teacher salaries can be paid through a combination of funding streams, depending on the percentage of children in a classroom enrolled in Pre-K, Head Start, or special education.
4   Programs are required to operate at least 2.5 hours per day and a total of 465 hours per school year.
5   Every child in the program must have at least one risk factor. Eligibility for free lunch (130% of poverty) is counted as a risk factor. This represents an income of $19,525 or below for a family of three during fiscal year 2002.
6   Priority enrollment is offered to children who are: eligible for free lunch, developmentally delayed, English Language Learners, referred from another agency, migrant children, or children of teen or single parents.
7   All children served present at least one risk factor such as eligibility for free lunch.
8   Children with IEPs are enrolled in the special education preschool.
9   Although not mandated by the state, programs are encouraged to follow NAEYC recommendations, as well as limit class size to 15 students with two teachers present. Many programs that combine special education and Pre-K children in the same classrooms require lower student to teacher ratios.
10 Vision, hearing, and other general health screenings and referrals are not explicitly required but must be included as part of the grant proposal. The schools must explain in their proposals how they will provide comprehensive health services in order to receive funding.
11 Parent activities include involvement with newsletters, planning activities, and general program decision making.
12 Due to insufficient funding, workshops for professional development are offered but not required. Teachers participate on a voluntary basis.
13 Local evaluation is required and reported to the state, but funds and personnel are not available to support a statewide evaluation.

KENTUCKY — Kentucky Preschool Program 2002–2003

1   State money provides the majority of funding but is often insufficient to fully support the program. Most districts contribute funds ranging from $10,000 to $1,000,000 depending on the size of the district. Contributions to the state-funded preschool program are provided at local school districts' discretion.
2   Federal funds are blended with state funds to provide additional support for extended-hours and comprehensive services.
3   The majority of programs are located in the public schools. The remainder are located in Head Start and private or faith-based centers.
4   Wrap-around services are provided by Family Resource Centers, Head Start, TANF, and CCDBG. These services are available to children not enrolled in the preschool program as well as to those who do participate.
5   Children under age 3 who are diagnosed with a disability are eligible to enter the program as of their third birthday. Four-year-olds with disabilities or otherwise at risk must meet an October 1st cut-off date.
6   A 5-year-old child with a disability would have the option of attending the program if the ARC committee decided the child would be best served in a preschool setting.
7   Four-year-olds at risk attend for one year. Three-year-olds identified with disabilities may attend for two years.
8   Districts may accept over-income children if space is available, and some districts charge tuition for these children.
9   The preschool program serves almost all 3- and 4-year-old children with disabilities who attend regular classrooms. Many preschool coordinators are also special education supervisors.
10 As of the 2004–2005 program year, all new teachers must have a BA and early childhood certification.
11 Teachers not hired by the public schools do not have to be paid on the public school salary scale. Teachers hired by Head Start in a blended program are paid on the Head Start scale.
12 In addition to the scholarship program, an income-based loan forgiveness program is available through the Kentucky Higher Education Authority.

LOUISIANA — 8(g) Student Enhancement Block Grant Program 2002–2003

1   There may be some duplication across different prekindergarten programs in the state, as some 8(g) funds are used to supplement funding in classrooms that also receive funds from the state's other prekindergarten programs such as LA4 and Starting Points.
2   A child enrolled in 8(g) in a school system that offers the LA4 program may attend wrap-around hours supported by LA4 funds.
3   The state does not set specific income eligibility criteria, but priority is given to children from low-income families.
4   Children at risk of being insufficiently ready for school are identified based on screening results. Priority is given to children from low-income families.
5   The staff-child ratio requirement changed from 1:15 to 1:10 effective as of the 2002–2003 program year.
6   Screening is conducted to determine which children are potentially eligible and to plan an appropriate program. The 8(g) program does not specifically require referrals, but programs refer children for services if needs are identified.
7   The 8(g) program does not specifically require translators to be available, but programs provide them if needed.
8   Louisiana 8(g) funds are allocated to the public school systems, which in turn determine which schools will receive funding for 4-year-old programs.

LOUISIANA — LA4 and Starting Points Programs 2002–2003

1   LA4 programs were offered in 19 school districts, while Starting Points was offered in 55 districts. Some districts offer both LA4 and Starting Points programs.
2   This total represents an enrollment of 5,717 children in LA4 and 1,505 children in Starting Points. Before- and/or after-school programming was provided to 2,075 children in LA4, approximately 717 of whom were not enrolled during regular operating hours.
3   All 251 tuition-paying children are in the LA4 program. These 251 children are not included in the total enrollment count.
4   Starting Points programs do not offer or support wrap-around services. However, services may be provided to any child who needs wrap-around in school systems that offer LA4.
5   Some families with incomes above this limit are able to enroll their children by paying tuition.
6   Teachers may also qualify with any of the following: an Elementary certificate and an Out-of-Field Authorization to Teach, a BA and a Temporary Authority to Teach, a Temporary Employment Permit, or an Out-of-State Provisional Certificate. Teachers qualifying under these conditions must be working toward obtaining a Louisiana teaching certificate specified in program requirements.
7   Starting Points relies to a large degree on other sources of funding. Children in Starting Points may be in classrooms with children funded by other sources, including LA4 as well as 8(g) or Title I.
8   Although the Starting Points program has provided funds directly to faith-based centers in the past, beginning in 2004–2005 the program will no longer contract with these agencies. The Nonpublic Schools Early Childhood Development Program is expected to pick up the contracts for Starting Points faith-based centers.
9   Public schools may subcontract with faith-based centers in both LA4 and Starting Points, but no LA4 contracts were established with faith-based centers during 2002–2003.
10 During 2002–2003, program quality in LA4 was assessed using the ECERS-R, SWOT analysis, and the Developmental Skills Checklist. A separate, less-intensive evaluation to collect demographic information was conducted for Starting Points. For the 2003–2004 school year, there will be a single evaluation covering both programs.
11 The special education staff are responsible for programs covering Pre-K–Grade 3.

LOUISIANA — Nonpublic Schools Early Childhood Development Program (NSECD) 2002–2003

1   This funding total consists of federal TANF funds that the state has chosen to direct toward prekindergarten. There are no additional state funds.

MAINE — Two-Year Kindergarten Program 2002–2003

1   Many programs are moving toward a 4-day-per-week schedule with Fridays used for parent outreach.
2   Most programs operate for the academic year.

APPENDIX A: STATE SURVEY DATA continued

MARYLAND — Extended Elementary Education Program 2002–2003

1 The enrollment total includes children served by public school districts through a combination of funds derived from the Prekindergarten Program as well as other federal, state, and local sources. Because districts blend these funding sources, a specific number of children supported by state Pre-K funds is not available. Additionally, 1,426 3-year-olds served in public school Pre-K programs are included in this enrollment total. These children were supported by sources other than Prekindergarten Program funds, which can only be used to serve 4-year-olds.

2 Federal Head Start funds supported 2,264 children who were in Head Start but served in public school facilities. While the use of child care and other community-based settings is currently very limited, the state plans to increase the use of these facilities as it expands availability of Pre-K to include all eligible 4-year-olds whose families choose to participate. The same standards that apply to school-based Pre-K programs will apply to other settings.

3 Children eligible for services supported directly by IDEA funds are not included in the total enrollment count. However, IDEA indirectly supports many children in state Pre-K because they often attend the same classrooms as children receiving IDEA services and therefore benefit from additional staff and materials provided to those inclusive classrooms.

4 The Judith P. Hoyer Early Care and Education Enhancement Program provides about $8 million in earmarked funds to support comprehensive early childhood centers that are school-based or school-linked.

5 Additional risk factors include homelessness, referral from another program, previous experience in Head Start, health issues, and specific home and family characteristics.

6 By policy, 3-year-olds are not eligible for the Prekindergarten Program, but the state reported the maximum class size and staff-child ratio requirement for 3-year-olds under child care regulations as 24 and 1:12, respectively.

7 Vision and health screening and referral are the responsibility of the school health services program in conjunction with the health department. These services are not all required by the Prekindergarten Program, but they are required under Title I, which applies to all children enrolled.

8 Programs are required to offer parent involvement activities as specified under NCLB. The statute defines parental involvement as the participation of parents in regular and meaningful communication involving student academic learning and other school activities. Such involvement is meant to ensure that parents play an integral role in assisting their child's learning both at home and at school. (NCLB does not apply directly to state Pre-K programs, but since all of Maryland's Pre-K programs are in Title I schools, and all Title I schools are subject to NCLB, the state's Pre-K programs all comply with NCLB.)

9 Some in-service requirements may be imposed locally. Also, all schools involved in the Prekindergarten Program have adopted the Maryland Model for School Readiness, which entails 5 days of training in teachers' first year, 4 days of training in their second, and 2-day institutes in their school-system-selected focus area in subsequent years. There are new professional development standards as of 2003–2004. In addition, teachers must meet the requirements for "highly qualified" teachers under NCLB.

10 Total spending was estimated based on half the average cost per student for the K–12 school system, since Pre-K is funded for a half-day. The per pupil estimate includes costs for the operation of the program, classroom activities, teacher salaries, materials, central administration, and other expenses but does not include transportation or facilities costs.

11 The estimate for local funding was calculated by subtracting federal and state expenditures from the total spending estimate.

12 Local school systems apply a consolidated planning process that uses blended funding and do not break down their operating costs by funding source.

13 The state conducted a longitudinal study that started in the 1980s and followed the children through 9th grade. The study was published in 1991, and the state has not conducted another evaluation since. However, an accountability system is now in place that uses selected measures from the Work Sampling System.

14 Students are assessed within seven domains of progress: social and personal, language and literacy, mathematical thinking, scientific thinking, social studies, the arts, physical development, and health.

MASSACHUSETTS — Community Partnerships for Children (CPC) 2002–2003

1 Exact data on the age breakdown of enrolled children are not available, but it is estimated that about 10% of the children are age 5 with the remainder split evenly between 3- and 4-year-olds.

2 Additional children are served in a public school preschool program that overlaps with the CPC initiative and is supported with special education funds, federal Title I dollars, local fees, and other resources. Classroom composition in the public school program is highly inclusive—in classes of 20, up to 30% of the children may have special needs, and in classes of 15 or smaller, up to 50% of the children may have special needs.

3 Local sources include parent fees through a sliding fee scale, in-kind contributions, and leveraging classrooms and staff in public schools and Head Start programs.

4 Some children are served through a combination of CPC and Head Start funding, with Head Start funding used for the core program day and CPC dollars used for wrap-around services.

5 TANF funds are blended with CPC dollars and may be used to fund support services rather than to provide direct prekindergarten services.

6 The sum of numbers for children served in different settings is greater than the total enrollment figure because children may be served in more than one setting.

7 Program operating schedules are determined by family needs and preferences.

8 An estimated 60% of programs operate for the calendar year.

9 Most of the 2,548 children served by Head Start are receiving wrap-around care, and additional children in other settings may also be receiving wrap-around care.

10 Risk factors include premature birth, low birth weight, homelessness, poverty, or having a parent with a disability.

11 Some communities may require children to have more than one risk factor to qualify.

12 The sliding fee scale does not apply to children in legal custody of grandparents or other family members, foster children, and children served through funding sources targeted to at-risk families.

13 Community Partnerships for Children funds cannot be used to supplant IDEA funding. However, CPC funding can be used for supplementary services that benefit all of the children in the classroom, including those with an IEP.

14 It is suggested that programs provide support to families in their own languages, but there is no requirement.

15 Required parent involvement activities include playgroups and enrichment activities. In addition, educational services for parents and transportation can be provided locally, based on need.

16 All teachers must be at least 21 years old. Furthermore, standards passed in 2003 require all newly hired teachers to attain at least an AA by 2010 and a BA by 2017.

17 Local funding that supports CPC programs is controlled locally and does not go to the state.

18 Total TANF funding used for the CPC program, including $21,000,000 in federal TANF funds as well as state MOE for TANF (which is counted as state funds), is $34,209,422.

19 Federal CCDF dollars are not used to support the CPC program, but 5% of CPC funds are counted toward the state match for CCDF.

20 In-kind expenditures include items such as staff fringe benefits, custodial services, space, utilities, maintenance, postage, paper, copying, supplies, mileage, administrative and transportation costs.

21 Roughly 70% of state and local funds are spent on direct services for children enrolled. Remaining funds support program components such as community outreach, comprehensive services, and quality enhancement. These indirect services benefit many children who are not counted in enrollment.

22 In addition to these requirements, the CPC program evaluation cycle requires sites to collect data on quality, council collaboration, capacity, and family needs every three years on a rotating basis. Programs are also evaluated as part of the process of accreditation, which is required for all programs within three years of serving a CPC child.

23 Data are collected on quality, council collaboration, capacity, and family needs. In addition, the Cost and Quality Study collected data on programs using the ECERS.

24 In addition to the evaluation conducted by the state, other evaluations include the Cost and Quality Study conducted by Wellesley College and the SWEEP study conducted by the National Center for Early Development and Learning.

25 This total includes 2,000 scholarships funded with CPC quality dollars and 400 scholarships that were granted through Advancing the Field and supported with early childhood special education and special education funds.

MICHIGAN — Michigan School Readiness Program 2002–2003

1 State funding is not always enough to fund School Readiness programs to operate for 2.5 or 3 hours per day. Parents cannot be charged in order to make up for gaps in funding, nor can Head Start or IDEA, but Title I funds can be used to supplement state money. Children who remain in Pre-K classrooms for a full day are considered to be in child care during the extended hours.

2 Providers may charge tuition if offering a fifth day. Most programs operate 4 half days, though some offer 2 full days.

3 There are 25 specified risk factors considered to place children at risk of becoming educationally disadvantaged.

4 Over 50% of enrollees are required to be low-income and have at least 1 other risk factor. In practice, more than 60% of children who attend meet the income criterion.

5 While data are not collected relevant to IEPs or IFSPs, 5% of children enrolled in state Pre-K are identified as having a handicapping condition.

6 The state provides $3,300 per child regardless of special needs. Special education can be charged for services such as speech or physical therapy, but special education teachers or aides cannot be paid to work with a child in the state Pre-K program.

7 A qualified teacher must be present, plus an associate teacher in rooms with 9–16 children. If more than 16 students are in a class, then a third adult (who does not have to meet any specified qualifications) must be present.

8 Programs must make referrals but are not required to conduct screenings. Screening is required before kindergarten entry.

9 Most teachers in nonpublic settings have a BA.

10 Associate (assistant) teachers are given 2 years to meet the requirements of their position.

11 Title I money may be used to supplement state spending, but no data on such supplements are collected.

12 Most local providers offer in-kind support, but no data regarding local contributions are collected.

13 Medical health and social service agencies may provide programs.

14 An effort is made to conduct site visits and reviews on 10% of public school programs and one-third of agency programs each year.

15 Comprehensive indicators were examined using PQA (High/Scope).

16 Child progress was measured for a sample study only, using COR and teacher and parent surveys.

17 Each person works on multiple programs.

MINNESOTA — State-Funded Head Start Model 2002–2003

1 In 2002–2003, state Head Start funding went to one school district; seven tribal governments; and 27 private, nonprofit agencies, each serving one or more counties. State Head Start grantees include all federally designated Head Start programs in Minnesota as of 1989.

2 This enrollment total includes 195 children under age 3 and 240 5-year-olds.

3 Total 2002–2003 federal Head Start funding for 3- to 5-year-olds in Minnesota was $72,447,486. Grantees were required to garner at least a 25% local match of $18,111,871. A local match is not required for state Head Start funds, and state funds cannot be used as a match for federal funds.

4 State funds support additional slots in classrooms that also receive federal Head Start money.

5 One school district, seven tribal governments, 24 community action agencies, and three other private nonprofit agencies receive state Head Start funding. Data are not available on the number of children served in each type of site.

6 Minimum operating hours must be consistent with the requirements of the federal Head Start Program Performance Standards. Programs must operate at least 3.5 hours per day, 4 days per week, and 32 weeks per year.

7 In 2002–2003, about 195 children from birth to age 3 were served with state Head Start funds. This number is not included in the total enrollment count reported here.

8 At least 10% of children served must have an identified disability.

9 Part-day programs are required to provide children with at least one-third of their daily nutritional needs, as determined by the USDA. Full-day programs must provide one-half to two-thirds of daily nutritional needs, depending on length of the program day.

10 Programs are required to provide all activities specified in the federal Head Start Program Performance Standards.

11 Assistant teachers in settings subject to child care regulations must work under the supervision of a teacher, be at least 18 years old, and meet one of nine combined credential, educational, and experience requirements, such as a high school diploma, 12 quarter credits in early childhood or a related field, and 2,080 hours of experience.

12 Non-degreed staff are required to complete 2% of their total working hours for in-service training (full-time employment requires 40 hours of in-service) and degreed staff are required to complete 1.5% of total working hours for in-service.

13 This total includes $1 million in state Head Start funds that was set aside in 2002–2003 to serve children birth to age 3. The set aside funds were eliminated in 2003, so that grantees now have the flexibility to serve children birth to age 5 with state Head Start funds.

14 All federal or state Head Start grantees have an in-depth federal peer review every three years that involves participation of a state monitor. In addition, every grantee receives an annual monitoring visit from a state monitor.

MISSOURI — Missouri Preschool Project (MPP) 2002–2003

1 Special education funds cover the prorated amount for special needs services.

2 Each program may choose to apply as either a full-day program (6.5 hours) or a half-day program (3 hours). Most programs offer extended-day services using other sources of funding.

3 Programs awarded in 1998–1999 had the option to operate 4 days per week with a fifth day for home visiting. This practice is being phased out and most programs awarded in 1998–1999 now operate 5 days per week.

4 Programs must operate a minimum of nine months but may choose to operate for up to 12 months.

5 Programs are funded through a competitive process and receive extra points in the scoring system for serving children with special needs or from low-income families.

6 Private providers generally use the sliding scale from the Department of Social Services, while school-based programs use free or reduced-price lunch eligibility to determine the sliding scale fee. Some districts offer free services to students qualifying for free lunch, while others charge minimal fees. All children who receive reduced-price meals pay some fee.

7 Child care licensing requires full-day programs to offer lunch and two snacks. Half-day programs must offer either a morning or afternoon snack.

8 Parent conferences are optional. Two hundred MPP programs involved a total of 4,109 families in some type of conference.

9 Although provision of such services is optional, MPP programs offered 1,579 parent involvement activities in which 3,613 families participated.

10 Teachers are also required to attend at least two full-day training programs and receive on-site technical assistance. All professional development opportunities paid for through MPP funds represent additional hours beyond the 12 clock hours required for licensure.

11 Certified teachers in nonpublic programs must be paid at a rate comparable to the local public school salary scale.

12 This figure includes professional development opportunities for teachers in programs located in private preschools or public schools. The amount of funding available to programs decreases after each year.

13 State monitoring in each of these areas occurs as needed and as budget constraints allow. A minimum frequency of monitoring is not specified.

14 Program quality was evaluated using the ECERS. Child progress/outcomes were examined using indicators that included: mathematical assessment, applied mathematical assessment, conventional knowledge, receptive language assessment, assessment of letter word recognition, other reading related skills, and social skills.

15 Programs may fund each teacher or assistant teacher up to $800 per year toward the acquisition of a BA in early childhood education.

NEBRASKA — Early Childhood Grant Program 2002–2003

1 Programs are also offered in 3 out of 19 Educational Service Units.

2 There were 176 children younger than 3 years old enrolled in the program.

3 Local sources are required to match 50% of the program funding. Due to limited state funding, local sources in practice provide an average of 66% of the program budget.

4 Children are primarily served in public schools. However, some schools subcontract with Head Start and private centers when program space is limited. Data are reported by individual programs and are not compiled as part of the statewide evaluation report.

5 All programs operate at least 12–15 hours per week and approximately half run full-day, 5 days per week.

6 Grants can either be for the academic or the calendar year.

7 Some programs provide extended services using local match funds, but state grant money does not support wrap-around.

8 Grants are competitive with priority given to districts with high English Language Learner or low-income populations. In addition, districts offer priority enrollment to children born prematurely or with low birth weights. Up to 30% of funds can be used to serve children without these risk factors.

9 Meal requirements depend on hours during which children attend the program. All programs provide snacks, most offer lunch, and some provide breakfast as well.

10 A translator is required if the majority of the children in the class speak a language other than English. If a smaller percentage is non-English speaking, the classroom must have a resource person available.

11 Parent involvement activities include: providing written information about program policy and procedures; parent orientation; at least two parent visits; opportunities to participate in dialogue, conferences, classroom volunteering, and advisory committees; and family development and support based on needs and interests.

12 Though there is no direct funding from Even Start, preschool programs and Even Start often serve the same families. Collaboration is therefore required for preschool programs operating in communities with Even Start.

13 The state funds up to 50% of the total cost per child, and districts provide the remainder with local resources and other funds from sources such as special education, Head Start, and Title I.

14 Educational Service Units are eligible to receive funding directly.

15 Environmental rating scales such as the ITERS-R, ECERS-R, and High/Scope PQA are used to assess program quality. Within 3 years, programs receiving state funds will be required to have NAEYC accreditation. In 2003–04, the ELLCO was added as a measure of program quality that may be used in evaluations.

16 The High/Scope Child Observation Record, Work Sampling System, or the Creative Curriculum Development Continuum has been employed to track child progress and outcomes.

17 TEACH scholarships are available to assistant teachers who are working towards an AA.

NEVADA — Nevada Early Childhood Education Comprehensive Plan 2002–2003

1   Total enrollment for 2002–2003 includes an estimated 88 children younger than 3 years of age. Breakdown of enrollment by age is approximate.
2   Students with IEPs are partially supported by special education funds, but those dollars do not replace state Pre-K funds.
3   Local education agencies may operate programs in elementary schools, high schools, or community centers. The breakdown of enrollment by these locations is unavailable.
4   A total of 171 children were served through home visits, and 34 were served in university settings.
5   This breakdown of enrollment by location is based on the total number of children served during the 2002–2003 school year, rather than a point-in-time count.
6   Most programs operate 2.5 hours per day, 4 days per week.
7   The yearly Pre-K schedule is based on local needs. During 2002–2003, children in center-based programs were served an average of 38.8 hours per month for 7.3 months out of the year.
8   In 2002–2003, the only home-based program was located in Las Vegas. This program has since been eliminated due to difficulty in meeting quality requirements.
9   Several programs offer home visits in addition to classroom experience, which benefits children not counted in home-based enrollment.
10 Children may theoretically enroll for 5 years, but most enter when they are 4 years old and spend 1 year in the program.
11 All programs give enrollment priority to students from low-income families and specify detailed eligibility criteria that align with individual program needs. Many programs offer priority enrollment to children with limited English proficiency.
12 Programs must provide a rationale for class size and staff-child ratio. The state recommends that programs follow NAEYC guidelines, and all sites maintained a staff-child ratio of 1:8 or better in 2002–2003.
13 Each program is required to have a parent involvement component that is sensitive to individual needs. A prescribed number of parent conferences is therefore deemed unnecessary. In 2002–2003, most programs provided home visits and parent conferences to the majority of families served.
14 Required parent involvement programs typically include, but are not limited to, any or all of the following options: workshops, classes or literacy nights, volunteer time in the classroom, home visits, parent education, ESL classes, or home parent involvement packets.
15 Teachers in Title I schools must fulfill degree requirements set forth by Title I.
16 Nevada Even Start Quality Indicators of program delivery and participant outcomes for children and parents were evaluated.
17 State-funded programs were required to set aside 3% of their total grant award to pay for evaluation costs.

NEW JERSEY — Abbott Preschool Program 2002–2003

1   Programs are required to operate for a minimum of 180 days per year. Funds from the Department of Human Services are combined with Department of Education funds to operate full-day, year-round programs.
2   While there are no income eligibility criteria for individual children, only districts where are least 40 percent of children qualify for free or reduced-price lunch receive funding through this initiative. All 3- and 4-year-old children within those districts are eligible to participate.
3   Parent involvement specialists organize family, student, and community program activities.
4   Teachers who worked in center-based programs before the degree requirement was implemented have until September 2004 to meet the requirement.
5   This total does not include contributions of $121 million from the Department of Human Services that were used to provide extended-day services to some Abbott program enrollees.
6   This amount represents DOE funds only.
7   Yearly classroom observations using the ECERS-R are conducted to monitor program quality. Also, districts must submit a revised three-year operational plan each year.
8   The ECERS-R, SELA, and PCMI were used to assess program quality.
9   Child progress was assessed using PPVT and TVIP tests, as well as a Get Ready to Read screening at Kindergarten entry.
10 State evaluators collaborated with universities to conduct evaluations.
11 This number does not include DHS staff who devote time to the Abbott program.

NEW JERSEY — Non-Abbott Early Childhood Program Aid 2002–2003

1   While there are no income eligibility criteria for individual children, only districts where 20 to 40 percent of children qualify for free or reduced-price lunch receive funding through this initiative. All 3- and 4-year-old children within those districts are eligible to participate.

NEW MEXICO — Child Development Program 2002–2003

1   This enrollment total includes children from birth to age 5. Some of the infants and toddlers received home-visiting or hospital-based services and did not attend a center-based program.
2   Child Development Program funds do not fully support any program or child, but rather are blended to supplement other sources of funding.
3   This is the approximate breakdown for the 540 children in some type of center-based program. In addition, 267 children are in specialized infant/toddler programs and receive home-visiting or hospital-based services. The sum of these figures does not equal total enrollment, as data on program location were only reported for 807 children. This figure also includes one program serving 32 infants of teen parents.
4   Most programs operate year-round. Out of 22 funded programs, 18 operate on a regular schedule. Of these 18 programs, 15 serve 3- and 4-year-olds, and eight serve 3- and 4-year-olds exclusively.
5   This number includes 55 children receiving one home visit every week through a Parents as Teachers program, 146 children served through a home-visiting program on a Navajo reservation, and 12 children participating in a program that offers home visiting and a play group. These home-visiting programs serve children from birth to age 3. In addition to the home-visiting programs, there is also a hospital-based program serving 54 high-risk infants.
6   The enrollment priorities of individual programs differ. While there are no standard criteria for eligibility, one goal is to fill enrollment gaps left by other programs. Some programs target children who are eligible for but not able to receive services from Head Start while others serve children from families just above the income eligibility for child care assistance. Individual programs may set priorities to be optimally inclusive and meet family needs.
7   These figures represent state child care licensing regulations. Child Development programs are required by contract to be accredited or working toward accreditation. Out of the 18 center-based programs in operation during 2002–2003, 10 are either accredited or awaiting validation. These 10 programs maintain lower class sizes and child-staff ratios than licensing regulations require.
8   Center-based programs that meet for at least a half-day session must provide meals. The home-visiting and hospital-based programs are not required to offer meals.
9   Parent involvement services that must be offered include family support services based on individual need (detailed in contract) and a parent advisory panel. Some programs have additional activities such as literacy sessions, field trips and classroom participation. Home-visiting programs are more focused on parents than center-based options.
10 Funding is blended such that a Child Development program may receive additional funds from IDEA for children with developmental delays or disabilities. All children in the program are served together in inclusive settings.
11 A consultant would not offer direct preschool services. A program may contract with a consultant for assistance in improving their program environment, their professional practices, their health services, or to provide a specific service such as counseling.
12 The state tracks teachers' ability to observe and document child growth in seven domains under the Focused Portfolio System in terms of objectivity, detail, and match to appropriate milestones. All domains have milestones at yearly benchmarks and are tied directly to kindergarten expectations. Staff use the benchmarks to plan developmentally appropriate curriculum activities. Parents receive a portfolio documenting their child's learning twice a year to encourage further learning at home.
13 A new TEACH initiative began in summer 2004.

NEW YORK — New York State Experimental Prekindergarten (EPK) 2002–2003

1   In most instances local funding is provided by local tax levy dollars. EPK has an 11% match requirement, but due to flat funding in the state budget for the last 10 years, many districts find it necessary to exceed the required match in order to operate the program and meet required standards.
2   Programs may be full- or half-day and operate 4 or 5 days per week.
3   Programs are funded per session. A half-day class counts as one session, while a full-day class is weighted as 1.45 sessions.
4   State law establishes a cut-off date of December 1, but local districts have the authority to establish a date between December 1 and January 1.
5   Most children enter the program as 4-year-olds and attend for only one year.
6   Economically disadvantaged children are those from families who are eligible for some form of assistance such as Aid to Families of Dependent Children, free or reduced-price school lunch, food stamps, Medicaid, unemployment compensation, or disability compensation.
7   LEAs are allowed to identify other risk factors to prioritize eligibility.
8   Programs must provide at least one meal per day regardless of the length of the program day.
9   Parent activities are determined locally and may include: workshops, ESL classes, opportunities to volunteer in classrooms, newsletters, advisory committees, readers in the classrooms, or field trips.
10 Additional services are provided, either directly or indirectly, as they are deemed necessary to meet the needs of enrolled families.
11 In February 2004, the required certification changed to cover Birth–Grade 2.
12 Effective February 2004, assistant teachers must have a Level 1 certification (one year non-renewable), which requires a high school diploma or equivalent and passing the Assessment of Teaching Assistant Skills Test.
13 The full amount of local and federal expenditures is unknown.
14 This number represents a minimum required match. Actual local expenditure is unknown.

NEW YORK — New York State Universal Prekindergarten (UPK) 2002–2003

1   Because programs are administered at the local level, there are many variations. Some Head Start/district collaborations use UPK funds to extend the Head Start day. Others use the UPK funds to add a certified teacher or additional curricular materials to Head Start programs.
2   UPK funds pay for the standard program while IDEA money provides support services in order to successfully mainstream children into UPK classrooms.
3   In addition, some UPK-funded families may receive a child care subsidy or TANF funds to pay for wrap-around service.
4   These children have an IEP that places them in approved special education programs that are fully funded by IDEA but located in UPK classrooms.
5   Programs may be full-day (5 hours) or half-day (2.5 hours). About 83% of enrollees attend a half-day program.
6   UPK programs may provide parents with access to extended-day services. These services are not generally paid for with UPK funds.
7   Although the number of children served is not available, 38% of classes offer parents the option of extended-day services.
8   State law establishes a cut-off date of December 1, but local districts have the authority to establish a date between December 1 and January 1.
9   UPK programs operating less than 3 hours must provide a nutritional meal or snack. Programs operating more than 3 hours must provide appropriate meals and snacks to ensure that the nutritional needs of children are met.
10 UPK policy requires every child to have a signed medical statement that the child is free from contagious or communicable diseases and has been immunized in accordance with Public Health Law. If a child does not meet this requirement, the family will be referred to resources in the community. The district does not directly provide exams or immunizations.
11 Parent activities are determined locally and may include: workshops, ESL classes, opportunities to volunteer in classrooms, newsletters, advisory committees, readers in the classrooms, or field trips.
12 Additional services are provided, either directly or indirectly, as they are deemed necessary to meet the needs of enrolled families.
13 Effective in September 2004, UPK teachers in nonpublic settings must meet the same degree and certification requirements as teachers in public settings.
14 For the 2002–2003 school year, districts reported 80% of all UPK teachers to be state certified. In February 2004, the required certification changed to cover Birth–Grade 2.
15 Effective February 2004, assistant teachers must have a Level 1 certification (one year non-renewable), which requires a high school diploma or equivalent and passing of the Assessment of Teaching Assistant Skills Test.
16 This number represents state funds. Federal and local funds were used, but data were not collected about these sources.
17 Agencies eligible for subcontracting include nursery schools, approved special education programs, BOCES, and nonpublic schools.
18 The Education Incentive Program through OCFS is open to Pre-K teachers in licensed and registered child care programs.

NORTH CAROLINA — *More at Four* 2002–2003

1   No wrap-around services are provided with *More at Four* funds. However, some sites may choose to provide wrap-around services with other resources including CCDF funds, local funds, and Smart Start funds.
2   In 2002–2003, low family income was one of the risk factors that could be considered for enrollment priority.
3   Risk factors considered are: family income, child health status, disability, parent education, parent employment, family composition, housing stability, English proficiency, and minority status. Children who have risk factors and have not previously participated in any early childhood education program are given first priority.
4   Counties determine how many risk factors must be present for eligibility but operate with the same priorities.
5   Providers are given 4 years to phase in the degree requirement after being recognized as a *More at Four* program. Teachers with degrees in other fields may be given provisional licenses but must work toward a Birth–K license.
6   An AA in early childhood or child development is encouraged for assistant teachers in both public and private settings. Teachers in public schools must meet the employment provisions of the No Child Left Behind law, which generally requires that assistant teachers have at least a 2-year degree. Assistant teachers in public schools who meet NCLB employment provisions but do not hold a CDA must also have 6 semesters of coursework in early childhood or 2 years in an early childhood classroom setting.
7   All licensed Pre-K teachers have a continuing education requirement to renew their licenses every 5 years. Teachers must either hold or be working toward a Birth–K license at a minimum rate of 6 semester hours per year.
8   Total funding was estimated based on the reported state funding figure and the proportion of total funding that this figure represented.
9   The figure reported for state funding represents actual expenditures and constitutes 51% of the total budget. The remaining 49% consists of other federal and local resources accessed by local school districts to support programs.
10 Legislation requires that local districts access resources other than state funding to support the program but does not specify an amount of federal or local funds that must be used.
11 Agencies funded directly are allowed to subcontract with faith-based centers that are licensed and do not provide religious instruction.
12 The evaluation examined such factors as global quality and curriculum implementation in a sample of classrooms.
13 The evaluation consisted of nine pre-post measures of language, math, cognitive abilities, and social-emotional skills.
14 The evaluation is no longer required by legislation but is now mandated by the State Office *More at Four*.
15 This number does not include early childhood staff in the Department of Public Instruction.

211

OHIO — State-Funded Head Start Model 2002–2003

1 Ohio Head Start programs follow federal Head Start Program Performance Standards for minimum hours of operation and yearly operating schedule. Programs must operate for at least 3.5 hours per day, 4 days per week, and 32 weeks per year.
2 This income requirement applies to children in partnership arrangements with child care.
3 Federal Head Start Program Performance Standards require that part-day programs provide children with at least one-third of their daily nutritional needs, as determined by the USDA. Full-day programs must provide one-half to two-thirds of daily nutritional needs, depending upon program length. All children in morning center-based settings must be given the opportunity to eat a nutritious breakfast.
4 As of 2003, the Ohio DOE requires all classroom teachers to be working toward obtaining an AA. All teachers are required to have obtained degrees by 2007.
5 In-service requirements associated with renewal of licenses or certificates take precedence. In these circumstances, the specific requirements for in-service depend upon the type of license or certificate.

OHIO — Public School Preschool Program 2002–2003

1 An additional 2,284 children from families who exceed the income requirement were served in the Public School Preschool Program using parent fees and/or district funds.
2 A sliding fee scale was used to determine fees for 2,629 children from families with incomes between 100% and 185% of poverty. Tuition was charged to families of 2,284 children with household incomes above 185% of poverty. These children were not included in total enrollment.
3 The enrollment breakdown by type of school is based on a total of 8,543 participants. The number of children served in Head Start settings is an estimate, as some Public School Preschool grantees sub-contract with Head Start.
4 Public School Preschool programs follow federal Head Start Program Performance Standards for minimum hours of operation and yearly operating schedule. Programs must operate for at least 3.5 hours per day, 4 days per week, and 32 weeks per year.
5 License types offered include: Pre-K Associate (2-year level), Pre-K (4-year-level), Kindergarten (with early childhood coursework), and the Early Childhood License (age 3–Grade 3). Teachers can also qualify with a BA including 20 credits in early childhood plus a supervised practicum with preschoolers.
6 In-service requirements associated with renewal of licenses or certificates take precedence. In these circumstances, the specific requirements depend upon the type of license or certificate.
7 Grant funds support per pupil costs ranging from $2,766 to $4,907, with an average of $3,836. These figures reflect the state contribution only and do not represent the total cost of the program.

OKLAHOMA — Early Childhood Four-Year-Old Program 2002–2003

1 State Department of Education (SDE) state aid funds support Pre-K, but Head Start funds are used to enhance services in some cases.
2 IDEA funds provide additional services to Pre-K students with an IEP.
3 Half-day programs operate for 2.5 hours, while full-day programs operate for 6 hours. Many districts offer full- and half-day programs, with both program types required to operate 5 days per week. Statewide, 15,746 children attend half-day programs, and 12,314 attend full-day programs.
4 The state aid funding formula weights a slot in a half-day program by a factor of .7 and a slot in a full-day program is weighted at 1.3.
5 Local districts decide educational placement based on need and ability. Although rare, some children attend the program for more than one year.
6 Pre-K programs are part of public school districts where breakfast and lunch are required to be available for all children.
7 Parent conferences are encouraged but not required. Most programs offer two per year.
8 At the local district level, public schools may collaborate with Head Start, private childcare centers and faith-based facilities. SDE public Pre-K standards are required in all locations.
9 Early childhood programs are expected to be appropriate for the age, developmental level and special needs of each child. Teaching strategies and learning environments that foster development in several areas, including cognitive and social/emotional, are considered indicative of program quality. For a more in-depth examination of indicators used for evaluations, visit http://www.sde.state.ok.us/home/defaultie.html.
10 A total of 21 professionals spend part of their time administering early childhood programs. In addition to three full-time positions, three staff members spend part of their time working with early childhood programs. Also, 15 regional accreditation officers visit school districts 3–4 times per year to monitor Pre-K programs and to ensure accreditation standards are being met.

OREGON — Oregon Head Start Prekindergarten 2002–2003

1 Most programs operate 3 to 4 days per week.
2 Most programs operate for the academic year.
3 The federal poverty line is $15,020 for a family of three according to the February 2002 DHHS poverty level, which was used for 2002–2003 enrollment. While state law allows up to 20% of families enrolled to be over-income, only 6% of enrolled children actually were from over-income families. These children generally had disabilities or were from isolated, rural areas.
4 Programs must offer at least 10% of their enrollment slots to children with diagnosed disabilities and their families.
5 In prioritizing eligibility, points are given to families with the lowest incomes. Other risk factors are considered in order so that the lowest income and highest need families are served first.
6 Programs must follow all federal Head Start Program Performance Standards for comprehensive services including parent involvement activities.
7 In nonpublic schools, half of grantee teachers must have at least an AA either in ECE or with a minimum of 15 ECE college credits.
8 Teachers in classrooms run by agencies other than the public schools, even if located in public schools through a collaborative partnership, are not required to meet public school requirements.
9 An assistant teacher paid through Title I funds must meet the Title I paraprofessional requirements, which include an AA degree or local district qualifying procedures.
10 Each program allocates 2.5% of its budget for training; these funds are used for professional development of staff.
11 This is the estimated state contribution to the Oregon Head Start Prekindergarten program, which is a state-funded Head Start model. All state Pre-K spending is therefore directed toward Head Start programs.
12 Total funding for the combined federal and state Head Start program included an estimated $47,288,346 in federal funds and an estimated $416,664 in local funds. Federal funding for Tribal or Migrant/Seasonal Head Start is not included.
13 Federal sources of funding for the combined federal and state Head Start program included $45,539,894 in Head Start funding, an estimated $609,594 in Title I funding, and an estimated $138,888 in migrant education funding.
14 Local sources of funding for the combined federal and state Head Start program included an estimated $416,664 in City of Portland funds and local tribal funds.
15 Any non-sectarian agency with the capacity to administer grants and deliver required comprehensive services is eligible for direct funding.
16 Any non-sectarian agency with the capacity to administer grants and deliver required comprehensive services is eligible for subcontracting.
17 Site visits, technical assistance, and follow-up reviews are provided as needed.

PENNSYLVANIA — Kindergarten for Four-Year-Olds 2002–2003

1 Programs using basic education funding must operate at least 2.5 hours per day, but there is no maximum number of hours per day that a program may operate. Programs must operate at least 180 days per year.
2 Pennsylvania has an Early Intervention (EI) program, and districts may coordinate Kindergarten for Four-Year-Olds with EI services. However, Kindergarten for Four-Year-Olds funds are not used to support special services.
3 Districts design and manage their own support services, but there is no program-wide requirement.
4 Assistant teachers are not required in classrooms.
5 For fiscal year 2003, money was available through the basic education formula to support prekindergarten programs, but the specific amount used for this purpose is not available.
6 Districts use money from various federal and local sources at their discretion. Amounts are not known.

SOUTH CAROLINA — Half-Day Child Development Program (4K) 2002–2003

1 State legislation requires each district to offer at least one class.
2 Local sources totaling $587,000 contributed to services for 2,348 children enrolled.
3 State funding for early intervention Pre-K totaled $3,973,584. Approximately $1,740,000 of those funds was used in 4K programs for 580 children with an IEP requiring 4K.
4 First Steps to School Readiness served an additional 260 children in public-private partnerships.
5 Full-day classes were offered in 18 districts using Title I or local funding and in 3 districts using state Education Improvement Act funds.
6 Three districts allow children other than those identified as most likely to experience school failure to be served supported by parent fees. Only about 80 children statewide are served in this manner.
7 Two districts that serve a total of 80 children operate for a 12-month calendar year.
8 Districts receive allocations based on the number of 5-year-old kindergarten children who are eligible for free or reduced-price lunch.
9 Some districts serve 4-year-olds in before- and after-school care, but these extended hours are not supported with 4K funds.
10 Children may be enrolled for a second year if required by an IEP. In rare cases an additional year is granted if parents and district personnel decide it would benefit the child.
11 Risk factors tied to eligibility include: limited parent education, enrollment in Even Start or a family literacy program, having an IEP, and low SES.
12 At least one meal and one snack are provided to all children. Children enrolled in half-day programs receive either breakfast or lunch plus a snack, and children in full-day programs receive breakfast and lunch plus a snack, as required by the Office of Food Service.
13 Every district must offer a family literacy or parenting program. Parents enrolled in family literacy programs receive education services or job training, parenting support, opportunities for parent involvement, and literacy support for children and the family.
14 It is recommended that assistant teachers complete an early childhood class within one year of their hiring date.
15 First Steps programs operating outside of public schools require teachers to be certified in early childhood but do not follow public school salary scales. All teachers in the 4K program are paid on the public school salary scale.
16 Three districts allow children other than those identified as most likely to experience school failure to be served supported by parent fees. Only about 80 children statewide are served in this manner.
17 The Office of School Quality randomly selects programs annually for paper audits and conducts site visits if a problem is detected. Additionally, any site that requests a waiver from the state requirements receives a visit.
18 While information on program quality was not collected in 2002, 154 classrooms in 23 primary schools were assessed using the ECERS during the Spring of 2004. Child progress is documented by tracking children through 3rd grade and through the use of an annual survey of teachers and parents. The Education Oversight Committee also conducted a review of 4K programs in 2003.
19 New legislation requires an annual evaluation of 4K, funded partially by the state and conducted by the SDE and the Education Oversight Committee, to be submitted to the EOC, Governor, and state legislators.
20 TEACH scholarships are only available to teachers attending 2-year programs, and are thus not applicable to 4K. Due to funding issues, TEACH is not yet available for 4K teaching assistants either.

TENNESSEE — Early Childhood Education Pilot Program 2002–2003

1 Federal Head Start and Pilot Pre-K funds were blended to support 415 slots.
2 For the 2002–2003 school year, 399 children were identified as having an IEP. No data on the amount of money spent to support special services for these children are available.
3 Although children typically attend for 1 year, 3-year-olds and children with an IEP may attend for two years if deemed appropriate.
4 Children eligible for free or reduced-price lunch receive highest priority for enrollment.
5 Other children offered priority enrollment include those who have been neglected, are at risk for abuse or in state custody, and those for whom the program is used as a Least Restrictive Environment specified in an IEP.
6 Although there is no sliding scale payments based on income for full-day programs, there is a locally determined sliding payment scale for wrap-around care.
7 When children with special needs are included in the program, money is available from the preschool grant as well as from special education.
8 A family advisory committee that meets at least twice per year is required, and parents complete a family satisfaction survey each year. Family involvement activities are determined locally. Agencies keep sign-in sheets from each activity.
9 Programs collaborating with Even Start must provide education and job training for parents and assist with school for older siblings through age 8.
10 This figure includes $9 million in TANF funds.
11 School-based programs are monitored by the DOE, whereas not-for-profit and Head Start programs are monitored by the Department of Human Services. Program rules and regulations are comparable across settings.
12 Indicators of program quality include teacher qualifications, staff to child ratios, curriculum, and collaboration with other agencies.
13 Child progress in the program was measured through authentic assessment. Follow-up assessments were conducted at entrance to kindergarten, first grade, and second grade.

TEXAS — Public School Prekindergarten 2002–2003

1 School districts are required to offer Pre-K if the district identifies 15 or more eligible children who are at least 4 years of age. To be eligible, a child must be: (1) eligible to participate in the national free or reduced-price lunch program; (2) homeless; or (3) unable to speak and comprehend the English language.
2 Age is not available for 108 students.
3 In general, the Pre-K program for eligible students is funded through the state's Foundation School Program, which includes both state and local money. Districts may open the program to non-eligible children and fund these slots with parent fees and/or local funds.
4 Legislation enacted in 2004 states that a school district must seek space from an existing Head Start or other child care site before establishing a new Pre-K program. If a district contracts with a private agency, the program must comply with the applicable child care licensing standards.
5 The Texas Education Code limits Foundation School Program funding for Pre-K to a half-day. School districts may operate full-day programs on a tuition basis, through grant funding, or supported by local revenue. Districts or campuses approved for the Pre-kindergarten Expansion Grant Program may report Pre-K eligible students as full-day if the students are scheduled for at least six hours of instruction each day.
6 Public School Pre-K follows an academic year schedule, but there is a separate summer program for students entering kindergarten who cannot speak or comprehend English.
7 Extended-day hours are financed and managed locally. Some children attend Public School Prekindergarten classrooms during wrap-around hours.
8 During 2002–2003, 72% of attendees were eligible for free or reduced-price lunch.
9 For children who meet eligibility criteria, the state pays for the standard 3-hour program while IDEA funds provide for special services and additional hours if full-day service is mandated by the IEP. Children who do not meet the program's eligibility criteria are entirely funded by IDEA.
10 There is no class size or staff-child ratio requirement for prekindergarten. Most classes do not exceed 18 children. A teacher and an aide are present in most classrooms, although the aide is optional.
11 Most school districts serve either breakfast or lunch and some serve both meals. School districts that offer a full-day program always provide lunch and often provide breakfast.
12 Districts with an enrollment of 20 or more students in the same grade level who are identified with limited English proficiency are required to offer a bilingual education or special language program regardless of the students' language classifications.
13 Teachers assigned to a bilingual education program must be appropriately certified for bilingual education. Teachers assigned to an English as a Second Language or other special language program must also be appropriately certified.
14 This figure includes $100 million in expansion grants provided by the state.
15 This figure represents the average amount generated by a student in preschool from the Foundation School Program, which funds K–12 education in Texas. Specific amounts per student vary by district and individual need.
16 The program evaluation assessed child progress by comparing school outcome measures for 200 children who had attended Pre-K with those for 600 children who were eligible but did not attend.
17 Texas currently has a federal loan forgiveness plan, but Pre-K teachers have been excluded from participation. This practice of exclusion is being legally challenged.

VERMONT — Early Education Initiative (EEI) 2002–2003

1 Children who would not have otherwise been able to participate in Pre-K were served in Head Start classrooms. Early Education Initiative paid for these slots, but the children benefited from additional Head Start services.
2 IDEA funds supplement state funds to provide enhanced services not necessarily specified in an IEP.
3 This breakdown of enrollment by location does not include 10 children the state classified as belonging to an age group other than 3- or 4-year-olds.
4 Public school and Head Start programs generally follow the academic year, while programs in child care centers usually operate throughout the calendar year.
5 Risk factors tied to eligibility include: developmental delay, being at risk for abuse or neglect, limited English proficiency, exposure to violence or substance abuse, social isolation, and poor educational attainment by parents.
6 One snack is required per 3-hour program, and a meal plus a snack must be offered to children attending for at least 4 hours.
7 All districts conduct vision, hearing and general health screenings for 3- to 5-year-olds in conjunction with district-wide developmental screening. As children participate in general preschool screenings to determine eligibility, they receive services (e.g., vision, health, etc.). Therefore, all children benefit from screening and referrals, even those not found to be eligible for EEI. General eligibility screenings are mandatory for participation in EEI.
8 Parent involvement activities include parent education, involvement in program decision-making, and opportunities to take part in program activities with children.

VIRGINIA — Virginia Preschool Initiative 2002–2003

1 Eligibility criteria are specified at the local level. Examples of risk factors considered for eligibility are: poverty, homelessness, parents who dropped out of school or have limited education, and parents who are chronically ill.
2 All staff must have some training in early childhood development. Minimum teacher qualifications depend on the location of the program: public school teachers must be certified, Head Start teachers must hold a CDA, and there is no specific degree requirement for teachers in child care settings.
3 In general, the composite index is designed so that counties with large low-income populations are required to contribute less of a local match than wealthier communities. The percentage of costs covered by matching funds varies by community, but more specific information was not reported.

WASHINGTON — Early Childhood Education and Assistance Program (ECEAP) 2002–2003

1 Early Childhood Education and Assistance Program allows enrollment year round with the majority of children enrolled by November 15.
2 CCDF funds are blended with state funds to support the ECEAP core program.
3 Children served by other agencies include children served by community organization facilities (181), colleges and universities (182), educational service districts (118), local government (41), tribal organizations (197), and other agencies (535).
4 Providers design initiatives based on community needs. All programs operate at least 2.5 hours per session. The majority of programs operate for 3 to 4 days per week.
5 Most programs operate for the academic year.
6 Direct services for children that count toward the 240-hour requirement can include group sessions, home education sessions, and peer experiences. Programs must provide a total of 32 weeks of direct services, which may also include educational planning meetings and adult contact.
7 After 1 year, family income is used to re-qualify a child who has not reached school age. Three-year-olds are only accepted after all eligible 4-year-olds whose families wish to participate have been enrolled.
8 This income cutoff would be equivalent to $16,522 per year for a family of three in 2002–2003.
9 At least 10% of enrollees must be children of migrant or seasonal farm workers or Native Americans. Environmental or developmental risks are also tied to eligibility.
10 Program standards are targeted to 4-year-olds, but since 3-year-olds are in blended classrooms, ECEAP standards apply to educational settings for both ages. In classes of 24 students, the staff to child ratio must be 1:6.
11 Program models are encouraged to be culturally and linguistically responsive to children and families.
12 Although not required, the Devereux Early Childhood Assessment Program, which is used to identify children's social and emotional strengths and build on their protective factors through classroom strategies, working with families, and continuous follow-up, is highly recommended.
13 The Early Childhood Education and Assistance Program requires in-service training but does not specify the number of hours required.
14 Local sources of support include the United Way, local business sponsors, Rotary, Lions, Kiwanis, foundations, and corporate giving programs. School districts, community-based organizations, and state and federal government offer in-kind contributions as well as grants. However, data are not kept on the amounts that each of these sources contributes.
15 Programs can be reviewed more often if necessary. The state also assesses programs through monthly and annual reporting.
16 Programs are required to meet applicable licensing requirements.
17 The Devereux Early Childhood Assessment Program is an optional assessment used to identify children's social and emotional strengths and build on their protective factors.

WEST VIRGINIA — Public School Early Childhood Education Program 2002–2003

1 Although Head Start funds may have supported some or all children in programs that are Head Start grantees, the number of children funded by Head Start is unavailable.
2 There are two prevailing models: one option provides two full-day classes each week while the other offers four full days with Friday reserved for activities such as home visits or planning.
3 Children with an IEP are served in classes designed specifically for that purpose.
4 As of the 2003–2004 program year, the staff-child ratio requirement is 1:10 with a certified teacher present at all times.
5 Programs that received state funding in 2002 primarily used the National School Lunch Program (NSLP) to support nutritional services in Pre-K. Meals and snacks were determined by NSLP guidelines based on the length of the program day.
6 Dental and developmental screening and referral were added for the 2003–2004 school year.
7 West Virginia Board of Education Policy 2525 went into effect February 12, 2003, requiring two face-to-face visits with parents, including one in the home. Many school systems did not institute full compliance with this policy until the 2003–2004 school year.
8 Scholarships are reserved for Head Start or child care teachers who are pursuing an AA or a BA. Public school Pre-K teachers are not eligible for scholarships or loan forgiveness programs.

WISCONSIN — Four-Year-Old Kindergarten Program (4K) 2002–2003

1 The local school board must approve the program. Generally, the first year a district makes a claim, they are reimbursed for one-third of all students. The second year they are reimbursed for two-thirds, and beginning in the third year a district will be reimbursed for all students enrolled. During the first 2 years, some districts take out short-term loans or borrow from their own funding to meet costs.

2 Local matching funds support all children enrolled in the 4K program.

3 Children receiving 4K membership aid and/or IDEA funding may also receive special education services. Four-Year-Old Kindergarten money does not fund services beyond the regular program requirements. Furthermore, IDEA funding is not a per-child allocation, but rather is used by districts to provide special education-related services, staff, equipment, or adaptations as specified by the IEP. These funds are available to children in all grades.

4 Schools may operate programs in other settings. Data regarding the number of children served in other settings are not available.

5 Several school districts run full calendar-year programs but receive the same funding as academic-year programs.

6 Programs must operate for a minimum of 437 hours per year and may add 87.5 hours for parent outreach. Most programs operate 2.5 hours per day, 5 days per week for 180 days per year. Some programs operate 4 days per week with parent outreach on the fifth day.

7 Districts claim .5 FTE membership aid when operating 5 days per week or 4 days per week plus 87.5 hours of parent outreach. They claim .6 FTE membership aid when operating 5 days plus parent outreach.

8 Districts may offer 87.5 hours of parent outreach in addition to regular 4K hours.

9 Age limits for eligibility are not written requirements, but standard practice is that children attend the program for 1 year and exit at age 5.

10 Of the 5,358 4-year-old children receiving early childhood special education services, 45% receive services in general education or part-time special education/part-time regular education settings including, but not limited to, 4K.

11 Vision, hearing and general health screenings are required at kindergarten entrance for all children. Typically they are provided by family physicians or through the state Women, Infants, and Children (WIC) program. LEAs follow up with children who do not receive these services. Referrals, however, are not mandatory.

12 Parent involvement activities are required for program models providing 87.5 hours of parent outreach, as per membership aid funding.

13 New licensing standards that take effect in 2004 create early-childhood-level licenses.

14 As of 2004, new teachers will be required to have professional development plans, mentors, and team support. Teachers hired before 2004 may use either the old system of credits (rather than clock hours) or the new system of professional development planning.

15 Other funding sources may supplement 4K programs but they are not used directly for 4K.

16 The Department of Health and Family Services monitors licensed child care programs. Depending on the grantee, Head Start centers may or may not be monitored licensed child care programs. Preschool programs in private schools or voucher "choice" schools are not monitored.

17 Wisconsin is currently part of the second phase of the National Center for Early Development & Learning study—State-Wide Early Education Programs (SWEEP). Additionally, the state and the Trust for Early Education are interested in studying the impact of 4K on school cost savings. Wisconsin is also part of the National Early Childhood Transition Center study—Opening Doors to Success, which would address 4K transitions.

18 TEACH scholarships are available to 4K assistant teachers working in a licensed child care facility with a 4K collaboration.

19 TEACH data are not collected that would specify the number of 4K assistants who received a scholarship.

WISCONSIN — State-Funded Head Start Model 2002–2003

1 A child in state-funded Head Start may receive services from his or her public school or federal Head Start grantee, but no funds go directly to augment the state contribution to Head Start.

2 School district staff and resources support children receiving special education services, but IDEA funding is not direct.

3 Although some Head Start programs operate in collaboration with public schools or child care centers, they are still considered Head Start locations. Data are not collected on the number of collaborations or the number of children served in each setting.

4 At least 10% of students must be identified with a disability.

5 Of the 5,358 4-year-old children receiving early childhood special education services, 45% receive services in general education or part-time special education/part-time regular education settings including, but not limited to, Head Start.

6 The federal Head Start Program Performance Standards require that part-day programs provide children with at least one-third of their daily nutritional needs, and full-day programs provide one-half to two-thirds of daily nutritional needs depending on the length of the program day. All children in morning center-based settings must be given the opportunity to have a nutritious breakfast.

7 Parent involvement activities are in accord with requirements indicated in the federal Head Start Program Performance Standards.

8 When a school district is the federal Head Start grantee, it may or may not require Head Start teachers to have a BA and appropriate licensure.

9 When a school district is the federal Head Start grantee, it may or may not require an AA degree and assistant teacher license.

10 Teacher compensation requirements for the Head Start state supplement follow federal Head Start guidelines. If the grantee is a school, however, Head Start teachers may be paid on the public school salary scale. In most cases the grantee is not a school.

11 This number represents the approximate amount paid to each Head Start program for each slot.

12 Because state funds are used in conjunction with federally funded programs, monitoring follows the federal process.

13 TEACH scholarships are available for teachers in a licensed child care facility including Head Start teachers.

14 This number reflects both federal Head Start and the state supplement. In most cases, Head Start teachers are not designated to be solely federally or state funded.

STATE	STATE-FUNDED HEAD START		FEDERAL HEAD START						
	State funding (Fiscal Year 2003)	State enrollment: additional funded slots for 3- and 4-year-olds[1]	Federal funding (Fiscal Year 2003)	Funded enrollment by state (Program Year 2002–2003)[2]		American Indian/Alaska Native enrollment (Program Year 2002–2003)[2]		Migrant enrollment (Program Year 2002–2003)[2]	
				3-year-olds[4]	4-year-olds[4]	3-year-olds	4-year-olds	3-year-olds	4-year-olds
Alabama			$103,588,331	5,605	10,136	0	0	30	33
Alaska	$6,276,000[6]	403	$12,126,424	1,036	1,287	547	704	0	0
Arizona			$100,173,750	5,681	11,214	1,843	2,954	234	261
Arkansas			$62,645,003	3,894	6,388	0	0	94	119
California			$811,486,631	31,430	59,065	308	353	1,204	1,149
Colorado			$66,427,807	3,378	5,755	76	64	131	110
Connecticut	$4,500,000	332[7]	$50,604,341	2,074	3,430	0	0	0	0
Delaware	$4,456,700	843	$12,536,909	588	952	0	0	7	6
District of Columbia			$24,407,526	1,418	1,335	0	0	0	0
Florida			$255,501,245	11,778	21,179	13	7	978	710
Georgia			$163,757,113	11,223	10,655	0	0	65	50
Hawaii	$390,000	0	$22,248,160	1,071	1,567	0	0	0	0
Idaho	$1,500,000	151	$21,819,720	736	2,345	103	155	168	200
Illinois			$263,047,115	13,954	18,638	0	0	74	72
Indiana			$93,523,057	4,085	7,330	0	0	0	0
Iowa			$50,108,568	2,618	3,819	0	0	0	0
Kansas	$0[8]		$49,503,208	2,812	3,498	32	34	0	0
Kentucky			$104,828,778	5,600	9,024	0	0	7	6
Louisiana			$141,891,707	8,704	10,127	0	0	0	0
Maine	$3,581,018[9]	199	$26,990,760	1,005	1,884	11	21	11	5
Maryland	$3,000,000	26[10]	$75,851,238	3,987	5,548	0	0	40	38
Massachusetts	$6,100,000	400[11]	$105,475,665	4,260	6,238	0	0	0	0
Michigan			$228,044,810	12,927	19,174	175	178	250	233
Minnesota	$17,620,000	2,641	$70,369,154	3,945	6,069	360	476	207	203
Mississippi			$157,164,747	10,498	15,188	125	113	0	0
Missouri			$115,662,551	6,913	8,102	0	0	0	0
Montana			$20,365,406	1,482	2,285	386	796	0	0
Nebraska			$35,008,457	1,844	2,562	117	110	126	198
Nevada			$23,315,025	935	1,394	123	180	0	0
New Hampshire	$241,337	0	$13,018,299	521	784	0	0	0	0
New Jersey			$126,711,091	5,696	7,445	0	0	35	23
New Mexico	$1,650,000[12]	0	$50,852,224	2,374	4,656	490	590	0	0
New York			$422,349,645	17,170	24,325	71	55	95	70
North Carolina			$137,403,001	6,438	11,247	37	91	143	129
North Dakota			$16,696,830	1,033	1,766	403	504	0	0
Ohio	$87,632,156[13]	17,284	$239,770,120	15,267	19,080	0	0	0	0
Oklahoma	$3,300,000	105[14]	$78,783,942	6,293	8,250	1,324	1,368	0	0
Oregon	$26,100,000	4,000	$57,703,995	2,876	4,968	172	196	467	437
Pennsylvania	$2,000,000[15]	0	$222,603,242	10,574	15,527	0	0	101	101
Rhode Island	$1,800,000	340	$21,445,541	676	1,713	0	0	0	0
South Carolina			$80,222,592	5,681	5,662	50	35	66	63
South Dakota			$18,301,095	1,506	1,841	578	630	0	0
Tennessee			$116,071,781	4,948	10,616	0	0	42	45
Texas			$465,421,856	27,586	36,364	13	8	2,229	1,993
Utah			$36,709,468	1,443	3,775	102	125	60	83
Vermont			$13,182,631	465	644	0	0	0	0
Virginia			$96,213,748	4,276	7,406	0	0	54	52
Washington			$98,022,295	3,803	7,536	468	580	555	617
West Virginia			$49,227,458	2,732	4,035	0	0	0	0
Wisconsin	$7,425,000	1,449	$88,082,140	5,967	6,933	354	353	82	81
Wyoming			$12,027,897	679	1,062	116	111	19	19
50 States + DC[16]	$177,572,211	28,173	$5,729,294,097[17]	293,487	441,825	8,397	10,791	7,574	7,106

STATE	Percent of children enrolled full-day, 5 days per week, all ages (Program Year 2002–2003)	AVERAGE SALARIES FOR HEAD START TEACHERS, DIRECTORS, AND ASSISTANT TEACHERS[3]						
		Teachers, all degree levels (2003)	Teachers with CDA credentials (2003)	Teachers with AA degrees (2003)	Teachers with BA degrees (2003)	Teachers with graduate degrees (2003)	Directors (2002)[5]	Assistant teachers (2003)
Alabama	68%	$18,333	$17,395	$19,325	$22,111	$23,573	$58,579	$13,877
Alaska	8%	$23,389	$24,139	$24,526	$24,471	Not applicable	$61,537	$16,982
Arizona	12%	$23,332	$21,991	$22,124	$26,866	$28,824	$60,861	$16,459
Arkansas	84%	$21,114	$19,829	$20,813	$24,561	$26,750	$48,687	$13,995
California	26%	$27,177	$23,807	$26,873	$32,106	$41,784	$70,104	$18,983
Colorado	23%	$22,620	$18,351	$20,925	$25,699	$38,813	$49,481	$14,748
Connecticut	57%	$26,316	$21,370	$26,224	$28,289	$42,311	$62,009	$17,305
Delaware	23%	$19,675	$18,547	$20,815	$20,963	$16,969	$54,663	$21,751
District of Columbia	15%	$32,237	$23,943	$27,958	$35,980	$48,516	$66,107	$19,571
Florida	92%	$24,155	$20,537	$22,609	$30,190	$37,236	$55,445	$16,507
Georgia	87%	$20,932	$18,604	$22,405	$27,105	$36,255	$58,615	$15,339
Hawaii	35%	$32,078	$31,116	$32,438	$34,533	$33,571	$54,865	$28,130
Idaho	24%	$16,599	$14,520	$17,977	$22,077	$25,104	$51,070	$10,829
Illinois	44%	$24,939	$20,168	$22,118	$28,770	$45,120	$52,320	$17,169
Indiana	21%	$20,533	$18,229	$20,406	$22,952	$29,486	$46,435	$13,654
Iowa	36%	$22,801	$18,556	$19,075	$24,413	$38,964	$48,156	$15,301
Kansas	14%	$21,516	$18,611	$20,522	$24,363	$33,027	$47,005	$12,822
Kentucky	37%	$20,700	$16,714	$19,142	$25,811	$36,464	$50,884	$13,086
Louisiana	74%	$20,578	$17,806	$20,008	$23,117	$22,839	$42,780	$13,805
Maine	18%	$21,939	$20,181	$23,571	$23,381	$17,753	$51,048	$15,981
Maryland	47%	$28,796	$21,183	$24,412	$34,056	$51,539	$51,662	$15,520
Massachusetts	33%	$23,290	$22,022	$24,118	$24,660	$24,658	$54,879	$17,107
Michigan	20%	$27,993	$22,138	$26,067	$31,519	$54,505	$58,054	$18,221
Minnesota	8%	$25,161	$26,250	$24,455	$24,705	$36,222	$48,346	$17,747
Mississippi	74%	$17,977	$15,992	$17,349	$20,597	$25,592	$64,443	$13,403
Missouri	31%	$21,642	$19,783	$22,415	$24,961	$29,800	$52,839	$14,509
Montana	26%	$16,934	$16,302	$17,346	$17,761	$17,412	$36,981	$11,318
Nebraska	20%	$20,654	$17,815	$19,705	$22,279	$28,361	$45,261	$11,967
Nevada	9%	$19,348	$17,268	$21,031	$24,392	$29,604	$41,766	$14,137
New Hampshire	13%	$19,254	$15,709	$19,836	$21,769	$21,394	$41,505	$14,001
New Jersey	82%	$30,854	$23,103	$24,152	$33,696	$39,888	$67,650	$17,428
New Mexico	29%	$21,339	$19,645	$21,733	$27,006	$36,012	$48,291	$13,628
New York	46%	$29,023	$19,914	$22,303	$29,559	$37,376	$55,852	$18,319
North Carolina	83%	$21,788	$19,010	$21,170	$25,399	$33,457	$49,692	$15,785
North Dakota	22%	$21,936	$17,312	$22,489	$23,536	$36,000	$39,709	$13,522
Ohio	24%	$22,056	$19,850	$21,316	$25,388	$37,680	$57,697	$15,111
Oklahoma	55%	$22,410	$19,586	$23,593	$27,288	$26,854	$46,486	$16,674
Oregon	36%	$19,989	$16,225	$20,376	$24,514	$33,007	$54,813	$15,121
Pennsylvania	35%	$25,244	$19,502	$20,427	$25,578	$40,726	$50,264	$14,820
Rhode Island	31%	$25,396	$21,378	$23,595	$30,654	$37,458	$63,186	$16,415
South Carolina	86%	$17,519	$15,486	$17,784	$20,563	$18,626	$62,751	$12,860
South Dakota	22%	$21,118	$19,654	$19,618	$23,083	$33,000	$49,407	$14,776
Tennessee	47%	$20,605	$16,808	$19,186	$26,919	$35,689	$51,202	$14,345
Texas	76%	$22,971	$19,212	$21,575	$30,661	$38,501	$53,752	$14,581
Utah	18%	$20,550	$18,027	$17,789	$24,390	$45,639	$52,498	$14,097
Vermont	20%	$25,274	$21,072	$27,688	$26,280	$29,961	$43,265	$15,352
Virginia	56%	$25,839	$19,085	$20,089	$31,010	$42,116	$52,534	$19,356
Washington	34%	$23,625	$22,463	$25,620	$26,874	$29,812	$54,948	$16,463
West Virginia	20%	$21,869	$17,448	$19,518	$24,471	$32,546	$41,971	$14,609
Wisconsin	15%	$24,445	$20,285	$21,293	$26,619	$36,763	$59,295	$15,736
Wyoming	18%	$19,602	$15,923	$19,537	$24,623	$23,161	$42,779	$11,334
50 States + DC[16]	46%	$23,620	$19,837	$22,480	$27,595	$38,315	$53,114	$16,027

Source:

Data are from Head Start Program Information Reports (PIR) for 2002–2003, unless otherwise noted.

Notes:

1   Several states providing Head Start supplements were not able to report the number of children served with these state funds. In some cases, this was because a portion of state funds were used to enhance services for federally funded Head Start participants rather than for separate, additional slots. For these states, enrollment was estimated based on non-ACYF funded enrollment and proportions of all enrollees who were age 3 or age 4, as reported in the 2002–2003 Head Start PIR.

2   Funded enrollment indicates the number of slots that are funded annually, which differs from the actual number of children served in a year (since, for example, a child may participate for only part of the year). In contrast, enrollment totals for American Indian and Migrant programs are the actual number of children served, and may count some children who participated for only a portion of the year. American Indian and Migrant enrollment are not included in the funded enrollment totals.

3   Salary figures for 2003 represent weighted averages, based on the average salary for degreed teachers at each level reported by grantees, and the number of teachers employed by grantees in each category.

4   Funded enrollment was not available by single year of age. Data shown here are estimates, calculated based on the percentage of total actual enrollment represented by 3-year-olds and by 4-year-olds in the 2002–2003 program year and the total ACYF-funded enrollment by state as reported on the 2002–2003 Head Start PIR.

5   Director salaries were not available in the 2002–2003 PIR, so data reported here represent figures from the 2001–2002 program year.

6   State Head Start funds in Alaska were used to enhance services, improve quality and wherever possible serve additional children and families.

7   In addition to supporting separate slots, Connecticut's state Head Start funding was also used to extend the program day for 683 children, and to enhance literacy-focused efforts in Head Start classrooms.

8   Kansas Early Head Start receives $7.8 million from CCDF to fund quality initiatives.

9   State Head Start funds in Maine support Early Start, wrap-around services, and extend eligibility for some families up to 135% FPL.

10 Maryland's state Head Start funds were also used to expand services or extend the program day for 484 children. Additionally, programs used state funds for professional development, parent education, mental health services, expanded transition services, and literacy projects.

11 In addition to supporting separate slots, Massachusetts' state Head Start funding was also used for quality enhancements in existing classrooms.

12 New Mexico's state Head Start funds were used to enhance services in federally funded Head Start classrooms.

13 This total funding for the Ohio Head Start program includes $69,229,403 of TANF dollars.

14 Oklahoma used its state Head Start funds to extend services, increase enrollment, and improve quality.

15 The Head Start State Collaboration Office in Pennsylvania received $2,000,000 in TANF funds to support extended-day child care for children in the federally funded Head Start program.

16 Data on the percentage of children enrolled in full-time programs include Puerto Rico, and other U.S. territories.

17 This sum for federal Head Start funding only represents the portion of funding provided to states and does not include funding for programs in U.S. territories, Native American programs, Migrant programs, or support activities such as research, training and technical assistance, and monitoring. Total federal Head Start funding, including all of these components, was $6,666,783,000 in FY 2003.

APPENDIX C: CHILD CARE DATA

STATE	CHILDREN RECEIVING CHILD CARE ASSISTANCE THROUGH THE CHILD CARE AND DEVELOPMENT FUND, PER MONTH (FY 2001)[1]			INCOME ELIGIBILITY LIMIT FOR CHILD CARE ASSISTANCE FOR A FAMILY OF 3 (FY 2002–2003)	
	3-year-olds	4-year-olds	5-year-olds	Eligibility limit as annual income figure	Eligibility limit as percent of state median income (SMI)
Alabama	4,936	4,536	3,114	$19,020	43%
Alaska	661	796	741	$53,772	85%
Arizona	3,540	3,597	3,285	$24,156	54%
Arkansas	1,490	1,215	809	$23,520	60%
California	28,235	34,564	25,044	$35,100	75%
Colorado	3,305	3,060	2,623	$32,916	62%[4]
Connecticut	1,427	1,512	1,171	$47,592	75%
Delaware	946	873	750	$29,280	80%
Florida	11,270	9,997	7,909	Not available	53%
Georgia	7,882	7,180	5,295	$42,828	85%
Hawaii	1,361	1,181	752	$39,288	80%
Idaho	1,294	1,182	1,169	$20,472	51%
Illinois	11,294	10,187	9,248	$21,816	39%
Indiana	4,796	4,279	4,254	$26,484	57%
Iowa	1,894	1,652	1,373	$22,680	47%
Kansas	2,044	1,927	1,540	$27,060	49%
Kentucky	5,192	4,617	3,564	$24,144	55%
Louisiana	6,008	4,471	3,067	$24,924	60%
Maine	300	321	268	$36,456	85%
Maryland	2,640	2,401	2,105	$25,140	40%
Massachusetts	4,312	4,240	3,116	$28,968	50%[5]
Michigan	4,920	5,140	4,247	Not available	Not available
Minnesota	3,399	3,167	2,538	$42,012	75%
Mississippi	1,202	1,018	844	$30,156	85%
Missouri	4,696	4,461	3,366	$17,784	42%
Montana	942	881	795	$21,948	51%
Nebraska	1,706	1,615	1,138	$25,260	53%
Nevada	954	855	803	$37,476	75%
New Hampshire	Not available	Not available	Not available	$31,776	62%
New Jersey	6,071	6,838	4,783	$36,576	61%
New Mexico	2,826	2,650	2,268	$29,256	78%
New York	23,687	26,143	19,892	$29,256	61%
North Carolina	11,628	10,313	7,083	$34,224	75%
North Dakota	639	605	486	$29,556	69%
Ohio	11,899	11,036	8,116	$27,060	57%
Oklahoma	5,654	4,767	3,959	$23,232	53%
Oregon	2,575	2,891	2,630	$27,060	60%
Pennsylvania	7,944	7,421	6,642	$29,256	58%
Rhode Island	516	562	423	$32,916	61%
South Carolina	2,749	2,931	2,550	$21,948	47%
South Dakota	449	461	349	$21,948	44%
Tennessee	7,960	7,050	5,946	$24,324	56%
Texas	13,821	12,707	10,050	$38,052	85%[4]
Utah	1,277	1,248	1,058	$26,928	56%
Vermont	437	422	414	$31,032	77%
Virginia	2,188	1,940	1,439	$23,400	43%
Washington	5,877	6,983	4,974	$32,916	64%
West Virginia	1,019	901	816	$28,296	75%
Wisconsin	3,349	3,148	2,413	$27,060	51%
Wyoming	405	368	324	$27,060	58%
Data sources	a	a	a	b	b

NR=Not regulated

STATE	FUNDING FOR CHILD CARE (FY 2003)				
	Child Care and Development Fund: Federal allocations [2]	Child Care and Development Fund: State maintenance of effort	Child Care and Development Fund: State matching funds	TANF transfers to the Child Care and Development Fund [3]	TANF direct spending on child care [3]
Alabama	$80,869,783	$6,896,417	$9,496,006	$20,545,839	$35,092,690
Alaska	$11,700,535	$3,544,811	$3,336,307	$15,737,700	$6,405,306
Arizona	$94,524,915	$10,032,936	$14,181,906	$0	$32,321,232
Arkansas	$44,262,908	$1,886,543	$4,876,895	$6,000,000	$4,163
California	$520,891,901	$85,593,217	$197,340,702	$572,514,000	$483,594,179
Colorado	$56,262,350	$8,985,901	$23,070,359	$22,241,896	$1,002,329
Connecticut	$51,607,411	$18,738,358	$17,855,826	$0	$1
Delaware	$13,725,976	$5,179,325	$4,097,057	$1,265,646	$0
Florida	$228,793,951	$33,415,872	$53,311,640	$122,549,160	$115,868,645
Georgia	$153,460,641	$22,182,651	$31,058,861	$32,200,000	$0
Hawaii	$19,604,845	$4,971,630	$4,366,746	$11,050,000	$0
Idaho	$21,557,581	$1,175,819	$3,050,022	$8,731,981	$1,462,112
Illinois	$204,347,853	$56,873,825	$68,416,685	$0	$152,662,453
Indiana	$99,254,410	$15,356,949	$20,253,505	$18,352,906	$2,127
Iowa	$42,379,907	$5,220,891	$8,466,820	$28,199,491	$5,113,184
Kansas	$43,363,002	$6,673,024	$8,951,683	$12,741,228	$0
Kentucky	$73,421,297	$7,274,579	$8,951,301	$47,135,000	$13,349,883
Louisiana	$87,371,840	$5,873,488	$9,801,173	$39,030,549	$2,920,266
Maine	$16,713,033	$1,749,818	$3,034,466	$10,699,122	$8,998,797
Maryland	$79,542,056	$23,301,407	$28,431,974	$48,884,560	$1,651,300
Massachusetts	$104,552,135	$44,973,368	$31,723,061	$91,874,222	$125,612,617
Michigan	$145,408,840	$24,411,364	$42,687,843	$0	$135,909,459
Minnesota	$76,461,076	$19,690,833	$26,487,248	$26,603,000	$3,620
Mississippi	$56,111,761	$1,715,420	$4,879,792	$19,323,838	$3,631,835
Missouri	$93,551,805	$16,548,755	$18,681,006	$24,882,439	$0
Montana	$13,963,728	$1,313,990	$1,702,889	$8,612,239	$162,422
Nebraska	$31,584,905	$6,498,998	$6,850,698	$9,000,000	$0
Nevada	$25,358,420	$2,580,421	$10,055,932	$0	$1,450,696
New Hampshire	$16,145,394	$4,581,866	$6,416,933	$1,195,910	$0
New Jersey	$110,047,985	$26,374,178	$44,479,288	$25,665,017	$9,388,750
New Mexico	$37,466,782	$2,895,259	$3,538,570	$29,813,209	$0
New York	$317,244,015	$101,983,998	$98,858,356	$39,900,000	$0
North Carolina	$173,118,151	$37,927,282	$24,999,195	$74,499,688	$27,137,424
North Dakota	$10,164,763	$1,017,036	$1,487,277	$0	$2,717,993
Ohio	$199,352,211	$45,403,943	$42,028,846	$0	$234,785,938
Oklahoma	$74,117,273	$10,630,233	$7,466,851	$30,822,071	$41,389,144
Oregon	$59,136,493	$11,714,966	$11,602,009	$0	$9,431,128
Pennsylvania	$181,445,171	$46,629,051	$49,979,288	$124,484,000	$11,522,200
Rhode Island	$17,573,933	$5,321,126	$4,200,594	$9,091,106	$0
South Carolina	$67,979,898	$4,085,269	$9,120,296	$1,300,000	$0
South Dakota	$11,923,170	$802,914	$2,171,900	$1,700,000	$0
Tennessee	$112,223,161	$18,975,782	$16,132,158	$52,025,586	$17,092,767
Texas	$382,905,511	$34,681,426	$81,473,392	-$2,349,075	$9,347,768
Utah	$43,232,266	$4,474,923	$3,965,006	$0	$5,083,261
Vermont	$10,279,148	$2,666,323	$1,791,954	$9,224,074	$3,123,269
Virginia	$97,063,350	$21,328,762	$34,810,122	-$8,189,221	$16,008
Washington	$106,705,285	$38,707,605	$30,720,798	$107,300,000	$63,478,641
West Virginia	$31,227,188	$2,971,392	$2,725,575	$0	$20,733,002
Wisconsin	$83,344,081	$16,449,406	$19,885,785	$65,308,581	$93,932,978
Wyoming	$8,504,843	$1,553,707	$1,568,988	$11,679,671	-$2,620,359
Data sources	c	c	c	c	c

NR=Not regulated

STATE	MAXIMUM CHILD: STAFF RATIOS IN CHILD CARE CENTERS (FEBRUARY 2004)		MAXIMUM GROUP SIZE IN CHILD CARE CENTERS (FEBRUARY 2004)	
	For 3-year-olds	For 4-year-olds	For 3-year-olds	For 4-year-olds
Alabama	10:1	16:1	NR	NR
Alaska	10:1	10:1	20	20
Arizona	13:1	15:1	NR	NR
Arkansas	12:1	15:1	24	30
California	12:1	12:1	NR	NR
Colorado	10:1	12:1	20	24
Connecticut	10:1	10:1	20	20
Delaware	12:1	15:1	NR	NR
Florida	15:1	20:1	NR	NR
Georgia	15:1	18:1	30	36
Hawaii	12:1	16:1	NR	NR
Idaho	12:1	12:1	NR	NR
Illinois	10:1	10:1	20	20
Indiana	10:1	12:1	20	24
Iowa	8:1	12:1	NR	NR
Kansas	12:1	12:1	24	24
Kentucky	12:1	14:1	24	28
Louisiana	13:1	15:1	13	15
Maine	8:1	10:1	24	30
Maryland	10:1	10:1	20	20
Massachusetts	10:1	10:1	20	20
Michigan	10:1	12:1	NR	NR
Minnesota	10:1	10:1	20	20
Mississippi	14:1	16:1	14	20
Missouri	10:1	10:1	NR	NR
Montana	8:1	10:1	NR	NR
Nebraska	10:1	12:1	NR	NR
Nevada	13:1	13:1	NR	NR
New Hampshire	8:1	12:1	24	24
New Jersey	10:1	12:1	20	20
New Mexico	12:1	12:1	NR	NR
New York	7:1	8:1	18	21
North Carolina	15:1	20:1	25	25
North Dakota	7:1	10:1	14	20
Ohio	12:1	14:1	24	28
Oklahoma	12:1	15:1	24	30
Oregon	10:1	10:1	20	20
Pennsylvania	10:1	10:1	20	20
Rhode Island	9:1	10:1	18	20
South Carolina	13:1	18:1	NR	NR
South Dakota	10:1	10:1	20	20
Tennessee	9:1	13:1	18	20
Texas	15:1	18:1	30	35
Utah	12:1	15:1	24	30
Vermont	10:1	10:1	20	20
Virginia	10:1	12:1	NR	NR
Washington	10:1	10:1	20	20
West Virginia	10:1	12:1	20	24
Wisconsin	10:1	13:1	20	24
Wyoming	10:1	12:1	24	30
Data sources	d	d	d	d

NR=Not regulated

STATE	CHILD CARE STAFF PRE-SERVICE QUALIFICATIONS (FEBRUARY 2004)			
	Child care center teachers: education/ training requirements	Child care center teachers: experience required?	Child care center directors: education/ training requirements	Child care center directors: experience required?
Alabama	12 hrs CC training	N	124 hrs CC training	Y (1 year)
Alaska	None	N	CDA	N
Arizona	None	N	60 hrs ECE/CD training	Y (2 years)
Arkansas	None	N	None	N
California	6 ECE/CD credits	N	12 EC credits	Y (4 years)
Colorado	None	N	18 ECE credits	Y (2 years)
Connecticut	None	N	CDA	Y (1,080 hrs)
Delaware	Vocational CC program	Y (6 months)	CDA	Y (2 years)
Florida	None	N	State Director's credential	N
Georgia	None	N	None	N
Hawaii	CDA or ECE certification	Y (1 year)	CDA	Y (4 years)
Idaho	None	N	None	N
Illinois	CDA or CCP certification	N	CDA or CCP + 12 credits	Y (2 years)
Indiana	None	N	AA in ECE	Y (3 years)
Iowa	None	N	75 hrs CD training	Y (> 1 year)
Kansas	CDA	Y (1 year)	CDA	Y (1 year)
Kentucky	None	N	None	N
Louisiana	None	N	30 hrs ECE	Y (1 year)
Maine	None	N	135 hrs training	Y (5 years)
Maryland	90 hrs ECD training	Y (1 year)	90 hrs ECD training	N
Massachusetts	2 yr CC course	N	CDA + 5 CD/ECE credits	Y (33 months)
Michigan	None	N	CDA + 12 child-related credits	N
Minnesota	CDA	Y (1,560 hrs)	90 hrs CD or Human Relations	Y (1,040 hrs)
Mississippi	None	N	CDA or CCP credential	Y (2 years)
Missouri	None	N	CDA + 6 child-related credits	Y (1 year)
Montana	None	N	None	N
Nebraska	None	N	None	N
Nevada	None	N	CDA	N
New Hampshire	2 yr CC course	N	CDA	Y (4,000 hrs)
New Jersey	CDA or CCP certification	N	None	N
New Mexico	None	N	1-year vocational certificate	Y (2 years)
New York	None	N	CDA	Y (4 years)
North Carolina	None	N	CDA	N
North Dakota	None	N	CDA	Y (1 year)
Ohio	None	N	CDA	Y (2 years)
Oklahoma	None	N	None	N
Oregon	None	N	None	N
Pennsylvania	None	N	AA with 30 child-related credits	Y (4 years)
Rhode Island	BA (24 ECE credits)	Y (6 credits student teach)	CDA + 4 college courses in ECE/CD	Y (3 years)
South Carolina	None	N	None	N
South Dakota	None	N	None	N
Tennessee	None	N	TECTA certificate + 4 hrs training	N
Texas	8 hrs EC training	N	CDA	Y (2 years)
Utah	None	N	CDA, CCP, or NAC credential	N
Vermont	CDA	N	CDA	Y (2 years)
Virginia	None	N	None	N
Washington	None	N	CDA	Y (2 years)
West Virginia	None	N	None	N
Wisconsin	4 ECE credits	Y (80 days)	2 ECE courses	Y (80 days)
Wyoming	None	N	100 hrs training	Y (1 year)
Data sources	d	d	d	d

NR=Not regulated

Data Sources:

a Child Care Bureau

b Information was compiled from state CCDF plans, FY 2002–2003.

c Data retrieved from the United States Department of Health and Human Services web site at http://www.acf.hhs.gov.

d LeMoine, S. (2004). Compiled from licensing regulations posted on the National Resource Center for Health and Safety in Child Care web site: http://nrc.uchsc.edu.

Notes:

1 The number of families and children served is the average number reported by each state on the monthly ACF-801 submission provided to the Child Care Bureau. The figures are adjusted in those states that report on all families and children, across multiple funding sources, to show an estimate of the number of families and children served only by CCDF. The number of children served is calculated based on the number of families served in each state and the ratio of families to children served. Monthly enrollment figures reported are for fiscal year 2001 because more recent data were not available at press time.

2 These data represent the sums of mandatory, discretionary, and federal shares of the matching funds.

3 Some states made adjustments to TANF spending reported between 1997 and 2002 when they reported figures for fiscal year 2003. These adjustments were applied to 2003 figures, which resulted in negative totals for 2003 TANF spending in some states.

4 In Colorado and Texas, localities determine income eligibility limits within state parameters. Localities may choose to set lower income cutoffs than this.

5 In Massachusetts, this is the income limit a family must meet to quality for assistance when they first apply. Once a family begins receiving assistance, they can continue to receive help until their income reaches 85% SMI ($49,248).

This publication is a product of the National Institute for Early Education Research (NIEER), a unit of Rutgers University, which supports early childhood education policy by providing objective, nonpartisan information based on research. NIEER is supported by grants from The Pew Charitable Trusts and others. Special appreciation is extended to Carol Shipp, Pat Ainsworth, Mary Meagher, Chris Gilbert, Judi Boyd, Vincent Costanza, Emily Giarelli, Erin Graves, Jennifer Fitzgerald and Nancy Lorince for their invaluable help.

ACKNOWLEDGEMENTS—This publication was made possible through the support of The Pew Charitable Trusts. The Trusts' *Starting Early, Starting Strong* initiative seeks to advance high-quality prekindergarten for all the nation's 3- and 4-year-olds through objective, policy-focused research, state public education campaigns and national outreach. The opinions expressed in this report are those of the authors and do not necessarily reflect the views of The Pew Charitable Trusts.

design: sk designworks/philadelphia www.skdesignworks.com

THE PEW CHARITABLE TRUSTS
Advancing Quality Pre-Kindergarten for All

THE STATE UNIVERSITY OF NEW JERSEY
RUTGERS